WHERE TO RIDE

1992-93

A Guide to BHS-Approved Establishments in the UK and Ireland

THE KEN[illegible] PRESS

in assoc[illegible] Society

Produced for The British Horse Society by
The Kenilworth Press Ltd
Addington , Buckingham, MK18 2JR

Design by Sandie Boccacci
Set in 9/9½ pt Helvetica Light
Typesetting and data conversion by Textype, Cambridge
Printed and bound in Great Britain by Hollen Street Press, Slough, Berks.

Contents

What is the British Horse Society?

The British Horse Society is a charity to promote the interests of horse and pony breeding, to further the art of riding and driving and to encourage horsemastership and the welfare of horses and ponies.

The Society is internationally recognised as the premier equestrian riding, training and examination organisation in the United Kingdom, and operates an Approvals scheme for riding establishments and trekking centres. It incorporates the Pony Club, and some 410 Riding Clubs are affiliated to the BHS. The Society is also the governing body for the sports of dressage, endurance riding, horse driving trials, horse trials and vaulting.

The BHS plays a major role in equine welfare, safety, provision of access to the countryside and protection of riding and driving rights of way. It represents riders to Government and the EEC in Brussels in all matters, especially those concerning taxation, rates, planning and the law.

Membership benefits include £2 million public liability insurance, personal accident insurance, a yearbook, magazines, special facilities and discounts at BHS functions, discounts with retailers and access to BHS advice and support. Membership is a prerequisite to competing in the disciplines or taking the Society's qualifications.

On the 1st September 1991 the BHS had 53,460 members which included 15,518 members of the major disciplines (Dressage 7,340, Endurance Riding 1,226, Horse Driving Trials 990, Horse Trials 8,717). In addition the Pony Club had 38,000 members and Affiliated Riding Clubs represented approximately 36,000 members.

By joining the Society you are helping all who ride. For further information and membership details write to: The British Horse Society, British Equestrian Centre, Stoneleigh, Kenilworth, Warwickshire, CV8 2LR, or phone 0203 696697. An application form is provided at the back of this book.

The BHS Approval Scheme and How it Works

For over twenty years the British Horse Society has been running a scheme for the approval of riding schools and other equine establishments throughout the British Isles.

The basis on which Approval is granted is that the establishment offers sound instruction in riding and horsemastership, and its premises, facilities, safety equipment, and animals are properly looked after.

Any riding establishment in Britain that offers instruction in riding, at whatever level, or provides riding on horses and/or ponies that are its property, requires a Local Authority Licence. This is required by the Riding Establishments Acts of 1964 and 1970, the Welfare of Animals Act (N.I.) 1972 (in Northern Ireland), and the Isle of Man Riding Establishment (Inspection) Acts 1968–1986. No BHS Approval can be granted unless such a licence is held. The only exception to this rule is in the case of training establishments which offer sound instruction and facilities, but which do not have horses for hire.

The BHS Approval Scheme has over 600 Approved establishments, with different classifications depending on the level of instruction on offer. The six classification levels are as follows:

1. Basic instruction in riding and/or jumping
2. Instruction in riding and jumping
3. Instruction in riding and jumping, and students to BHSAI
4. Instruction in riding and jumping, and students to BHSII
5. Instruction in riding and jumping, and students to BHSI
6. Instruction in riding and jumping, and students to all BHS exams including Fellowship

Each application for inclusion in the scheme is formally considered by the Riding Establishments Policy Committee of the British Horse Society after an initial visit by one of the Society's inspectors. Thereafter it is reconsidered after periodic visiting or after the investigation of a complaint. Approval is withheld from establishments which allow clients to ride without hats or which provide hats which are not of a current BSI Standard and/or not in good condition.

The aims of the scheme

Through the administration of this Approval Scheme the BHS hopes to provide members of the public with reliable information as to where, in the opinion of the Society, good riding can be obtained, together with an accurate description of the facilities on offer at any Approved centre.

By visiting and inspecting riding establishments and providing an advisory service for their proprietors, the Society hopes to assist in raising the standard of riding instruction, horsemastership and horsemanship.

For their part, the proprietors are given publicity for their business through the medium of *Where to Ride* and the equestrian press, plus advantageous rates for public liability insurance.

Why Choose a BHS-Approved Establishment?

Whatever your reason for seeking out a riding centre – be it for a pleasant hour's hacking, or training up to advanced level – you will want to choose an establishment that is both reputable and well run.

By selecting one of the establishments listed in *Where to Ride,* you will not only be able to satisfy yourself on that point but you will also be able to discover a good deal about the centre before you pick up the telephone to discuss your ride.

Each of the establishments listed in *Where to Ride* has been inspected by a fully qualified representative of the British Horse Society, who will have looked carefully at the level of instruction available to clients, the on-site facilities and equipment, and the standards of safety, horse care and management.

A riding centre will not be approved by the BHS unless it has a Local Authority Licence. As a general rule, *every* riding establishment is supposed to have a Local Authority Licence; without this licence it will not have proper third party insurance cover. To hold such a licence, granted annually, the establishment will have been inspected by a council representative who will have concerned himself primarily with riders' safety and the welfare of the animals being used. Unlike the BHS inspector, the council inspector will of course *not* have assessed the standard of the instructors or whether the horses are well-schooled and forward-going.

It is also reassuring to know that at an Approved establishment you will not be allowed to ride without the correct protective head gear. An Approved centre will be able to supply you with an appropriate hard hat if you do not already possess one of the correct standard. And newcomers to riding can expect to be offered helpful advice on what to wear so that their first lessons are safe and enjoyable.

Another advantage is that many BHS-Approved establishments run the BHS Progressive Riding Tests, a scheme of instruction and assessment designed for riders of all ages and abilities. Further details of these tests – which can be administered only by an Approved centre – are given on page 11.

Riding Holidays

The establishments listed in *Where to Ride* include many which offer a variety of activities for those wishing to spend their holidays riding or learning more about horses.

Riding courses give riders the chance for more rapid learning, with the opportunity to ride more than once a day under the skilful eye of a qualified instructor. By choosing a BHS-Approved establishment offering specialised courses it is possible to feel confident that the level of tuition will be appropriate and that the horses will be well schooled. Some centres will allow you to take your own horse for training, which means that you can learn and improve together.

An afternoon's **trekking** in beautiful countryside or along the coastline is the dream of many weekend and urban riders. This sort of ride can be easily arranged – and possibly fitted into a weekend break or as part of a longer holiday. The regional organisation of the entries in *Where to Ride* enables you quickly to identify the centres in your chosen location and for a dream to become a reality.

Trekking ponies are usually sure-footed animals that are sturdy and safe, but be sure to tell the riding centre about your own level of riding so that you can be matched to an appropriate horse or pony. Treks can vary in length from an hour or two up to a full day's ride, and are a marvellous way to explore the more scenic areas of Britain.

Trail riding holidays, often covering quite long distances with organised stopping points for picnics and overnight rests, can give the more adventurous and experienced rider an exhilarating holiday that will be hard to beat.

Trail riding horses are usually pretty fit and capable of maintaining a fast pace over a variety of terrain. In order to enjoy this type of riding, you will need to be fairly experienced and reasonably fit yourself, so never be tempted to exaggerate your riding ability when booking such a holiday. Day trails, weekend trails and five-day trails are all options for consideration.

Some centres offer the pony-mad youngster a chance to '**own a pony**' for a week. Here a child can be given responsibility, under supervision, for a pony's grooming, mucking-out, feeding and exercise, and thereby can experience the joys – and hard work – that pony ownership entails. Many of these holidays are for unaccompanied children, giving parents and children an enjoyable break. As stated elsewhere, all the centres included in *Where to Ride* have been inspected and approved by the British Horse Society, but it makes sense to discuss at length your child's requirements and the amount of supervision that will be on hand. The proprietors of all the riding holiday establishments listed here will be happy to talk to you about such matters and show you around the centre if you prefer to visit.

BHS Examinations and Training

The British Horse Society administers an examination structure designed to meet the requirements of both the riding instructor and those who wish to further their knowledge in riding, stable management and horse care. It runs these examinations – aimed primarily at career students – at BHS-Approved centres throughout the British Isles.

Before embarking on a career with horses it is important to select carefully the place of training. Whilst it is not obligatory for candidates to receive their training at a BHS-Approved centre it is certainly advisable to do so. *Where to Ride* gives details of the establishments which are approved to train students, and provides a list of examination centres (see page 13). It also includes details of colleges where equestrian courses, often combined with other studies, are on offer.

Candidates work up the examination ladder, tackling the Horse Knowledge and Riding examinations Stages I–IV progressively. In order to achieve the first certificate on the instructor's ladder (the BHSAI – awarded to those passing the BHS Assistant Instructor's examination), candidates must pass the 1986 Horse Knowledge and Riding Stage III examination and the Preliminary Teaching Test. It is also a requirement for candidates to have successfully completed the Riding and Road Safety Test prior to taking the riding section of the Stage II examination. Holders of the BHSAI certificate are able to teach basic riding and stable management under supervision.

Thereafter, trainees can continue to gain experience before taking the next examination on the ladder – the Intermediate Instructor's Certificate (BHSII). This requires a high standard of horsemanship and teaching and is aimed at producing an instructor who can work without supervision. The next step is the main professional qualification of the British Horse Society – the Instructor's Certificate (BHSI). This requires a very high standard of stable management, horsemanship and teaching. There is only one more senior qualification – Fellowship of the British Horse Society (FBHS) – of which there are only forty-odd holders in the world.

For those not involved in teaching, there is the BHS Stable Manager's qualification (BHSSM). In addition, a new series of National Vocational Qualifications (NVQs) is being introduced and developed.

The present structure of the BHS examination system is shown by the diagram opposite. If you wish to find out more about the syllabi and requirements of the different exams, you should contact the Examinations Office, The British Horse Society, Stoneleigh, Kenilworth, Warwickshire CV8 2LR.

BHS Instructional Qualifications and Certificates

FBHS – *Fellow of the British Horse Society*
Highest qualification awarded by the British Horse Society

Before the BHSI, BHSII and BHSAI qualifications can be used, the following must be passed:

BHSI – *British Horse Society Instructor*
BHS Stable Manager Certificate – BHS(SM)
Equestrian Teaching Exam

BHSII – *British Horse Society Intermediate Instructor's Certificate*
BHS Intermediate Training Certificate
BHS Horse Knowledge & Riding Stage IV Certificate
The British Pony Club 'A' Test Certificate

BHSAI – *British Horse Society Assistant Instructor's Certificate*
BHS Preliminary Teaching Test
BHS Horse Knowledge & Riding Stage III Certificate

BRITISH SOCIETY EXAMINATION SYSTEM

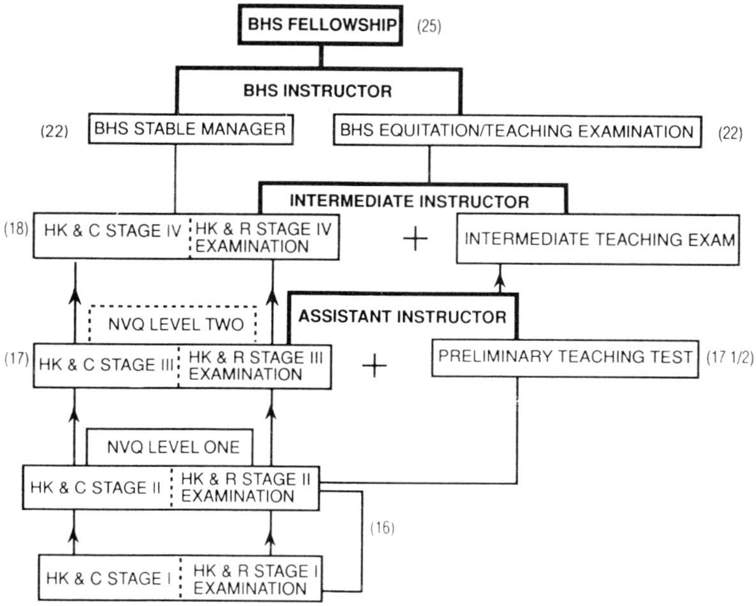

Notes
1. ( ) Minimum age for entry.
2. HK & C = Horse Knowledge and Care.
   HK & R =Horse Knowledge and Riding.
3. NVQ Level Two is being developed.
4. The Riding and Road Safety Test is a pre-requisite to entry for HK & R Stage II.

The Link between HK & R Stages and NVQs is being reviewed.

Progressive Riding Tests

Many BHS-Approved establishments operate a training system for their clients, known as the Progressive Riding Tests. The aim of the tests, which can be taken by riders of all ages and abilities, is to encourage riders to improve their riding and stable management skills and to show progress from early stages up to a reasonable standard of proficiency in school work and outdoor riding, including jumping.

Every rider has a personal record card on which details of each test passed are recorded, and there is a series of awards of achievement. The tests are administered only by BHS-Approved establishments, and those wishing to participate should contact their nearest BHS-Approved centre for further details.

The BHS Register of Instructors

The British Horse Society is concerned that the public should be able to expect a high standard of both teaching and safety from riding instructors. To this end the BHS now operates a 'Register of Instructors', open to holders of BHS teaching qualifications from Assistant Instructor (BHSAI) level upward.

Members of the Register agree to keep their teaching methods up to date by attending a training course every three years, and also undertake to abide by a legally binding code of conduct which sets out guidelines for professional behaviour.

Teachers whose names appear on the register are entitled to use the abbreviation 'Regd' as a suffix to their qualification, e.g. BHSAI Regd.

A full list of Registered instructors in your area is available at your main library or from The BHS Examinations Office, Stoneleigh, Kenilworth, Warwickshire, CV8 2LR (Tel: 0203 696697).

BHS Examinations Centres

The North
Blackdyke Farm Riding Centre, Carlisle.
New Moors Training and Livery Centre, Bishop Auckland.

Yorkshire
Bishop Burton College of Agriculture, Beverley.
Harrogate Equestrian Centre, Harrogate.
Moor House Riding Centre, Wiggington.
Snainton Riding Centre, Scarborough.
Yorkshire Riding Centre, Markington.

The North West
Bold Heath Equestrian Centre, Widnes.
Eccleston Equestrian Centre, Chorley.
Longacres Riding School, Lydiate.

The East Midlands
Brackenhurst College of Agriculture, Southwell.
Brampton Stables, Northampton.
Causeway Farm, Nr Matlock.
Four Winds Equestrian Centre, West Pinchbeck.
Hill House Riding School, Market Rasen.
Stone Lodge Equestrian Centre, Oadby.
Wellow Park Stables, Newark.

The West Midlands
Berriewood Stud Farm, Shrewsbury.
Field House Equestrian Centre, Uttoxeter.
Ingestre Stables, Ingestre.
Pittern Hill Stables, Kineton.
The Mounts Equestrian Centre, Kidderminster.
Tong Riding Centre, Tong.
Waverley Riding School, Leamington Spa.
Warwickshire College of Agriculture, Warwick.

Eastern
Aldborough Hall Equestrian Centre, Ilford.
Cambridgeshire College of Agriculture, Milton.
Hallingbury Hall Equestrian Centre, Bishops Stortford.
Lynch Farm Equestrian Centre, Peterborough.
North Herts Equestrian Centre, Baldock.
Patchetts Equestrian Centre, Watford.
Ponsbourne Riding Centre, Hertford.
Salhouse Equestrian Centre, Norwich.

Greater London
Lea Bridge Riding School, Leyton.
Suzannes Riding School, Harrow Weald.

The South East
Bedgebury Park Riding Centre, Cranbrook.
Blue Barn Stables, Ashford.
Ditchling Common Stud, Burgess Hill.
Limes Farm Equestrian Centre, Hawkinge.
Plumpton Agricultural College, Lewes.
West Sussex College of Agriculture, Brinsbury.

The South
Catherston Stud, Brockenhurst.
Loughton Manor Equestrian Centre, Milton Keynes.
Naval Riding Centre, Fareham.
Rycroft School of Equitation, Eversley.
Spanish Bit Riding School, Windsor.
Wellington Riding (Ltd). Basingstoke.

The South West
Bicton College of Agriculture, Budleigh Salterton.
Chiverton Riding Centre, Truro.
Duchy College of Agriculture, Plymouth.
Fortune Centre, Christchurch.
Huntley School of Equitation, Huntley.
Leigh Equestrian Centre, Sherborne.
Pewsey Vale Riding Centre, Marlborough.
Summerhouse Equestrian Centre, Hardwicke.
The Talland School of Equitation, Circencester.
Urchinwood Manor Equestrian Centre, Congresbury.

Scotland
Gleneagles Mark Phillips Equestrian Centre, Perth.
Hayfield Riding School, Aberdeen.
Loch Ness Equicentre, Dores.
Tower Farm Riding School, Edinburgh.

Wales
Bowling Riding School, Haverfordwest.
The Equestrian Centre, Wrexham.

Ireland
Brennanstown Riding School, Co Wicklow.
Calliaghstown Riding School, Co Dublin.

BHS–Approved Establishments

Key to Abbreviations

Accom	Accommodation
Av No	Average number
Break	Breaking
Chng	Changing
Cov Sch	Covered school
CC	Cross-country
CT	Combined Training
DRG	Dressage
F/T	Full time
Fl Lit	Floodlit
Gly 20	Gallery with 20 seats
HT	Horse Trials
Int	Intermediate
Inst	Instructor
Jump Pd	Jumping Paddock
Lec Rm	Lecture Room
Man	Manege
Nov	Novice
NVQ	National Vocational Qualification
Out Man	Outdoor Manege
P/T	Part time
Regd	BHS Registered Instructor
Resid	Residential
Schlg	Schooling
Sh Jmper	Show jumper
Sh Jmpg	Show jumping
Sh Jmps	Show jumps
Std	Standard
Unqual	Unqualified
Vis Aids	Visual Aids
Wkg Students	Working Students
43 x 22m	Size in metres
*	Available for hire

Using the Listings

The list of Approved establishments which follows is divided into regional areas for easy reference, and provides a detailed profile of each of the centres featured. Simply by studying the listings, you can find out, for example:

- How many horses or ponies a centre has
- The level of instruction on offer
- How many qualified staff are employed
- The type of riding it specialises in – e.g., hacking, dressage, show-jumping, cross-country etc.
- What facilities the centre has
- Whether evening classes are available

In addition to the full address and telephone number, basic directions to the location are given.

Standard of Horses
Levels of Schooling for Horse Trials, Dressage and Show Jumping are:
Advanced (A), Grade A (A)
Intermediate (I), Grade B (B)
Elementary (E)
Novice (N), Grade C (C)
General-purpose riding school horses and ponies are animals which are trained to a sufficient standard to enable instruction to be given in riding and jumping and are safe and tractable mounts for hacking out and pleasure riding.

Definitions Used in 'Where to Ride'

Riding Establishment
A Riding School which offers instruction in riding and horsemastership, at whatever level, on horses and ponies that are the property of that Establishment.

Training Centre
An Establishment, without horses or ponies of its own for hire, that is fully equipped and capable of giving specialist instruction and training in equitation.

Livery Yard
An Establishment which offers adequate facilities for the accommodation and care of horses and ponies. Such service can be on Full, Part or DIY basis.

Trekking Centre
An Establishment which offers for hire, horses, and/or ponies for conducted tours. Such centres are normally situated in areas of Outstanding Natural Beauty.

Stud
An Establishment specialising in the breeding of horses and/or ponies and training students in the branch of husbandry.

Riding in the North

CLEVELAND ♦ CUMBRIA ♦ DURHAM ♦ NORTHUMBERLAND ♦ TYNE AND WEAR

CLEVELAND

ESTON EQUITATION CENTRE
Occupation Road, Eston, Cleveland
Tel: Eston Grange (0642) 452260
Proprietors: J & E Thomson
Chief Inst: Mrs Elvia Thomson (BHSII)
Other Staff: 1 (BHSAI) 2 (BHSAI) P/T
Instruction in Riding and Jumping & Students to BHSAI Exam
Av No: Horses 16 Ponies 14
Std of Schlg: General Purpose
Livery: Full/Hunt/Hack/Trek – Forest/Moorland/Open Country
Ev Classes
Courses: Resid Inst Hol
Facilities: Cov Sch: 20 x 40m* Fl Lit/ Jmp Pd* one acre/Sh Jmps 10*/CC Fences/Lec Rm/Refresh/Wash Rm/Chng Rm/WC/Car Park
Accom: 8–10 Dormitory Catering: Full
Specialities: RDA/AI Students
Exclusions: Weight limit 14 stone
Location: Off Jubilee Road under A174

FORD CLOSE RIDING CENTRE
Brass Castle Lane, Marton, Middlesborough, Cleveland, TS8 9EE
Tel: Middlesbrough (0642) 300257
Proprietor: Miss S Ritchie BHSI **Other Staff:** 1 (BHSAI) 2 (BHSAI) P/T
Instruction in Riding and Jumping & Students to BHSII Exam
Av No: Horses 6 Ponies 6
Std of Schlg: General Purpose Break/School
Ev Classes
Courses: Inst/Wkg Students
Facilities: Cov Sch: 22 x 37m* Fl Lit/Out Man: 22 x 46m* Fl Lt/Jmp Pd two acres/ Sh Jmps*/CC Fences */CC Course*/Lec Rm/Vis Aids/Rest Rm/WC/Wash Rm/Chng Rm/Car Park
Specialities: Eventing/Dressage/Cross Country schooling
Exclusions: No children under 5 years/No Riders over 12.5 Stone/No YTS
Location: West of A172 5 miles south of Middlesborough

STAINSBY GRANGE RIDING CENTRE
Stainsby Grange Farm, Thornaby, Cleveland, TS17 9AB
Tel: 0642 762233
Proprietor & Chief Inst: Mrs P Allen (BHSAI) **Other Staff:** 1 (BHSAI) P/T
Instruction in Riding and Jumping
Av No: Horses 4 Ponies 15
Std of Schlg: General Purpose Std of Specialist Schlg: Sh Jmpg – Grade B
Livery: Full/Part/Grass/DIY/School
Ev Classes
Courses: YT – 2/3
Facilities: Cov Sch: 55 x 24m*/Out Man:76 x 37m/Lec Rm – Video/ Cafeteria/Gallery/Wash Rm/WC/ Car Park
Specialities: Show Jumping
Exclusions: No children under 5
Location: At Junc of A19/A1130 3 miles west of Middlesborough

WHISPERS EQUESTRIAN CENTRE
Whispers, Whinney Hill, Stockton, Cleveland, TS21 1BQ
Tel: 0642 582 896
Proprietor & Chief Inst: Miss M K Jackson (BHSII) **Other Staff:** 1 (BHSAI) P/T
Instruction in Riding and Jumping
Av No Horses 4 Ponies 10
Std of Schlg: General Purpose Std of Specialist Schlg: Sh Jmp – Novice
Livery: Full/Part/Grass/School/Hack – Open Country
Courses: Residential/YT – 2
Facilities: Out Man: 30 x 25m Fl Lit/Jmp Pd/Lec Rm – Seat 8/Vis Aids/Wash Rm/ WC/Chng Rm/Car Park
Accom: Camp Site – 8 Catering: Full
Specialities: Competitions
Location: 1 mile north off A66 midway btwn Stockton & Darlington

CUMBRIA

BIGLAND HALL RIDING CENTRE
Backbarrow, Nr Ulverston, Cumbria, LA12 8PB
Tel: 05395 31728
Proprietor: R Bigland
Chief Inst: Mrs L Potter (BHSAI) **Other Staff:** 1 (BHSI) Visiting
Instruction in Riding and Jumping
Av No: Horses 8 Ponies 16
Std of Schlg: General Purpose
Livery: Full/Part/Grass/School/Hack/Trek – 1,100 acre private estate (fells)
Ev Classes
Facilities: Cov Sch: 37 x 19m* Gly 60/Jmp Pd 37 x 28m/Sh Jmps 10/CC Fences*/CC Course*/Lec Rm/Vis Aids/Club Rm/Refresh/WC/Car Park
Specialities: Trekking/Hacking/21 Fence Cross-Country Course/Equitation/Jumping tuition/RDA
Exclusions: No children under 7 for hacking or trekking or under 6 for lessons

BLACKDYKE FARM & RIDING SCHOOL
Blackdyke Farm, Blackford, Carlisle, Cumbria, CA6 4EY
Tel: Rockcliffe (022874) 633
Proprietors: Mr & Mrs J Collier
Chief Inst: Mrs Collier (BHSAI) **Other Staff:** 2 (BHSAI)
Instruction in Riding and Jumping & Students to BHSAI Exam
Av No: Horses 15 Ponies 12
Std of Schlg: General Purpose
Livery: Full/Part/Hack – Country Lanes
Ev Lessons
Courses: YT 2
Facilities: Cov Sch: 49 x 25m*/Fl Lit 100 Seats/Out Man: 56 x 26m Fl Lit/CC Fences/Jmp Pd/Sh Jmps*/WC/Tack Shop/Car Park
Specialities: Instruction in Riding and Jumping/RDA
Location: Off A7 2 miles from Junc 44 on M6

CALTHWAITE RIDING SCHOOL
Hill House, Calthwaite, Cumbria, CA11 9PY
Tel: 0768 85374
Proprietor: Mrs M C Tuck
Chief Inst: Mrs M C Tuck (BHSAI)
Other Staff: 1
Basic Instruction in Riding and Jumping
Av No: Horses 4 Ponies 7
Std of Schlg: General purpose
Livery: Full/Part/Schooling
Ev Classes
Courses: Residential/Working Pupil Courses
Facilities: Out Man 20x40m Fl Lit/Jmp Pd/Lec Rm/Lunging Area/Wash Rm/WC/Refreshments/Car Park
Accom: Dormitory/Cottage Catering: Self
Exclusions: No children under 6 years of age

HOLMESCALES RIDING CENTRE
Old Hutton, Nr Kendal, Cumbria, LA8 0NB
Tel: Kendal (0539) 729388
Proprietors: Mr & Mrs P Jones
Chief Inst: Eleanor Jones (BHSII)
Instruction in Riding and Jumping
Av No: Horses 10 Ponies 12
Std of Schlg: General Purpose Break/School/Hunt/Hack/Trek – Hills/Woods/Farmland
Ev Classes
Courses: Inst
Facilities: Cov Sch: 43 x 19m Gly Fl Lit/Out Man: 37 x 19m Seats Fl Lit/CC Fences/Jmp Pd 2 acres/Sh Jmps/Feed Rm/Rest Rm/Refresh/WC/RDA Toilet Block/Chng Rm/Car Park
Accom: Family House 6 (Children & Teenagers up to 17yrs on Riding Holidays)
Specialities: Superb hacking on good horses/Instruction for all types of riders in jumping/dressage etc/Instruction on own horse/RDA

SIDE FARM TREKKING CENTRE
Side Farm, Patterdale, Penrith, Cumbria, CA11 0NP
Tel: 0768 482337
Proprietors: Mr & Mrs Taylforth
Pony Trekking
Av No: Horses 8 Ponies 19
Std of Schlg: General Purpose Hack/Trek – Lakeland/Hills/Fells
Facilities: Refresh/WC/Chng Rm/Car Park
Specialities: Trekking on Lakeland Hills/Fells
Exclusions: No YT
Location: Off A592 15 miles from Junc 40 on M6

STONERIGG RIDING CENTRE
Great Orton, Carlisle, Cumbria, CA5 6NA
Tel: 0228 576232
Proprietor: Mr G Johnstone

Chief Inst: Mrs M Kendall **Other Staff:** Mrs C Flynn (BHSAI) P/T 1 (BHSAI)
Instruction in Riding and Jumping
Av No: Horses 1 Ponies 10
Std of Schlg: General Purpose
Livery: Full/Part/Break/School/Hack
Facilities: Out Man: 19 x 37m*/Jmp Pd* 3 acres/Sh Jmps 9*/Cov Sch: 37 x 19m* Fl Lit/Wash Rm
Specialities: Jumping
Exclusions: No YT
Location: 5 miles west of Carlisle

WYNLASS BECK STABLES

Lakeland Equestrian Enterprises Ltd, Wynlass Beck, Windermere, Cumbria, LA23 1EU
Tel: Windermere (09662) 3811
Proprietor: Mrs W M Oakden (BHSAI)(YT Agency – 30) **Other Staff:** 1 (BHSII) 1 (BHSAI)
Instruction in Riding and Jumping
Av No: Horses 7 Ponies 8
Std of Schlg: General Purpose
Livery: Full/Part/Grass/DIY/Break/School/Hunt/Hack/Trek – Lanes/Bridlepaths over fell/Woodland
Courses: Resid Hol Inst/YT 8
Facilities: Out Man: 138 x 37m* Fl Lit/Jmp Pd/CC Course/CC Fences 7/Lec Rm/Vis Aids/Video/Showers/WC/Chng Rm/Car Park
Accom: 6 – Country House (Unaccompanied children only) Catering: Full
Specialities: Riding holidays
Location: In Windermere on A591

DURHAM

CENTURION EQUESTRIAN CENTRE

Birtley Lane, Hunwick, Bishop Auckland, County Durham
Tel: 0388 603057/606463
Proprietor: B Thexton Esq
Chief Inst: Mrs B Scott (BHSAI) **Other Staff:** 1 (Unqual)
Instruction in Riding and Jumping
Av No: Horses 10 Ponies 6
Std of Schlg: General Purpose Std of Specialist Schlg: CT – All levels/Sh Jmpg – Grade A
Livery: Full/School/Hack – Licenced Right of Way
Ev Classes
Facilities: Cov Sch: 42 x 30m* Gly/Out Man: 30 x 20m* Fl Lit/CC Course* – Nov/Int/Adv/Jmp Pd*/Snacks/Wash Rm/WC/Full facilities for the Disabled

DURHAM EQUESTRIAN SKILLS LTD

New Moors Training & Livery Centre, Bishop Auckland, County Durham, DL14 9NN
Tel: 0388 833542
Proprietors: Messrs A & M A & Miss G Lewis
Approved Training Organisation YT
Chief Inst: Mrs M Watts BHSI **Other Staff:** 1 (BHSAI) 1 (BHSII) P/T
Instruction in Riding and Jumping
Av No: Horses 12 Ponies 4 Specialist Horses: 2 Drg
Std of Schlg: General Purpose Std of Specialist Schlg: Drg – Grand Prix/CT & Sh Jmpg: Novice
Livery: Full/Part/Grass/DIY/School/Break
Ev Classes
Courses: up to BHS Stage III/Dressage to Grand Prix/YT – 3/4/Resid – YT only
Facilities: Cov Sch: 20 x 40m*/Out Man: 20 x 6 0m*/CC Course* – 20 CC Fences – Basic/Sh Jmps*/Lec Rm – Seating/Library/Refreshments/Wash Rm/WC/Showers/Waiting Rm/Car Park
Accom: Caravan/house – YT only/4 Catering: Part
Specialities: Dressage – Grand Prix/Approved Training Organisation YT
Exclusions: No hiring for hunting/No children under 10 years

LOW FOLD FARM RIDING CENTRE

Sunnybrow, Crook, Co Durham
Tel: Bishop Auckland (0388) 747313
Proprietor: Miss M J Hedley (BHSII)
Chief Inst: Miss V Deacon (BHSII)
Other Staff: 1 (BHSAI) 1 (BHS(PTT))
Instruction in Riding and Jumping
Av No: Horses 17 Ponies 11
Std of Schlg: General Purpose
Livery: Full/Part/Grass/Hunter/School/Hunt
Ev Classes
Courses: YT 2/Restart 2/Wkg Pupils 2
Facilities: Cov Sch: 15 x 30m*/Jmp Pd/Sh Jmps/CC Course/CC Fences/WC/Change Rm/Car Park
Specialities: Cross Country Training
Exclusions: No children under seven years
Location: On B6286 1 mile from Willington & 4 miles from Bishop Auckland

NORTHUMBERLAND

BENRIDGE RIDING CENTRE

Benridge Hagg, Morpeth, Northumberland, NE61 3SB
Tel: 0670 518507

Proprietor: D M Mancey Esq
Manager & Chief Inst: Miss J Mancey
Other Staff: 1 (BHSAI) P/T
Basic Instruction in Riding and Jumping
Av No: Horses 6 Ponies 6
Std of Schlg: General Purpose Std of Specialist Schlg: Sh Jmpg/Drg – Novice
Livery: Part/Grass/School/Break/Hack – Bridlepaths/Minor Roads
Ev Classes
Facilities: Out Man: 42 x 22m* Fl Lit/ Jmp Pd*/Lec Rm/Club Rm/Wash Rm/ WC/Showers/Changing Rm/Car Park
Accom: Cottages – 15 Catering: Self

EQUI STUDY
Hole House, Haltwhistle, Northumberland, NE49 0LQ
Tel: 069 72 577
Proprietor: Mrs A L Midgley
Chief Inst: Henri Plag BHSI
Instruction in Riding and Jumping
Av No: Horses – Ponies –
Std of Schlg: General Purpose Std of Specialist Schlg: CT – Basic/Sh Jmp – Novice
School
Courses: Private lessons/YT – 3
Facilities: Out Man: 60 x 20m*/Wash Rm/WC/Changing Rm/Lec Rm*/Vis Aids*/Film Projector*/Library/Car Park
Specialities: Youth Training
Exclusions: No complete Novices taken
Location: On A69 between Haltwistle & Greenhead

KIELDER ADVENTURE CENTRE
Kielder Water, Hexham, Northumberland, NE48 1BS
Tel: 0434 250232
Director: P J V Cockerill Esq
Chief Inst. & Manageress: Other Staff: 1 (BHSAI)
Basic Instruction in Riding and Jumping
Av No: Horses 2 Ponies 4
Std of Schlg: Basic
Livery: DIY/School/Hack & Trek – Forestry Commision
Courses: Resid/YT – 2
Facilities: Cov Sch: 20 x 60m Gly*/Club Rm/Bar/Refreshments/Wash Rm/WC/ Showers/Changing Rm/Wait Rm/ Car Park
Accom: Single/Shared Rms – 35 Catering: Full
Specialities: Integration of normal able bodied & RDA activities/Hacking/ Novices/unaccompanied Children

Exclusions: No children under 4/Riders over 18 stone

KIMMERSTON RIDING CENTRE
Kimmerston, Wooler, Northumberland, NE71 6JH
Tel: 06686 283
Proprietors: Mr & Mrs R Jeffreys
Manager & Chief Inst: Mrs R Jeffreys (BHSAI) **Other Staff:** 2 P/T
Basic Instruction in Riding and Jumping
Av No: Horses 20 Ponies 10
Std of Schlg: General Purpose
Livery: Full/Part/Grass/School/Hunt/ Hack – Beach/Moorland/Woodland/ Bridleways
Courses: YT 1/Resid
Facilities: 15 Schooling Fences* – Basic/Jmp Pd
Accom: House – 4 Catering: Full
Specialities: Cheviot & Beach Rides
Location: 1.5 miles from Ford village & 2 miles from Millfield (on A697)

WHITTON FARM HOUSE HOTEL
Whitton Farm, Rothbury, Northumberland, NE65 7RL
Tel: Rothbury (0669) 20811
Proprietor: Mr T Clubley
Stable Manager: Anne Bailey (BHSAI)
Other Staff: 1 (BHSAI) 1 (BHSAI) P/T 1 (BHSII) P/T
Basic Instruction in Riding and Jumping
Av No: Horses 10 Ponies 6
Std of Schlg: General Purpose
Hack/Trek – Moors/Bridle Paths/Trail Riding
Courses: YT – 2
Facilities: Lic Bar – members only/WC/Wash Rm/Showers/Wait Rm/ Car Park
Accom: 42 – Hotel/Double rooms Catering: Full
Specialities: Private fishing/Shooting/ Farm cooking/Informal atmosphere/ Riding Holidays

WINDY EDGE STABLES
Alnmouth Road, Alnwick, Northumberland, NE66 2QB
Tel: Alnwick (0665) 602284
Proprietors: Miss I White & Miss I Sisterson
Chief Inst: Miss I White **Other Staff:** 1 (BHSAI) – Visiting
Basic Instruction in Riding and Jumping
Av No: Horses 6 Ponies 8
Std of Schlg: General Purpose

Livery: Full/Part/Hunter/Hunt/Hack – Farmland
Courses: YT 1
Facilities: Out Man: 31 x 31m/Jmp Pd/ Sh Jmps/CC Fences/WC/Car Park
Specialities: Good hacking country/Livery Service/RDA
Exclusions: No children under 5 years/ Open April – August
Location: 1.5 miles from A1/30 miles from Berwick & 17 miles from Morpeth

TYNE & WEAR

BARTON STUD & SCHOOL OF EQUITATION
Middle Brunton, Newcastle upon Tyne, NE3 5NA
Tel: 091 2362088
Proprietors: Mr L N Barrass (BHSAI) & Mrs L Barrass (BHS T & SM)
Instruction in Riding and Jumping & Students to BHSII Exam
Av No: Horses 9 Ponies 5
Std of Schlg: General Purpose Break/School/Hunt/Hack – varied
Ev Classes
Courses: Wkg Students/YT – 2
Facilities: Cov Sch: 28 x 20m* Gly 12/Jmp Pd/CC F ences
Accom: 1 or hotels locally
Specialities: Breaking/Training your own horse/One day events
Exclusions: No children under 8 years/No long term liveries/Weight restriction 10 stone
Location: Off A6125 3 miles north of Newcastle

WHITTINGTON MILL RIDING STABLES
Whittington Mill, Great Whittington, Newcastle upon Tyne, NE19 2HU
Tel: 0434 672264
Proprietor & Chief Inst: Mrs J Findeisen (BHSAI) **Other Staff:** 1 (BHSI(T & SM))
Instruction in Riding and Jumping
Av No: Horses 8 Ponies 10
Std of Schlg: General Purpose Std of Specialist Schlg: CT – Basic/Sh Jmpg – Novice
School/Hack – Country Roads/Lanes
Ev Classes
Courses: Wkg Pupils: 2/3
Facilities: Out Man: 25 x 35m Fl Lit/CC Course & Fences (Basic)/Wash Rm/WC/ Car Park
Specialities: Children Day Courses/ Camps with full catering
Exclusions: No Riders over 11 stone/ No children under 6 years
Location: 6 miles from Corbridge & 8 miles from Hexham

Riding in Yorkshire

HUMBERSIDE ♦ NORTH YORKSHIRE ♦ SOUTH YORKSHIRE ♦ WEST YORKSHIRE

HUMBERSIDE

BISHOP BURTON COLLEGE OF AGRICULTURE
Bishop Burton, Beverley, North Humberside, HU17 8QG
Tel: 0964 550481
Proprietor: Mr H W Petch
Managing YT Agent
Chief Inst: Mr N Mumby (BHSI) **Stable Managers:** A Parkin/T Vaughan-Taylor
Other Staff: 4 (BHSI) 2 (BHSII)
Instruction in Riding and Jumping & Students to BHSII Exam
Av No: Horses 40
Std of Schlg: General Purpose
Livery: Full/Part/School/Break
Ev Classes
Courses: Pre – BHS Exams
Facilities: Cov Sch: 60 x 20m*/Out Man: 50 x 50m/CC Course/60 CC Fences*/Jmp Pd*/Lec Rm/Club Rm/ Vis Aids/Video/Wash Rm/WC/Showers/ Chng Rm/Waiting Rm/Car Park
Specialities: Courses for College of Agriculture
Students/National Cert – Management of Horses(inc BHSAI)/National Dip in Equine & Business Studies(inc BHSII)/ Adv Nat Cert in Equine Business Man (incl (BHSII) or Stud Man)/YTS Man Agent/Competition
Training for Dressage/Show Jumping/ Eventing/BTEC First Diploma
Location: 3 miles West of Beverley

CARRIER HOUSE RIDING SCHOOL
Main Street, Newton-on-Derwent, North Humberside, Y04 5DA
Tel: Elvington (090485) 373
Proprietors: Mr & Mrs P Teasdale
Other Staff: Miss L Sleight (Unqual)
Basic Instruction in Riding and Jumping
Av No: Horses 9 Ponies 7
Std of Schlg: General Purpose
Livery: Full/Break/School/Hack – Forestry Land/Bridleways/Commons/ Riverbank/Country Lanes
Facilities: Cov Sch: 41 x 14m* Fl Lit/ Jmp Pd/Sh Jmps*/CC Fences/ Refresh/WC/Car Park
Specialities: Tuition for beginners/ Children/Teenagers a speciality/Livery Facilities/Schooling/Show Jumpers/ Show Hunters
Location: 1 mile off the York – Beverley Road

CHESTNUT FARM RIDING SCHOOL
Brigsley Road, Ashby – Cum – Fenby, Grimsby, South Humberside, DN37 0QN
Tel: 0472 825777
Proprietor & Chief Inst: Mrs I Pettigrew (BHSAI)
Other Staff: 1 (BHSAI)
Basic Instruction in Riding and Jumping
Av No: Horses 6 Ponies 10
Std of Schlg: General Purpose Std of Specialist Schlg: CT – Basic/Sh Jmpg – Novice
Livery: Full/Part/School/Hack – flat arable land with some Woodland
Ev Classes
Courses: Wkg Pupils/YT
Facilities: Cov Sch: 18 x 36m* Gly/10 Basic CC Schooling Fences – small obstacles only/Jmpg Pd*/Lec Rm – seating 6/Drinks Machine/WC/ Car Park
Specialities: Family Instruction/ Competitions
Location: Adjoining B1203 at Brigsley

NORTH HUMBERSIDE RIDING CENTRE
Easington, Nr Hull, Humberside, HU12 0UA
Tel: (0964) 650250
Proprietor: Mrs T Biglin BHS SM (Regd) NPSSAC

Other Staff: 1 (BHSAI) 1 (BHSAI) P/T
Instruction in Riding and Jumping & Students to BHSAI Exam
Av No: Horses 10 Ponies 16
Std of Schlg: General Purpose
Livery: Full/Part/Grass/Break/School/Hack – Beach/River Banks
Ev Classes
Courses: Resid Inst Hol/Wkg Students
Facilities: Cov Sch: 37 x 34m* Gly 50 Fl Lit/Sh Jmps/CC Fences*/CC Course/Lec Rm/WC/Wash Rm/Showe rs/Chng Rm/Refresh/Wait Rm/Car Park
Accom: 12 – House – Unaccompanied children
Specialities: Competition Training
Location: Approx 3/4 Mile from Easington Church

SKERNE LEYS FARM
Driffield, Humberside, YO25 9HN
Tel: 0377 43102
Proprietors: Mr & Mrs T A Watson
D I Y Livery Yard
Livery: DIY
Facilities: Wash Rm/WC/Car Park
Specialities: Secluded Yard for DIY Livery Owners with turnout facility and personal supervision on site
Location: 1 mile south of Great Driffield

NORTH YORKSHIRE

BARROWBY RIDING CENTRE
Kirkby Overblow, Nr Harrogate, North Yorks, HG3 1HU
Tel: Leeds (0532) 886201
Proprietors: Mrs S J & Miss J A Caley
Chief Inst: Mrs S J Caley (BHSAI)
Other Staff: 1 (BHSAI)
Instruction in Riding and Jumping & Students to BHSAI Exam – for clients on their own horses
Std of Schlg: General Purpose
Livery: Full/Part/Grass/Hunter/School/Hunt/Hack – Bridlepaths/Country Lanes
Courses: Inst/Wkg Students/YT
Facilities: Out Man: 21 x 42m*/Jmp Pd 2 acres*/Sh Jmps*/CC Fences*/Vis Aids/Refresh/WC/Change Rm/Car Park
Accom: 3 – as family (students)
Specialities: Livery/Training horse and rider/Production of eventers/Convalescent horses taken/Stabling & nursing/Hunter liveries
Exclusions: No hiring out– Cnly for clients with own horses
Location: 5 miles from A1 at Wetherby/12 miles from M1 & M62

BLEACH FARM STABLES
Bridlington Road, Stamford Bridge, York, North Yorkshire, YO4 1HA
Tel: 0759 71846
Proprietors: Miss S Crompton & Mr J Hutchinson
Chief Inst: Miss S Crompton (BHS(PTT))
Basic Instruction in Riding and Jumping
Av No: Horses 4 Ponies 10
Std of Schlg: General Purpose
Livery: Full/Hunter/Hack – Tracks/Bridleways
Ev Classes
Facilities: Out Man: 24 x 40m* Fl Lit/WC/Car Park
Exclusion: No riders under 3 years of age

BRECKONBROUGH EQUESTRIAN CENTRE
Breckonbrough Farm, Brough Park, Richmond, North Yorkshire, DL10 7PL
Tel: 0748 811629 Fax: 0748 818019
Proprietors: Messrs K A & M & Mrs P C Acaster
Chief Inst: Martin Acaster (Unqual)
Hacking – Basic instruction for only
Av No: Horses 16 Ponies 16
Std of Schlg: General Purpose Std of specialist Schlg: Sh Jmpg – Novice School/Hunting/Hack– edge of Dales/Bridleways/Country Roads
Ev Classes
Courses: Riding Hols
Facilities: Cov Sch: 24 x 12m/Out Man: 37m x 19m/Refreshments/Lec Rm – 30 seats/Club Rm – Vis Aids/Video/Horse Walker – 4/Wait Rm/Laundry Rm/Showers/Wash Rm/WC/Changing Rm/Tack Shop/Car Park
Accom: Cottages 8/Bunkhouse – 20 Catering: Full
Specialities: RDA/Courses/Holidays/Driving Instruction
Location: 1.5 miles North West of Tunstall Village

CATTERICK ARMY SADDLE CLUB
Headquarters Catterick Garrison, Scotton Road, Catterick Garrison, North Yorkshire, DL9 3JS
Tel: 0748 832521 Ext 2661/225
Secretary: Mrs B Riley (BHSAI)
Manager: Hazel Webb (BHSAI) **Other Staff:** 3 (BHSAI) – All P/T
Instruction in Riding and Jumping
Av No: Horses 8 Ponies 8
Std of Schlg: General Purpose Std of Specialist Schlg: CT – Novice/Sh Jmpg – C

Livery: Part/DIY/School/Hack – Moors
Ev Classes
Courses: YT – 2
Facilities: Cov Sch: 46 x 19m* Gly/Out Man: 35 x 25m* Fl Lit/CC Course/CC Fences(Nov)*/Video Camera*/ Recorder*/TV*/Wash Rm/WC/Changing Rm/Waiting Rm/Car Park
Specialities: Dressage/Hunter Trials/ Pony/Riding Clubs/RDA
Exclusions: Club Members only/No Children under 7 years
Location: 3 miles west of A1

FARSYDE STUD AND RIDING CENTRE

Farsyde House, Robin Hood's Bay, Whitby, North Yorkshire, YO22 4UG
Tel: 0947 880249
Proprietors: Mr & Mrs R V Green
Other Staff: 1 (BHSAI) – (available on request)
Basic Instruction in Riding and Jumping
Av No: Horses 10 Ponies 2
Std of Schlg: General Purpose
Livery: Full/Hunter/Hack – Beach/ Moors/Bridlepaths/Forest
Courses: Resid Hol
Facilities: Out Man: 18 x 36m/Jmp Pd/ Sh Jmps/Car Park
Accom: 4 x 2 bedroom Cottages/1 Bungalow Catering: Self/Full
Specialities: Self catering holidays/With English Tourist Board/Show Jumps/ Resid Hols for adults with full board
Exclusions: No hiring without escort/No Hacking for Novices
Location: Off Middlewood Lane/Fyling Thorpe/Robin Hood's Bay

FRIAR'S HILL RIDING STABLES

Friars Hill, Sinnington, Nr Pickering, North Yorkshire, YO6 6NF
Tel: 0751 32758/31583
Proprietor: Mrs C Gamble
Chief Inst: Miss A Gamble (BHSAI)
Basic Instruction in Riding and Jumping
Av No: Horses 8 Ponies 10
Std of Schlg: General Purpose Std of Specialist Schlg: Sh Jmp – Novice
Livery: Part/Grass/DIY/School/Hack – Woodlands/Moorland
Ev Classes – Summer only
Facilities: Out Man: 40 x 27m*/Jmp Pd/Lec Rm – seating 10/Wash Rm/WC/Car Park
Specialities: RDA/Side Saddle
Location: Off A170 5 miles from Pickering & 2 miles from Kirby Moorside

HARROGATE EQUESTRIAN CENTRE

Brackenthwaite Lane, Burn Bridge, Harrogate, North Yorkshire, HG3 1PW
Tel: Harrogate (0423) 871894
Proprietor: Major J N D Birtwistle T D FBHS
Other Staff: 2 (BHSI) P/T 1 (BHSII) 3 (BHSAI)
Instruction in Riding and Jumping & Students prepared for all BHS Exams including Fellowship
Av No: Horses 15 Ponies 12 Specialist Horses 4
Std of Schlg: General Purpose/ Advanced
Livery: Full/Part/Grass/Hunter/Break/School/ Hack/Trek – Rural
Ev Classes
Courses: Resid Inst Hol/Wkg Students/YT 4
Facilities: Cov Sch: 62 x 22m* Gly Fl Lit/Out Man : 43 x 22m* Seats Fl Lit/ Jmp Pd/CC Course/80 CC F ences*/ Sh Jmps/Lec Rm/Vis Aids/Refresh/ Lic Bar/Wait Rm/WC/Showers/Wash Rm/Chng Rm/Shop/Car Park
Accom: 24 Porta Kabin/Rooms/Local hotel/Lodgings/2 Mobile Homes Catering: Full
Specialities: Complete training for all exams/Horse Trials/Show Jumping/ Ponies & Horses Schooled
Exclusions: No hiring for hunting/Weight limit 15 Stone
Location: 3 miles from centre of Harrogate

LACYS COTTAGE RIDING SCHOOL

Scrayingham, York, North Yorkshire, YO4 1JD
Tel: 0759 71586 & Fax No: 0759 71028
Proprietor: Mrs N Pimlott
Basic Instruction in Riding and Jumping
Av No: Horses 5 Ponies 18 Specialist Horses – Race horses
Std of Schlg: Basic Instruction Std of Specialist Schlg: Sh Jmpg – Novice
Livery: Full/Grass/School/Break/Hack – mainly flat riverside country/quiet roads
Ev Classes
Courses: Stable Management/Riding Courses
Facilities: Out Man: 28 x 23m* Fl Lit/ Basic CC Schooling fences/Sh Jmp Pd/Wash Rm/WC/4 furlong gallop alongside river – (dog leg & natural surface not prepared)
Specialities: Children/Nervous riders/Stable Management courses/Riding courses/working

towards Riding School & BHS Stages/ Progressive Riding Tests
Exclusions: No riders under 3 years of age/No unescorted rides
Location: Approx 3 miles off A166

MOOR HOUSE RIDING CENTRE
Sutton Road, Wigginton, York, YO3 8RB
Tel: York (0904) 769029
Proprietor: Mrs S Kemp-Welch
Chief Inst: Miss Philippa Kemp-Welch BHS(SM) **Other Staff:** 1 (BHSAI) 1 (BHSI) Visiting 1 (BHSAI)P/T
Instruction in Riding and Jumping & Students to BHSAI Exam
Av No: Horses 9 Ponies 8
Std of Schlg: General Purpose Std of Specialist Schlg: Drsg I/HT – E
Livery: Part/Hack – Lanes/Farmland
Ev Classes
Courses: Inst Hol/Wkg Students
Facilities: Cov Sch: 37 x 28m Gly small Fl Lit/2 Out Mans: 41 x 21m Fl Lit/41 x 21m(Sand)/Jmp Pds/Sh Jmps 10/CC Fences/CC Course/Lec Rm/Vis Aids/ Club Rm/Rest Rm/WC/Wash Rm/Chng Rm/Car Park
Specialities: Non-residential courses for adults/children/Nervous Riders
Exclusions: No hire of horses without supervision/No rides on Thursdays
Location: On B1363 2 miles north of Ring Road

NABURN GRANGE RIDING CENTRE
Naburn, North Yorkshire, YO1 4RU
Tel: Escrick (090487) 283
Proprietor: Mrs D Horn (BHSAI)
Chief Inst: Mrs Denise Claydon (BHSAI) **Other Staff:** Visiting (BHSI) 1 (BHSAI)
Instruction in Riding and Jumping
Av No: Horses 8 Ponies 9
Std of Schlg: General Purpose
Livery: Full/Part/Grass/Hunter/Break/ School/Hack/Trek – Woodland/Parkland/ quiet Country Lanes
Evening Lessons
Courses: Resid Inst Hol/YTS – 4
Facilities: Cov Sch: 40 x 21.5m Fl Lit/ Out Man: 60 x 40m/CC Fences 14/Jmp Pd/Sh Jmps 10/Lec Rm/W. C/Shop/ Car Park
Accom: 10 – Farmhouse Catering: Full
Specialities: Instruction & training for PC tests/Weekly residential or daily holiday riding/Stable Management Courses
Location: On B1222 off A19 4 miles from York

QUEEN MARGARET'S RIDING SCHOOL
Escrick Park, York, North Yorkshire, YO4 6EA
Tel: Escrick (090487) 632
Proprietor: Miss G M Sanders (BHSAI)
Other Staff: Weekends Only
Instruction in Riding and Jumping
Av No: Horses 6 Ponies 6
Std of Schlg: General Purpose
Hack – Farm/Woodland
Courses: YT – 1
Facilities: Out Man: 40 x 20m Fl Lit/Jmp Pd 50 x 50m/Sh Jmps 10/15 CC Fences/WC/Car Park
Specialities: Instructional courses for children/Small friendly groups for lessons/Individual requirements catered for/Hacking with little road work
Exclusions: No Riders over 12 stone/ No children under 8
Location: Off A19 between York & Selby

RILLINGTON MANOR RIDING SCHOOL
Rillington Manor, Rillington, Malton, North Yorks, YO17 8LL
Tel: Rillington (09442) 246
Proprietor: Mrs G T Russell
Chief Inst: Mrs P J Ireland (BHSAI) Regd
Basic Instruction in Riding and Jumping
Av No: Horses 7 Ponies 9
Std of Schlg: General Purpose
Livery: Full/Part/Grass/DIY/Break/ School/Hunt/Hack – Varied
Ev Classes
Courses: YT – 1
Facilities: Out Man:(Field) 60 x 20m/ Jmp Pd (1 acre)/Sh Jmps*/CC Course*/ CC Fences/WC/Car Park
Accom: Small caravan site
Specialities: Individual attention/One day event & hunter trials on own 82 acres/Dressage & CT
Location: On A64 4 miles from Malton (Off Sands Lane)

SNAINTON RIDING CENTRE
Snainton, Nr Scarborough, North Yorks
Tel & Fax No: Scarborough (0723) 859218
Proprietors: Mr & Mrs A L Lyall
Chief Inst: Mr A L Lyall (BHSI) **Other Staff:** Mrs C Lyall (BHSII) Regd Miss M Wilding (BHSAI) Miss P MacCheon (BHSAI)
Instruction in Riding and Jumping & Students to BHSI Exam

Av No: Horses 17 Ponies 9 Spec Horses – H T/Dressage – I/Sh Jmp – B
Std of Schlg: General Purpose
Livery: Full/Hunter/Break/School/Hunt/Hack – Varied country
Ev Classes
Courses: Resid Inst/Wkg Students/YT
Facilities: Cov Sch: 42 x 25m Gly 200 Fl Lit/Out Man: 52 x 22m Fl Lit/Jmp Pd/Sh Jmps/CC Course/CC Fences/Lec Rm – Vis Aids/Video/Refresh on Comp Days/Chng Rm/Hot Drinks/Wash Rm/Wait Rm/Car Park
Accom: 13 – Cottage – Students Catering: Self
Specialities: Training horse and rider for all competitions/Breaking/Schooling/Difficult horses reschooled/RDA/Exam Centre to BHSII level
Location: Off A170 10 miles from Scarborough

SPRINGFIELD EQUESTRIAN CENTRE
Springfield Farm, Fylingdales, Nr Whitby, North Yorkshire, YO22 4QH
Tel: 0947 880393
Proprietor/Chief Inst: Mrs S M Richardson (BHSII) Regd **Other Staff:** Mrs F Robinson (BHSAI) Regd 3 F/T
Instruction in Riding and Jumping
Av No: Horses 8 Ponies 2 Specialist Horses – 3 Drg – 1 Nov/1 Sh Jmper – Grade A/1 Nov Eventer
Std of Schlg: General Purpose Std of Specialist Schlg: Drg – Nov/CT – Basic/Sh Jmpg – Novice
Livery: Full/Part/DIY/Hunter/School/Break/Hunting/Hacking – Forest/Moorland/Beach
Ev Classes
Courses: Up to BHSII/Road Safety/Pony & Riding Club/Resid/Wkg Pupils – 3
Facilities: Out Man: 40 x 20m*/17 Basic CC Fences/Lec Rm* – Vis Aids/Seating – 15/Library/WC/Washing/Changing Facilities/Car Park
Accom: Shared Rms – 6 Catering: Full
Specialities: General Instruction/Competition Preparation/Riding Holidays/Breaking/Schooling

THE YORKSHIRE RIDING CENTRE LTD
Markington, Harrogate, North Yorks, HG3 3PE
Tel: Ripon (0765) 677207/677497 – Students only
Fax No: 0765 677065
Managing Director: Mr C Bartle (BHSI) Regd **Chief Inst:** Mrs J Bartle-Wilson (BHSI)
Other Staff: Mrs G Bartle (BHSI) Regd Miss M Digby-Ovens (BHSI) Regd Miss L Potts (BHSII) Regd Miss S Daly (BHSII) Regd M Nicholson (BHSII) Regd Miss B Hurrell (BHSII) Regd Mr S Metcalfe BHSI(SM) Regd
Instruction in Riding and Jumping & Students to BHSI Exam
Av No: Horses 55 Ponies 12
Std of Schlg: General Purpose Std of Specialist Schlg: Drg/Evt: Advanced
Livery: Full/Part/DIY/Break/School/Edge of Dales
Ev Classes
Courses: Resid Inst Hol/Wkg Students/YT – 40 (Agency)/Career Training
Facilities: Cov Schs: 49 x 22m* Gly* 100 & 49 x 2 8m Gly 200/Out Man: 70 x 37m*/Jmp Pd/Sh Jmps 30*/CC Fences*/CC Course/Lec Rm/Audio video/Club Rm/Refresh/WC/Wash Rm/Chng Rm/Wait Rm/Tennis Court/Car Park
Accom: Guest House: 9 Luxury Bedrooms – 4 Priv Bath/Shower/35 Single/Twin Rooms Catering: Full/Part
Specialities: Training for careers/Adults & Children's riding holidays/Competition training for dressage/Show jumping & eventing/YT
Exclusions: No hiring for hacking or hunting
Location: Off A61 5 miles from Ripon & 8 miles from Harrogate

YORK RIDING SCHOOL
Wigginton Road, York, North Yorkshire, YO3 8RH
Tel: 0904 763686
Proprietor/Chief Inst: Mrs L A Holstead (BHSI) Regd
Manager: Miss H Worthington (BHSAI) Regd **Other Staff:** Mr R Holstead (BHSAI) Regd
Instruction in Riding and Jumping & Students to BHSAI Exam
Av No: Horses 10 Ponies 11 Specialist Horses: 1 A – 2 B Sh Jmpers/1 Adv Event
Std of Schlg: General Purpose Std of Specialist Schlg: CT – Int/Sh Jmpg – A
Livery: Full/Hunter/School
Ev Classes
Courses: Resid/Wkg Pupils/YT/up to BHSI
Facilities: Cov Sch: 80 x 20m* Gly/Out Man: 60 x 25m* Fl Lit/Jmpg Pd*/Int CC Courses*/Lec Rm/Club Rm – Vis Aids/Video/Seating – 75/Snacks/Wash Rm/Lic Bar/WC/Showers/Changing Rm/Tack Shop – Res ident Saddler/Car Park

Accom: 1 Single/2 Shared Rms – 5 Catering: Full
Specialities: Career Student Training/Training Horse & Rider for all Competitions/General Instruction
Exclusions: No Hacking
Location: Off the Ring Road North of York

SOUTH YORKSHIRE

ROCKINGHAM HOUSE FARM

Upper Haugh, Rawmarsh, Rotherham, South Yorks, S62 7DP
Tel: Rotherham (0709) 524045
Proprietors: Mrs J E Lindsey (BHSAI) & Mr G C Knight
Basic Instruction in Riding and Jumping
Av No: Horses 4 Ponies 6 Specialist Horses: 1/2 Sh Jmpers
Std of Schlg: General Purpose
Livery: Full/Part/Grass/Hunter/Break/School/Hack – Bridlepaths/Country Roads
Ev Classes
Courses: Inst
Facilities: Cov Sch: 18.5 x 23m* Fl Lit/Out Man: 31 x 21.5m Only used in Summer/Sh Jmps*/Jmp Pd/WC/Car Park
Specialities: Escorted hacking/Production of Show Animals/All types of livery/Preparation for Pony Club Tests/RDA
Exclusions: No unescorted riders
Location: 5 miles from Rotherham & 15 miles from Sheffield

BARNES GREEN RIDING SCHOOL

Woodseats Farm, Barnes Green, Grenoside, Nr Sheffield, South Yorkshire
Tel: 0742 402548
Proprietor: Miss C Walker
Chief Inst: Miss S Turner (BHSAI)
Other Staff: 3 (BHSAI) 2 (BHSII) P/T 2 (BHSAI) P/T
Instruction in Riding & Jumping
Av No: Horses 11 Ponies 10
Std of Schlg: General Purpose Std of Specialist Schlg: CT – Basic/Sh Jmpg – C
Livery: Full/School/Break/Hack – Woodlands/Forest Rides
Ev Classes
Courses: Wkg Pupils/YT – 3
Facilities: Out Man: 47 x 24m* Fl Lit/12 Basic Schooling CC Fences*/Jmp Pd/2 full sets BSJA Sh Jmps*/Lec Rm – Seating 10 – 15/Vis Aids/Library/Wash Rm/WC/Car Park
Specialities: Managing Agent for the YT Scheme
Location: 5 miles north of Sheffield/Off A61

BROCKHOLES FARM RIDING CENTRE

Branton, Doncaster, South Yorkshire, DN3 3QS
Tel: 0302 535057/535450
Proprietor: Miss J H Turner
Chief Inst: Miss P Lane (BHSAI) P/T
Other Staff: 2 (BHSAI) 2 (BHSAI) P/T
Instruction in Riding and Jumping
Av No: Horses 10 Ponies 25 Mules 2
Std of Schlg: General Purpose Std of Specialist Schlg: Sh Jmpg – Grade C
Livery: Full/Part/Grass/School/Break/Hack – Farmland/Bridleways
Ev Classes
Courses: YT – 1
Facilities: Out Man: 20 x 40m Fl Lit/Cov Sch: 14 x 32m/Jmp Pd/Snacks/Wash Rm/WC/Car Park
Specialities: Show Jumping/RDA
Exclusions: No children under 3 years
Location: 2 miles east of Doncaster

FINNINGLEY SCHOOL OF EQUITATION

Finningley, Doncaster, South Yorkshire, DN9 3BU
Tel: Doncaster (0302) 770259
Proprietors: Mrs C M Baddiley & Mrs J C Cartwright
(BHSAI) Chief Insts: Mrs M Mearns (BHSII(T)) & Mrs P Hinchliff (BHSII(T))
Other Staff: Miss J Taylor(BHSAI) Mrs J Peel (BHSAI) Mrs P Keenan (BH S SM) Miss J Furr Mrs A Woodland (BHSII) P/T Miss C Evans (BHSAI) P/T Miss P Rowling (BHSAI) P/T
Instruction in Riding and Jumping & Students to BHSII Exam
Av No: Horses 35 Ponies 25
Std of Schlg: General Purpose Std of Specialist Schlg: Drg – Elem
Livery: Full/Part/Grass/Hunter/Break/School/Hunt/Hack – Open country
Ev Classes
Courses: Resid Inst Hol/Wkg Students/YT – 4
Facilities: Cov Sch: 42 x 19m* Gly Fl Lit/Sh Jmps/CC Course/Lec Rm/Rest Rm/Refresh/WC/Wash Rm/Clu b Rm/Car Park
Accom: 10 – Cottage/Guest House 6 to 8 Catering: Full
Specialities: Adults & Childrens courses/BHS Stages I & II Exams/RDA

Location: Off A614 6 miles south of M18/M180 Junction

MASSARELLA SCHOOL OF RIDING
Thurcroft Hall, Brookhouse, Laughton, Sheffield, South Yorkshire, S31 9YO
Tel: Dinnington (0909) 566429
Proprietors: Mr S Massarella & Miss G Liggins
Chief Inst: Miss G Liggins (BHSII(T))
Other Staff: 3 (BHSAI)
Instruction in Riding and Jumping
Av No: Horses 10 Ponies 15
Std of Schlg: General Purpose
Livery: Full/Part/Grass/Break/School/ Hack – Lanes/Bridlepaths/Woodlands
Ev Classes
Courses: Inst/YT 4
Facilities: Cov Sch: 37 x 25m* Fl Lit/Out Man: 53 x 22m* Fl Lit/Jmp Pd/Sh Jmps*/ Lec Rm/Tack Shop/Wait Rm/WC/Chng Rm/Car Park
Accom: 4 House Catering: Full
Specialities: Show jumping for clients with own horses/Schooling/Show jumping
Location: 2 miles East of M1/M18 Junction

MILLVIEW EQUESTRIAN CENTRE
Mark Lane, Fulwood, Sheffield, South Yorkshire, S10 4PY
Tel: Sheffield (0742) 305093
Proprietor: Mrs H M Greenwood (BHSAI)
Chief Inst: Miss Alison Baggaley(BHSAI) **Other Staff:** 1 (BHSAI)
Instruction in Riding and Jumping
Av No: Horses 2 Ponies 11
Std of Schlg: General Purpose Break/School/Hack – Bridlepaths/ Moorland
Courses: YT 1
Facilities: Out Man: 40 x 20m*/Jump Pd/Sh Jumps/CC Fences/Vis Aids/ Video/Refresh/WC/Chng Rm/Shop/ Car Park
Specialities: Children's riding/Riding & Stable Management day courses/ Shows/Riding & Road Safety Tests/RDA
Exclusions: No casual hire
Location: 3 miles from Centre of Sheffield

MOORHOUSE EQUESTRIAN CENTRE
Gap Farm, Moorhouse, Doncaster, South Yorkshire, DN6 7HA
Tel: 0977 642109
Proprietors: Mr & Mrs W & Miss V Hobson & Mrs DJ Harris
Manager & Chief Inst: Miss T Harmer (BHSAI) Regd **Other Staff:** Miss D Harris (BHSAI) Regd Miss S Corkwell (BHSAI) P/T Miss S miles (BHSAI) P/T G Bartle BHSi Regd – Visiting
Instruction in Riding and Jumping & Students to BHSAI Exam
Av No: Horses 10 Ponies 10 Specialist Horses: 2 Elem Drg/6 B & C Sh Jmpers/ 2 Nov Eventers
Std of Schlg: General Purpose Std of Specialist Schlg: Drg – Elem/CT – Nov/ Sh Jmpg – A
Livery: Full/Part/Hunter/School
Ev Classes
Courses: up to BHSII/Pony Club/Wkg Pupils/YT
Facilities: 2 Cov Schs: 77 x 36m* Gly & 27 x 19 m* Gly/Use of Novice nearby CC Course/Lec Rm – Seating – 12/ Library/Video/Vis Aids/Snacks/Wash Rm/WC/Waiting Rm/Tack Shop/Horse Walker in Stable area for 4/Horse Transport/Car Park/Facilities for Disabled
Accom: 1 Caravan – 1 single & 3 Shared Rms – 9 Catering: Self/Part
Specialities: Competitions – BSJA & Dressage/Preparation for BHS Exams/ Liveries
Location: 1.5 miles East of S Elmsall

PARKLANDS RIDING SCHOOL LTD
Worksop Road, Aston, Sheffield, South Yorkshire, S31 0AD
Tel: 0742 875278
Proprietor & Chief Inst: Mrs R Sampson (BHSAI)
Other Staff: 2 (BHSAI) 1 (BHSI(SM & T)) P/T 1 (BHSAI) P/T
Instruction in Riding and Jumping
Av No: Horses 9 Ponies 14
Std of Schlg: General Purpose Std of Specialist Schlg: Sh Jmpg – Novice
Livery: Full/School/Hack – mainly across own land/adjoining fields for shorter rides
Ev Classes
Courses: YT – 2/towards BHS Stages I & II & Road Safety Test
Facilities: Cov Sch: 33 x 46m*/Out Man: 25 x 40m*/20 Basic CC Fences*/ Jmpg Pd/Wash Rm/WC/Tack Shop/ Horse Feed/Car Park
Specialities: Disabled Riders/Under privileged & Youth Groups
Location: 5 miles East of Sheffield off A57

SMELTINGS FARM RIDING CENTRE
Ringinglow Road, Sheffield, South Yorkshire, S11 7TD
Tel: 0742 307661

Proprietor & Chief Inst: Mrs S V Stenton (BHSAI)
Other Staff: Miss N Keeley (BHSAI) Miss A Lesson Miss K Green (BHSII) P/T Miss C Ballantyne (BHSAI) P/T Miss C Coghlan P/T Miss N Danson Mr D J Stenton
Instruction in Riding and Jumping
Av No: Horses 5 Ponies 11
Std of Schlg: General Purpose Std of Specialist Schlg: CT – Basic/Sh Jmpg – Nov
Livery: Full/Part/Grass/School/Break/Hack – Moorland
Ev Classes
Courses: Up to & including (BHSAI) & NVQ/Wkg Pupil
Facilities: Out Man: 40 x 20m* Fl Lit/SH Jmps*/Lec Rm* – Vis Aids/Seating – 20/Library/Video/Snacks/Wash Rm/WC/Chng Rm/Car Park
Specialities: General Instruction/Road Safety/Pony Club Work/Livery
Location: 4 miles from Sheffield off the A625

WEST YORKSHIRE

ACRE CLIFFE RIDING SCHOOL

Ellar Ghyll, Bradford Road, Otley, West Yorkshire, LS21 3DN
Tel: 0943 73912
Proprietor & Chief Inst: Mrs A Everall (BHSII(T))
Other Staff: 2 (BHSAI) P/T 1 UQ
Instruction in Riding and Jumping
Av No: Horses 12 Ponies 10 Specialist Horses: 1 Drg – E
Std of Schlg: General Purpose Std of Specialist Schlg: Drg – Novice/Sh Jmp – C
Livery: Full/Wkg Livery/School
Ev Classes
Courses: Up to BHS Stage III/YT
Facilities: Cov Sch: 40 x 20m*/Out Man: 40 x 20m* Fl Lit/14 Schooling Fences* – Novice/Jmpg Pd*/Refreshments on Show Days/WC/Car Park
Specialities: Side Saddle Instruction/RDA/Private & Handicapped Riders/Monthly Horse Shows/Weekly practice shows (May – September)/Training for BHS Exams
Location: Between Otley & Menston

CHERRY TREE LIVERY STABLES

Gill Lane, Kearby, Nr Wetherby, West Yorkshire, LS22 4BS
Tel: 0532 886460
Proprietor & Chief Inst: Miss R A Search (BHSAI)
Other Staff: Miss R Headey (BHSII(T))
Training & Facility Centre & Students to BHSAI Exam
Av No: Horses 7 Ponies –
Std of Schlg: General Purpose Std of Specialist Schlg: Sh Jmpg – Novice/Drg – Elem
Livery: Full/School/Break
Courses: Up to & including BHSAI/Pony Club Tests/Wkg Pupils – 3/Resid – Students only
Facilities: Out Man: 43 x 23m* Fl Lit/13 Novice Schlg CC Fences/Jmpg Pd*/Vis Aids/Video
Accom: C/H Flat – 4 Catering: main meal provided
Specialities: Livery/Training of Horse & Rider/Breaking/Career Training/Dressage Training
Exclusions: External Riders unless with own horses – except Students
Location: 4 miles from Wetherby

J – SIX S C RIDING SCHOOL

Thorpe Lane, Tingley, Nr Wakefield, West Yorkshire, WF3 1QY
Tel: 0532 520429
Proprietor & Chief Inst: Miss J Howarth (BHSAI)
Other Staff: Mrs J Senior (BHSAI)
Instruction in Riding and Jumping
Av No: Horses 4 Ponies 6 Specialist Horses: 1 Grade C Sh Jmper/3 Side Saddle
Std of Schlg: General Purpose Std of Specialist Schlg: Sh Jmpg – Novice
Livery: Full/Part/School
Courses: Wkg Pupils
Facilities: Cov Sch: 44 x 18m* Gly/Jmpg Pd/Lec Rm – Vis Aids/Library/Video/Snacks/WC/Showers/Wait Rm/Tack Shop/Car Park
Specialities: Show Jumping/Side Saddle Instruction/RDA
Exclusions: No Rider over 13 Stone
Location: Nr Junc 28 off M62

LONGFIELD STABLES

Middle Longfield Farm, Todmorden, West Yorkshire
Tel: 0706 812736
Proprietor & Chief Inst: Miss C Farnaby (BHSAI)
Other Staff: N Arnott (BHSI(SM & T)) – Visiting
Instruction in Riding and Jumping
Av No: Horses 5 Ponies 8
Std of Schlg: General Purpose Std of Specialist Schlg: Showing

Livery: Full/Grass/Working/School/Break/Hack – Moorland with country tracks
Ev Classes
Courses: Wkg Pupils – 3
Facilities: Cov Sch: 20 x 14m/Out Man: 39 x 18 m/8 Basic Schooling CC Fences/Lec Rm – Seating – 30/Vis Aids/Video/WC/Car Park
Specialities: Breaking/Schooling – Show Production (Horses)
Exclusions: No unaccompanied hacking
Location: 1 mile East of Todmorden

MOORSIDE EQUESTRIAN CENTRE
Moorside Farm, Baildon, Shipley, West Yorkshire, BD17 6BJ
Tel: 0274 587849
Proprietor: Mrs K Metcalfe
Chief Inst: Miss Katie Butters (BHSII)
Other Staff: Miss S Robinson (BHSAI) Miss K Firth (BHSAI) Miss E Jack (BHSAI) P/T
Instruction in Riding and Jumping & Students to BHSAI Exam
Av No: Horses 12 Ponies 12 Specialist Horses: 3 Drg – Elm/2 Sh Jmp C/3 HT Nov
Std of Schlg: General Purpose Std of Specialist Schlg: CT – Basic/Sh Jmp – Novice
Livery: Full/Part/School/Break/Hack – Open Moorland
Ev Classes
Courses: BHS Stages including BHSAI/NVQ/YT – 1/Wkg Pupil – 3
Facilities: Out Man: 35 x 55m* Fl Lit/24 CC Fences/CC Course/Jmp Pd/Lec Rm – Vis Aids/Snacks/Wash Rm/WC/Waiting Rm/Car Park
Accom: 2 Prefab Buildings – 20 (Staff & Students Only) Catering: Full
Specialities: Dressage/Show Jumping/YT Man Agent
Location: 4 miles north Bradford/Signed for Moorside

PARK STABLES
Ewood Lane, Todmorden, West Yorkshire, Corres: Ewood Lane Todmorden, Lancs, OL14 7DF
Tel: Todmorden (0706) 812564
Proprietor: Mr R Miller
Instruction in Riding and Jumping & Students to BHSAI Exam
Av No: Horses 8 Ponies 9
Std of Schlg: General Purpose
Livery: Full/Break/School/Hunt/Hack/Trek – Rural uplands/Moorland
Courses: Resid Inst Hol
Facilities: Jmp Pd/Sh Jmps/CC Fences/CC Course/Lec Rm/WC/Car Park
Accom: Local hotels/guesthouses
Specialities: Show jumping/Hunter Trials/Showing
Location: 1 mile from Todmorden on edge of moor

SHAY LANE STABLES
Ovenden, Halifax, West Yorks
Tel: Halifax (0422) 363069
Proprietors: Mr & Mrs S Yates
Chief Inst: Mr S Yates
Instruction in Riding and Jumping
Av No: Horses 6 Ponies 8
Std of Schlg: General Purpose
Livery: Full/Hunter/Break/School/Hack – Moorland
Ev Classes
Courses: Short/School Holiday
Facilities: Cov Sch: 74 x 19m*/Sh Jmps/Lec Rm/WC/Car Park
Specialities: Schooling of ponies/Showing hacks ponies & hunters/Show jumping competitions
Location: 2 miles from Halifax off A629

THROSTLE NEST FARM RIDING SCHOOL
Fagley Lane, Bradford, West Yorkshire, BD2 3NU
Tel: 0274 639390
Proprietor: Mrs B Howorth
Chief Inst: Mrs J Wheeler (BHSAI) Regd
Instruction in Riding and Jumping
Av No: Horses 8 Ponies 9
Std of Schlg: General Purpose Std of Specialist Schlg: Sh Jmpg – Novice
Livery: Full/Part/DIY/School/Hack – Country Lanes/Woodland
Ev Classes
Courses: YT
Facilities: Out Man: 40 x 20m*/Jmp Pd/Lec Rm/Tack Shop
Exclusions: No Riders over 14 Stone
Location: 2 miles from Bradford/Off A658

WESTWAYS RIDING SCHOOL
The Homestead, Carr Lane, Thorner, Leeds, West Yorks, LS14 3HD
Tel: Leeds (0532) 892598
Proprietor: Miss Yolande Catherine Beaumont
Other Staff: 2 (BHSAI) P/T Miss S Brown (BHSII) – visiting
Basic Instruction in Riding and Jumping
Av No: Horses 10 Ponies 16
Std of Schlg: General Purpose
School/Hack/Trek – Bridle Paths

Ev Classes
Courses: Hol Inst (Non Residential)/YT
Facilities: Out Man:(3)* 2 Fl Lit/Jmp Pd*/Sh Jmps/CC Fences*/CC Course/ Vis Aids/Video/Chng Rm/WC/Wash Rm/ Car Park
Specialities: Teaching riding and basic jumping/Stable Management and pony care to children and adults/Small shows and events of an improving nature
Exclusions: No Riders over 12 stone
Location: Between A58 & A64 5 miles from centre of Leeds

WILLOW ROYD STABLES
Luddenden Foot, Halifax, West Yorks, HX2 6LG
Tel: Halifax (0422) 884095
Proprietor: Mrs J Ambler
Chief Inst: Mrs L Baldwin (BHSAI)
Other Staff: 1 (BHSAI) P/T
Instruction in Riding and Jumping
Av No: Horses 10 Ponies 7
Std of Schlg: General Purpose
Livery: Full/School/Break/Hack – Open moorland
Ev Classes
Courses: YT – 2
Facilities: Cov Sch: 43 x 22m*/Jmp Pd/Sh Jmps/Vis Aids/WC/H & C/ Refresh/Wait Rm/Car Park
Specialities: Show Ponies/Buying & Selling Horses & Ponies
Location: 6 miles from Halifax/off Sowerby Lane

Riding in the North West

CHESHIRE ♦ GREATER MANCHESTER ♦ ISLE OF MAN ♦ LANCASHIRE ♦ MERSEYSIDE

CHESHIRE

B 1st RIDING SCHOOL & EQUITATION CENTRE
1 Higherfold Farm, Windlehurst Road, High Lane, Stockport, Cheshire, SK6 8AQ
Tel: 061 427 3737
Proprietor: P M Booth Esq
Chief Insts: Miss J Gardner (BHSAI) & Miss E Dronsfield (BHSAI) **Other Staff:** 1 (BHSAI) P/T
Instruction in Riding and Jumping
Av No: Horses 10 Ponies 7
Std of Schlg: General Purpose Std of Specialist Schlg: Sh Jmp – Novice
Livery: Full/Part/School/Break/Hack – Bridleways – National Trust/Country Park
Ev Classes
Courses: Wkg Pupils/YTS 2/ET 2
Facilities: Cov Sch: 41 x 20m*/Jmp Pd/Lec Rm – Seating/Vis Aids/Video/Wash Rm/WC/Changing Rm/Car Park
Location: Off A6 3 miles from Stockport

BARNSTON RIDING CENTRE
Gills Lane Farm, Barnston, Wirral, Cheshire, L61 1AH
Tel: 051 648 2911
Proprietors: Mr & Mrs A Wlodarski
Chief Inst: Mrs P Boyd (BHSAI) P/T – 4 days per week **Yard Manager:** Miss H Jones (BHSAI) **Other Staff:** 3 (BHSAI) P/T
Basic Instruction in Riding and Jumping
Av No: Horses 12 Ponies 8
Std of Schlg: Basic Std of Specialist Schlg: Sh Jmpg – Novice
Livery: Full/Part/DIY/School/Hack – Beach/Bridle paths
Ev Classes
Courses: YT – 2/ET – 4
Facilities: Cov Sch: 25 x 56m Gly/Out Man: 20 x 60m Fl Lit/Jmpg Pd/Lec Rm – Seating – 20/Video/Snacks/Wash Rm/WC/Changing Rm/Wait Rm/Tack Shop/Car Park
Location: Leave A540 Nr Heswall/Gills Lane is off A551 through Barnston

BOLD HEATH EQUESTRIAN CENTRE
Heath House Farm, Bold Heath, Nr Widnes, Cheshire, WA8 0XT
Tel: 051 424 5151
Proprietor: Mrs J E Baker (BHSII) YTS (Agency)
Other Staff: 4 (BHSAI) 1 (BHSII) Miss M Hawley (BHSI) – Visiting Mrs J Basil (BHSI) – Visiting
Instruction in Riding and Jumping & Students to BHSII Exam
Av No: Horses 17 Ponies 15
Std of Schlg: General Purpose School – Farmland/Grassland
Ev Classes
Courses: Inst/Wkg Students/Non-resid Inst Courses/YT 18
Facilities: Cov Schs: 28 x 65m* Gly 300 Seats Fl Lit & adjacent School 25 x 43m*/Jmp Pd* Fl Lit/Sh Jmps*/CC Course*/CC Fences/Lec Rm/Vis Aids/Video/Club Rm*/Lic Bar/Rest Rm/Refresh/WC/Wash Rm/Chn g Rm/Shop/Car Park
Accom: 1 – Mobile Home Catering: Self
Specialities: Competitions/Dressage/Teaching/Indoor & Outdoor shows/RDA/BHS H K & R Exams I – III
Exclusions: No hacking out/No casual hiring
Location: 2 miles from Junc 7 on M62

BROOMHALL RIDING SCHOOL
Heatley Lane, Broomhall, Nr Nantwich, Cheshire, CW5 8BA
Tel: Crewe (0270) 780392
Proprietor: Mr C D Garside (BHSII(T))
Other Staff: 2 (BHSAI) P/T
Instruction in Riding and Jumping
Av No: Horses 7 Ponies 10
Std of Schlg: General Purpose

Livery: Full/Part/Grass/DIY/Break/School/Hack
Ev Classes
Courses: Resid Inst Hol/Wkg Students
Facilities: Cov Sch: 32 x 22m Gly 120*/Out Man: 3 6 x 23m*/Jmp Pd/Sh Jmps/CC Fences/Lec Rm/Vis Aids/WC/Car Park
Accom: 3 – House Catering: Part
Specialities: Riding Club
Exclusions: No YTS
Location: Off A530 3 miles from Nantwich & 6 miles from Whitchurch

CROFT RIDING SCHOOL
Spring Lane, Croft, Nr Warrington, Cheshire, WA3 7AS
Tel: 0925 763715
Proprietors: Mr & Mrs A Daniels
Chief Inst: Miss M Dickinson (BHSII)
Other Staff: Miss J Glover (BHSAI) Miss L Woolaston (BHSAI) Miss R Rudge (Unqual)
Basic Instruction in Riding and Jumping
Av No: Horses 8 Ponies 10
Std of Schlg: Basic Std of Specialist Schlg: CT – Novice/Sh Jmpg – C
Livery: Part/DIY/School
Facilities: Cov Sch: 21 x 42m* Gly/Novice CC Course*/Jmp Pd*/Club Rm/Lec Rm* – Seating – 40/Vis Aids/Video/Snacks/Wash Rm/WC/Changing Rm/Waiting Rm/Car Park

THE FOXES RIDING SCHOOL
Badgersrake Lane, Ledsham, South Wirral, Cheshire, L66 8PF
Tel: 051 339 6797
Proprietor: Mrs J E Davey (BHSAI)
Chief Inst: Mrs S Hinchcliffe (BHSII)
Other Staff: 1 (BHSI) P/T 3 (BHSAI) 3 (BHSAI) P/T 1 FBHS P/T
Instruction in Riding and Jumping & Students to BHSII Exam
Av No: Horses 25 Ponies 15 Std of Specialist Horses: 1 Drg – E
Std of Schlg: General Purpose
Livery: Full/Part/Break/School
Ev Classes
Courses: Inst/Wkg Students/YTS 5/ET 5
Facilities: 2 Cov Schs: 18.5 x 37m* Gly 60 Fl Lit & 23 x 42m/Out Man: 23 x 46m*/Jmp Pd/Sh Jmps/Lec Rm/Vis Aids*/Video/Refresh/WC/Wash Rm/Chng Rm/Car Park
Specialities: RDA/Dressage
Location: 3 miles from M56 towards Hoylake on A540 Rt at Two Mills for 5 mile

HOLLY TREE RIDING STABLES
Plumley Moor Road, Plumley, Nr Knutsford, Cheshire, WA16 9RU
Tel: Lower Peover (0565) 72188
Proprietors: Mr P Long & Mr D Long
Chief Inst: Miss S Littler (BHSAI) P/T
Instruction in Riding and Jumping
Av No: Horses 5 Ponies 9
Std of Schlg: General Purpose
Hack – Country Lanes/Bridlepaths/Park
Ev Classes
Courses: Inst
Facilities: Cov Sch: 32 x 25m Gly 20/Jmp Pd*/Lec Rm/Vis Aids/WC/H & C/Chng Rm/Refresh/Car Park
Specialities: RDA
Exclusions: No casual hiring/No YTS
Location: Off A556 3 miles south of Junc 19 on M6

MOBBERLEY RIDING SCHOOL
Oak House, Newton Hall Lane, Mobberley, Cheshire, WA16 7LQ
Tel: Mobberley (056587) 3123
Proprietor: Miss P Rigby (BHSII)
Instruction in Riding and Jumping
Av No: Horses 14 Ponies 11 Spec Horses: Dsrg – M
Std of Schlg: General Purpose
Livery: Full
Courses: YTS – 2
Facilities: Cov Sch: 46 x 21.5m* Gly30/Out Man: 40 x 20m*/WC/H & C/Car Park
Specialities: General instruction/Novices/Livery/Riding Club/RDA
Location: On B5085 between Mobberly & Wimslow

POOL BANK FARM
Bow Lane, Bowdon, Altrincham, Cheshire, WA14 3BY
Tel: 061 929 9713 – evening
Proprietors: N P Kennerley Esq – (B Kennerley & Son (Stables))
Managers: Mr & Mrs Kennerley
D I Y Livery Yard
Std of Specialist Schlg: Sh Jmpg – Novice
Livery: DIY/Hack – for riders on own horses – Tatton Park/Bridlepaths/Country Roads
Facilities: Out Man: 20 x 44m Fl Lit/WC/Car Park
Specialities: D I Y Liveries
Exclusions: For riders on their own horses only
Location: 2 miles from Tatton Park

THE WIRRAL RIDING CENTRE
Haddon Lane, Ness, South Wirral, Cheshire, L64 8TA
Tel: 051 336 3638

Proprietor: Mrs M Ward
Chief Inst: Miss C Church (BHSAI)
Other Staff: Mrs J Carrathers (BHSI) P/T Mrs D Johnson (FBHS) – Visiting
Instruction in Riding and Jumping & Students to BHSII Exam
Av No: Horses 16 Ponies Std/No of Specialist Horses: 12
Std of Schlg: General Purpose Std of Specialist Schlg: Sh Jmpg – B
Livery: Full/Part/DIY/Break/School
Ev Classes
Courses: Hol Inst/Wkg Students – 2/YT – 2
Facilities: Cov Sch: 44 x 22m* Gly 300/Out Man:60 x 20m* Fl Lit/Jmp Pd/Sh Jmps/Lec Rm/WC/Chng Rm/Refresh/Wait Rm/Car Park
Specialities: Indoor Shows/Demonstrations/Competition training/General Instruction/Livery/RDA/National Training Centre for Special Olympics
Exclusions: No casual hiring
Location: 7 miles from M56/8 miles from Chester

GREATER MANCHESTER

CARRINGTON RIDING CENTRE
Nursery Farm, Isherwood Road, Carrington, Urmston, Manchester, M31 4BH
Tel: 061 969 5853
Proprietor: Mr B Groos
Chief Inst: Miss H Shaw (BHSII(T)) P/T
Other Staff: 2 (BHSAI)
Instruction in Riding and Jumping & Students to BHSAI Exam
Av No: Horses 12 Ponies 10
Std of Schlg: General Purpose
Livery: DIY/Break/School/Hack – Bridlepaths/Parkland
Ev Classes
Courses: Inst/Wkg Students
Facilities: Cov Sch: 40 x 15m* Gly 40/Out Man: 40 x 45m Fl Lit/Jmp Pd 20/Sh jumps 6/School Fences/Lec Rm/Vis Aids/Video/Club Rm/Wash Rm/Refresh/WC/Chng Rm/Wait Rm/Tack Shop/Car Park
Accom: 4 – Mobile Home/Locally
Catering: Self
Specialities: Show Jumping/Student courses
Exclusions: No YT
Location: Off A6144 7 miles east of Warrington

DEANDANE RIDING STABLES
397 Gathurst Road, Orrell, Wigan, Gt Manchester
Tel: Appleby Bridge (02575) 3086
Proprietor: Mr M Whalley (BHSII(T))
Chief Inst: Miss A Brook (BHSAI) **Other Staff:** 2 (BHSAI) P/T
Basic Instruction in Riding and Jumping
Av No: Horses 8 Ponies 10
Std of Schlg: General Purpose School/Hack – Woodlands/Bridlepaths
Ev Classes
Courses: Inst/YT
Facilities: Cov Sch: 20 x 32 m* Fl Lit Gly/Out Man: 30 x 15m/Jmp Pd/Sh Jmps/CC Fences 22/CC Course 1.5 mile/WC/Car Park
Specialities: Hacking/Non-residential courses/RDA work
Location: 4 miles west of Wigan

LASSELL HOUSE RIDING CENTRE
Mossey Lea Road, Wrightington, Nr Wigan, Lancashire, WN6 9RE
Tel: 0257 427319
Proprietor: Mrs P S Brightcliffe
Chief Inst: Mr A Wong (BHSII) **Other Staff:** 2 (BHSAI) 1 (BHSAI BHS IT)
Instruction in Riding and Jumping
Av No: Horses 15 Ponies 10 Specialist Horses: 5 RDA Ponies
Std of Schlg: General Purpose Std of Specialist Schlg: Sh Jmp–Novice/Newcomers/Drg – E
Livery: Full/Part/School/Break/Hack – Bridleways/Country Lanes/Country Park
Ev Classes
Courses: BHS Stages I & II & III/Wkg Students/YT 3
Facilities: Cov Sch: 55 x 19m* Gly/Out Man: 40 x 20m*/Jmp Pd/Wash Rm/Changing Rm/WC/Car Park
Specialities: Adult Novice Courses/Courses tailored to suit the individual/Lecture/Demonstrations/Preparation for BHS Stages Exams I – III
Location: 0.5 mile from Junc 27 on M6

ISLE OF MAN

AULDYN EQUESTRIAN CENTRE
Rydings, Glen Auldyn, Ramsey, Isle of Man
Tel: 0624 812259
Proprietors: Mrs J & Mr N Barham
Chief Inst: Mrs J Barham (BHSII(SM))
Other Staff: 1 (BHSAI)
Instruction in Riding and Jumping & Students to BHSAI Exam

Av No: Horses 4 Ponies 6
Std of Schlg: General Purpose Std od Specialist Schlg: Drg – Elem/CT – Nov
Livery: Full/Grass/School/Break/Hack – Glen/Open Mountain Side
Ev Classes
Facilities: Out Man: 35 x 18m Fl Lit/ Novice Schooling Fences/Seats in House – Video/WC
Exclusions: No Rider over 12 stone

G G H EQUITATION CENTRE
Ballacallin Beg, Crosby, Marown, Isle of Man
Tel: Marown (0624) 851574/851450
Correspondence to: Mrs C Matthews & Mrs Gilbey
Proprietors: Mrs S Matthews/Mrs J Gilbey/Mr W A Gilbey
Head Girl: Miss F Walker (BHSAI)
Other Staff: 2 (BHSAI) 1 (BHSAI) P/T
Instruction in Riding and Jumping & Students to BHSAI Exam
Av No: horses 10 Ponies 26
Std of Schlg: General Purpose
Livery: Full/Part/Grass/Break/School/ Hunt/Hack – Farmland/Forestry
Ev Classes
Courses: Inst Hol/Wkg Students/YTS/ Side Saddle
Facilities: Cov Sch: 37 x 22m* Gly/2 Out Man: 37 x 25m & 60 x 25m/Jmp Pd Seats Fl Lit/Sh Jmps/CC Course/WC/ Chng Rm/Refresh/Lec Rm/Vis Aids/ Video/Car Park
Specialities: Instruction given in general riding and jumping/Student Training/Side Saddle/2 day Events/RDA
Location: 2 miles South St Mark Braaide Cross Roads

LANCASHIRE

CHORLEY EQUESTRIAN CENTRE
Higher Garstang Farm, Chapel Lane, Heapey, Chorley, Lancs, PR6 8TB
Tel: 0257 268801
Proprietor & Chief Inst: Mrs J E Berry (BHSII(T))
Other Staff: 1 (BHSII(T)) P/T 1 (BHSI) P/T
Instruction in Riding and Jumping
Av No: Horses 10 Ponies 7
Std of Schlg: General Purpose Std of Specialist Schlg: CT – Basic/Sh Jmpg – Nov
Livery: Full/Part/Hunter/School/Hack – Parkland/Tracks/Woodland
Ev Classes
Courses: BHS Stages I & II/YT – 2
Facilities: Out Man: 20 x 40m* Fl Lit/5 Basic Schooling CC Fences/Jmp Pd*/Snacks/Vending Machine/ Microwave/Wash Rm/WC/Car Park
Specialities: Escorted hacking/General Instruction
Location: Off the A674 near Wheelton 2 miles from Junc 8 on M61

CROOKLANDS RIDING ESTABLISHMENT
Langley Lane, Goosnargh, Nr Preston, Lancashire, PR3 2JU
Tel: Broughton (0772) 863017
Partners: Mrs J Ward (BHSI) Mrs S A C Ward (BHSII) & Miss A C Turner (BHSII)
Chief Inst: Miss Turner (BHSII) **Other Staff:** 3 (BHSAI)
Instruction in Riding and Jumping & Students to BHSAI Exam
Av No: Horses 11 Ponies 7 Spec Horses: 2 Dsg – E
Std of Schlg: General Purpose
Livery: Full/Grass/DIY/Hunter/Break/ School/Hack – Bridlepaths
Ev Classes
Courses: Inst Hol/Wkg Students/YT 2
Facilities: Cov Sch: 37 x 15m* Gly 15/ Out Man: 41 x 20m* Seats Fl Lit/Sh Jmps/CC Fences/Lec Rm/Vis Aids*/ Chng Rm/Rest Rm/WC
Specialities: General instruction/ Training for competitions/Riding & Pony Club/RDA
Exclusions: No unaccompanied riding
Location: 2 miles from Junc 32 off M6

EARNSDALE FARM RIDING SCHOOL
Earnsdale Farm, Darwen, Lancashire, BB3 0LB
Tel: 0254 702647
Proprietors: Mrs M Comer & Mrs J Crook
Chief Inst: Mrs J Crook (BHSAI) (NDHM)
Other Staff: 1 (BHSAI) 1 (BHSII)
Basic Instruction in Riding and Jumping
Av No: Horses 8 Ponies 12
Std of Schlg: Basic Instruction Std of Specialist Schlg: Sh Jmpg – Novice
Livery: Full/Part/School/Break
Ev Classes
Courses: YT – 4
Facilities: Cov Sch: 20 x 40m/Out Man: 40 x 20m* Fl Lit/WC/Small place for Car Park
Specialities: Children & Novice Adults
Exclusions: No casual hire
Location: Off A666 Blackburn – Darwen Road up Lynwood Avenue/Dudden Avenue adj Darwen Golf course

ECCLESTON EQUESTRIAN CENTRE
Ulnes Walton Lane, Leyland, Preston, Lancashire, PR5 3LT
Tel: 0772 600 093
Proprietor & Chief Inst: Miss K A Green (BHSII)
Managing Agent for YT
Other Staff: 1 (BHSAI) 1 (BHSII(T)) 2 (BHSAI) P/T
Instruction in Riding and Jumping
Av No: Horses 15 Ponies 9
Std of Schlg: General Purpose
Livery: Full/Grass (summer only) Break/School/Hack – Country lanes/ Beach
Ev Classes
Courses: Inst Hol/YT 6
Facilities: Out Man: 43 x 21m Fl Lit/ Cov Sch: 6 0 x 24m Gly – 250/Sh Jmps/18 CC Fences/Canteen/Bar/WC/ RDA WC/Lec Rm/Staff Rm/Rest Rm/ Tack Shop/Large Car & Box Park
Specialities: General Instruction/ Hacking/Livery/Show Preparation/RDA
Exclusions: No casual hiring
Location: Off A581 Chorley – Croston 1 mile from Croston

FIR TREE RIDING CENTRE
Fir Tree Lane, Aughton, Nr Ormskirk, Lancashire, L39 7HH
Tel: Aughton Green (0695) 423655
Proprietor: Mrs S Temme
Chief Inst: Miss L Lemmon (BHSII(T))
Other Staff: 2 (BHSAI)
Instruction in Riding and Jumping
Av No: Horses 6 Ponies 5
Std of Schlg: General Purpose
Livery: Full/School/Break/Hack – Roads/Tracks/Farmland
Ev Classes
Courses: Wkg Students
Facilities: Cov Sch: 37 x 22m* Fl Lit/Club Rm/Rest Rm/Refresh/WC
Specialities: Training Students/Nervous Riders
Exclusions: No casual hiring/Weight Limit 14 stone
Location: A59 from Ormskirk 3rd turning on right dual carriageway & 1st right into Fir Tree Lane

HALSALL RIDING & LIVERY CENTRE
Terra Nova, Gregory Lane, Halsall, Nr Ormskirk, Lancs, L39 8SP
Tel: 0704 840001
Proprietors: Mr & Mrs B Beilensohn
Manager & Chief Inst: Mrs J Beilensohn (BHSAI) **Other Staff:** 1 (BHSAI) – Visiting Mrs Johnson (FBHS) – Visiting
Instruction in Riding and Jumping
Av No: Horses 18 Ponies 2
Std of Schlg: General Purpose Std of Spec Schlg: Drg – Novice/Sh Jmp – Novice
Livery: Full/Part/Grass/School/Hack – Country Lanes/Beach
Ev Classes
Facilities: Cov Sch: 43 x 25m Gly*/ Out Man: 42 x 22m Fl Lit*/WC/Car Park
Specialities: Show Eventing/Dressage Competitions
Location: Gregory Lane is off the A5147 at Halsall

OSBALDESTON HALL FARM RIDING CENTRE
Osbaldeston, Nr Blackburn, Lancashire, BB2 7LZ
Tel: 0254 813159 (Centre)/878452 (Home)
Proprietors: Mr & Mrs N Bargh
Facility Centre & Livery Yard
Specialist Schlg: CT – Novice/Sh Jmpg – A
Livery: Full/Part/Grass/DIY/School/Hack – on the Farm/Quiet roads
Facilities: 2 Cov Schs:61 x 31m* Gly – 320 & 37 x 17m/Novice & Pre Novice CC Course*/Jmpg Pd*/Club Rm/Lec Rm – Seating – 100/Film Projector/Full Meals/Lic Bar/Changing RmShowers/ Wash Rm/WC/Car Park
Specialities: Facility Centre/Livery/ Indoor & Outdoor Shows/Seminars/ Courses/Lectures/Demonstrations etc
Location: Near M6 Junction 31 just off the A59

WHITEMOOR STABLES
Whitemoor Bottom Farm, Foulridge, Colne, Lancashire, BB8 7LX
Tel: 0282 861890
Proprietor/Chief Inst: Mrs R M Stanworth (BHSAI)
Basic Instruction in Riding and Jumping – Livery Owners Only
Av No: Horses 18 Ponies 7
Std of Schlg: General Purpose
Livery: Full/Part/School
Ev Classes
Courses: YTS – 3
Facilities: Out Man: 23 x 37m Fl Lit/WC/ Car Park
Specialities: Livery including Show Horses & Ponies/All kinds of horse feed for sale
Exclusions: No horses for hire
Location: Between Barrowsford & Barnoldswick on the B6251

WREA GREEN EQUITATION CENTRE
Bryning Lane, Wrea Green, Nr Kirkham, Lancashire, PR4 1TN
Tel: Kirkham (0772) 686576
Proprietor: Miss C A Pollitt (BHSII(T))
Other Staff: Mrs S Pimbley (BHSI) – Visiting 1(BHSAI)
Instruction in Riding and Jumping
Av No: Horses 14 Ponies 7
Std of Schlg: General Purpose
Livery: Full/School/Break
Ev Classes
Courses: YT 2
Facilities: Cov Sch: 37 x 19m* Gly 30/ a few Small CC Fences/Lec Rm/WC/ Chng Rm/Refresh/Car Park
Accom: 5
Specialities: Riding for the Disabled/ Side Saddle/General Instruction
Exclusions: No casual hire or hack
Location: 4 miles from Junc 4 on M55/ 10 miles from Blackpool & 15 miles from Preston

MERSEYSIDE

LONGACRES RIDING SCHOOL
290 Southport Road, Lydiate, Nr Liverpool, Merseyside, L31 4EQ
Tel: 051 526 0327
Proprietors: Mr & Mrs J Kirkham
Other Staff: 3 (BHSAI) 2 (BHSII) Mrs Johnson (FBHS) – Visiting
Instruction in Riding and Jumping & Students to BHSII Exam
Av No: Horses 12 Ponies 12
Std of Schlg: General Purpose
Livery: Full/Part/School/Hack – Mainly arable
Ev Classes
Courses: Inst/Wkg Students/YT/ET
Facilities: Cov Sch: 40 x 20m Gly 20/Jmp Pd/Sh Jmps 20*/CC Course/ Lec Rm/Vis Aids/Video/Refresh/WC/ Wash Rm/Car Park
Specialities: Non residential courses/ RDA/Indoor and outdoor shows/ Preparation for exams
Location: On the A5147 at Lydiate

NORTHFIELD RIDING CENTRE
Northfield Farm, Gorsey Lane, Bold, Nr St Helens, Merseyside, WA9 4SW
Tel: Marshalls Cross (0744) 816075
Proprietors: Mr & Mrs Cotterill
Chief Inst: Miss H Cotterill (BHSII)
Other Staff: 4 (BHSAI) 2 (BHSII) Mrs J Basil (BHSI) – visiting 2 daysper week
Instruction in Riding and Jumping & Students to BHSII Exam
Av No: Horses 35 Ponies 11 Spec Horses: Drg – 4 E/1 M
Std of Schlg: General Purpose
Livery: Full/Break/School
Ev Classes
Courses: Resid Inst Hol/Wkg Students/ YT/ET
Facilities: Cov Sch: 46 x 22m Gly 260 Fl Lit/Out Man: 55 x 28m/Jmp Pd/Sh Jmps 20 BSJA/CC Course/Lec Rm/ Vis Aids/Video/Refresh/Rest Rm/WC/ Showers/Wash Rm/Chng Rm/Car Park
Accom: 15 – Cottage Catering: Full
Specialities: Student Training/Eventing/ RDA
Location: 5 miles from Junc 7 on M62/ A57 2 miles + A570 + Gorsey Lane

WOODVILLE RIDING SCHOOL
Raby Road, Thornton Hough, Wirral, Merseyside, L63 4JR
Tel: 051 336 4800
Proprietor: Mrs M P Walton
Livery Yard, Inst. under the direction of Mr T Thompson BHSI
Av No: Horses 6 Ponies 2
Std of Schlg: General Purpose
Livery: Full/DIY/Hunter/School/Hack – Bridlepaths/The Wirral Way
Facilities: Cov Sch: 20 x 36m* Fl Lit/WC/Car Park
Specialities: Nervous riders/Novice riders/Horse transport/Horses/Ponies for sale/Lessons on own horses
Exclusion: No unescorted rides
Location: 300 yds off the main road through Thornton Haugh

Riding in the East Midlands

DERBYSHIRE ♦ LEICESTERSHIRE ♦ LINCOLNSHIRE ♦ NORTHAMPTONSHIRE ♦ NOTTINGHAMSHIRE

DERBYSHIRE

ALTON RIDING SCHOOL
Alton, Chesterfield, Derbyshire, S42 6AW
Tel: 0246 590267
Proprietor: Mrs J D Fisher
Chief Inst: Mrs J Fisher (BHSAI) **Other Staff:** 1 (BHSII) P/T 1 (BHSI) Visiting
Instruction in Riding and Jumping
Av No: Horses 14 Ponies 14
Std of Schlg: General Purpose Std of Specialist Schlg: Sh Jmps – Grade C
Livery: Full/Grass/School/Hack/Trek – Bridleways/Lanes
Ev Classes
Courses: YTS – 23
Facilities: Cov Sch: 20m x 40m*/Out Man: 20m x 45m * Fl Lit/Jmp Pd/ Snacks/Wash Rm/WC/Car Park
Specialities: Side Saddle/Show Jumping Clincs/RDA
Location: 5 miles from Chesterfield & 5 miles from Matlock

AMBER HILLS EQUESTRIAN
Whitehouse Farm, Belper Lane, Belper, Derbyshire, DE5 2UJ
Tel: 0773 824080
Proprietors: Mrs V Cooke & Miss V Morris
Manager & Chief Inst: Mrs V Cooke (BHSAI) **Other Staff:** 2 (BHSAI) P/T
Instruction in Riding and Jumping
Av No: Horses 8 Ponies 6 Specialist Horses: 1 Drgs – E/HT – N/Sh Jmper – C
Std of Schlg: General Purpose Std of Specialist Schlg: Sh Jmp – Novice/Drg – Elem
Livery: Full/Part/School/Break/Hack – Stone Wall Country on edge of Peak District
Ev Classes
Courses: Available up to Stage 3/Res Rid Hols/YT – 2
Facilities: Out Mans: 40 x 20m* Fl Lit & 35 x 20m/Jmp Pd/Refreshments/Wash Rm/WC/Car Park
Accom: Dormitory – Children 8/Adults 6 Catering: Full
Specialities: Children Riding Holidays/ Equestrian days/Short Breaks for adults – (off peak) with high class cuisine
Exclusions: No Children under 4 years
Location: Off A517 1 mile from centre of Belper

BIRCHWOOD RIDING CENTRE
140 Birchwood Lane, Somercotes, Derbyshire, DE55 4NE
Tel: 0773 604305
Proprietor & Chief Inst: Mrs L Coyle (BHSII(T))
Instruction in Riding and Jumping
Av No: Horses 6 Ponies 3
Std of Schlg: General Purpose Std of Specialist Schlg: Drg – Novice/C T – Basic/Sh Jmpg – Novice
Livery: Full/Part/School/Break
Ev Classes
Courses: BHS Stages 1 & 2/Riding & Road Safety Test/YT – 1/Wkg Pupil – 1
Facilities: Out Man: 20 x 60m* Fl Lit/12 Schooling Fences/Jmp Pd/Refreshments/ Wash Rm/WC/Changing Rm/Tack Shop/ Car Park/Lec Rm – Vis Aids/Seating
Accom: House – 6 Catering: Full Children's Riding Holidays – Summer only
Specialities: Childrens Riding Holiday
Location: Off A38 2 miles from Junc 28 on M1

BREASTON EQUESTRIAN CENTRE
Sawley Road, Breaston, Derbyshire, DE7 3EF
Tel: 03317 2934
Proprietor & Chief Inst: Mrs S M Davison (BHSII SM)
Other Staff: Miss L O'Brian (BHSAI) L Smith (BHS AI) Miss S Baxter (BHSAI)
Instruction in Riding and Jumping & Students to BHSII Exam
Av No: Horses 10 Ponies 8 Std of Specialist Horses: 1 Int & 2 Nov Eventer
Std of Schlg: General Purpose Std of Specialist Schlg: Drg – Elem/CT – Novice/Sh Jmpg – C
Livery: Full/Part/DIY/Hunter/School/ Break/Hack – Country Roads/Lanes
Ev Classes
Courses: Wkg Pupils/YT – 1/Up to & including BHSII
Facilities: 2 Out Mans: Both 40 x 20m* Fl Lit/C C Course* – 23 Novice/Int CC Fences/Jmpg Pd*/Club Rm/Lec Rm – Vis Aids/Seating/Library/Video/Film Projector/Snacks/Wash Rm/WC/Waiting Rm/Car Park
Accom: for Staff only – Self Contained – 2 Catering: Full
Specialities: Competitions & Competition coaching
Location: Bewteen Exits 24 & 25 0n M1 off A6005 0.5 mile from Breaston Village Centre

BRIMINGTON EQUESTRIAN CENTRE
130 Manor Road, Brimington, Chesterfield, Derbyshire, S43 1NN
Tel: 0246 235465/566132
Proprietor/Chief Inst: Miss T E Priest (BHSII(T))
Other Staff: 1 (BHSAI) 1 (BHSII) P/T
Instruction in Riding and Jumping & Students to BHSAI Exam
Av No: Horses 9 Ponies 7
Std of Schlg: General Purpose Std of Specialist Schlg: Sh Jmpg – Novice
Livery: Full/Part/School/Hack – Bridleways/Woodlands
Ev Classes
Courses: YT – 1/ET – 2/Childrens 'Own a Pony'
Facilities: Out Man: 40 x 20m Fl Lit/Jmp Pd*/Lec Rm/Refreshments/WC/Car Park
Specialities: Childrens 'Own a Pony Courses'/Single Driving Turnout
Location: 4 miles from Junc 29 on M1

BUXTON RIDING SCHOOL
Fern Farm, Fern Road, Buxton, Derbyshire, SK17 9NG
Tel: 0298 72319
Proprietor & Chief Inst: Miss F L Andrew (BHSAI)
Other Staff: 1 (BHSAI) P/T
Instruction in Riding and Jumping
Av No: Horses 7 Ponies 9
Std of Schlg: General Purpose Specialist Schooling: Sh Jmp – A
Livery: Full/Part/Grass/Schl/Break/Hack – Open Country/Quiet Lanes
Ev Classes– Summer only
Courses: YT – 2
Facilities: Out Man: 26 x 19m*/Lec Rm WC/Car Park
Location: Off A515 1 mile from centre of Buxton opposite Haddon Hall Hotel

CAUSEWAY FARM
Plaistow Green, Crich, Nr Matlock, Derbyshire
Tel: 0629 534248
Proprietors: Mrs G St John Bell–Heather & A C Bell Esq
Manager & Chief Inst: Mrs G St John Bell-Heather (BHSII SM) **Other Staff:** 2 (BHSI) Visiting 3 (BHSAI) 2 (BHSAI) P/T 1 (BHS SM) P/T
Instruction in Riding and Jumping & Students to BHSII Exam
Av No: Horses 17 Ponies 3 Specialist Horses: 2 Drg M – 1 Drg E/ 2 Sh Jmpers C – 1 Sh Jmper A/1 CT N
Std of Schlg: General Purpose Std of Specialist Schlg: Drg – N/CT – Basic/Sh Jmpg – Grade C
Livery: Full/Part/Grass/DIY/Hunter/ School/Hack – Bridlepaths
Ev Classes
Courses: BHS Stages I/II/III/IV & (BHSII(T))/Resid Riding Holidays/YT – 1/2 Wkg Pupils/ET – 5
Facilities: Cov Sch: 50 x 20m* Gly/Out Man: 60 x 25m Fl Lit/20 Basic CC Fences*/Jmp Pd*/Lec Rm/Club Rm – Vis Aids/Seating/Film Projector/Library/ Snacks/Wash Rm/Bar/WC/Changing Rm/Waiting Rm/Car Park
Accom: 4 Self contained Chalets – 8 – for Staff & Holiday riders only Catering: Self
Specialities: Side Saddle/Show Jumping/Shows
Location: 4 miles from Matlock between Plaistow & Crich

THE EAST MIDLANDS RIDING ASSOCIATION FOR HANDICAPPED CHILDREN AND ADULTS
Leathersley Lane, Scropton, Derby, DE6 5PN
Tel: Burton-on-Trent (0283) 812753
Proprietor: Mrs Y Austin (BHSAI)

Other Staff: 2 (BHS(PTT))
Instruction in Riding and Jumping
Av No: Horses 10 Ponies 12
Std of Schlg: General Purpose
Livery: Full/Part/Break/School/Hack – Bridleways
Ev Classes
Facilities: Cov Sch: 37 x 22m Fl Lit 150 Seats/Out Man: 40m x20m Fl Lit/Jmp Pd/Sh Jmps/Lec Rm/Chng Rm/Wait Rm/Car Park
Specialities: Handicapped riders of all ages/Beginners/Children
Exclusions: No YTS
Location: Off A50 5 miles from Burton upon Trent between Uttoxeter & Derby

ELVASTON CASTLE RIDING CENTRE
Thulston, Derby, Derbyshire, DE7 3EP
Tel: Derby (0332) 751927/753481
Proprietors: Mr & Mrs P J Coe & Mr & Mrs F F Anderson
Chief Inst: Mr P Coe (BHSII)
Other Staff: Miss K Haden (BHSAI) 4 (BHSAI) P/T
Instruction in Riding and Jumping & Students to BHSAI Exam
Av No: Horses 17 Ponies 12
Std of Schlg: General Purpose
Livery: Part/Break/School/Hack – Castle Country Park – Grounds – 250 acres
Ev Classes
Courses: Resid Inst Hol/Wkg Students – 3/YT – 2
Facilities: 2 Out Man: 56 dia* & 43 x 22m* Fl Lit/Sh Jmps/2 CC Courses*/CC Fences/Lec Rm/Vis Aids/Videos/ Refresh/WC/Tack shop/Car Park
Accom: 6 (Annexe – Students & Staff) Catering – Self/Limited for clients as family/Catering– full
Specialities: All round equestrian tuition plus regular competitions/RDA
Exclusions: No hunting/No hacking unless client of sufficient standard
Location: Nr Borrowash on B501
5 miles from Derby & 10 from Nottingham

FIELD FARM STABLES
The Field, Shipley, Nr Heanor, Derbyshire, DE7 7JH
Tel: 0773 713164
Proprietors: Mr & Mrs D G Barker
Chief Inst: Miss V Barker (BHS Int Teach Cert) **Other Staff:** Miss S Graham (BHS Int Teach Cert)
Instruction in Riding and Jumping
Av No: Horses 9 Ponies 7
Std of Schlg: General Purpose Std of Specialist Schlg: Sh Jmpg Grade C
Livery: DIY/School/Hack – Bridleways/ Farm Land
Ev Classes
Courses: YT – 1/Wkg Pupil – 1
Facilities: 2 Out Man: 40 x 20m Fl Lit & 22 x 2 2m Fl Lit/Wash Rm/WC/Changing Rm/Car Park
Exclusions: No children under 4 years
Location: Off A6007 between Nottingham & Derby

HARGATE HILL RIDING SCHOOL
Hargate Hill, Glossop, Derbyshire, SK13 9JL
Tel: 0457 865518
Proprietors: Mr & Mrs M C Tyldesley
Chief Inst: Mrs E Taylor (BHSII) **Yard Manager:** Miss M Mitchell (BHSAI)
Other Staff: Miss A Brown (BHSAI) Miss L Belston (BHSAI) Miss J Roath (BHSAI)
Instruction in Riding and Jumping
Av No: Horses 8 Ponies 12
Std of Schlg: General Purpose Std of Specialist Schlg: Sh Jmpg – Novice
Livery: Full/Part/Grass/DIY/Hunter/ School/Hack – Country Lanes/ Bridlepaths
Ev Classes
Courses: Stable Management/YT – 3
Facilities: Out Man: 40 x 20m* Fl Lit/ Jmp Pd/WC/Car Park
Specialities: Childrens Riding/Stable Management
Location: Off A626 3 miles from Glossop

NORTHFIELD FARM RIDING & TREKKING CENTRE
Northfield Farm, Flash, Nr Buxton, Derbyshire
Tel: Buxton (0298) 22543
Proprietors: Mr D C & Mrs M E Andrews (BHSAI)
Basic Instruction in Riding and Jumping
Av No: Horses 15 Ponies 10
Std of Schlg: General Purpose
Livery: Full/Part/Grass/DIY/Break/ School/Hunt/Hack/Trek – Moorland valley/Pack Horse Trails
Ev Classes
Courses: Hol/YT – 1
Facilities: Sh Jmps 8/WC/Wash Rm/ Chng Rm/Car Park
Accom: 3 – Self contained flats Catering: Self
Specialities: Hacking/Trekking all ages & standards including RDA/Large groups catered for/Weekend Trail rides – experienced riders only

Exclusions: No accommodation for unaccompanied children
Location: Just off A53 5 miles South of Buxton

PARK HALL FARM EQUESTRIAN CENTRE
Park Hall Farm, Mapperley, Nr Ilkeston, Derbyshire, DE7 6DA
Tel: 0602 301581
Proprietor: A Morgan Esq
Livery Yard
Livery: Full/Part/Grass/DIY
Facilities: Wash Rm/WC/Car Park
Location: Off A609 7 miles from Derby & 7 miles from Nottingham

RED HOUSE STABLES
Old Road, Darley Dale, Matlock, Derbyshire, DE4 2ER
Tel: Matlock (0629) 733583
Proprietor: Mrs Caroline Dale-Leech
Chief Inst: Miss J Green (BHSII) P/T
Other Staff: Miss S Hares (BHSAI)
Instruction in Riding and Jumping
Av No: Horses 12 Ponies 10
Std of Schlg: General Purpose
Livery: Full/Part/Grass/Hunter/Break/School/Hack/Trek – Country Lanes/Moorland
Ev Classes
Courses: Inst Hol – unaccompanied Children/Horse Driving/YT – 2
Facilities: Jmp Pd/Sh Jmps/CC Fences/Lec Rm/Refresh/WC/Chng Rm/Car Park
Specialities: Stage coach and four/Tours around the Peak District/Driving instruction/TV & Film work
Location: Just off A6 between Matlock & Bakewell on edge of Peak National Park

RINGER VILLA EQUESTRIAN CENTRE
Ringer Lane, Clowne, Derbyshire, S43 4BX
Tel: 0246 810456
Proprietor: Miss Y M Evans
Manager & Chief Inst: Miss J Eastwood (BHSAI) **Other Staff:** Mr C White (BHSII)
Instruction in Riding and Jumping
Av No: Horses 9 Ponies 14
Std of Schlg: General Purpose Std of Specialist Schlg: Sh Jmpg – Nov
Livery: Full/Part/Grass/DIY/School/Hack – unmade lanes
Ev Classes
Courses: Wkg – 1
Facilities: Out Man: 40 x 20m Fl Lit/3 Basic Schooling CC Fences/Lec Rm – Vis Aids/Library/Video/Seating – 20/Snacks/WC/Car Park
Specialities: Children & Beginners
Location: Off A616 2 miles east of Exit 30 on M1

STUBLEY HOLLOW RIDING CENTRE
Stubley Hollow, Dronfield, Woodhouse, Nr Sheffield, South Yorkshire
Tel: Dronfield (0246) 419207
Proprietors: Mr & Mrs E H Mosley
Chief Inst: Mrs E Salt (BHSAI) **Head Girl:** Miss S Morrison **Other Staff:** Miss S Berry (BHSI) Visiting
Instruction in Riding and Jumping
Av No: Horses 12 Ponies 15
Std of Schlg: General Purpose
Livery: Full/DIY/Hack – Bridlepaths/Woodland/Moorland
Courses: YT – 2/Wkg Students – 1/ET – 2
Facilities: Cov Sch: 25 x 19m* Fl Lit/Out Man: 43 x 25m* Fl Lit/Jmp Pd*/Sh Jmps*/CC Fences 20*/Lec Rm/Club Rm/Showers/WC
Accom: 12 – Flat & Caravan – Families & Children Catering: Full/Self
Specialities: Riding for all ages/Livery/Riding Holidays
Location: Just off A61 between Chesterfield & Sheffield

YEW TREE FARM STABLES
Hazelwood, Derbyshire, DE6 4AE
Tel: Derby (0332) 841364
Proprietors: M & H Lester
Chief Inst: Miss S J Harby (BHSII) P/T
Other Staff: 1 (BHSAI) P/T
Instruction in Riding and Jumping
Av No: Horses 10 Ponies 10
Std of Schlg: General Purpose
Livery: Full/Part/Grass/Hunter/Hunt/Hack – Open Country
Ev Classes
Courses: ET – 1
Facilities: Cov Sch: 25 x 32m Fl Lit/Jmp Pd/Sh Jmps/CC Fences/WC/Car Park
Specialities: Pupils with own horses/Childrens courses/Prof tests/Horses for sale and hire
Location: 2 miles from Belper between A6 & A517

LEICESTERSHIRE

BROOKLANDS FARM RIDING SCHOOL
Kirkby Lane, Barwell, Leics, LE9 8FT
Tel: 0455 844599

Proprietors: Mr T J Golding & Miss D L Yates
Manager & Chief Inst: Miss D L Yates (BHSII(T)) **Other Staff:** Miss J Coe (BHSAI) Mr N Creaton BHSI P/T Mr M White (BHSII) P/T
Instruction in Riding and Jumping & Students to BHSAI Exam
Av No: Horses 11 Ponies 7
Specialist Horses: Drg – 3 I & 2 N/2 CT – Nov
Std of Schlg: General Purpose Std of Specialist Schlg: Sh Jmpg – Grade C
Livery: Full/Part/Grass/School/Hack – Bridleways/Country Lanes
Ev Classes
Courses: Up to & including BHSAI/Wkg Pupils/YT
Facilities: Cov Sch: 50 x 25m Gly*/Out Man: 40 x 20m*/8 Basic Schooling CC Fences/Jmpg Pd/Lec Rm – Seating – 12/ Library/Vis Aids/Refreshments/Wash Rm/ WC/Waiting Rm/Car Park
Specialities: Dressage/Shows
Location: Off A47 10 miles from Leicester & 4 miles from Hinckley

CANAAN FARM RIDING SCHOOL
Loughborough Road, Costock, Loughborough, Leicestershire, LE12 6XB
Tel: East Leake (0509) 853351
Proprietor & Chief Inst: Mrs J Chiasserini (BHSAI)
Other Staff: 1 (BHSAI) Miss J Bream (FBHS) – Visiting in Winter
Instruction in Riding and Jumping
Av No: Horses 7 Ponies 7
Std of Schlg: General Purpose
Livery: Full/School/Hack – Farm Track/ Roads/Bridlepaths
Ev Lessons
Courses: YT
Facilities: Cov Sch: 51 x 25m Fl Lit 50 seats/Out Man: 19 x 37m Fl Lit/Jmp Pd/Sh Jmps/CC Fences/Refresh/WC/H & C/Chng Rm/Car Park
Specialities: General Instruction
Location: On A60 between Nottingham & Loughborough

COLEORTON RIDING SCHOOL
The Old Vicarage, Loughborough Road, Coleorton, Leics, LE6 4HJ
Tel: 0530 223337/223663
Proprietor: Mrs J A Unwin
Manager: Mrs C A Fox (BHSAI) **Other Staff:** Miss L Thorpe (BHSAI) P/T Mr M White (BHSII) P/T
Instruction in Riding and Jumping
Av No: Horses 3 Ponies 8
Std of Schlg: General Purpose Std of Specialist Schlg: Sh Jmpg – C
Livery: Full/Part/Grass/DIY/Working/ School
Ev Classes
Courses: YT – 2/ET – 1
Facilities: 2 Out Mans: 42 x 22* Fl Lit & 42 x 22m*/Wash Rm/WC/Car Park
Specialities: Side-Saddle
Location: On A512 7 miles from Loughborough & 4 miles from Ashby de la Zouch

IVANHOE EQUESTRIAN CENTRE
Ivanhoe House, Smisby Road, Ashby De La Zouch, Leics, LE6 5UG
Tel: 0530 413629
Proprietors: Mr & Mrs J D Lebutt
Manager: Mrs J D Lebutt **Chief Inst:** Miss F Armstrong (BHSII) P/T **Other Staff:** Mr D Saddler (BHSAI) P/T Mr N Creaton (BHSI) – Visiting
Instruction in Riding and Jumping
Av No: Horses 3 Ponies 8 Specialist Ponies: 2 JA
Std of Schlg: General Purpose Std of Specialist Schlg: Sh Jmpg – Novice Schooling Liveries/Hack – Bridleways/ Farm Tracks
Ev Classes
Courses: Resid Riding Hols
Facilities: Cov Sch: 43 x 25m* Gly/Sh Jmps*/Video/Snacks/Wash Rm/WC/ Showers/Changing Rm/Shop/Car Park
Accom: 6 – House & Caravan Catering: Full
Specialities: Children/Native Ponies
Exclusions: No Riders over 12 stone
Location: Off B5006 1.5 miles from centre of Ashby De La Zouch

THE LIMES EQUESTRIAN CENTRE
Hinkley Road, Sapcote, Leicestershire, LE9 6LG
Tel: Sapcote (045527) 2271
Proprietor: Mrs P Brown
Chief Inst: Miss S Malin (BHSAI) **Other Staff:** 1 (BHSII) P/T
Instruction in Riding and Jumping & Students to BHSAI Exam
Av No: Horses 12 Ponies 16 Spec Horses: Sh Jmp – A
Std of Schlg: General Purpose
Livery: Full/Break/School/Hack – Flat/Wooded
Ev Classes
Courses: Inst/Wkg Students – 3/YT – 1/ET – 2
Facilities: Cov Schs:(1) 52 x 22m Gly 90/(2) 25 x 12m*/Jmp Pd/CC Course/CC Fences 21/Lec Rm/Vis

Aids/Showers/Chng Rm/Wash Rm/WC/ Wait Rm/Car Park
Accom: 10 – Flat/Mobile Home & Local Hotels Catering: Full/Part/Self
Specialities: Close personal attention/ Training/Show Jumping/Private instruction/RDA
Exclusions: No hiring for unaccompanied hacking
Location: 1 mile from Junc 2 on M69

MARKFIELD EQUESTRIAN CENTRE
Stanton Lane Farm, Markfield, Leicestershire, LE6 0TT
Tel: Markfield (0530) 242373
Proprietors: J & P Duffield
Chief Inst/Manager: Mr G Savory (BHSII)
Other Staff: 1 (BHSAI) P/T 2 (BHSAI)
Instruction in Riding and Jumping
Av No: Horses 14 Ponies 15 Specialist Horses: 1 Sh Jmper Grade B
Std of Schlg: General Purpose
Livery: Part/School/Break/Hack – Roadwork/Forestry
Courses: Inst
Facilities: Cov Schs: 62 x 31m* Gly 80 & 43 x 22 m* Fl Lit/CC Fences/Jmp Pd/ WC/Refresh/Car Park
Specialities: General instruction/ Coaching – competition/Riding Club

MARSDEN HOUSE STABLES
Marsden House, Huncote Road, Stoney Stanton, Leicestershire, LE9 6DJ
Tel: Sapcote (045527) 3093
Proprietor: Mrs L Dilkes (BHSAI)
Chief Inst: Miss J A Fray (BHSII(T))
Other Staff: 1 (BHSAI) P/T – weekends
Instruction in Riding and Jumping
Av No: Horses 6 Ponies 6
Std of Schlg: General Purpose
Livery: Full/DIY/Hack – Bridlepaths/ Common Land
Courses: YT – taken
Facilities: Cov Sch: 37 x 14m Fl Lit/Out Man: 60 x 20m Fl Lit/12 CC Fences/Jmp Pd/Sh Jmps/WC/Showers/Chng Rm/ Refresh/Wait Rm/Car Park
Specialities: Training for Show Jumping on own horses
Location: 7 miles from centre of Leicester

MEADOWS SCHOOL OF RIDING
Stanford on Soar, Loughborough, Leicestershire, LE12 5PY
Tel: Loughborough (0509) 263782
Proprietor: Mr D Allonby
Chief Inst: Miss D Whitmore (BHSAI)
Other Staff: 1 (BHSAI) P/T
Basic Instruction in Riding and Jumping
Av No: Horses 8 Ponies 12
Std of Schlg: General Purpose
Livery: Full/Break/School/Hunt/Hack – Bridlepaths
Ev Classes
Courses: Childrens – one day
Facilities: Cov Sch: 32 x 22m Fl Lit/Jmp Pd/Sh Jmps/CC Course/WC/Chng Rm/ Car Park
Specialities: Producing native Highland ponies/RDA
Exclusions: No YT
Location: 1 mile from Loughborough between the A6 & A60

THE MEADOWS RIDING CENTRE
Kilby Road, Fleckney, Leics, LE8 0BQ
Tel: 0533 402336
Proprietor: Mr & Mrs J Bowie
Manager: Mrs S Hood **Chief Inst:** Mrs V Saul (BHSAI) P/T **Other Staff:** Mrs D Varley (BHSAI) P/T
Instruction in Riding and Jumping
Av No: Horses 10 Ponies 7
Std of Schlg: General Purpose Std of Specialist Schlg: CT – Basic/Sh Jmpg – Nov
Livery: Full/Part/Grass/DIY/School/Hack – Bridleways/Lanes
Ev Classes
Courses: BHS Stages I & II/YT – 2
Facilities: Cov Sch: 23 x 46m* Gly/Out Man: 23 x 60m*/CC Course* – 21 Basic CC Fences/Jmp Pd*/Drinks Dispenser/ Wash Rm/WC/Changing Rm/Car Park
Location: Btwn A6 & A50 about 8 miles from Leicester & 6 miles from Market Harborough

PARK VIEW LEICESTER EQUESTRIAN CENTRE
Anstey Lane, Thurcaston, Leicester, LE7 7JA
Tel: 0533 364858
Proprietors: Mr & Mrs J L Mc Donald
Chief Inst: Mrs A Timlock (BHSAI)
Other Staff: Mrs J Payne (BHSI) – Visiting
Instruction in Riding and Jumping
Av No: Horses 25 Ponies 25
Std of Schlg: General Purpose Std of Specialist Schlg: CT – Novice/Sh Jmpg – Grade C
Livery: Part/Hunt/School/Hack – Park Land/National Trust Land
Ev Classes
Facilities: Cov Sch: 37 x 18m/Out Man: 37 x 21 m Fl Lit/30 CC Fences/CC Course – Novice/Jmp Pd/Refreshments/

Wash Rm/WC/Changing Rm/Tack Shop/ Car Park
Specialities: Livery
Location: 5 miles north of centre of Leicester

SCHOOL OF NATIONAL EQUITATION
Bunny Hill Top, Costock, Loughborough, Leicestershire
Tel: East Leake (0509) 852366
Proprietors: Mr R J Humphrey BHSI Mrs F M Humphrey Mr M Humphrey & Mrs E L Humphrey
Chief Inst: Mr R J Humphrey BHSI
Other Staff: 4 (BHSAI) 1 (BHSII) P/T
Instruction in Riding and Jumping & Students to BHSII Exam
Av No: Horses 20 Ponies 9
Std of Schlg: General Purpose Spec Horses: Drg – Med/Sh Jmp – C
Livery: Full/Part/Grass/Hunter/Break/ School/Hunt/Hack – Hilly woodland
Ev Classes
Facilities: Cov Schs: 46 x 19m Gly Fl Lit & 46 x 6m Fl Lit Gly 80/Out Man: 68 x 25m* Fl Lit/Jmp Pd/Sh Jmps*/CC Fences/CC Course/Lec Rm*/Vis Aids*/ Club Rm*/Lic Bar/Refresh/WC/ Showers/Chng Rm/Wash Rm/Tack Shop/Car Park
Accom: 8 – Rooms Local Catering: Full
Specialities: Showjumping & indoor shows lectures/demonstrations by riding personalities/RDA/Film work/ Riding Club
Location: On A60 between Nottingham & Loughborough

SOUTH LEICESTERSHIRE RIDING ESTABLISHMENT
Kimberley House, Frolesworth Road, Leire, Nr Lutterworth, Leicestershire, LE17 5HP
Tel: (0455) 209407
Proprietor: Mr K W Clawson BHSI
Other Staff: 2 (BHSAI) P/T
Training & Competition Centre
Av No: Horses 5 Ponies 2 Spec Horses: Sh Jmpg Grade A – 2
Std of Schlg: General Purpose
Livery: Full/Break/School/Hack/Trek
Courses: Wkg Students
Facilities: Cov Sch: 37 x 19* Fl Lit Gly/Out Man: 62 x 19m*/Jmp pd/Sh Jmps/CC Fences*/Lec Rm/Vis Aids/ Club Rm/Refresh/WC/Showers/Wash Rm/Chng Rm/Wait Rm/Car Park
Specialities: All competitive training especially Young Riders/RDA
Exclusions: No YT taken

STONE LODGE EQUESTRIAN CENTRE
Stone Lodge, Mere Lane, Oadby, Leicestershire
Tel: Leicester (0533) 712314/715292
Proprietor & Chief Inst: Miss Jones-Fenleigh (BHSI(SM))
Yard Manager: Francis Hutchinson (BHSII(T)) **Other Staff:** Miss L Machin (BHSAI) Miss S Fairie (BHSAI) Miss C Marclew (BHSII) P/T 3 (BHSAI) P/T Mr K Clawson (BHSI) – Visiting one day per week
Instruction in Riding and Jumping & Students to BHSII Exam
Av No: Horses 16 Ponies 3 Std of Spec Horses: 2 Drg I/2 HT I/1 Sh Jmp Grade A – 1 Sh Jmp Grade B
Std of Schlg: General Purpose
Livery: Full/Part/DIY/Hunter/Break/ School/Hack – Farmland/Country Lanes/ Bridlepaths
Courses: Resid Inst Hol/Wkg Students – 6/YT 12
Facilities: Cov Sch: 50 x 23m* Fl Lit/Out Man:20 x 40m*/Jmp Pd*/Sh Jmps 12*/ CC Course*/CC Fences*/Lec Rm/Vis Aids*/Club Rm/Rest Rm/WC/Showers/ Wash Rm/Chng Rm/Video/Car Park
Accom: 12– Farmhouse – Catering: Full – Holidays 5 – Shared Rooms – Catering: Self – Students
Specialities: Residential courses/ Working pupils
Exclusions: No Unaccompanied hacking or hunting/No main road riding
Location: Off A6 next to Glen Corse Golf Course

STRETTON RIDING CENTRE
Manor Bungalow Farm, Stretton, Oakham, Leicestershire
Tel: (0780) 410 323
Proprietor: Mrs J L Ward
Other Staff: Mrs S Dalby (BHS(PTT))
Basic Instruction in Riding and Jumping
Av No: Horses 13 Ponies 14
Std of Schlg: General Purpose Hack/Woodland/Bridleways
Ev Classes
Courses: Inst/YT – 1
Facilities: Out Man: 22 x 11m Fl Lit/Jmp Pd/Sh Jmps 3/CC Fences 11/Lec Rm/ Showers/WC/Wash Rm/Chng Rm/Car Park
Specialities: Driving (Governess cart) including instruction in harnessing/ Adults and children taught responsibility in caring for and riding a pony/Private lessons
Location: Off A41 within the triangle of Granth am/Oakham/Stamford

THE WHARF
Market Overton, Oakham,
Leicestershire, LE15 7PW
Tel: Thistleton (057 283) 279
Proprietor: Mrs J M Sturrock FBHS
Other Staff: 1 (BHSAI) Miss Sturrocks (BHSI) P/T
Instruction in Riding and Jumping & Students for all BHS Exams including Fellowship
Av No: Horses 3 Ponies – Specialist Horses: 3 HT I/3 Drg I
Std of Schlg: General Purpose Std of Specialist Schlg: Drg – Med
Livery: Full/Break/School
Ev Classes
Courses: Resid Inst/Wkg Students
Facilities: Cov Sch: 42 x 23m Gly Fl Lit/ Jmp Pd 4 acres/CC Course/Rest Rm/ WC/Showers/Wash Rm/Chng Rm/ Car Park
Accom: 7 – Family House Catering: Self/Part
Specialities: Training for competitions and all examinations on own horse
Exclusions: No YT

LINCOLNSHIRE

AUSTER LODGE RIDING STABLES
Edenham, Bourne, Lincolnshire, PE10 0LH
Tel: Edenham (077 832) 287
Proprietor: Mr R W Haddow
Chief Inst: Ms W Dykstra (BHSII(T))
Other Staff: 1 (BHSAI)
Basic Instruction in Riding and Jumping
Av No: Horses 12 Ponies 8
Std of Schlg: General Purpose
Livery: Full/Part/Grass/DIY/Break/ School/Hunt/Hack – Farm/Forestry
Ev Classes
Courses: Resid Inst Hol/YTS 1
Facilities: Cov Sch: 28 x 18.5m* Fl Lit (only open in Winter)/Out Man: 37 x 28m*/Jmp Pd*/Sh Jmps*/CC Fences*/ CC Course/Refresh/Rest Rm/WC/ Showers/Wash Rm/Chng Rm/Car Park
Accom: 10 – Farmhouse/Local Catering: Full
Specialities: Hacking

BECKS LANE RIDING CENTRE
Becks Lane, Scotter, Gainsborough, Lincs
Tel: 0724 764475
Proprietors: Mr R D & Miss S J Harbour
Manager: Miss S J Harbour **Chief Inst:** Miss K Rimes (BHSAI)
Instruction in Riding and Jumping
Av No: Horses 7 Ponies 7
Std of Schlg: General Purpose Std of Specialist Schlg: Sh Jmpg – Novice
Livery: Full/Part/Working/School/Hack – Woodlands/Bridleways
Ev Classes
Courses: YT – 1
Facilities: Out Man: 30 x 35* Fl Lit/Jmp Pd/Snacks/Wash Rm/WC/Spectators Viewing Box overlooking Manege/Car Park
Specialities: RDA – Riding & Driving
Location: Off A159 10 miles south of Scunthorpe

BETTER TACK RIDING CENTRE
Middledene, Surfleet Road, Surfleet, Spalding, Lincolnshire, PE11 4AG
Tel: 0775 85368
Proprietors: Mr & Mrs J P Bettinson
Chief Inst: Miss C Moore (BHSII) **Other Staff:** 1 (BHSAI)
Instruction in Riding and Jumping
Av no: Horses 11 Ponies 5 Spec Horses: 2 Med Drg
Std of Schlg: General Purpose Std of Specialist Schlg: Sh Jmpg – Novice
Livery: Full/Part/Hack – Lanes/Track
Ev Classes
Courses: BHS Stages 1 & 2/YT – 4/Wkg Students – 1
Facilities: Out Man(2): 44 x 25m* Fl Lit/ 42 x 25m Fl Lit/Jmp Pd/Wash Rm/WC/ Tack Shop/Car Park
Accom: 3 Staff/Students – Portacabin Catering: Self
Specialities: Saddlery Shop
Exclusions: No Children under 5 years
Location: On A16 3 miles north of Spalding/12 miles south of Boston

BUCKMINSTER EQUESTRIAN CENTRE
Sewston, Grantham, Lincolnshire, NG33 5RW
Tel: 057 284 544
Proprietors: Mr & Mrs V Gillingham
Chief Inst: Miss A Gillingham (BHSAI)
Instruction in Riding and Jumping
Av No: Horses 10 Ponies 6
Std of Schlg: General Purpose Std of Specialist Schlg: Sh Jmp – Novice
Livery: Full/Part/Grass/School/Hack– Bridleways/Broad Verges
Ev Classes
Courses: Resid/Driving/YT – 1
Facilities: Cov Sch: 20 x 28m/Jmp Pd/CC Fences/Snacks/Wash Rm/WC/Car Park
Accom: Residential Wing for 6 –

Bedrooms/Sitting Rm/Dining Rm/ Kitchen/Shower Rms/Catering: Self
Specialities: Pony Days/Weekly Courses/Driving – Governess/Exercise Carts/Landau/RDA
Location: On Sewstern to Wymondham road

FOUR WINDS EQUITATION CENTRE
Leaveslake Drove, West Pinchbeck, Spalding, Lincolnshire
Tel: 0775 87533
Proprietors: Miss P V & Mrs E D Matthews
Manager & Chief Inst: Miss P V Matthews (BHSII) **Other Staff:** Miss E Smith (BHSAI)
Instruction on Riding and Jumping Students to BHSAI
Av no: Horses 8 Ponies 8 Spec Horses: 2 Novice Eventers
Std of Schlg: General Purpose Std of Specialist Schlg: Drg/CT/Sh Jmp – all novice
Livery: Full/Part/Grass/School/Hack – Fens
Ev Classes
Courses: Wkg Pupil – 3/YTS– 3
Facilities: Cov Sch: 43 x 20m* Fl Lit/Out Man: 25 x 50m* Fl Lit/CC Course/Jmp Pd/Lec Rm/Vis Aids/Video/Wash Rm/ WC/Chng Rm/Tack Shop/Car Park
Accom: Shared rooms – 6 For Staff/Pupils/YT only Catering: Self
Specialities: Novice Competitions
Location: Off A1511 4 miles from Spalding & 6 miles from Bourne

HILL HOUSE RIDING SCHOOL
Sand Lane, Osgodby, Market Rasen, Lincolnshire, LN8 3TE
Tel: 0673 843407
Proprietor: A D Pennell Esq
Manager/Chief Inst: Miss K Pennell (BHSAI) **Other Staff:** 1 (BHSI(E & T)) 1 (BHSII) P/T Miss T Thornton (BHSAI) Miss S Moss (BHSAI)
Instruction in Riding and Jumping & Students to BHSAI Exam
Av No: Horses 20 Ponies 10
Std of Schlg: General Purpose Std of Specialist Schlg: Sh Jmp – C
Livery: Full/Part/DIY/School/Hack – Forestry Commission Land/Bridleways
Ev Classes
Courses: YT
Facilities: 2 Cov Sch: 67 x 25m* & 37 x 18m/Out Man: 40 x 23m Fl Lit/12 CC Fences/Jmp Pds*/Refreshments/Wash Rm/Club Rm*/Lec Rm*/Vis Aids*/ Library*/Video*/Film Projector*/WC/Wait Rm/Tack Shop/Car Park
Specialities: Show Jumping & Dressage & Showing Competitions/Instruction for all ages/Handicapped riders
Location: Off A46 2.5 miles from Market Rasen

LINCOLNSHIRE COLLEGE OF AGRICULTURE & HORTICULTURE
Caythorpe Court, Caythorpe, Grantham, Lincolnshire, NG32 3EP
Tel: 0400 72521
Principal: J Moverley Esq
Equine Course Manager: Mr N Locke (BHS SM) **Chief Inst:** Mrs S Burt BHSI
Other Staff: 1 (BHSII SM) 1 (BHSII) 2 (BHSAI) 1 (BHSI) P/T
Instruction in Riding and Jumping & Students to BHSAI Exam
Av No: Horses 29
Std of Schlg: General Purpose Std of Specialist Schlg: CT – Basic/Sh Jmpg – C School
Courses: Up to & including (BHSAI) Exam & NCMH/Pupils – 14/YTS 60
Facilities: Cov Sch: 20 x 38m* Gly/Out Man: 60 x 30m/16 Basic Schooling CC Fences*/Lec Rm – Vis Aids/Seating/Film Projector/Library/Video
Accom: Hall of Residence 150 Catering: Full
Exclusions: No casual clients
Location: Off A17 15 miles from Lincoln & 9 miles from Grantham

LINESIDE RIDING STABLES
Lineside Farm, Amberhill, Boston, Lincolnshire
Tel: Boston (0205) 820744
Proprietor: Miss J Key
Chief Inst: Miss N Beck (BHSAI) **Other Staff:** 1 (BHSAI) P/T 1 (BHSAI)
Basic Instruction in Riding and Jumping
Av No: Horses 7 Ponies 10
Std of Schlg: General Purpose
Livery: Full/Grass/School/Break/Hack – Farm Tracks
Ev Classes
Courses: Inst/YTS/ET – 2
Facilities: Cov Sch: 31 x 21.5m*/Gly 20/Jmp Pd/Sh Jmps/Refresh/WC/H & C/Car Park
Exclusions: No children under 7 years
Location: On A1122 6 miles from Boston

REDNIL FARM EQUESTRIAN CENTRE
Lincoln Road, Welton, Nr Lincoln, LN2 3JE
Tel: Welton (0673) 60548

Proprietors: Mr & Mrs P J Linder
Chief Inst: Mrs J Beaumont (BHSI) P/T
Other Staff: Mrs E Bingham (BHSAI) Mrs E Bell (BHSII) P/T Miss R Evans (BHSAI) P/T
Instruction in Riding and Jumping & Students to BHSAI Exam
Av No: Horses 12 Ponies 7
Std of Schlg: General Purpose Break/School/Hack – Open Countryside
Ev Classes
Courses: Inst Hol Driving Side-saddle
Facilities: Cov Sch: 14 x 28m Fl Lit Gly/Out Man: 19 x 37m Fl Lit/Jmp Pd/ Sh Jmps/CC Course/CC Fences/Club Rm*/Lec Rm/Vis Aids/Video/Showers/ Wash Rm/Chng Rm/WC/Shop/Car Park
Specialities: Friendly atmosphere – offering wide range of activities
Exclusions: No children under the age of six years
Location: 1 mile from A46/6 miles from Lincoln

SAXILBY RIDING CLUB
High Street, Saxilby, Lincoln, LN1 2HA
Tel: Lincoln (0522) 702240
Proprietors: Mr & Mrs M J Scott
Chief Inst: Mr M J Scott **Other Staff:** 2 (BHSAI) P/T 1 (BHSAI)
Basic Instruction in Riding and Jumping
Av No: Horses 16 Ponies 14
Std of Schlg: General Purpose
Livery: Full/Grass/Hacking – Farm Land
Ev Classes
Courses: Hol/YT – 3
Facilities: Cov Sch: 39 x 9m/Out Man: 2/3rds Acre/Fl Lit/CC Fences/Jmp Pd/ Sh Jmps/Lec Rm/Club Rm/W. C/H & C/ Chng Rm/Refresh/Wait Rm/Car Park
Accom: 16 – Dormitory Catering: Full
Specialities: Show Jumping/Children's Riding Holidays
Exclusions: No children over 16 years on riding holidays
Location: Off A57 6 miles from Lincoln

SPRINGFIELD FARM
Springfield Farm Stables, Benniworth, Lincoln, LN3 6JN
Tel: 0507 313234
Proprietors: Messrs D L Martin & M A Pinney
Livery Yard
Livery: Full/Grass/Hunter/Mares & Foals/Hack – Available for Livery Owners Only
Facilities: Wash Rm/WC/Car Park
Exclusions: Facilities available for Livery Owners Only
Location: Off A157 btwn Louth & Wragby 8 miles from Market Rasen & 16 miles from Lincoln

THORPE GRANGE EQUESTRIAN CENTRE
Newark Road, Aubourn, Lincoln, LN5 9EJ
Tel: Lincoln (0522) 680159
Proprietor: Mrs E Poskitt
Chief Inst: Mr S Cruikshank (BHS SM)
Other Staff: 2 (BHSAI) 1 (BHSI) – Visiting
Instruction in Riding and Jumping & Students to BHSAI Exam
Av No: Horses 25 Ponies 5
Std of Schlg: General Purpose
Ev Classes
Courses: YT – 3
Facilities: Cov Schs: 74 x 28m* Gly 300 Fl Lit & 40 x 20m*/Jmp Pd/CC Fences/ Lec Rm/Club Rm/Vis Aids/Refresh/Wash Rm/Wait Rm/WC/Chng Rm/Car Park
Specialities: Indoor shows
Location: Off A46 4 miles from Lincoln & 8 miles from Newark

UFFINGTON LIVERY STABLES
Essendine Road, Uffington, Stamford, Lincs, PE9 4SN
Tel: 0780 64013
Proprietor & Chief Inst: Mrs J Musgrove
Basic Instruction in Riding and Jumping
Av No: Horses 2 Ponies 3
Std of Schlg: General Purpose Std of Specialist Schlg: Sh Jmpg – Novice
Livery: Working/School/Hack – Bridleways
Ev Classes
Facilities: Out Man: 20 x 40m* Fl Lit/2 Small Schooling CC Fences/Jmp Pd/ Wash Rm/WC/Car Park
Exclusions: No children under 5 years
Location: Off A16 1.5 miles from Stamford

NORTHAMPTONSHIRE

BRAMPTON STABLES
Church Brampton, Northampton, NN6 8AU
Tel: Northampton (0604) 842051
Proprietors: Mr & Mrs D A Ward
Managing Agent YT
Chief Inst: Mrs J Ward (BHSI) **Other**

Staff: Miss V Boyce (BHSII) Miss J Yargleson (BHSII) Mr C Macintyre (BHSII) Mr M Townsend (BHSAI) Miss A Davidson (BHSAI) Miss J Davis (BHSAI) Mr N Creaton (BHSI) P/T 2 (BHSII(T)) P/T 1 (BHSAI) P/T
Instruction in Riding and Jumping & Students to BHSII Exam
Av No: Horses 25 Ponies 15 Specialist Horses: Drg: 1 Med – 1 Elm/Sh Jmpg B/1 HT – Adv
Std of Schlg: General Purpose
Livery: Full/Part/Grass/School/Hunt/ Hack –Pytchley Hunt country
Ev Classes
Courses: Resid Inst Hol/Wkg Students/ YT – 6
Facilities: Cov Sch: 20 x 40m* Gly Fl Lit/2 Out Man: 20 x 40m/60 x 20m Fl Lit/ Sh Jmps/CC Fences/Video/Lec Rm/ Wait Rm/Refresh/WC/Wash Rm/Chng Rm/Car Park
Accom: 6 – Cottage 8 – Flat Catering: Self
Specialities: Sound instruction/Side Saddle/Career Student Courses/RDA
Exclusions: No hiring of hunters/No children under 5/Escorted hacks only/No riders over 13.5 Stone
Location: 5 miles North of Northampton 1 mile from Junc 18 on M1

EAST LODGE FARM RIDING ESTABLISHMENT
East Lodge Farm, Ecton, Northamptonshire, NN6 0QU
Tel: 0604 810244
Proprietors: Mr & Mrs R D White
Other Staff: 1 (BHSAI) P/T
Basic Instruction in Riding and Jumping
Av No: Horses 8 Ponies 8
Std of Schlg: General Purpose Std of Specialist Schlg: Sh Jmpg – Novice
Livery: Full/Part/Grass/Hunter/DIY/ School/Hack – Farm Land/Bridleways
Ev Classes
Courses: Childrens one day
Facilities: Cov Sch: 18 x 14m*/Out Man: 40 x 40m & 60 x 40m/23 CC Fences*/Club Rm/Refreshments/Wash Rm/WC/Car Park
Specialities: Children's one day courses/Adult Stable management Courses
Location: Off A4500 5 miles north east of Northampton

FOXHILL FARM EQUESTRIAN CENTRE
Sywell Road, Holcot, Northants, NN6 9SN
Tel: 0604 781191
Proprietors: Miss L J Stephenson (BHSI) & Mr M E Woolman
Chief Inst: Miss L J Stephenson (BHSI)
Other Staff: 1 (FBHS) Mrs J Knowles (Visiting) 1 (BHSAI)
Instruction in Riding and Jumping & Students to BHSII Exam
Av No: Horses 10 Ponies 10 Std of Specialist Horses: 3 Drg E
Std of Schlg: General Purpose School/Hunt/Hack – Farm Tracks/ Fields
Ev Classes (Summer)
Courses: Inst Hol/YT – 1
Facilities: 2 Out Mans: 45 x 23m & 40 x 20m/Jmp Pd/Sh Jmps/CC Fences/Lec Rm/Vis Aids/Video/Wash Rm/WC/Chng Rm/Car Park
Specialities: General Instruction/ Side-saddle/Road Safety Tests/Progressive Riding Tests
Exclusions: No Riders over 13 stones/ No unescorted Hacks/No Children under 6
Location: 1 mile off A43/7 miles north of Northampton

GREENACRES RIDING CENTRE
Green Farm, Puxley, Potterspury, Nr Towcester, Northants, NN12 7QS
Tel: 0908 566092
Proprietor: T Smith Esq
Manager/Chief Inst: Mrs M Carman (BHSAI) **Other Staff:** 2 (BHSAI) 1 (BHSII) P/T 2 (BHSAI) P/T Visiting (BHSI) – Mrs L Eaton
Instruction in Riding and Jumping
Av No: Horses 8 Ponies 12
Std of Schlg: General Purpose Std of Specialist Schlg: CT – Basic/Sh Jmpg – Nov
Livery: Full/Part/Grass/DIY/School/Hack – Own Farm Land/Bridleways
Ev Classes
Facilities: Cov Schs: 30 x 15m* Gly & 25 x 12m/Out Man: 40 x 20m* Fl Lit/36 Basic CC Fences over 25 miles/Jmp Pd/ Lec Rm/Wash Rm/WC/Car Park
Specialities: RDA
Location: Off A5 5 miles from Towcester & 10 from Milton Keynes

HOLDENBY RIDING SCHOOL
Holdenby, Northampton, NN6 8DJ
Tel: 0604 770752 – Home/770003 – Stables
Proprietors: Mr M J Watkins & Miss T M Watkins
Chief Inst: Miss T M Watkins (BHSII)

Other Staff: 3 (BHSAI) Miss S Watkins (BHSII(T)) P/T 2 (BHSAI) P/T
Instruction in Riding and Jumping & Students to BHSAI Exam
Av No: Horses 12 Ponies 20
Std of Schlg: General Purpose
Livery: Full/Hunter/School/Break/Hunt/Hack – Bridleways
Courses: Wkg Students – 5
Facilities: Cov Sch: 40 x 20m Fl Lit/Out Man: 40 x 20m/Jmp Pd/7 CC Fences/Lec Rm/Vis Aids/Refresh/Wash Rm/WC/Chng Rm/Wait Rm/Car Park
Specialities: Children from 7 years/Adult Novices
Location: 9 miles from centre of Northampton & 2 miles from the A428

MANOR FARM EQUESTRIAN CENTRE
Manor Farm, Maidwell, Northamptonshire, NN6 9JB
Tel: Maidwell (060 128) 221
Proprietor/Chief Inst: Miss S Stanier LVO
Other Staff: 1 (BHSAI)
Instruction in Riding and Jumping
Av No: Horses 4 Ponies 1
Std of Schlg: General Purpose Std of Specialist Schlg: Drg – Adv
Livery: Full/School/Break
Ev Classes
Courses: Non – Resid/YT taken
Facilities: Cov Sch: 34 x 23m* Gly Fl Lit/Out Man/Jmp Pd/Sh Jmps*/CC Fences/Lec Rm/Refresh/WC/Chng Rm/Car Park
Specialities: Side-Saddle/Long Reining/Breaking/S chooling/Demos/Film Work
Location: On A508 5 miles South of Market Harborough

MOULTON COLLEGE
Moulton, Northampton, NN3 1RR
Tel: 0604 491131/492653
Principal: D T Rowe Esq
Yard Manager: Miss C Hill (BHS SM)
Chief Inst & Head of Dept: Mr D Hamer (BHSI) **Other Staff:** 1 (BHSII) P/T 1 (BHSI) 1 (BHS SM) Visiting (FBHS) Mrs Gardiner
Instruction in Riding and Jumping & Students to BHSII Exam
Av No: Horses 16 Ponies 2 Std of Specialist Horses: 2 Drg I – 2 Drg N/ 2 Grade C Sh Jmpers
Std of Schlg: General Purpose Std of Specialist Schlg: Drg – I/Sh Jmpg – C
Livery: Full/Working/School
Ev Classes
Courses: Up to & including BHSII Exam & NCMH/Resid – for College Students only
Facilities: Cov Sch: 60 x 20m* Gly/2 Out Mans: 60 x 20m* & 40 x 20m*/Lec Rm*– Seating/Vis Aids/Film Projector/Library/Video/Wash Rm/WC/Showers/Car Park/CC
Accom: Single Rms – 100 Catering: Full
Specialities: Outside clients by arrangement
Exclusions: No casual clients
Location: Between A508 & A43 5 miles north of Northampton

SHUCKBURGH HOUSE RIDING CENTRE
Shuckburgh House, Naseby, Northampton, NN6 7DA
Tel: Northampton (0604) 740481
Proprietor: Mrs S Muirhead
Other Staff: 2 (BHSAI)
Instruction in Riding and Jumping & Students to BHSAI Exam
Av No: Horses 12 Specialist Horses: HT 1(Int) – 4(Novice)
Std of Schlg: General Purpose
Livery: Full/Hunter/Break/School
Courses: Resid Inst
Facilities: Out Man: 40 x 23m* Fl Lit/CC Fences/Lec Rm/Vis Aids/Video/Wash Rm/Showers/Chng Rm/WC/Car Park
Accom: 3 – House 4 – Cottage Catering: Full/Part
Specialities: Livery/Breaking/Schooling for Competition
Exclusions: No Casual Hiring
Location: in Naseby Village

NOTTINGHAMSHIRE

BLOOMSGORSE TREKKING CENTRE
Bloomsgorse Farm, Bilsthorpe, Nr Newark, Nottinghamshire, ND22 8TA
Tel: 0623 870276
Proprietors: S R Bowring Esq & Mrs Z Grant
Head Girl: Miss Jane Martin **Other Staff:** Miss A Dawn (BHSAI) 4 Trek Leaders
Trekking
Av No: Horses 15 Ponies 15
Std of Schlg: Basic Trekking
Trek – Clipston Forest
Courses: Resid/YT – 2
Facilities: Wash Rm/WC/Car Park
Accom: Bungalows in Centre Park
Catering: Self
Exclusions: No Children under 7 years
Location: Off A614 4 miles south of Ollerton

BRACKENHURST COLLEGE
Brackenhurst, Southwell,
Nottinghamshire, NG25 0QF
Tel: 0636 812252
Principal: J P Benson Esq
Manager: R H J Wall Esq **Chief Inst:** Miss C Elvin (BHSI) **Other Staff:** 2 (BHSI) 1 (Unqual) Mr R Leyland (BSJA Coach) P/T 4 (BHSI) P/T 2 (BHSI(SM)) P/T 6 (BHSII) P/T 1 UQ P/T
Instruction in Riding and Jumping & Students to BHSII Exam
Av No: Horses 40 Ponies –
Std of Schlg: General Purpose Std of Specialist Schlg: Sh Jmpg Grade C/Drg – E
School
Ev Classes
Courses: up to BHSII/Resid for College Students only
Facilities: Cov Sch: 60 x 40m* Gly/ Out Man: 60 x 40m*/Lec Rm – Vis Aids/Film Projector/Library/Video/Wash Rm/WC/ Showers/Chng Rm/Waiting Rm/ Car Park
Accom: Local – 120 Catering: Full
Specialities: Residential & Non Residential Courses during College Breaks
Exclusions: College Students only during term time
Location: On A612 just south of Southwell

COLLEGE FARM EQUESTRIAN CENTRE
West Markham, Tuxford, Nr Newark,
Nottingham, NG22 0PN
Tel: 0777 870886
Proprietor: Mrs L J Hayton
Manager & Chief Inst: Mrs L J Hayton (BHSAI) **Other Staff:** Miss P Nicol (BHSAI) 2 (BHSAI) P/T
Instruction in Riding and Jumping
Av No: Horses 12 Ponies 11 Std of Specialist Horses: 1 Drg prelim
Std of Schlg: General Purpose Std of Specialist Schlg: Drg – Adv/CT – Basic/ Sh Jmpg – Novice
Livery: Full/Part/Hunter/School/Break/ Hack – Bridleways/Clumber Park
Ev Classes
Courses: Up to BHSAI/Wkg Pupils – 2/YT – 2
Facilities: Out Man: 40 x 20m* Fl Lit/ Jmp Pd/CC Fences/Lec Rm – Vis Aids/ Video/Snacks/WC/Car Park
Accom: Live as a Family – 2
Specialities: Dressage/Show Jumping
Location: Off A1 10 miles north of Newark

NOTTINGHAM EQUESTRIAN CENTRE
Asher Lane, Ruddington,
Nottinghamshire, NG11 6U
Tel: 0602 842854
Proprietor & Chief Inst: Mrs M J Worthington (BHSAI)
Head Girl: Miss F Jenkins (BHSAI)
Other Staff: Miss J Turner (BHSI) 1 (BHSII) P/T 2(BHSAI) P/T
Instruction in Riding and Jumping
Av No: Horses 15 Ponies 15
Std of Schlg: General Purpose Std of Specialist Schlg: CT – Basic
Livery: Full/Part/Grass/School/Break/ Hunt/Hack – Bridleways
Ev Classes
Courses: Up to & including Stage III & PTT/YT & ET –4/YT Day release training
Facilities: Cov Sch: 42 x 19m Gly*/Out Man: 20 x 40m Fl Lit*/CC Course – Basic/Sh Jmps*/Snacks/Wash Rm/WC/ Car Park
Specialities: Weekly Summer & Winter Competitions & Shows
Exclusions: No children under 4 years
Location: Off A60 4 miles south of Nottingham

SELSTON EQUESTRIAN CENTRE
Hillbank Farm, Common Side, Selston,
Nottinghamshire, NG16 6FJ
Tel: (0773) 813817
Proprietor/Principal: Mrs Wild & Mr Burr
Chief Inst: Mr E Burr (BHSI) **Other Staff:** Mrs Burr (BHSII) Miss N Simpson (BHAI) 1 (BHSAI) P/T
Instruction in Riding and Jumping & Students to BHSII Exam
Av No: Horses 16 Ponies 8
Std of Schlg: General Purpose Spec Horses: 2 Drg Int/3 Sh Jmp C
Livery: Full/Part/Hunter/School/Break
Ev Classes
Courses: Inst/YT – 3
Facilities: Cov Sch: 40 x 20m* Gly/Out Man: 40 x 20m* Fl Lit/CC Fences/Jmp Pd/Sh Jmps/Lec Rm/Vis Aids/WC/Club Rm/Change Rm/Wait Rm/Tack Shop/ Car Park
Specialities: Show Jumping/ Preparation for BHS Exams
Location: 1.5 miles from Junc 28 on M1

ST CLEMENTS LODGE RIDING SCHOOL
Woods Lane, Calverton,
Nottinghamshire, NG14 6FF
Tel: Nottingham (0602) 652524
Proprietors: Mr G Burrows & Mr N Burrows

Chief Inst: Mr N Burrows (BHSII) **Other Staff:** 2 (BHSAI) 1 (BHSII) P/T
Instruction in Riding and Jumping & Students to BHSAI Exam
Av No: Horses 10 Ponies 10
Std of Schlg: General Purpose
Hack – Hilly/Woods
Ev Classes
Courses: Inst/Wkg Students
Facilities: Cov Sch: 60 x 21m Gly 50 Fl Lit/Out Man: 26 x 18m/Refresh/Jmp Pd/ Lec Rm/Vis Aids/WC/Chng Rm/ Reception Rm/Car Park
Specialities: Gymkhanas for pupils/ Special rates schools/Stable management courses/Lessons on own horse/video service
Location: Off A614 8 miles north of Nottingham

WELLOW PARK STABLES & SADDLERY
Rufford Lane, Wellow, Nr Newark, Nottinghamshire, NG22 0EQ
Tel: Mansfield (0623) 861040
Proprietor: Mrs M Willett
Chief Inst: Miss F Donaldson (BHSAI)
Other Staff: Miss L Smith (BHSAI) Miss C McGuigan Miss J Turner (BHSI) – Visiting Miss S Lowe (BHSI) – Visiting
Instruction in Riding and Jumping & Students to BHSII Exam
Av No: Horses 20 Ponies 9
Std of Schlg: General Purpose
Livery: Full/Part/Hunter/Break/School/ Hunt/Hack – Open country/Woodland
Ev Classes
Courses: Resid Inst/Wkg Students/YT – 4
Facilities: Out Man: 60 x 20m* Fl Lit/ Jmp Pd*/Sh Jmps 2 sets/CC Fences 12*/CC Course – BHS Novice HT standard/Lec Rm/Vis Aids/Video/WC/ Wait Rm/Tack Shop/Car Park
Accom: 8 – Student Block Catering: Part
Specialities: Hunter hire/Dressage/ Riders trained on own horses/Horses & ponies broken to harness/Driving instruction
Location: 1 mile from Ollerton Roundabout/9 miles from Newark on A616

Riding in the West Midlands

HEREFORD AND WORCESTER ♦ SHROPSHIRE ♦ STAFFORDSHIRE ♦ WARWICKSHIRE ♦ WEST MIDLANDS

HEREFORD AND WORCESTER

CAMPUS CENTRES LTD
Hope under Dinmore, Leominster, Herefordshire, HR6 0PW
Tel: (0568) 611412
Proprietor/Manager: Mr G Stansbridge
Riding Holidays and Trekking
Av No: Horses 3 Ponies 17
Trekking – Common/Woodland
Facilities: Out Man:40 x 25m/Lec Rm/Vis Aids/Club Rm/WC/H & C/Showers/Chng Rm/Refresh/Car Park
Accom: 100 – Dormitory Catering: Full
Specialities: Riding Holidays/Trekking
Exclusions: No YT/Open February – November incl
Location: Off A49 3 miles south of Leominster

CASTLE FARM LIVERY YARD
Castle Farm Stables, Lea Castle Farm, Cookley, Kidderminster, Worcester, DY10 3RD
Tel: 0562 851459
Proprietors: G Knight Esq & Miss W Wedgbury
Livery Yard
Av No Horses – Ponies – Specialist Horses: 5 Sh Jmpers (Livery)
Std of Schlg: General Purpose Std of Specialist Schlg: Sh Jmpg – Grade A
Livery: Full/Grass/School/Break
Facilities: Out Man: 60 x 25m* Fl Lit/CC Course/WC/Car Park
Specialities: Livery/Show Jumping
Exclusions: No Casual Clients
Location: On A499 1 mile from Kidderminster

COUNTY COMPETITION STUD & LIVERY YARD
Home Farm, Munderfield Harold, Bromyard, Herefordshire, HR7 4SZ
Tel: 0885 482062
Proprietor: Mrs Y L Wall
Other Staff: 1 F/T
Livery & Training Centre
Std of Specialist Schlg: Drg/CT/Sh Jmpg – all Nov
Livery: Full/Part/Grass/Hunter/Stallion/School/Break
Facilities: Out Man: 20 x 30m* Fl Lit/Sh Jmps*/Video – to record birth of Foals – Owners have Mares at Livery/Snacks/Wash Rm/WC/Tack Shop/Car Park
Accom: Local Hotel Catering: Full
Location: Off A44 2 miles from Bromyard & 11 miles from Leominster

FAR FOREST EQUESTRIAN CENTRE
Far Forest Stables, James Place, Far Forest, Nr Kidderminster, Worcester, DY14 9DG
Tel: Rock (0299) 266438
Proprietors: Mr & Mrs A Fitzpatrick
Chief Inst: Mr Andrew Fitzpatrick (BHSII) **Other Staff:** 2 (BHSAI) P/T
Instruction in Riding and Jumping & Students to BHSAI Exam
Av No: Horses 7 Ponies 3 Specialist Horses: 1 Drg I – 2 Drg E/ Sh Jmper Grade C
Std of Schlg: General Purpose Std of Specialist Schlg: Drg – E
Livery: Full/Part/Hunter/School/Break/Hack – Wyre Forest (6000 acres)
Ev Classes
Courses: Res Inst/ET 1/Wkg Student – 2
Facilities: Out Man: 40 x 30m* Fl Lit/Jmp Pd/CC Course (x 2)/CC

Fences/Lec Rm/Refresh/Wash Rm/ WC/Tack Shop/Car Park
Accom: 4/6 – Rooms Catering: Part
Specialities: All levels of instruction on well – schooled horses/small groups/ Courses tailored to individual requirements/Good hacking country/ Adv riders – Sh Jmpg/Drg/Shows un/affiliated – May – October
Exclusions: No hiring for unaccompanied hacking
Location: 4 miles west of Bewdley

HALLOW MILL EQUESTRIAN CENTRE
Hallow, Nr Worcester, Hereford & Worcester, WR2 6PR
Tel: Worcester (0905) 640373
Principals: Mrs I Auty (BHSI) & Mrs R Johnson BHSI
Instruction in Riding and Jumping & Students to BHSII Exam
Av No: Horses 6 Ponies 10
Std of Schlg: General Purpose Std of Specialist Schlg: Drg – M
Livery: Full/Hunter/Break/School/Hack – Arable Wo odland/Bridlepaths
Ev Classes
Courses: Resid Hol/Wkg Students – 4
Facilities: Out Man: 49 x 31m* and 12 x 18m*/Jmp Pd/CC Fences*/Lec Rm/Vis Aids/Club Rm/Refresh/WC/Car Park
Accom: 4 Catering: Full
Specialities: Short individual courses/ Professional qualifications/Prep courses/Pony Club tests/Holiday courses
Exclusions: No hiring for hunting/No riders under 7 years/No YT
Location: 2 miles from Worcester west of River Severn

MOYFIELD RIDING SCHOOL
South Littleton, Evesham, Worcestershire, WR11
Tel: Evesham (0386) 830207/830252
Proprietor: Joan Bomford
Other Staff: 2 (BHSAI) P/T
Instruction in Riding and Jumping
Av No: Horses 40 Ponies 50
Std of Schlg: General Purpose
Livery: Part/Hunter/Break/School/ Hack/Trek
Ev Classes
Courses: Resid Inst Hol
Facilities: Cov Sch: 12 x 6m* Gly 50/Out Man: 12 x 6m*/Jmp Pd/Sh Jmps/ CC Fences*/Lec Rm/Vis Aids*/Club Rm/Refresh/Games Rm/WC/Chng Rm/ Car Park
Accom: 10 Bunk House/Dormitory 12
Catering: Full
Specialities: Beginners/Holidays/Gymkhanas/Golden Horse Shoe Rides/Team CC/RDA/Side Saddle/Western Style Riding
Exclusions: No unaccompanied rides/No YT
Location: 4 miles east of Evesham & 12 miles from Stratford on Avon

PORTMANS FARM
Newbridge Green, Upton-on-Severn, Worcester, WR8 0QP
Tel: Upton (068 46) 2873
Proprietor: Mrs J Challens BHSI
Instruction in Riding and Jumping & Students to BHSII Exam
Av No: horses 6 Ponies 6
Std of Schlg: General Purpose Std of Specialist Schlg: Drg – Adv/Sh Jmp – A
Livery: Full/Break/School/Hack/Country Lanes
Ev Classes
Courses: YT – 1
Facilities: Cov Sch: 37 x 22m* Fl Lit/ Jmp Pd/Sh Jmps/CC Course/Lec Rm/ Vis Aids/WC
Accom: Hotels/lodgings locally
Specialities: Individual instruction beginners/Advanced instruction/RDA
Exclusions: No hiring for Hunting/ Hacking
Location: On B4211 4 miles from Junc 1 on M50

ROCKMOOR STABLES
Rock, Nr Kidderminster, Worcestershire, DY14 9RY
Tel: Clows Top (029 922) 214/556
Proprietor: H D Maidment
Other Staff: 1 (BHSII) P/T
Instruction in Riding and Jumping
Av No: Horses 5 Ponies 12
Std of Schlg: General Purpose
Livery: Full/Part/Grass/Hack/Trek– Varied Country
Ev Classes – Summer Only
Facilities: Out Man: 50m x 30m* Fl Lit/ Jmp Pd 100 x 80 Seats/Sh Jmps full set/ CC Fences/CC Course/Vis Aids/WC/ Refresh/Showers/Chng Rm/Car Park
Specialities: Beginners all ages/CC Competitions/Show Jumping
Exclusions: No casual hiring
Location: In Rock south of A456 & 5 miles west of Bewdley

SEECHEM EQUESTRIAN CENTRE
Rowney Green Lane, Alvechurch, Nr Birmingham, Worcestershire
Tel: 021 445 2333

Proprietor: Mrs Joan Willetts (BHSAI)
YTS Managing Agency
Chief Inst: Miss L Thomas (BHSAI)
Other Staff: 3 (BHSAI) 1 (BHSII) 1 (BHSII) P/T
Instruction in Riding and Jumping & Students to BHSAI Exam
Av No: Horses 13 Ponies 14
Std of Schlg: General Purpose
Livery: Full/Part/Hunter/Break/ School/Hack – Lanes Bridleways
Ev Classes
Courses: Inst Hol/Wkg Students/YT – 4
Facilities: Cov Sch: 37 x 20m* Fl Lit Gly 300/Out Man: 20m x 40m Fl Lit/Jmp Pd/ Sh Jumps* Full BSJA/CC Course/Lec Rm/Vis Aids/Refresh/Rest Rm/WC/Wash Rm/Chng Rm/Car Park
Specialities: Show Jumping/Show Horses/RDA/General Instruction
Location: 10 minutes from M42

ST RICHARD'S SCHOOL
Bredenbury Court, Nr Bromyard, Herefordshire, HR7 4TD
Tel: 0885 482491
Head Master: R E H Coghlan Esq (BHSAI)
Chief Inst: Miss J Bettely (BHSII)
Instruction in Riding and Jumping
Av No: Ponies 9
Std of Schlg: General Purpose Std of Specialist Schlg: CT – Basic/Sh Jmpg – Nov
School/Hack – Own land – Bridleways – School Pupils only
Courses: Resid – Boarding facilities for school pupils only
Facilities: Out Man: 40 x 20m/Basic CC Course – 20 fences/Jmp Pd/Lec Rm – Vis Aids/Seating/Film Projector/ Library/Video
Accom: Dormitory – 100 Catering: Full
Exclusions: No casual Clients/For pupils of St Richards School Only
Location: On A44 between Leominster & Bromyard

SUE ADAM'S RIDING SCHOOL
The Ox House, Shobdon, Herefordshire, HR6 9HY
Tel: 056881 8973
Proprietor & Chief Inst: Mrs S E Adams (BHSAI)
Other Staff: 1 (BHSII) P/T 1 (BHSI) – visiting
Instruction in Riding and Jumping
Av No: Horses 6 Ponies 3 Spec Horses: 2 Med Drg
Std of Schlg: General Purpose Std of Specialist Schlg: CT/Drg/Sh Jmpg – all Nov
Livery: Full/Part/Hunter/School/Hack – Forestry/Farm Land
Ev Classes
Courses: ET – 1
Facilities: Cov Sch: 50 x 20m*/Out Man: 30 x 8 0m/Nov CC Courses* – 18 CC Fences/Jmp Pd/Lec Rm – Vis Aids/Seating/Library/Snacks/Wash Rm/WC/Chng Rm/Wait Rm/Car Park
Specialities: Lunge Lessons/Nervous Riders/Remedial Riding
Exclusions: No children under 5 years
Location: Off B4362 7 miles from Leominster & 7 miles from Presteigne

SHROPSHIRE

BERRIEWOOD STUD FARM
Condover, Shrewsbury, Shropshire, SY5 7NN
Tel: Dorrington (074 373) 252
Proprietors: Mrs W J Lock (BHSAI) & Mrs P Cowdy (BHS SM)
YT Managing Agent (32)
Chief Inst: Miss Ella - Louise Webb (BHSII) **Other Staff:** 3 (BHSAI) Mrs S Charters (BHSI) P/T
Instruction in Riding and Jumping & Students to BHSII Exam
Av No: Horses 23 Ponies 18 Spec Horses: 4 Drg E/1 Sh Jmper Grade B
Std of Schlg: General Purpose Hack – Farmland
Ev Classes
Courses: Res Hol Inst/Wkg Students/YT – 8 on site
Facilities: Cov Sch: 46 x 22m* Gly Fl Lit/Out Mans: 60 x 20m* Fl Lit & 40 x 40m* Fl Lit/Jmp Pd/Sh Jmps/CC Course/Lec Rm/Vis Aids/Office/Refresh/ Wash Rm/WC/Car Park
Accom: 4 – House/2 – Cottage/New Block – YT & Students Catering: Full
Specialities: General Instruction/Career Students/Hacking/Livery/Pony Club/Riding Holidays
Exclusions: No Casual Hiring
Location: Off A49 6 miles south of Shrewsbury

FRESHFIELDS EQUESTRIAN CENTRE
Longford Turning, Market Drayton, Shropshire
Tel: 0630 652495
Proprietor & Chief Inst: Miss J A Arnold
Instruction in Riding and Jumping
Av No: Horses 4 Ponies: 12 Specialist Horses: 4 JA/5 Prince Phillip Cup

Ponies/1 Sh Jmper Grade A & 1 Sh Jmper B/2 Nov Eventers
Std of Schlg: General Purpose/Std of Specialist Schlg: CT & Sh Jmpg – Nov
Livery: Full/Part/Grass/DIY/School/Break/Hack – Bridleways/Country Lanes
Ev Classes
Facilities: Out Man: 40 x 40m*/1 Schooling CC Fence/Sh Jmps*/Club Rm – Library/Video/Refreshments/Chng Rm/Car Park
Specialities: Loan a Pony Scheme/Driving/Musical Riding Displays/Competitions
Location: Off A53 1.5 miles south of Market Drayton

LILLESHALL RIDING AND LIVERY STABLES
Child Pit Lane, Nr Newport, Shropshire, TF10 9AR
Tel: Telford (0952) 677166
Proprietors: Mr & Mrs Francis
Chief Inst: Miss S Francis (BHSAI)
Other Staff: 1 (BHSAI)
Instruction in Riding and Jumping
Av No: Horses 9 Ponies 6
Std of Schlg: General Purpose
Livery: Full/Part/School/Break/Hack – Farm Lanes/Tracks/Bridleways
Ev Classes
Courses: Inst/YT
Facilities: Out Man: 20 x 40m*/Sh Jmps/CC Fences/Lec Rm/Club Rm/Vis Aids/WC/Car Park
Specialities: General Instruction/Children/Hacking/Livery/Family rides/School contract work
Exclusions: No riders over 14 stones/All riding escorted
Location: 1 mile from A41 within grounds of Lilleshall Hall National Sports Centre

MILL FARM RIDING CENTRE
Hughley, Shrewsbury, Shropshire, SY5 6NT
Tel: 074 636 645
Proprietor: Mrs E Bosworth
Chief Inst: Mrs J Kerswell (BHSII) P/T
Instruction in Riding and Jumping
Av No: Horses 10 Ponies 12
Std of Schlg: General Purpose Std of Specialist Schlg: Sh Jmp – Novice
Livery: Full/Part/Grass/DIY/Hack– Bridleways/Disused Railway Line/Wenlock Edge
Ev Classes
Courses: Resid/YT 3
Facilities: Out Man: 47 x 27m Fl Lit*/Jmp Pd/Snacks/WC/Wash Rm/Showers/Changing Rm/Tack Shop/Car Park
Accom: Dormitory – 20/House – 6 Catering: Full/Part
Specialities: Riding Holidays for Adults & Children/Bed & Breakfast Accom
Exclusions: No Riders over 15 stone
Location: 3 miles from Much Wenlock off B4371

THE MOUNTS EQUITATION CENTRE
Crumpsbrook, Nr Cleobury Mortimer, Nr Kidderminster, Worcestershire
Tel: 074 632 677
Proprietors: Mr & Mrs B Linington-Payne (BHSI(SM))
Chief Inst: Mrs M Lingington-Payne (BHSI(SM)) **Other Staff:** Mrs S Charters (BHSI) P/T 2 (BHSAI)
Instruction in Riding and Jumping & Students to BHSII Exam
Av No: Horses 15 Ponies 5 Specalist Horses: 2 Drg – E/1 HT – Int
Std of Schlg: General Purpose Std of Specialist Schlg: Drg – E
Livery: Full/Part/Schooling/Breaking/Hacking – Common Land
Ev Classes
Courses: YT/Wkg Student – 1
Facilities: Cov Sch: 42 x 22m* Gly 20/Out Man: 6 0 x 30m/CC* Basic/Jmp Pd/Sh Jmps*/Wash Rm/WC/Showers/Chng Rm/Wait Rm/Car Park
Accom: Shared – 6 – For Staff/YT/Holiday Riders Catering: Full
Specialities: Excellent Riding Country/Individual Service
Exclusions: Unaccompanied young children not taken
Location: Off A4117 5 miles from Cleobury Mortimer 8 miles from Ludlow

NORTH FARM RIDING ESTABLISHMENT
North Farm, Whitcliffe, Ludlow, Shropshire, SY8 2HD
Tel: Ludlow (0584) 872026
Proprietor: Mr P Dickin
Basic Instruction in Riding and Jumping
Av No: Horses 7 Ponies 8
Std of Schlg: General Purpose Break/School/Hack – Mortimer Forest/Bringewood Chase
Facilities: Jmp Pd/CC Fences/Vis Aids/Rest Rm/WC/Wash Rm/Showers/Chng Rm/Car Park
Accom: Caravan Club – camping facilities
Specialities: Beginners/School

parties/Riding holidays for unaccompanied children/RDA
Exclusions: No unescorted riding/No YT
Location: 1 mile west of Ludlow

P G L YOUNG ADVENTURE LTD
Boreatton Park, Baschurch, Nr Shrewsbury, Shropshire, SY4 2EZ
Tel: Baschurch 0939 260 551
Proprietor/Director: Mr B F Knell
Chief Inst: Miss K Eccles
Basic Instruction in Riding and Jumping
Av No: Horses 7 Ponies 60
Std of Schlg: General Purpose
Courses: Resid Hol
Facilities: WC/Wash Rm/Showers/Chng Rm/Club Rm/Refresh/Car Park
Accom: House/Caravan/Campsite
Specialities: Adventure/Riding Holidays
Exclusions: Children 8 – 12 years only/ Closed in Winter – October to February

PRESCOTT EQUESTRIAN CENTRE
Prescott Farm, Baschurch, Nr Shrewsbury, Shropshire
Tel: 0939 260712
Proprietors: Mrs J C Haydon & R W Stone Esq
Manager: Mrs J C Haydon **Chief Inst:** Miss C Hayes (BHSAI)
Yard Manager: Mr N Targett (BHSAI)
Other Staff: Miss V Yatt (BHSAI) 2 (BHSAI) P/T Mr A Tyler (BHSI) – Visiting
Instruction in Riding and Jumping
Av No: Horses 15 Ponies 13
Std of Schlg: General Purpose
Livery: Full/Part/Grass/DIY/School/Hack – Bridle paths/Country Roads/Farmland
Ev Classes
Courses: YT taken/ET – 1
Facilities: 2 Cov Schs: 46 x 26m Gly* & 24 x 10m/Out Man: 60 x 20m Fl Lit/Sh Jmps*/5/6 CC Fences/Lec Rm/Snacks/ Wash Rm/WC/Changing Rm/Saddlery Shop/Car Park
Accom: Self Contained Flats – 6 Catering: Self
Specialities: Show Jumping & Dressage Competitions/Demonstrations/Trout Pool/Course Fishing
Location: Between A5 & A528 7 miles from centre of Shrewsbury

TONG RIDING CENTRE LIMITED
Church Farm, Tong, Shifnal, Shropshire, TF11 8PW
Tel: 0902 372352
Proprietors: Mrs M J Garside-Bates M A (BHSI) & MrsD M K Russell
Chief Inst: Mrs Garside-Bates (BHSI)
Other Staff: 1 (BHSI) 1 (BHSII SM) 1 (BHSAI)
Instruction in Riding and Jumping & Students to BHSI Exam
Av No: Horses 25 Ponies 7
Std of Schlg: General Purpose Std of Specialist Schlg: Drg – I/HT – I/Sh Jmp – Grade C
Livery: Full/Break/School/Hack – Bridlepaths
Ev Classes
Courses: Resid Inst Hol/Working Pupil/ YT/Students for all Exams up to BHSI
Facilities: Cov Sch: 37 x 19m*/2 Out Man: 62 x 25 m* & 34 x 15m/Jmp Pd/Sh Jmps 14*/2 CC Courses/Lec Rm/Club Rm/Refresh/WC
Accom: 10 Rooms Catering: Self
Specialities: Dressage/Cross Country/ Sh Jumping/Equitation at all levels/RDA
Location: Just off A41 1 mile from Junc 3 on M54

THE WYKE EQUESTRIAN CENTRE
Shifnal, Shropshire, TF11 9PP
Tel:(Telford) 0952 460560/461823
Proprietors: L Phillips (BHSAI) & R J C Phillips (BHS SM)
Other Staff: 2 (BHSAI) 1 (BHSII) P/T
Instruction in Riding and Jumping & Students to BHSII Exam
Av No: Horses 17 Ponies 10 Specalist Horses: 1 Drg
Std of Schlg: General Purpose Std of Specialist Schlg: Drg M & E/HT Adv.
Livery: Full/Hunter/Part/Break/School/ Hack – Countryside
Courses: Resid Inst/Wkg Students/ Approved Training Oganisation for up to 18 YTS/8 YTS on site
Facilities: Out Man(2): 40 x 20m* Fl Lit/ 60 x 25m * Fl Lit/Cov Sch: 40 x 20m/Jmp Pd/Sh Jmps*/CC Course/Lec Rm/Vis Aids/Club Rm/Refresh/WC/Chng Rm/ Car Park/Video/Saddlery Company
Accom: 8 Farmhouse Catering: Full
Specialities: Good instruction on well schooled horses/RDA/Side Saddle
Exclusions: Hacking only for Clients & Students
Location: Just off A4169 1 Mile South West of Shifnal & 3 miles from Junc 4 on M54

STAFFORDSHIRE

ASHMORE BROOK DAIRY FARM
Cross Hand Lane, Lichfield, Staffordshire, WS13 8DY
Tel: 0543 254479

Proprietors: Mrs M A & Mr R C Bailye
Manager: Mr R C Bailye
D I Y Livery Service
Livery: D I Y
Specialities: D I Y Livery
Location: Off A51 1 mile north of Litchfield

DALE SCHOOL OF EQUITATION
White House Farm, Bradley, Stafford, Staffordshire, ST18 9EA
Tel: Stafford (0785) 780279
Proprietor: Miss H Kesson (BHSAI)
Other Staff: Mrs W Coupland (BHSII) P/T Miss K W ilson (BHSAI) P/T
Instruction in Riding and Jumping & Students to BHSAI Exam
Av No: Horses 7 Ponies 12
Std of Schlg: General Purpose
Livery: Full/Part/Break/School/Hack – Farmland/Country road work
Ev Lessons
Courses: YT 2
Facilities: Cov Sch: 45 x 30m* Fl Lit/ Sh Jmps/Lec Rm/Vis Aids/Club Rm/ Rest Rm/Wash Rm/Chng Rm/Car Park
Specialities: RDA Stafford Group
Location: Off A518 4 miles from centre of Stafford

ENDON RIDING SCHOOL
Coltslow Farm, Stanley Moss Lane, Stockton Brook, Stoke-on-Trent, Staffordshire, ST9 9LR
Tel: Stoke on Trent (0782) 502114
Proprietors: Mr A W Asplin & Mr D Machin
Chief Inst: Miss A Powell (BHSAI)
Other Staff: Miss Y Warmsley (BHSAI) Mrs Y Williams (BHSI) – visiting
Instruction in Riding and Jumping & Students to BHSAI Exam
Av No: horses 18 Ponies 12
Std of Schlg: General Purpose
Livery: Full/Part/DIY/Hunter/School/ Hack – Moorland/Bridlepaths
Courses: Resid Inst Hol/YT – 4/ET – 1
Facilities: Cov Sch: 37 x 23m* Gly 40/ Out Man: 42 x 26m/Jmp Pd/CC Fences/ Lec Rm/Vis Aids/Video/Club Rm/Lic Bar/Refresh/Rest Rm/WC/ Showers/Chng Rm/Car Park
Accom: 20 – Flat & Student block Catering: Full
Specialities: Residential Riding Holidays for Children/Livery services/ Pony Club courses/RDA
Location: Off A53 midway between Leek & Stoke on Trent

FIELD HOUSE EQUESTRIAN CENTRE
Marchington, Uttoxeter, Stafffordshire, ST14 8NX
Tel: Burton-on-Trent (0283) 820310
Proprietors: Mrs M Snow & Miss S Snow
Chief Inst: Miss S J Snow (BHSII) **Other Staff:** Miss J Nash (BHSAI) 2 (BHSAI) P/T
Instruction in Riding and Jumping & Students to BHSAI Exam
Av No: Horses 24 Ponies 12
Std of Schlg: General Purpose
Livery: Full/Part/Hunter/Break/School/ Hack/Rural
Ev Classes
Courses: Resid Inst/Wkg Students/YT
Facilities: Cov Schs: 65 x 31m Fl Lit Gly & 60 x 19m/Jmp Pd/Sh Jmps/CC Fences/Lec Rm/Vis Aids/Club Rm/ Refresh/Rest Rm/WC/Wash Rm/Shop/ Car Park
Accom: Room – 4 – For Wkg Students & YT only Catering – Self
Specialities: Eventing/Show jumping competitions/Student Training
Location: On B5017 between Uttoxeter & Burton on Trent

GARTMORE RIDING SCHOOL
Hall Lane, Hammerwich, Burntwood, Nr Walsall, Staffordshire
Tel: Burntwood (054 36) 86117
Proprietors: Miss T & Miss M Evans
Inst: Miss T Evans (BHSAI) & Miss M Evans (BHSAI) **Other Staff:** Mrs V Williams (BHSI) – once a week
Instruction in Riding and Jumping
Av No: Horses 11 Ponies 10
Std of Schlg: General Purpose Schooling/Breaking/Hack – Outdoor riding on own land
Ev Classes
Facilities: Cov Sch: 40 x 20m*/Jmp Pd/ Sh Jmps/CC Fences/Lec Rm/Vis Aids/ Refresh/WC/Change Rm/Wait Rm/Car Park
Specialities: Day courses/RDA
Exclusions: No YT
Location: Approx 2 miles from Lichfield

HURST VALE RIDING SCHOOL
Grange Road, Biddulph, Stoke on Trent, Staffordshire, ST8 7RZ
Tel: 0782 522281
Proprietors: Mr & Mrs R Attenborough
Manager: Mrs R Attenborough (BHSAI)
Chief Inst: Mrs N Arnott (BHSI(SM)) P/T
Other Staff: 1 (BHSII(T)) & (BHS SM) 3 (BHSAI) P/T

Instruction in Riding and Jumping
Av No: Horses 10 Ponies 12 Std of Specialist Horses: 4 Drg – E/1 Nov Eventer
Std of Schlg: General Purpose Std of Specialist Schlg: Drg – E/Sh Jmpg – Nov School/Hack – Bridleways
Ev Classes
Courses: YT – 2/ET – 2
Facilities: 3 Out Mans: 55 x 35m* Fl Lit & 20 x 35m* Fl Lit & 35m Cir* Fl Lit/20 small Basic CC Fences/Wash Rm/WC/ Car Park
Location: Off A527 3 miles south of Congleton

INGESTRE RIDING AND LIVERY STABLES
Ingestre, Stafford, ST18 0RE
Tel: Weston (0889) 271165
Proprietors: Mr T Downes (BHSI) & Mr R Lovatt(BHSAI)
Chief Inst: Mr T Downes (BHSI) **Other Staff:** Miss S Baker (BHSAI) Miss E Round (BHSAI) Miss D Cartwright (BHSAI) Mrs J Plant (BHSI) – visiting
Instruction in Riding and Jumping & Students to BHSII Exam
Av No: Horses 12 Ponies 8
Std of Schlg: General Purpose
Livery: Full/Part/Hunter/School/Break/ Hack/Trek – Cannock Chase
Ev Classes
Courses: Hol/Inst/YT – 3/ET – 2/Wkg Students – 11
Facilities: Cov Sch: 20 x 40m*/Jmp Pd/ Sh Jmps*/CC Fences/WC/Saddlery Shop/Lec Rm/Car Park
Accom: 8 Students 12 Flats/Hol Flats Catering: Full
Specialities: Breaking and schooling/Livery/General Instruction
Location: 5 miles from Stafford/1 mile off A51

MIDDLETON EQUESTRIAN CENTRE
Vicarage Hill, Middleton, Nr Tamworth, Staffordshire, B78 2AT
Tel: 021 311 1601
Proprietors: Mr & Mrs J Everill
Manager & Chief Inst: Miss L Cooke (BHSAI) **Other Staff:** Mrs J Warr I of H P/T
Basic Instruction in Riding and Jumping
Av No: Horses 7 Ponies 15
Std of Schlg: General Purpose Std of Specialist Schlg: Sh Jmpg – Novice
Livery: Working/School/Hack – Country Lanes
Ev Classes
Courses: YT – 2
Facilities: Cov Sch: 40 x 20m* Gly – bench seats/Snacks/Wash Rm/WC/Car Park
Location: Off A4091 4 miles south of Tamworth

OFFLEY BROOK RIDING SCHOOL
Heath House, Offley Brook, Eccleshall, Staffordshire, ST21 6HA
Tel: Adbaston (0785) 280318
Proprietor: Mrs N J Eyre–Walker
Chief Inst: Miss C Eyre–Walker (BHSII) P/T **Other Staff:** 1 (BHSAI) P/T
Basic Instruction in Riding and Jumping
Av No: Horses 6 Ponies 6
Std of Schlg: General Purpose.
Livery: Part/Grass/Summer/Hack – Woods/Fields/Tracks/Quiet Lanes
Ev Classes
Courses: Inst School holidays/YT
Facilities: Out Man: 44 x 22m*/Jmp Pd/ Sh Jmps/CC Course/WC/Car Park
Specialities: Basic instruction/Good hacking/Private instruction on own horse
Exclusions: No unaccompanied hacks
Location: 4 miles from Eccleshall

STAFFORDSHIRE COLLEGE OF AGRICULTURE
Rodbaston Stables, Rodbaston, Penkridge, Stafford, ST19 5PH
Tel: 0785 712209
Principal: R A Holtom Esq BSc Cert Ed
Chief Inst: Miss S M Vickers (BHSII)
Other Staff: Miss S Brand (BHSAI) Miss D Wallett (BHSAI) Mrs Y Williams (BHSI) P/T
Instruction in Riding and Jumping & Students to BHSAI Exam
Av No: Horses 9 Ponies 5
Std of Schlg: General Purpose Std of Specialist Schlg: Sh Jmpg – C
Livery: Working/School
Ev Classes
Courses: Resid/Students up to & including BHSAI/NVQ Exams
Facilities: Out Man: 20 x 50m Fl Lit/Lec Rm – Vis aids/Seating/Film Projector/ Library/Video – all other facilites within College complex
Accom: Student Block – Single Rms – 100 Catering: Full
Exclusions: No casual clients
Location: On A449 6 miles from Stafford

WESTWOOD RIDING CENTRE
Westwood Hall Farm, Leek, Staffordshire, ST13 8NW
Tel: 0538 384367

Proprietors: Mr & Mrs R Plant
Livery Yard
Std of Specialist Schlg: Sh Jmpg – Novice
Livery: Full/Grass/DIY/School/Hack – Own Farmland/Bridleways
Facilities: Cov Sch: 49m x 23m* Gly/ Out Man:20 x 40m/CC Course – small fences/Jmp Pd/Snacks/Wash Rm/WC/ Car Park
Location: 1.5 miles from centre of Leek

WARWICKSHIRE

BRITISH EQUESTRIAN CENTRE
Stoneleigh, Kenilworth, Warwickshire, CV8 2LR
Tel: (0203) 696867
Facilities Manager: Mrs J Williams
Training & Facility Centre
Courses: Various – contact The Training Office for further information
Facilities: Cov Sch:(1) 62 x 25m* (2) 43 x 21.5m*/Out Man:(1) 23 x 44m Fl Lit* (2) 25 x 65m*/Jmp Pd/Sh Jmps/CC Course/CC Fences/Lec Rm/Vis Aids*/ Video*/Refresh/Wash Rm/Lic Bar/WC/ Chng Rm/Wait Rm/Book Shop/Car Park
Specialities: Demonstrations/Shows/ Facilities for hire/Courses
Exclusions: This is not a commercial Riding School

CALDECOTE RIDING SCHOOL
Anker Cottage Farm, Caldecote, Nr Nuneaton, Warwickshire, CV10 0TN
Tel: 0203 383103
Proprietor & Chief Inst: Mrs S Sandon (BHSAI)
Other Staff: 1 FT
Basic Instruction in Riding and Jumping
Av No: Horses 5 Ponies 9
Std of Schlg: General Purpose Std of Specialist Schlg: Sh Jmpg – Novice
Livery: Full/Part/Hunter/School/Hack – Bridleways/Country Lanes
Courses: Resid/Riding Holidays
Facilities: Out Man: 30 x 20m/Jmp Pd/Lec Rm – Vis Aids/Snacks/WC/Tack Shop/Car Park
Accom: Shared Rms – Caravan – 6 Catering: Full
Specialities: Nervous Riders & RDA welcomed/Childrens Riding Holidays
Location: 2 miles from Nuneaton just south of Junc A5/A444

CARRY ON STABLES
Birmingham Road, Hertford Hill, Nr Warwick, Warwicks
Tel: Warwick (0926) 492477
Proprietor: Miss J A Cook
Livery and Training Centre
Av No: Horses 3 Ponies 2
Livery: Full/Grass/Break/School
Courses: YT – 1
Facilities: Out Man: 20 x 61m/Jmp Pd/ CC Fences 5 + wall/WC/Car Park
Specialities: Liveries/Schooling/ Breaking/Instruction on own horse
Exclusion: No Rider under 7 years accepted
Location: Off A41 between Warwick & Hatton

CASTLE HILL RIDING SCHOOL
Brandon, Coventry, Warwickshire, CV8 3HQ
Tel: Wolston (0203) 542762
Proprietor: Mrs P Potter (BHSII(T))
Other Staff: Mrs C Duff (BHSAI) Miss C Neil (BHS AI) 2 (BHSAI) P/T
Instruction in Riding and Jumping & Students to BHSAI Exam
Av No: Horses 15 Ponies 20 Specialist Horses: Drg – M
Std of Schlg: General Purpose Break/School/Hack/Trek – Bridlepaths
Ev Classes
Courses: Inst/Wkg Students/YT – 2
Facilities: Cov Sch: 43 x 14m* Fl Lit/Out Man: 55 x 41m* Fl Lit/Jmp Pd 1 acre Fl Lit/Sh Jmps 20/CC Course/Lec Rm/Vis Aids/Video/Refresh/Rest Rm/WC/Wash Rm/Chng Rm
Accom: Camp – 15 Catering – Full (Only for Children)
Specialities: General Instruction/ Children/Dressage/Show Jumping/Side Saddle/Summer Camps/Show Ponies/ Driving
Exclusions: No casual hiring
Location: Off B4029 6 miles from Coventry & 6 miles from Stoneleigh

KINGSWOOD SCHOOL OF RIDING
Dalehouse Lane, Kenilworth, Warwickshire, CV8 2JZ
Tel: Coventry (0203) 418121
Proprietor: Mrs Pauling (BHSAI)
Other Staff: 1 (BHSAI) P/T
Instruction in Riding and Jumping
Av No: Horses 2 Ponies 5
Std of Schlg: General Purpose
Livery: Full/School
Evening Lessons – Summer
Courses: Inst Hol/YT – Taken
Facilities: Out Man: 20 x 40m*/Jmp Pd/

Sh Jmps/CC Course/Refresh/WC/Wash Rm/Car Park
Specialities: Dressage training & frequent dressage competitions/Beginners welcome/Schooling on own horse/Jumping training & competitions in summer/Side Saddle
Exclusions: No Casual Hiring
Location: Just off A46 at Warwick University turn off

MOAT HOUSE FARM
Ullenhall, Henley in Arden, Warwickshire
Tel: 05642 2560
Proprietor: Mrs P G Westwood
Other Staff: 1 (BHS(Stage III))
Instruction in Riding and Jumping
Av No: Horses 7 Ponies 1
Std of Schlg: General Purpose
Livery: Full/Grass/School/Break/Hack – Bridleways/No main roads
Ev Classes
Courses: Wkg Students/YT – 4
Facilities: Out Man: 35 x 15m Fl Lit/Jmp Pd/Lec Rm/Vis Aids/Refresh/Wash Rm/WC/Chng Rm/Wait Rm/Car Park
Specialities: Breeding/Showing & Racing Arab Horses/Breeding Anglo Arabs
Location: Off B4480 4 miles from Henley in Arden

PITTERN HILL STABLES LIMITED
Pittern Hill, Kineton, Warwickshire, CV35 OJF
Tel: Kineton (0926) 640370
Proprietors: Mr R L Philpot & Miss P Lewis (FBHS)
Chief Inst: Miss P Lewis (FBHS) **Other Staff:** 2 (BHSII) 1 (BHSII) P/T 1 (BHSAI)
Instruction in Riding and Jumping & Students to BHSII Exam
Av No: Horses 25 Ponies 13
Std of Schlg: General Purpose Std of Specialist Schlg: Drg – M/Event – Int/Sh Jmp – Grade A
Livery: Full/Part/Grass/Hunter/Break/School/Hack – Bridlepaths Common/Farmland
Ev Classes
Courses: Inst Hol/Wkg Students/YT – 4
Facilities: Cov Sch: 22 x 46m* Fl Lit Gly 80/Out Man: 22 x 43m Fl Lit*/Jmp Pd/Sh Jmps/CC Fences/Lec Rm/Vis Aids/Refresh/Wash Rm/Shop/WC/Chng Rm/Car Park
Specialities: General riding instruction for Students/Side Saddle/Shows/RDA/Show Jumping to Grade A
Exclusions: No hiring for hunting/No casual hire
Location: On B4086 between Kineton & Wellesbourne

UMBERSLADE RIDING SCHOOL
Blunts Green Farm, Blunts Green, Nr Henley in Arden, Warwickshire
Tel: 0564 794609
Proprietor: P W Pettitt Esq
Manager: Mrs C M Pettitt **Chief Inst:** Miss V Townsend (BHSAI) **Other Staff:** 2 (BHSII) P/T 1 (BHSAI)
Instruction in Riding and Jumping
Av No: Horses 20 Ponies 6 Specialist Horses: 1 Drg – E/2 HT – N
Std of Schlg: General Purpose
Livery: Full/Part/School/Break/Hunt/Hack – Quiet Lanes/Bridleways
Ev Classes
Courses: YT Taken/Wkg Students – 2
Facilities: Cov Sch: 19 x 28m/Out Man: 85 x 40m Fl Lit/School Fences 10/Jmp Pd/Lec Rm/Film/Projector/Snacks/Wash Rm/WC/Tack Shop/Car Park
Specialities: Dressage Instruction up to Elementary Level/Show Jumping to Grade B/Nervous Riders
Location: 2 miles from A34 between Henley in Arden & Tanworth in Arden

WARWICKSHIRE COLLEGE OF AGRICULTURE
Moreton Hall, Moreton Morrell, Warwick, Warwickshire, CV35 9BL
Tel: 0926 651 367/Fax No – 0926 651190
Principal: Mr R H G Suggett
Manager: Mr J Houghton–Brown **Chief Inst:** Mrs J Houghton–Brown (FBHS)
Other Staff: Miss L Freeman (BHSI) 1 (BHSII)
Instruction in Riding and Jumping & Students to BHSII Exam
Av No: Horses 26 Ponies 4
Std of Schlg: General Purpose School/Break/Hack – College land
Courses: Resid/Inst
Facilities: Cov Sch: 18 x 22m seats 40*/Out Man: 60 x 26m Fl Lit/Jmp Pd/Lec Rm/Vis Aids
Accom: 150 – rooms Catering: Full
Exclusions: Warwickshire College of Agriculture Students only **Location:** Just outside village of Moreton Morrell

WAVERLEY RIDING SCHOOL
Coventry Road, Cubbington, Leamington Spa, Warwickshire
Tel: 0926 422876
Proprietors: Mr & Mrs Ruyssevelt

Chief Inst: Mrs Ruyssevelt (BHSAI)
Other Staff: 1 (BHSII(T)) 1 (BHSAI) 2 (BHSAI) P/T
Instruction in Riding and Jumping/Students to BHSAI
Av No: Horses 16 Ponies 9
Std of Schlg: General Purpose Std of Spec Sch 2 Show Jumping Grade C/2 HT Novice
Ev Classes
Courses: Resid/Wkg Pupil – 4/YT – 1
Facilities: Cov Sch: 37 x 20m*/Out Man: 40 x 20m* CC Course* – Fences 12/Jmp Pd/Sh Jumps/WC/Chng Rm/ Waing Rm/Car Park/Lecture Room
Accom: Caravan – 4 Catering: Self
Exclusions: No Riders under 6 Years
Location: 1 Mile from Stoneleigh

WITHYBROOK STABLES
Featherbed Lane, Withybrook, Nr Coventry, Warwickshire
Tel: 0455 220198
Proprietors: Miss S J Smallman & Mr D Dobson
Manager & Chief Inst: Miss S J Smallman (BHSAI) **Other Staff:** Miss L Irvine
Instruction in Riding and Jumping
Av No: Horses 7 Ponies 1 Specialist Horses: 2 Int Drg/2 Grade C Sh Jmpers/ 1 Nov Eventer
Std of Schlg: General Purpose Std of Specialist Schlg: Drg – Int/CT – Nov/Sh Jmpg – C
Livery: Full/DIY/Working/School
Ev Classes
Courses: YT – 3
Facilities: Cov Sch: 39 x 17m/Out Man: 41 x 22 m Fl Lit/Refreshments/Wash Rm/WC/Car Park
Specialities: Training for competitions
Location: Off the Fosse 5 miles from Hinckley & 8 miles from Coventry

WEST MIDLANDS

BEECHWOOD LIVERY & TRAINING CENTRE
Hodgetts Lane, Berkswell, West Midlands, CV7 7DG
Tel: 0676 34869
Proprietors: P Roberts Esq (FBHS) & Mr & Mrs B Fischer **Other Staff:** 1 (BHSII)F/T
Livery & Training Centre
Std of Specialist Schlg: CT – Int/Sh Jmpg – C
Livery: Full/School/Break
Courses: Wkg Students
Facilities: Out Man: 50 x 30m Fl Lit/Int CC Course/30 CC Fences/Snacks/Wash Rm/WC/Changing Rm/Car Park
Specialities: Livery/Schooling for competitions Cross Country/CT
Exclusions: No Casual Hire
Location: Off A452 between Birmingham & Stoneleigh

BOURNE VALE STABLES
Bourne Vale, Aldridge, Nr Walsall, West Midlands
Tel: 021 353 7174
Proprietor: Mrs P Cooper (BHSII(T))
Chief Instructor: Mr P Waterhouse (BHSII) **Other Staff:** Mrs Waterhouse (BHSII(T)) Miss S Symonds (BHSAI)
Instruction in Riding and Jumping & Students to BHSAI Exam
Av No: Horses 10 Ponies 5
Std of Schlg: General Purpose
Livery: Full/Hunter/Break/School/Hack – Parkland
Ev Classes
Courses: Hol Inst/Wkg Students
Facilities: Cov Sch: 43 x 25m Gly/ Jmp Pd/Out Man: 40 x 25m Fl Lit/Sh Jumps/3 CC Fences/Lec Rm/Video/ Vis Aids/WC/Wash Rm/Wait Rm/Car Park
Specialities: Non–residential children's holiday courses/RDA
Exclusions: No hiring for hunting/ Escorted Hacks only/No Children under 8 years/No YT
Location: 3 miles from Junc 7 on M6

COTTAGE FARM STABLES
Illshaw Heath Road, Warings Green, Earlswood, Solihull, West Midlands, B94 6DL
Tel: 05646 3314
Proprietor: Mr V Perry
Manager: Mrs H Perry
Instruction in Riding and Jumping
Av No: Horses 12 Ponies 12
Std of Schlg: General Purpose Std of Specialist Schooling: Sh Jmpg – Novice School/Break/Hack – Bridleways/ Woodland
Courses: Resid/Wkg Pupil
Facilities: Jmp Pd/Refresh/Wash Rm/ WC/Chng Rm/Wait Rm/Tack Shop/ Lec Rm*/Vis Aids*/Car Park
Accom: Portacabin – Shared – 6 Children on Riding Holidays Catering: Full
Exclusions: No Riders Over 14 Stone/No YT
Location: 1 mile from Junc 6 on M6 between Shirley & Henley in Arden

FARM HOUSE STABLES
The Farm House, Marston, Nr Sutton Coldfield, West Midlands, B76 0DW
Tel: 0675 470621
Proprietors: Mr M P J & Mrs D W Gee
Manager & Chief Inst: Mr M P J Gee (BHSII) **Other Staff:** 1 F/T 1 P/T
Training Centre
Av No: Horses 9 Ponies – Specialist Horses: 1 Grade B & C Sh Jmper/2 Novice Eventers
Std of Schlg: General Purpose Std of Specialist Schlg: CT – Novice/Sh Jmpg – C
Livery: Full/Hunter/School/Break
Ev Classes
Facilities: Out Man: 43 x 25m/Novice CC Course/Lec Rm/Wash Rm/WC/Car Park
Specialities: Breaking/Schooling
Location: Off A4097 2 miles from Exit 9 on M42

KINGSWOOD EQUESTRIAN CLUB
Kingswood Lodge, County Lane, Albrighton, Nr Wolverhampton, West Midlands, WV7 3AH
Tel: 0902 374480
Proprietor: R Lickley Esq MSc
Secretary: Miss S C Yeomans BA **Chief Inst:** Miss C Furnival (BHSII)
Other Staff: 1 (BHSAI) Miss B Williams (BHSI) P/T J Sainsbury (BHSI) P/T
Instruction in Riding and Jumping
Av No: Horses 4 Ponies 6
Std of Schlg: General Purpose Specialist Schlg: Eventing – Adv/Drg – Med/Sh Jmpg – Grade B/School/Sh Jmping – Novice
Ev Classes
Courses: YT – 2/Wkg Pupils
Facilities: Cov Sch: 34 x 22m Gly/Out Man: 44 x 22m/Jmp Pd/Sh Jmp: 60 x 40m/CC Course – Pre Novice Course/Chg Rm/Refreshments/Wash Rm/WC/Wait Rm/Lec Rm – Vis Aids/Video Cameras/Car Park
Specialities: Training Youngsters/Progressive Riding Tests
Exclusions: Club Membership is not restricted in any way & is open to anyone who rides or wishes to learn to ride
Location: Off A41 4 miles from Junc 3 on M54 & 3 miles from Wolverhampton

SILVRETTA HAFLINGER STUD & LONG DISTANCE RIDING CENTRE
Shangri – La, Woodfield Lane, Romsley, Halesowen, West Midlands, B62 0LR
Tel: 0562 710245
Proprietor & Chief Inst: Miss H Y Blair (BHSAI) Regd
Other Staff: Mrs J A Houghton (BHSI) 3/4 days per week
Instruction in Riding and Jumping
Av No: Horses 3 Ponies 8
Std of Schlg: General Purpose Std of Specialist Schlg: Sh Jmpg – Novice
Livery: Full/Grass/School/Break/Hack – National Trust Woodland/Hills
Courses: Wkg Pupils/YT – 1
Facilities: Cov Sch: 13 x 24m*/Jmp Pd*/Lec Rm/Snacks/Wash Rm/WC/Car Park
Specialities: Haflingers Display Team/Long Distance Riding
Location: Off A491 btwn Kidderminster & Bromsgrove/Halesowen & Stourbridge

STOURTON HILL STABLES
Bridgnorth Road, Stourton, Stourbridge, West Midlands, DY7 5BQ
Tel: 0384 872865
Proprietor: Mrs P A Knight
Chief Inst: Miss J A Knight (BHSAI)
Other Staff: 3 (BHSAI) P/T
Instruction in Riding and Jumping
Av No: Ponies 12
Std of Schlg: General Purpose Hack – Bridleways/County Lanes
Ev Classes
Facilities: Out Man: 40 x 20m Fl Lit/Sh Jmps/Jmp Pd/CC Fences 10/Refresh/WC/Waiting Rm/Car Park
Specialities: Teaching Children/Riding & Pony Care on well schooled ponies/Small classes/Summer Camp
Exclusions: No Riders over 10.5 stone/Riders under 7 years not accepted/Children only
Location: On A458 (Bridgnorth Rd) & 4 miles from Stourbridge

WISHAW RIDING CENTRE
Bulls Lane, Wishaw, Sutton Coldfield, West Midlands, B76 9QW
Tel: 021 313 1663
Proprietor: Mrs M Bevan
Chief Inst: Miss A Pine (BHSAI) **Other Staff:** Miss E Walpole (BHSAI) Mr N Rogers BHSI P/T – attends for staff only Miss J Yardley (BHSII) P/T
Instruction in Riding and Jumping
Av No: Horses 10 Ponies 6 Specialist Horses: 1 Drg – Nov/1 Sh Jmper – C/1 Eventer – Nov
Std of Schlg: General Purpose Std of Specialist Schlg: Drg – Nov/Sh Jmpg – C
Livery: Full/Working/School/Hack – Own land/Country Lanes

Ev Classes
Courses: Adult Training Days/Days for Children
Facilities: Cov Sch: 43 x 18m* Gly/ 2 Out Mans: 20 x 40m* & 23 x 45m*/ Wash Rm/WC/Waiting Rm/Car Park
Accom: Single Rms – Staff Only - 3
Catering: Self
Specialities: Adult Training Days/Day Courses for Children/RDA
Location: 8 miles from Birmingham & 2.5 miles from Sutton Coldfield

Riding in the East

BEDFORDSHIRE ♦ CAMBRIDGESHIRE ♦ ESSEX ♦ HERTFORDSHIRE ♦ NORFOLK ♦ SUFFOLK

BEDFORDSHIRE

ROCKLANE RIDING CENTRE
Soulbury Road, Wing, Leighton Buzzard, Bedfordshire, LU7 0JL
Tel: 0296 688673
Proprietors: Mrs J Joyce & Mr J Tossell (BHSAI)
Other Staff: 2 (BHSAI) P/T
Instruction in Riding and Jumping
Av No: Horses 6 Ponies 6
Std of Schlg: General Purpose
Livery: School
Ev Classes
Courses: Stage I & II/YT taken
Facilities: Cov Sch: 25 x 18m/Sh Jmp Pd/Lec Rm/Refreshments/Wash Rm/W C/Changing Rm/Waiting Rm/Car Park
Specialities: Day Courses
Exclusions: No Hiring for Hunting
Location: Off A418 3 miles from Leighton Buzzard & 9 miles from Aylesbury

ROWAN LODGE SCHOOL OF EQUITATION
Fildyke Close, Fildyke Road, Meppershall, Bedford, SG17 5LF
Tel: 0462 812151
Proprietor & Chief Inst: Mrs J V Hirsh (BHSII)
Other Staff: 1 (BHSAI) John Lassetter (BHSI) – Visiting
Instruction in Riding and Jumping & Students to BHSII Exam
Av No: Horses 10 Ponies 5 Specialist Horses: 2 Drg – E/1 Sh Jmpg – C
Std of Schlg: General Purpose
Livery: Full/Part/Schlg
Ev Classes
Courses: YT – 3/ET – 3
Facilities: Cov Sch:19 x 34m* Gly Fl Lit/2 Out Mans: 40m x 20 Fl Lit & 60 x 20m/Jmp Pd/Sh Jmps*/Refresh/WC/Car Park
Specialities: General Instruction/ Individual Courses/Dressage
Exclusions: No Riders over 14 stone/ No Hacking
Location: Centre of Village 1.5 miles off A600 Shefford/Hitchin

TINSLEYS RIDING SCHOOL
Green Lane, Clapham, Bedford, Bedfordshire
Tel: Bedford (0234) 268556
Proprietors: Mrs F Thody & Mr J Thody
Chief Inst: Mrs S Black (BHSAI)
Basic Instruction in Riding and Jumping
Av No: Horses 5 Ponies 5
Std of Schlg: General Purpose
Livery: Grass/DIY/Break/School/Hack – Bridlepaths/Park
Ev Classes
Facilities: Out Man:40m x 20m* Fl Lit/ Jmp Pd/Sh Jmps*/a few CC Fences/Wash Rm/WC/Car Park
Specialities: Basic Instruction/Hacking/Livery
Exclusions: No children under 6 years

CAMBRIDGESHIRE

CAMBRIDGESHIRE COLLEGE OF AGRICULTURE & HORTICULTURE
Landbeach Road, Milton, Cambridge, CB4 4DB
Tel: 0223 860701
Principal: R Lancaster Esq
Manager: Mrs J Walker (BHSII) RDAI
Other Staff: Miss C A Ratcliffe (BHSII) Msc Equine Studies Miss G Rowbury (BHSII) Mr E Bourgoin (BHSII) Miss S Merry (BHSAI) Mr G Boreham (BHSAI) PC
A Test 1 MSc Equine 3 (BHSII) P/T 2 (BHSAI) P/T

Instruction in Riding and Jumping & Students to BHSII Exam
Av No: Horses 18 Ponies 5 Specialist Horses: 3 Drg Int/2 Sh Jmp Grade C
Std of Schlg: General Purpose Std of Specialist Schooling: Drg–Int/Sh Jmp C School
Ev Classes
Courses: Resid/BHSAI Exam/Students – 60/YT – 3
Facilities: Out Man: 40 x 20m*/Cov Sch: 40m x 20m Fl Lit Gly/Jmp Pd/CC Fences/Lec Rm*/Club Rm*/Vis Aids*/ Library*/Film Projector*/Seating/Wash Rm/WC/Car Park
Accom: Single/Shared – 11 Catering: Full
Specialities: RDA/Full–time National Certificate in Management of Horses/ BHSAI/YTS Working with Horses/Part-time Courses/Clinics
Location: Just off Junc of A45 – A10

GRANGE FARM EQUESTRIAN CENTRE
Wittering Grange, Wansford, Peterborough, Cambridge, PE8 6NR
Tel: 0780 782459
Proprietors: Mr & Mrs R Dunlop & Miss J M Walford
Chief Inst: Miss J M Walford (BHSAI)
Other Staff: 2 (BHSII(T)) P/T 3 (BHSAI) P/T 2 Visiting FBHS – Mr J Michaels & Mrs S C Roughton
Instruction in Riding and Jumping
Av No: Horses 21 Ponies: 30 Specialist Horses: 4 Drg – 2 E/1 Grade B & C Sh Jmpers
Std of Schlg: General Purpose Std of Specialist Schlg: Drg – Elem/CT – Nov/ Sh Jmpg
Livery: Full/Part/Grass/School/Hack – Own Farmla nd/Woodland/Bridleways
Ev Classes
Courses: YT – 2
Facilities: Cov Sch: 40 x 20m*/2 Outdoor Mans: 110 x 44m* Fl Lit/40 x 20m* Fl Lit/Novice CC Course*/Snacks/ Wash Rm/WC/Car Park
Specialities: Side Saddle
Location: Bewteen A1 & A47 10 miles from Peterborough & 5 from Stamford

HAGGIS FARM STABLES
Cambridge Road, Barton, Cambridge, CB3 7AT
Tel: 0223 460353
Proprietor & Chief Inst: Mrs B J Morris – Lowe
Other Staff: Miss L Cooke (BHSII) P/T
Instruction in Riding and Jumping
Av No: Horses 10 Ponies 15
Std of Schlg: General Purpose Std of Specialist Schlg: Sh Jmpg – Novice
Livery: Full/Part/School/Hack – Bridleways
Ev Classes
Courses: YT – 1/Childrens Stable Management
Facilities: 2 Cov Sch: 18 x 14m*/31 x 14m*/Out Man: 25 x 45m/CC Course/ Snacks/Wash Rm/WC/Wait Rm/Car Park
Specialities: Children/Childrens Stable Management Courses
Location: Adjacent to Junc 12 on M11/2 miles from Cambridge

LYNCH FARM EQUITATION CENTRE
Wistow Way, Orton Wistow, Peterborough, Cambridgeshire, PE2 0XA
Tel: 0733 234445
Proprietors: Mr & Mrs D M Brown
Chief Inst: Mr D M Brown (BHSI) **Other Staff:** Mrs D M Brown (BHSI(T)) 2 (BHSAI) 1ABRS PD
Instruction in Riding and Jumping & Students to BHSII Exam
Av No: Horses 15 Ponies 9 Spec Horses: 3 Drg M/1 Sh Jmp C
Std of Schlg: General Purpose
Livery: Full/School/Break/Hack – Park Land
Ev Classes
Courses: Long/Short/Students up to BHSII Exam/YT – 3/6 Students
Facilities: Cov Sch: 37 x 20m/Jmp Pd/ Lec Rm/Vis Ai ds/Library/Film Projector/ Wash Rm/WC/Chang Rm/Car Park
Specialities: The Short Course Specialists/Short courses in wide range of subjects – send SAE
Exclusions: No unescorted Hacking/No Children under 7 years
Location: 1 mile from A1/3 miles from Centre of Peterborough

MILL COTTAGE RIDING & LIVERY STABLES
Mill Cottage, Gidding Road, Sawtry, Cambridge, Cambridgeshire, PE17 5UJ
Tel: 0487 831497
Proprietors: Mr & Mrs T Scott
Manager: Mrs T Scott **Inst:** Miss K Scott
Other Staff: Mrs B Johnson (BHSAI) P/T & Miss Z Bedford (BHSAI) P/T
Basic Instruction in Riding and Jumping
Av No: Horses 2 Ponies 4
Std of Schlg: General Purpose Std of Specialist Schlg: Sh Jmpg – Novice
Livery: Full/Part/DIY/School

Ev Classes
Facilities: Out Man: 25 x 40m* Fl Lit/Jmp Pd/W ash Rm/WC/Car Park
Exclusions: No riders over 13 stone
Location: 3/4 mile from A1 between Huntingdon & Peterborough

PARADISE RIDING CENTRE
Paradise Farm, Witchford Road, Ely, Cambridge, Cambridgeshire, CB6 3NN
Tel: 0353 662453/662499
Proprietor: Mrs E L Bedford
Chief Inst: Mr T Martin **Other Staff:** Mrs S Whittaker (BHSII) – 3 days per week
Instruction in Riding and Jumping
Av No: Horses 6 Ponies 13
Std of Schlg: General Purpose Std of Specialist Schlg: Sh Jmpg – Novice
Livery: Full/Part/Grass/School/Hack – own farmland
Ev Classes
Courses: YT – 1
Facilities: 2 Out Man: 33 x 17m* Fl Lit & 44 x 2 2m/Wash Rm/WC/Shower/ Waiting Rm/Car Park
Specialities: RDA
Location: On A142 1.5 miles from Ely

MISS E A PICKARD
New Farm, Fox Road, Bourn, Cambridge, CB3 7TY
Tel: Caxton (095 44) 501
Proprietor: Miss E A Pickard
Other Staff: 1 (BHSAI) P/T
Instruction in Riding and Jumping & Students to BHSAI Exam
Av No: Horses 3 Ponies 10
Std of Schlg: General Purpose
Livery: Full/Part/Grass/Hunter/Break/ School/Hack – Country Lanes/Bridlepaths
Ev Classes
Courses: Inst/Wkg Students/YT – 1
Facilities: Out Man:40m x 20m Fl Lit/CC Fences/Jmp Pd/Sh Jmps/WC/Car Park
Accom: 3 By arrangement in family house Catering – Self
Specialities: Dressage training/ Children/Pony Club activities/ Schooling/Eventing/Horse Walker
Location: On B1046 off A14 3 miles from A45 between Huntington/ Cambridge & Royston

THE WINDMILL STABLES
Shepreth Road, Barrington, Cambridge, CB2 5SB
Tel: Cambridge (0223) 871487
Proprietor & Chief Inst: Mrs S A Tydeman (BHSAI)
Other Staff: 1 (BHSII(T)) 1 (BHSAI) 1 (BHSAI) P/T
Instruction in Riding and Jumping & Students to BHSAI Exam
Av No: Horses 6 Ponies 9
Std of Schlg: General Purpose
Livery: Full/Part/Grass/Break/School/ Hack/Trek – Bridlepaths
Ev Classes
Courses: Resid Inst Hol Children only/ Wkg Students – 2
Facilities: Out Man(2): 38m x 17m Fl Lit & 45m x 25 m/Jmp Pd/Sh Jmps/CC Course/CC Fences/Lec Rm/Vis Aids/ Video/Refresh/Wash Rm/WC/Car Park
Accom: 8 – Caravan & in house Catering: Full (Childrens holiday courses and 2 students)
Specialities: Children/Horsemastership courses
Exclusions: No YT
Location: Between Cambridge & Royston/off A603 & A10

ESSEX

ALDBOROUGH HALL EQUESTRIAN CENTRE LIMITED
Aldborough Hall, Aldborough Hatch, Newbury Park, Ilford, Essex, IG2 7TE
Tel: 081 590 1433
Proprietor: A R S Garrett (BHS SM)
Other Staff: 3 (BHSAI) 1 (BHSII)
Instruction in Riding and Jumping & Students to BHSII Exam
Av No: Horses 20 Ponies 14 Specialist Horses: 6
Std of Schlg: General Purpose Std of Specialist Schlg: Drg & HT – Int/Sh Jmp – A
Livery: Full/Hunter/Break/School/Hunt – Farm/Forest
Ev Classes
Courses: Resid Inst Hol/8 Wkg Students
Facilities: Cov Sch: 24 x 60m Gly 400 Fl Lit/Out Man: (1) 50 x 90m (2) 20 x 40m Fl Lit/Jmp Pd/Sh Jmps 30/CC Fences 100/CC Course/Lec Rm/Vis Aids/Video/Refreshments/WC/Wash Rm/Chng Rm/Wait Rm/Car Park
Accom: 7 – Rooms Catering: Self
Specialities: Dressage/Show Jumping/ Cross Country/Instruction on own horses/Riding & Pony Club activities
Location: Just off A12 (Redbridge Roundabout) 3 miles East of M11

BROOK FARM EQUESTRIAN CENTRE
Stock Road, Stock, Essex, CM4 9PH
Tel: 0277 840425

Proprietors: Mr & Mrs C Stenbacka
Manager: Mrs C Johnson (BHSAI)
Other Staff: 1 (BHSAI)
Instruction in Riding and Jumping
Av No: Horses 15 Ponies 15
Std of Schlg: General Purpose
Livery: Full/Part/School/Hack – Bridleways
Ev Classes
Courses: Non – Resid Holidays
Facilities: Cov Sch: 37 x 25m* Gly/Refreshments/Wash Rm/WC/ Showers/Changing Rm/Waiting Rm/ Car Park
Specialities: Non Residential childrens riding holidays/RDA/Internal Gymkhanas
Location: On B186 3 miles from Billericay & 5 miles from Chelmsford

BROOK FARM EQUESTRIAN CENTRE

Radwinter, Saffron Walden, Essex, CB10 2TH
Tel: 079987 262
Proprietors: Mr & Mrs M Gay
Manager/Chief Inst: Miss K A Gay (BHSAI)
Instruction in Riding and Jumping
Av No: Horses 9 Ponies 9
Std of Schlg: General Purpose Std of Specialist Schlg: Sh Jmp – Novice
Livery: Full/Part/School/Hack– Bridleways/Farm Track
Ev Classes
Courses: Wkg Students – 2/YT – 1
Facilities: Cov Sch: 42 x 22m Gly – seating 30/Snacks/Wash Rm/WC/ Waiting Rm/Tack Shop/Car Park
Accom: 5 – House – 3 Portacabin – 2 (For staff & Students only)
Specialities: Special 3 year old class/ Indoor Shows/RDA
Exclusions: No Riders over 14 Stone
Location: On B1054 5 miles from Saffron Walden & 8 from Haverhill

CARLTON EQUESTRIAN CENTRE LTD

Beehive Lane, Galleywood, Chelmsford, Essex, CM2 8RJ
Tel: 0245 358116
Proprietors: Mrs S Dickinson & Mrs A Pirie
Manager: Mrs S Dickinson **Chief Inst:** Miss J Keough (BHSAI)
Other Staff: Mrs M Tovim (BHSII) Mrs J Miles (BHSAI) both 2 days per week
Instruction in Riding and Jumping
Av No: Horses 14 Ponies 14
Std of Schlg: General Purpose Std of Specialist Schlg: CT – Basic/Sh Jmpg – Novice
Livery: Working/School/Hack – Bridleways
Ev Classes
Courses: Wkg Pupils – 5/Childrens Day
Facilities: Out Man: 20 x 40m Fl Lit/ Jmpg Pd/Lec Rm – Vis Aids/Library/ Video/Wash Rm/WC/Waiting Rm/Tack Shop/Car Park
Specialities: Show Jumping/Childrens Day Courses
Location: Close to Galleywood Common/2 miles from centre of Chelmsford

DE'BEAUVOIR FARM LIVERY YARD

Church Road, Ramsden Heath, Nr Billericay, Essex, CM11 1PW
Tel: (0268) 710534/711302
Proprietor/Principal: Mr B Greenan
Manageress: Miss S Painter
Livery Yard
Av No: Horses – Ponies – (Liveries only) – 31
Livery: Full/Part/Grass/DIY
Courses: YT – taken
Facilities: Cov Sch: 19 x 9m* Fl Lit/Out Man: 14 x 14m* Fl Lit/Jmp Pd 92 x 92m/ Sh Jmps 15/CC Fences/Refresh/WC/ Wash Rm/Car Park

EASTERN EQUITATION

Brickhouse Farm, Colne Engaine, Nr Colchester, Essex, CO6 2HJ
Tel: 0787 222542
Proprietor: Mr J M Roberts
Managing Agent YT
Chief Inst: Miss C A Jones (BHSI(SM))
Other Staff: Miss L CLark (BHSAI)
Instruction in Riding and Jumping & Students to BHSII Exam
Av No: Horses 8 Ponies 2 Spec Horses: Drg N/Sh Jmp C
Std of Schlg: General Purpose
Livery: Full/Break/School/Hack – Farmland/Bridlepaths
Ev Classes
Courses: Day Half-day Inst/8 Wkg Students
Facilities: Cov Sch: 60 x 25m Gly 100 Fl Lit/Sh Jmps/CC Fences 12/Vis Aids/ Video/Wash Rm/Refresh/WC/Car Park
Specialities: Livery/Career Training/Dressage
Exclusions: No hiring/No unaccompanied riding/No Riders over 13 stone/No children under 13 years
Location: A mile from A604 btwn Colchester/Halstead

EASTMINSTER SCHOOL OF RIDING LIMITED
Hooks Hall Farm, The Chase, Rush Green, Romford, Essex, RM7 OSS
Tel: Hornchurch (04024) 47423/73980
Proprietor/Chief Inst: Mrs A Ackland (BHSAI)
Other Staff: 1 (BHSII) P/T 2 (BHSAI) P/T
Basic Instruction in Riding and Jumping
Av No: Horses 14 Ponies 15
Std of Schlg: General Purpose
Livery: Full/Grass/DIY/Hack – Private Land/varying terrain (no road work)
Ev Classes
Courses: Children two day courses
Facilities: Out Man: 31 x 18.5m Fl Lit/Cov Sch: 25 x 12.5m Fl Lit/Jmp Pd Seats Fl Lit Sh Jmps* 1 Set/CC Course*/Lec Rm/Vis Aids/Video/Club Rm/Refresh/WC/Chng Rm/Car Park
Specialities: Basic instruction/Hacking/Instruction on own horses/Riding & Pony Club activities
Exclusions: Weight limit 14 stones/No children under 6 years
Location: On A125 15 miles from London & 2 miles from Romford

FOLKES FARM RIDING & LIVERY STABLES
Folkes Lane, Upminster, Essex, RM14 1TH
Tel: Brentwood (0277) 212002
Proprietor: Mr R A Nightingale
Chief Inst: Mrs D Sheppard (BHSAI)
Other Staff: (BHSI) – Visiting
Instruction in Riding and Jumping
Av No: Horses 6 Ponies 6
Std of Schlg: General Purpose
Livery: Part/Break/School/Hack – Rural
Ev Classes
Courses: Resid Inst Hol
Facilities: Cov Sch: 31 x 25m Gly 60/Jmp Pd/CC Fences/Lec Rm/Vis Aids/Video/Club Rm/Refresh/WC/Chng Rm/Wait Rm/Car Park
Accom: 6 – Self contained flat/lodgings locally
Specialities: General Instruction/RDA
Exclusions: All riding Escorted/No YT

FOXHOUND RIDING SCHOOL LIMITED
Baker Street, Orsett, Essex
Tel: Grays Thurrock (0375) 891367
Proprietor/Director/Principal: Mrs M Cox (BHSII)
Other Staff: 1 (BHSII(T)) 1 (BHSAI) 1 (BHSI) – Visiting
Instruction in Riding and Jumping
Av No: Horses 7 Ponies 8
Std of Schlg: General Purpose
Livery: Full/Part/Break/School/Hack – Fenland/Bridleways
Ev Classes
Courses: Res Inst Hol/YTS – Taken
Facilities: Cov Sch: 31 x 20m* Gly Fl Lit/Out Man: 25 x 18m* Fl Lit/Jmp Pd/Sh Jmps/CC Fences/Refresh/WC/Chng Rm/Tack Shop/Car Park
Specialities: Riding Club tests/Children's courses/open shows/RDA
Exclusions: No Riders over 13 stones
Location: 4 miles from M25 & 1 mile from A13

GLEBE EQUESTRIAN CENTRE
Mope Lane, Wickham Bishops, Witham, Essex
Tel: Maldon (0621) 892375
Proprietors: Miss R Osborne & Miss J Osborne
Other Staff: 3 (BHSAI) P/T
Instruction in Riding and Jumping
Av No: Horses 2 Ponies 14
Std of Schlg: General Purpose
Livery: Full/Part/Grass/Hunter/Break/School/Hack – Lanes/Farmland
Ev Classes – None
Facilities: Cov Sch: 52 x 25m* Gly 150/Out Man: 52 x 25m* Fl Lit/Jmp Pd Seats Fl Lit/Sh Jmps/CC Fences/Lec Rm/Vis Aids/Video/Club Rm/Refresh/WC/Chng Rm/Car Park
Specialities: Children all ages/Sh horses/Lessons by appointment/General Instruction
Exclusions: No casual hiring/No YTS
Location: 5 minutes by car from A12 & 40 minutes by rail from London

HERON STREAM STUD
Church Road, Rawreth, Wickford, Essex, SS11 8SH
Tel: 0268 733008
Proprietor: Miss J R Van Lennep MSc (BHS SM) NPS Dip
Chief Inst: Mrs F Gillott (BHSII) NPS Dip P/T **Other Staff:** 1 (BHSII)
Instruction in Riding and Jumping & Students to BHSAI Exam
Av No: Horses 7 Ponies 3
Std of Schlg: General Purpose
Livery: Full/Part/Break/School
Courses: Resid Inst/Wkg Students/YT – 6/BHS & NVQ Exams
Facilities: Cov Schs: 32 x 19m* Gly 40 & 28 x 1 2m Fl Lit/Jmp Pd 2 acres Seats/Out Man: 60 x 20m/Sh Jmps 2 full sets/CC Fences/Lec Rm/Vis Aids/Refresh/WC/Wash Rm/Tack Shop

Accom: 5 Shared Catering: Full
Specialities: Breaking/Schooling/Livery/RDA/Stud Work
Exclusions: No Casual Hiring
Location: 0.5 mile West of A130 10 miles South of Chelmsford

HIGH BEECH RIDING SCHOOL
Pynest Green Lane, Waltham Abbey, Essex, EN9 3QL
Tel: 081 508 8866
Proprietors: A J & G J Taylor
Chief Inst: Mr A J Taylor **Other Staff:** 1 (BHSAI) P/T
Basic Instruction in Riding and Jumping
Av No: Horses 11 Ponies 10
Std of Schlg: General Purpose
Livery: Full/Hack – Epping Forest
Ev Classes
Courses: Non Resid/Children's Hol/YT – 1
Facilities: Cov Sch: 37 x 19m*/CC Fences/Sh Jmps/WC/Tack Shop/Car Park
Specialities: Hacking/Novice/Nervous riders/Hacking Holidays in Forest/HQ for 1st Epping Troop of the Horses Rangers Association
Exclusions: No riders over 13.5 stone
Location: 1 mile from Junc 26 on M25 between Waltham Abbey & Loughton

HILL FARM
Pan Lane, East Hanningfield, Chelmsford, Essex, CM3 8BJ
Tel: Chelmsford (0245) 400115
Proprietor: R Lawrence Esq
Manager & Chief Inst: Miss S Norris (BHSII(T)) **Other Staff:** 2 (BHSAI)
Instruction in Riding and Jumping & Students to BHSAI Exam
Av No: Horses 12 Ponies 12
Std of Schlg: General Purpose School
Ev Classes
Courses: Wkg students/YTS – 7
Facilities: Out Man: 50 x 20m Fl Lit/Jmp Pd/Lec Rm/Club Rm/WC/Wash Rm/Car Park
Specialities: RDA/YTS Managing Agent
Location: 5 miles south of Chelmsford off A130

LILLYPUTTS EQUESTRIAN CENTRE
272 Wingletye Lane, Hornchurch, Essex, RM11 3BL
Tel: Hornchurch (040 24) 53908
Proprietor: Mrs S J Ellis
Manager & Chief Inst: Mrs S A Ellis (BHSI(SM)) **Other Staff:** Mr C Evans (BHSAI)
Instruction in Riding and Jumping
Av No: Horses 2 Ponies –
Std of Schlg: General Purpose
Livery: Full/Part/Grass/DIY/Break/School/Hack
Ev Classes
Courses: Inst Hol
Facilities: Cov Sch: 37 x 19m* Gly 50/Out Man:40m x 20m Fl Lit/Jmp Pd/Sh Jmps full set/Lec Rm/WC/Wash Rm/Showers/Chng Rm/Car Park
Specialities: General Instruction/Liveries/Hacking
Exclusions: No Casual Hiring/No YT
Location: 20 miles from centre of London

LITTLE PADDOCKS
Frating Road, Great Bromley, Colchester, Essex, CO7 7JL
Tel: 0206 250921
Proprietors: Mr & Mrs J A Grant
Other Staff: 1 (BHSAI) P/T – Sat & Sun & Childrens Hols
Instruction in Riding and Jumping
Av No: Horses 12 Ponies 6
Std of Schlg: General Purpose Std of Specialist Schlg: Sh Jmpg – Novice/Basic
Livery: Part/School/Hack – Bridlepaths/Farm Land
Ev Classes
Facilities: 2 Out Man: 49 x 24m Fl Lit*/37 x 18m Fl Lit*/Sh Jmp Pd/WC/Car Park
Specialities: Driving/Western Style Riding
Location: Between A120 & A133 5 miles East of Colchester

LONGWOOD EQUESTRIAN CENTRE
Lelant, Dry Street, Laindon, Basildon, Essex, SS16 5NG
Tel: Basildon (0268) 412184 Fax No – 0268 534611
Proprietors: Mr & Mrs Boutler & Mr & Mrs Hooton
Chief Inst: Miss S Finley (BHSAI) **Other Staff:** 1 (BHSAI) P/T Mr D Arthur (BHSI) – Visiting
Basic Instruction in Riding and Jumping
Av No: Horses 5 Ponies 6
Std of Schlg: General Purpose
Livery: DIY/Hunt/Hack – Country Roads & Common
Ev Classes
Courses: YT – 2
Facilities: Cov Sch: 51 x 40m* Gly Fl Lit/Out Man: 50 x 45m Fl Lit*/Jmp Pd 54 x 46m* Fl Lit/Sh Jmps 2 full sets/CC

Fences/Lec Rm/Vis Aids/Club Rm*/Lic Bar/Refresh/WC/Wash Rm/Chng Rm/ Shop/Tack Shop/Car Park
Specialities: Indoor & Outdoor Shows
Exclusions: No unescorted hacking
Location: Off A176 2 miles from Basildon

LYNFORDS LIVERIES
Lynfords New Farm, Runwell, Wickford, Essex, SS11 7PS
Tel: 0268 769669
Proprietor: D S Knox Esq
Manager: Mrs C Brunt
D I Y Livery Yard
Std of Specialist Schlg: Sh Jmpg – Novice
Livery: Part/DIY/School & Hack – for owners only – Farmland/Bridleways
Facilities: Out Man: 27 x 27m Fl Lit/Sh Jmps – available for owners/Snacks/ Wash Rm/WC/Car Park
Exclusions: Facilities for use of Livery Owners Only
Location: On A132 1 mile north of Wickford

MEDWAY RIDING CENTRE
Medway Farm, Southminster Road, Althorne, Nr Chelmsford, Essex, CM3 6EN
Tel: Maldon (0621) 740419
Proprietor: Mr J S Castle
Other Staff: 2 (BHSAI) P/T
Instruction in Riding and Jumping
Av No: Horses 13 Ponies 14
Std of Schlg: General Purpose
Livery: Full/Part/Grass/Break/School
Ev Classes
Courses: Inst Hol
Facilities: Cov Sch: 40 x 19m* Gly Fl Lit/Out Man: 40 x 19m* Seats Fl Lit/Jmp Pd* 2 acres/Sh Jmps/Lec Rm/Vis Aids/ Club Rm/Tack Shop/Refresh/WC/ WashRm/Chng Rm/Car Park
Specialities: Basic instruction in riding/Livery/Nervous riders
Exclusions: No children under 4 years

MOOR END STABLES
Moor End, Great Sampford, Saffron Walden, Essex, CB10 2RQ
Tel: 079986 338/262
Proprietor: Miss S J Green (BHSAI)
Chief Inst: Miss S Aulguist (BHSII(T))
Other Staff: 1 (BHSII) P/T
Instruction in Riding and Jumping
Av No: Horses 9 Ponies 9
Std of Schlg: General Purpose Std of Specialist Schlg: Sh Jmpg – Novice
Livery: Full/Part/Grass/DIY/School/ Break/Hunt/Hack – Bridleways/Country Lanes
Ev Classes
Courses: YT/Wkg Pupil – 2
Facilities: Cov Sch: 28 x 15m*/Out Man: 40 x 20m* Fl Lit/CC Course*(Novice)/Sh Jmps*/Lec Rm/ Snacks/Wash Rm/WC/Car Park
Specialities: Hunter Hire/Hunter Liveries/RDA
Location: Off B1053 9 miles from Saffron Walden & 3 miles from Finchingfield

PAGLESHAM SCHOOL OF EQUITATION
Ingulfs, Paglesham, Rochford, Essex, SS4 2DG
Tel: 0702 258 285
Proprietor & Chief Inst: Mr A K Judge (BHS SM)
Instruction in Riding and Jumping & Students to BHSAI Exam
Av No: Horses 6 Ponies – Spec Horse: Drg – E
Std of Schlg: General Purpose
Livery: Full/Part/Break/School
Ev Classes
Courses: Resid Inst/Wkg Students – 2/ YTS – 4
Facilities: Cov Sch: 26m dia* Gly Fl Lit/ Out Man: 46 x 38.5m*/Jmp Pd*/Sh Jmps/ CC Course/Lec Rm/Vis Aids/Club Rm/ Rest Rm/WC/Wash Rm/Chng Rm/ Car Park
Accom: House – 6 Catering: Self
Specialities: Breaking/Schooling/ Instruction on own horses
Location: 11 miles from Southend/4 miles from Rochford

PARK LANE RIDING & LIVERY STABLES
Park Lane, Ramsden Heath, Billericay, Essex, CM11 1NN
Tel: Basildon (0268) 710145/711177
Proprietors: Mr W White & Mrs P Needham
Chief Inst: Mrs Needham (BHSAI)
Other Staff: 2 (BHSAI) P/T
Basic Instruction in Riding and Jumping
Av No: Horses 8 Ponies 16
Std of Schlg: General Purpose
Livery: Full/Part/Grass/DIY/Break/ School/Hack – Bridlepaths/Woodland
Ev Classes
Facilities: Cov Sch: 32 x 19m* Gly 300 Fl Lit/Jmp Pd/Sh Jmps/CC Fences/WC/ Refresh/Tack Shop/Car Park

Specialities: Young children/Nervous adults/Show jumping/Basic Dressage
Exclusions: No YT
Location: 4 miles from A127 & 11 miles from Chelmsford

PINE LODGE RIDING CENTRE
Springfield Farm, Lippitts Hill, High Beech, Loughton, Essex, IG10 4AL
Tel: 081 508 7070
Proprietor: Mrs S A Stavrou
Manager: Miss S J Dulwich (BHSAI)
Chief Inst: Miss J Atkins (BHSAI) **Other Staff:** Mr M Brown (BHSI) – Visiting/ Miss G Trew FBHS – Visiting
Instruction in Riding and Jumping
Av No: Horses 9 Ponies 4 Specialist Horses: 1 Med Drg/1 Grade C Sh Jmper
Std of Schlg: General Purpose Std of Specialist Schlg: Drg – Med/Sh Jmpg – Nov
Livery: Full/DIY/School/Hunter/Hack – Forest
Ev Classes
Facilities: 35 x 21m*/Out Man: 40 x 40m* Fl Lit/Jmp Pd*/12 small CC Fences/Lec Rm – Seating – 20/Vis Aids/ Film Projector/Snacks/WC/Car Park
Specialities: General Instruction/ Hacking/Livery/Dressage Training
Exclusions: All riding supervised

RAYNE RIDING CENTRE
Fairy Hall Lane, Rayne, Braintree, Essex, CM7 8SZ
Tel: 0376 22231
Proprietors: Mr & Mrs B R Pewter
Chief Inst: Mrs C Armstrong (BHSII(T))
Other Staff: Mrs A Shynn (BHSAI) 1 (BHSII(T)) P/T Miss J Curd (BHSI) – visiting
Instruction in Riding and Jumping & Students to BHSAI Exam
Av No: Horses 9 Ponies 10
Std of Schlg: General Purpose
Livery: Full/Hack – Lanes/Bridlepaths
Ev Lessons
Courses: Inst/YT – 1/Wkg Students – 2
Facilities: Cov Sch:40m x 20m/Gly 20*/Out Man:60m x 20m/Fl Lit*/Lec Rm/ Vis Aids/Video/WC/Wash Rm/Refresh/ Saddlery Shop/Car Park
Specialities: General Instruction/ Schooling for Competition/Livery
Exclusions: No hiring without assessment lesson
Location: On A120 2 miles from Braintree

RUNNINGWELL STUD
Warren Road, Rettendon, Chelmsford, Essex, CM3 5DG
Tel: 0268 711221
Proprietors: Mr & Mrs A I Bowman
Manager & Chief Inst: Mr V Radford (BHSII) **Other Staff:** Miss A Woodhams (BHSAI) Miss K Marshall (BHSAI) Miss S Sillery (BHSAI) 1 (BHSII) P/T
Instruction in Riding and Jumping
Av No: Horses 23 Ponies 9 Spec Horses: 2 Drg N/3 Sh Jmpers C
Std of Schlg: General Purpose Std of Specialist Schlg: Sh Jmpg – Grade B
Livery: Full/Part/DIY/School/Break/Hack – on Farm – Summer only
Ev Classes
Courses: Wkg Students – 4/YT – 4/ET – 3 – taking both BHS & NVQ Exams
Facilities: 2 Cov Schs: 41 x 18m Gly 6 & 38 x 1 8m/Out Man: 40 x 20m* Fl Lit/ Jmpg Pd with permanent Arena including Ditches/Devils Dyke/Water Jmps etc/Lec Rm – Vis Aids/Film Projector/Library/Video/Refreshments/ Wash Rm/WC/Changing Rm/Waiting Rm/Car Park
Accom: Shared Rms 10 (Staff & Students only) Catering: Self
Specialities: Show Jumping
Exclusions: No children under 5 years
Location: Off A130 6 miles south of Chelmsford & 2 miles from Wickford

WOODREDON RIDING SCHOOL
Woodredon Farm, Upshire, Nr Waltham Abbey, Essex, EN9 3QT
Tel: Lea Valley (0992) 714312/711144
Proprietors: Mr & Mrs D L Gill
Chief Inst: Mrs D L Gill (BHSI(T)) **Other Staff:** 1 (BHSAI) 1 (BHSII) P/T Miss J Drummond (BHSI) – Visiting
Instruction in Riding and Jumping & Students to BHSAI Exam
Av No: Horses 12 Ponies 14 Specialist Horses: Drg E
Std of Schlg: General Purpose
Livery: Full/Part/Hunter/Break/ School/Hack – Epping Forest
Ev Classes
Courses: Non-Resid Inst Hol For children only/Wkg Students
Facilities: Cov Sch: 37 x 22m* Gly/Jmp Pd* Seats Fl Lit/Sh Jmps 12/CC Fences 16/Lec Rm/Vis Aids/Video/Club Rm/WC/ Chng Rm/Wash Rm/Tack Shop/Car Park
Accom: 9 – Only for Staff
Specialities: Good forest Hacking/Livery/Dressage/Point to Point Training
Exclusions: No unescorted Hacking/No YT

Location: Off A121 0.5 mile from Junc 26 on M25

WRITTLE COLLEGE

Cow Watering Lane, Writtle, Essex, CM1 3SD
0245 420705
Proprietors: Mrs E M Warr/Mrs P A Wallace
Chief Inst: Mrs P Wallace (BHSAI)
Other Staff: 2 (BHSAI)
Courses: BHS Stages I,II,III
Av No: Horses 9 Ponies 2 Specialist Horses: 2 Drg/2Sh Jmper C
Facilities: Out Man: 40x20m
Specialities: Facilities for Ingatestone & Blackmore Riding Club, Road Safety, Training/Exams
Exclusions: No Casual Clients

HERTFORDSHIRE

ASHRIDGE EQUESTRIAN CENTRE

Ashridge Farm (Berkhamsted) Ltd, Ringshall, Berkhamsted, Hertfordshire, HP4 1ND
Tel: Little Gaddesden (044 284) 3443
Proprietors: Mrs E Craib and Miss Margie Craib (BHSI)
Chief Inst: Miss Margie Craib (BHSI) + a visiting Chief Examiner **Other Staff:** 1 (BHSAI) 1 (BHSII) 1 (BHSI)
Instruction in Riding and Jumping & Students to BHSII Exam
Av No: Horses 2 Ponies 2
Std of Schlg: General Purpose Std of Specialist Schlg: Drg – Nov/HT – Int
Livery: Grass/Break/SchooL
Ev Classes
Courses: Inst/Wkg Students/YT – 7
Facilities: Cov Sch: 20m x 40m* Gly Fl Lit/Jmp Pd* Seats Fl Lit/Sh Jumps/CC Fences*/CC Course/Lec Rm */Vis Aids/WC/Chng Rm/Wash Rm/Car Park
Accom: 4 – Single rooms/2 double rooms Catering: Self (Students)
Specialities: Non residential adult & children's courses/Preparation for all competitions/BHS Ridi ng Club/Pony Club activities/Exams
Exclusions: No hiring of horses for unaccompanied hacking/No children under 7 years

BAMBERS GREEN RIDING CENTRE

Takeley, Bishop's Stortford, Herts, CM22 6PE
Tel: 0279 870320
Proprietor: Mr & Mrs I Dobson
Chief Inst: Mrs I Dobson (BHSII) **Other Staff:** Miss V Page (BHSAI)
Instruction in Riding and Jumping
Av No: Horses 6 Ponies 6
Std of Schlg: General Purpose
Livery: Part/Hack – Bridleways
Ev Lessons
Courses: YT – 1
Facilities: Cov Sch:22 x 17m*/Out Man: 12 x 6m Fl Lit*/Jump Pd/Sh Jmps/CC Fences/WC/Car Park
Specialities: General Instruction/RDA/Hacking
Exclusions: No riders over 14 stone
Location: 1/2 mile off A120

BIRCH FARM SCHOOL OF EQUITATION

White Stubbs Lane, Broxbourne, Hertfordshire, EN10 7QA
Tel: 0992 467738
Proprietor: Mr A P Mead
Chief Inst: Miss M Lincoln (BHSII)
Other Staff: 2 (BHSII) P/T
Basic Instruction in Riding and Jumping
Av No: Horses 7 Ponies 7
Std of Schlg: General Purpose
Livery: Full/Part/Hack - Woodland/Bridlepaths
Ev Classes
Courses: Inst Hol/YT taken
Facilities: Cov Sch:21m x 28m* Gly Fl Lit/Out Man: 20m x 45m*/Jmp Pd/Sh Jmps*/CC Course*/Lec Rm/Vis Aids/Refresh/WC/Car Park
Specialities: Children/Novice adults/RDA/Hacking
Exclusions: No unaccompanied hacks
Location: Between Enfield and Hoddesdon

CHORLEYWOOD EQUESTRIAN CENTRE LTD

Chenies Road, Chorleywood, Hertfordshire
Tel: 0923 282713
Proprietor: Ms S Paret
Chief Inst: Mr Rudi Paret **Head Girl:** Miss Clare S Buckland (BHSAI) **Other Staff:** 1 (BHSAI) P/T 4 F/T 2 P/T
Basic Instruction in Riding and Jumping
Av No: Horses 7 Ponies 12
Std of Schlg: General Purpose
Livery: Full/Part/Grass/Hack – Parks
Ev Classes in summer only
Courses: YT – 1
Facilities: Jmp Pd/Sh Jmps/Refresh/WC/Car Park

Specialities: Livery/Basic Instruction/Hacking/Regular shows
Exclusions: No hacking by non-competent riders/No unaccompanied hacks
Location: Off A404 between Little Chalfont & Rickmansworth

CONTESSA ARABIAN AND RIDING CENTRE
Willow Tree Farm, Colliers End, Nr Ware, Hertfordshire, SG11 1EN
Tel: Ware (0920) 821 496/792
Proprietors: Miss T Layton & Mr & Mrs Layton
Chief Inst: Miss T Layton (BHSI) (YT Trng Officer) **Other Staff:** 2 (BHSAI IT)
Instruction in Riding and Jumping & Students to BHSII Exam
Av No: Horses 15 Ponies 6 Spec Horse: 2 Drg A – 1 Drg M
Std of Schlg: General Purpose School/Break
Ev Classes
Courses: Resid Inst Hol/Wkg Students/YT/GCSE in Horsemastership
Facilities: Cov Sch: 20 x 45m/Out Man:25m x 60m/Jmp Pd/Sh Jmps/CC Fences/Lec Rm/Video/WC/Car Park
Accom: Students/Rooms/Caravans Catering: Self
Specialities: Student training/Dressage/Schooling & Breaking/General instruction
Exclusions: No casual Hiring
Location: On A10 btween Ware/Puckeridge

HADHAM MILL RIDING CENTRE
Widford Road, Much Hadham, Hertfordshire, SG10 6EY
Tel: Much Hadham (027-984) 2682/2768
Proprietors: Mr C & Ms L Wymer
Manager: Ms M Wymer **Other Staff:** 3 (BHSAI) P/T 1 (BHSII)
Instruction in Riding and Jumping
Av No: Horses 14 Ponies 5
Std of Schlg: General Purpose
Livery: Full/Part/Grass/DIY/School/Hack – Bridlep aths/Farmland/Woods
Ev Classes
Courses: Hol Inst/YT 2
Facilities: Cov Sch:31 x 15m Gly 20/Jmp Pd/WC/Chng Rm/Club Rm/Refreshments/Car Park
Specialities: Childrens Courses/General Instruction/Hacking/Livery/RDA
Location: Off B1004 between Ware/Bishops Stortford

HALLINGBURY HALL EQUESTRIAN CENTRE
Little Hallingbury, Bishop's Stortford, Hertfordshire, CM22 2RP
Tel: Bishops Stortford (0279) 730348
Proprietor: Mrs Hardwick (BHS SM)
Yard Manager: Mrs S Morgab (BHS SM) **Chief Inst:** Miss E Firth (BHSII)
Other Staff: 3 (BHSAI)
Instruction in Riding and Jumping & Students to BHSII Exam
Av No: Horses 30 Ponies 14 Specialist Horses: 1 Drg Adv – 1 Med/5 Sh Jmper B & C
Std of Schlg: General Purpose Std of Specialist Schlg: Drg – Adv/Sh Jmpg B & C Break/School/Hack – Grassland/Forest
Ev Classes
Courses: Resid Hol/Wkg Pupil 2/YT 9/ET 2/NVQ/GC SE/Riding & Road Safety/First Aid/Short Intensive
Facilities: 2 Out Mans: 30m x 45m/30 x 20m Fl Lit/Cov Sch: 20 x 40m Fl Lit Gly/Sh Jmps 2 Full Sets/CC Course/CC Fences & Course/Tack Shop/Lec Rm/Wait Rm/Refresh/WC/Showers/Vis Aids/Swimmimg Pool/Tennis Court/Sun Bed/Car Park
Accom: House – 10
Specialities: Show Jumping/Dressage/Cross Country/One Day Event/Student Training/All standards of riders
Exclusions: No casual hiring/No Hunting
Location: On A1060 3 miles South of Bishop's Stortford

HASTOE HILL RIDING SCHOOL
Tring, Hertfordshire, HP23 6LU
Tel: Tring (044282) 3378
Proprietor: Mr L R N Lewis
Other Staff: 2 (BHSAI)
Instruction in Riding and Jumping
Av No: Horses 10 Ponies 8
Std of Schlg: General Purpose
Livery: Full/Grass/Break/School/Hack–Bridle paths
Ev Classes
Courses: Inst Hol
Facilities: Cov Sch:37 x 18m*/Jmp Pd/Sh Jmps/CC Course/Lec Rm/WC/Wait Rm/Car Park
Specialities: Side–Saddle/General Instruction/Shows/Day Courses
Exclusions: All rides accompanied/No YT taken

HIGH HERTS FARM RIDING SCHOOL
High Herts Farm, Pimlico, Hemel Hempstead, Hertfordshire, HP3 8ST
Tel: Kings Langley (0923) 269265

Proprietors: High Herts Farm Riding School Ltd
Manager: Mrs P Couldridge **Secretary:** Mr Peter Waterhouse (BHSII) **Other Staff:** 2 (BHSAI) 1 (BHSAI) P/T 1 (BHSII)
Instruction in Riding and Jumping
Av No: Horses 8 Ponies 14 Specialist Horses: 1 HT
Std of Schlg: General Purpose
Livery: Full/Part/DIY/Break/School/Hack – Bridlepaths
Ev Classes
Courses: Inst Hol/YTS 1
Facilities: Cov Sch: 20m x 40m* Fl Lit/Out Man:40m x 20m*/Lec Rm/Vis Aids/CC Fences/Sh Jmps/Wash Rm/WC/Tack Shop/Car Park
Specialities: Instruction for competition/training or pleasure/Holiday Courses
Exclusions: No casual hire
Location: Btwn Hemel Hempstead & Junc 8 M1

MILL GREEN RIDING SCHOOL
Millgreen, Hatfield, Hertfordshire
Tel: Hatfield (0707) 263434/262118
Proprietors: Mrs Reeve & Mrs Reeve-Smith (BHSI(SM& E))
Chief Inst: S L Reeve-Smith (BHSI(SM & E)) **Other Staff:** 1 (BHSAI)
Instruction in Riding and Jumping
Av No: Horses 4 Ponies 8
Std of Schlg: General Purpose
Livery: Full/Part/Break/School/Hunt/Hack
Ev Classes
Courses: YTS taken
Facilities: Out Man:(2) 40 x 20m and 30 x 20m/Jmp Pd/Video
Specialities: Young children/Adults/Show Jumping Dressage
Location: Off A1000 Btwn Hatfield & Welwyn Garden City

NORTH HERTS EQUITATION CENTRE
Norton Road, Baldock, Herts, SG7 5AU
Tel: Baldock (0462) 892626
Proprietors: Mrs D Deerness & Miss L Deerness
Chief Inst: Miss K Taylor (BHSII BHS SM) **Other Staff:** 1 (BHSII) 4 (BHSAI)
Instruction in Riding and Jumping & Students to BHSII Exam
Av No: Horses 14 Ponies 16 Specialist Horses: Drg M/HT Int/Sh Jmp A
Std of Schlg: General Purpose
Livery: Full/Part/Hunter/Break/School
Ev Classes
Courses: Resid Inst Hol/Wkg Students – 4/YT – 19
Facilities: Cov Sch:42 x 23m* Gly 400/Out Man: 60m x 20m Fl Lit/Jmp Pd/Sh Jmps 20/CC Fences/Lec Rm/Vis Aids/Refresh/Wash Rm/Showers/Change Rm/Car Park
Accom: 16 – Chalet Catering: Full
Specialities: Show jumping/Breaking/Schooling/Livery/Young Stock/General Instruction
Exclusions: No casual hiring
Location: Off A505 5 miles south of Biggleswade

PATCHETTS EQUESTRIAN CENTRE
Hilfield Lane, Aldenham, Watford, Hertfordshire, WD2 8DP
Tel: 0923 855776
Proprietor: Patchetts Green Ltd
Manager: Mrs Collins **Other Staff:** 5 (BHSAI) 8 (BHSII) 3 (BHSI) 1 FBHS P/T
Instruction in Riding and Jumping & Students to BHSI Exam
Av No: Horses 25 Ponies 15 Spec horses: Drg A/CT N/Sh Jmp B & 'C'
Std of Schlg: General Purpose/Advanced
Livery: Full/Part/Grass/Hunter/Break/School/Hack – Bridleways
Ev Classes
Courses: Resid Hol Inst/Wkg Students/YTS
Facilities: Cov Sch: 40m x 15m/Cov Sch: 20m x 50 m* Gly 100*/Out Man: 40m x 20m* Fl Lit/Jmp Pd/Sh Jmps*/CC Course/Lec Rm*/Vis Aids*/Club Rm*/Snacks/WC/Chng Rm/Wash Rm/Lic Bar/Car Park
Accom: 22 Single/double rooms – Catering: Full Caravan – 2 Self catering
Specialities: Dressage/Combined training/Examination preparation/Show Jumping/Side Saddle/Film work
Exclusions: Hunting for known clients only
Location: Junc 5 M1/A41 – B556 to Aldenham

PONSBOURNE RIDING CENTRE
Newgate Street Village, Nr Hertford, Hertfordshire
Tel: Cuffley (0707) 874777
Proprietors: Mrs K D Godwin (BHSI(T & SM)) & Mrs S Fitzgerald (BHSI)
Chief Inst: Mrs S Fitzgerald (BHSI)
Other Staff: 2 (BHSAI) 2 (BHSII) 1 BHSI
Instruction in Riding and Jumping & Students to BHSII Exam
Av No: Horses 24 Ponies 8 Specialist Horses: 1 Drg M – 2 Drg E/ 1 CT Adv
Std of Schlg: General Purpose

Livery: Full/Part/DIY/Break/School/Hack – Bridleways/Park/Forest
Ev Classes
Courses: Resid Inst Hol/Wkg Students/ YTS 6
Facilities: Cov Sch:42 x 22m* Gly Fl Lit/Jmp Pd/Sh Jmps*/CC Fences/Lec Rm/Vis Aids/Video/Refresh/WC/Tack Shop/Car Park
Accom: 10 – House Catering: Self
Specialities: Residential student Courses/Novice/Advanced tuition
Exclusions: No casual hire
Location: Btwn Cuffley/Hertford

POTTERSHEATH RIDING CENTRE
Arnold's Farm, Potters Heath Road, Welwyn, Hertfordshire, AL6 9SZ
Tel: Stevenage (0438) 813070
Proprietors: Mr & Mrs Gudgin (BHSII)
Chief Inst: Mrs D Gudgin (BHSII) **Other Staff:** 3 (BHSAI) 2 (BHSAI) P/T 1 (BHSII) P/T 1 (BHSI) – Visiting
Instruction in Riding and Jumping & Students to BHSAI Exam
Av No: Horses 15 Ponies 12
Std of Schlg: General Purpose
Livery: Full/Part/Hunter/School/Break/ Hack – Heath/Woodland
Ev Classes
Courses: Inst
Facilities: Cov Sch:51 x 26m* Gly 80/2 Out Man:40 x 20m* Fl Lit/CC Course/ Lec Rm/WC/Car Park
Specialities: General Instruction/ Dressage/Livery/Pony Club/RDA
Exclusions: All clients must be suitably dressed (No jeans etc)
Location: Btwn Stevanage/Welwyn 2 miles A1 Exit 6

ROSE HALL FARM RIDING AND LIVERY STABLES
Sarratt, Rickmansworth, Hertfordshire, WD3 4PA
Tel: Hemel Hempstead (0442) 833269
Proprietor: Mr R Higgs
Manager & Chief Inst: Mrs Coleman (BHSAI) **Other Staff:** 3 (BHSAI)
Instruction in Riding and Jumping
Av No: Horses 9 Ponies 7
Std of Schlg: General Purpose
Livery: Full/Grass/Hunter/Break/School/ Hunt/Hack – Bridlepaths/Farmland
Evening Lessons – Summer
Courses: Hol Inst
Facilities: Out Man:50m x 25m*/Jmp Pd/Sh Jmps/CC Course/Gallops/WC/ Refresh/Car park
Specialities: Livery service/General Instruction/Hunter Hirelings/Horse Walker
Exclusions: Hiring for known clients only

THORLEY RIDING CENTRE
Brook Farm, Thorley, Bishop's Stortford, Hertfordshire
Tel: 0279 652484
Proprietor: Mrs D A James
Chief Insts: Mrs A Mailings (BHSAI) & Miss J Hollingworth (BHSII) – both P/T
Other Staff: 3 (BHSAI) P/T
Instruction in Riding and Jumping
Av No: Horses 1 Ponies 9
Std of Schlg: General Purpose Std of Specialist Schlg: CT – Novice/Sh Jmp – Basic
Livery: Full/Part/Grass/School/Hack – Lanes/Bridleways/Farm Land
Ev Classes – Summer only
Facilities: Out Man: 40 x 20m/20 CC Fences (Basic)/Jmp Pd*/Wash Rm/WC/ Car Park
Specialities: Childrens Riding Courses/ Pony Club Holiday Courses/Livery
Exclusions: No Rider over 12 stone

WARRENWOOD STABLES
Kentish Lane, Nr Hatfield, Hertfordshire, AL9 6JQ
Tel: Potters Bar (0707) 55103
Proprietor: Mr S Robinson
Managers: Mr & Mrs Monaghan (BHSAI) **Chief Inst:** Miss L Monaghan (BHSAI) 2 (BHSAI)
Instruction in Riding and Jumping & Students to BHSAI Exam
Av No: Horses 4 Ponies 11
Std of Schlg: General Purpose
Livery: Full/Break/School/Hack – Varied
Ev Classes
Courses: Hol Inst/YTS 5
Facilities: Cov Sch: 32 x 15m* Gly Fl Lit/Out Man: 37 x 22m*Fl Lit/Jmp Pd*/Sh Jmps/CC Fences/WC/Car Park
Specialities: Short courses for children/ Daily courses for adults/Ponies hired for shows/Pony Club activities/RDA
Location: On B158 between Essendon/Potters Bar

NORFOLK

BLACKBOROUGH END EQUESTRIAN CENTRE
The Stables, East Winch Road, Blackborough End, Kings's Lynn, Norfolk, PE32 1SF
Tel: 0553 841212
Proprietors: Mr & Mrs C G Nash

Manager: Mr C G Nash **Chief Inst:** Miss M Capon (BHSAI) **Other Staff:** Mrs S Whittaker (BHSII) P/T – 2 or 3 days per week
Instruction in Riding and Jumping
Av No: Horses 10 Ponies 10
Std of Schlg: General Purpose Std of Specialist Schlg: Sh Jmpg – Novice
Livery: Full/Part/School/Hack – Bridleways/Farm Tracks/Woodland
Ev Classes
Courses: Resid Childrens Pony Camps
Facilities: Cov Sch: 40 x 20m* Gly/Out Man: 40 x 20m/Club Rm/Refreshments/Wash Rm/WC/Car Park
Accom: Dormitory – 12 Catering: Full
Specialities: Indoor Shows/Dressage Competitions
Location: Off A47 Swaffham Road/ 3 miles from King's Lynn

EDEN MEADOWS RIDING CENTRE
Sandy Lane, Rocklands, Attleborough, Norfolk, NR17 1XF
Tel: 095 383 545
Proprietors: Mr & Mrs J M Dothie
Manager: Mrs J M Dothie **Chief Inst:** Mrs S Watson (BHSAI) **Other Staff:** Miss Z Pawley (BHSI(SM)) P/T 1 (BHSAI) P/T
Instruction in Riding and Jumping
Av No: Horses 6 Ponies 8
Std of Schlg: General Purpose Std of Specialist Schlg: Sh Jmpg – Novice School/Hack – Forestry Land/ Bridleways
Ev Classes
Facilities: Cov Sch: 40 x 20m* Gly/Jmp Pd/Club Rm – Vis Aids/Video Camera/ Monitor/Snacks/WC/Car Park
Location: 3 miles from A11 between Attleborough & Watton

HARDINGHAM FARMS LIMITED
Hardingham Hall, Norwich, NR9 4AE
0953 850523/8520301
Proprietor: Mr H Edwards
Manager: Mr C Mason
Facilities: WC/Car Park
Specialities: Livery Yard
Location: Off B1108 12 miles From Norwich

HILLCREST RIDING SCHOOL LTD
Hillcrest Farm, Yarmouth Road, Filby Heath, Nr Great Yarmouth, Norfolk, NR29 3JS
Tel: 0493 730394
Proprietor & Chief Inst: Mrs N Wilkes (BHSAI)
Other Staff: 1 (BHSAI) P/T
Basic Instruction in Riding and Jumping
Av No: Horses 10 Ponies 8
Std of Schlg: General Purpose Std of Specialist Schlg: Drg – Nov/Sh Jmpg – Nov
Livery: Full/Part/DIY/School/Hack – Beaches/Quiet Lanes
Ev Classes
Courses: YT
Facilities: Wash Rm/WC/Waiting Rm/ Car Park
Specialities: Unaffilated Dressage/ Jumping Competitions
Location: On A1064 between Acle & Caister on Sea 5 miles from Great Yarmouth

HOCKWOLD LODGE RIDING SCHOOL
Davey Lodge, Cowles Drove, Hockwold, Thetford, Norfolk, IP20 4JQ
Tel: 0842 828376
Proprietor: K M Ladell Esq
Manager/Chief Inst: Mrs L Fielder (BHSI(SM)) P/T **Other Staff:** J Jacks (BHSI) – Once a week
Instruction in Riding and Jumping
Av No: Horses 15 Ponies 10 Specialist Horses: 2 Drg Prelim/2 Sh Jmpers Grade C
Std of Schlg: General Purpose Std of Specialist Schlg: CT – Basic/Sh Jmpg – C
Livery: Full/Part/Grass/DIY/Hunt/School/ Hack – Fenland/Forestry
Ev Classes
Courses: Up to BHS Stage II/Wkg Pupils/YT – 2
Facilities: Cov Sch: 15 x 50m*/Out Man: 30 x 32m/10 Basic CC Schooling Fences/Jmp Pd/Lec Rm – Vis Aids/ Seating/Film Projector/Library/Video/ Snacks/Wash Rm/WC/Showers/ Changing Rm/Waiting Rm/Tack Shop/ Car Park
Accom: for Wkg Pupils/YT – Caravan – 2/Local Accom available Catering: Part
Exclusions: No Children under 7 years/No riders over 13 stone
Location: On B 1112 10 miles from Thetford

HOME FARM RIDING STABLES
Holme-next-the-Sea, Hunstanton, Norfolk, PF36 6LF
Tel: Holme (048 525) 233
Proprietor: Miss N R Wheeler
Other Staff: 1 (BHSAI) P/T

Basic Instruction in Riding and Jumping
Av No: Horses 15 Ponies 15
Std of Schlg: General Purpose
Livery: Full/Part/Hack – Beach
Ev Classes
Courses: YT taken
Facilities: Cov Sch: 31 x 15m Fl Lit 25 seats/Jmp Pd
Specialities: RDA
Exclusions: No unaccompanied rides
Location: Off A149 2 miles from Hunstanton

MILL FARM STABLES
Mill Farm, Great Witchingham, Norfolk, NR9 5PQ
Tel: 0603 870236/871941
Proprietors: Mr N H Carey & Miss S Fox
Other Staff: 3 P/T
Livery Yard
Livery: Full/Grass/Hunter/Break/Hunt/ Hack – Farm Track/Lanes/Wodds/ Jumps – for clients only
Courses: YT – 2
Facilities: Snacks/Wash Rm/WC/Car Park
Specialities: Livery Yard
Exclusions: No casual hire/Facilities for use of Livery Clients only
Location: Off A1067 10 miles from Norwich

NEWIN EQUESTRIAN CENTRE
Woodrow Lane, Great Moulton, Norwich, Norfolk, NR15 2HZ
Tel: 037 977 715
Proprietor & Chief Inst: Mrs M S Harvey (BHSII)
Other Staff: Miss R Mollenux (BHSAI) 2 (BHSAI) P/T
Instruction in Riding and Jumping
Av No: Horses 4 Ponies 5
Std of Schlg: General Purpose Std of Specialist Schlg: Sh Jmpg – Grade A
Livery: Full/Part/DIY/Hunter/School/ Hack – Country Roads
Ev Classes
Courses: YT – 1/ET – 1
Facilities: Out Man: 20 x 40m* Fl Lit/ Jmp Pd/WC/Car Park
Specialities: Show Jumping
Location: Off A140 3 miles from Long Stratton & 8 miles from Diss

RECTORY ROAD RIDING SCHOOL
Old Rectory, Suffield, Norwich, Norfolk, NR11 7ER
Tel: 0263 761367
Proprietor: Mrs W Garrett
Chief Inst: Mrs E Coller (BHSAI) P/T
Instruction in Riding and Jumping
Av No: Horses 3 Ponies 17
Std of Schlg: General Purpose Std of Specialist Schlg: Sh Jmpg – Novice
Livery: Full/Part/DIY/School/Hack – Country Lanes/Farm Tracks/Bridlepaths
Ev Classes
Courses: Resid – childrens only
Facilities: Cov Sch: 19 x 25m*/Jmp Pd/ Lec Rm/Snacks/WC/Car Park
Accom: House – 6 Catering: Full
Specialities: Children Riding Holidays
Exclusions: No riders over 12 stone
Location: Off B145 between North Walsham & Aylesham

REEVES HALL
Hepworth, Diss, Norfolk, IP22 2PP
Tel: Stanton (Suffolk) 0359 50217
Proprietors: Mrs Richards & Mr & Mrs Allen
Chief Inst: Mrs C Feakes (BHSII(T))
Other Staff: Miss A Wakelin (BHSAI) Miss S Wick s (BHSII) P/T 1 (BHSAI) P/T
Instruction in Riding and Jumping & Students to BHSAI Exam
Av No: Horses 10 Ponies 7
Std of Schlg: General Purpose
Livery: Part/Break/School/Hack – Bridle Paths/Forestry Land
Evening Lessons
Courses: Resid Inst Hol/YT – 3
Facilities: Cov Sch: 42m x 22m * Fl Lit/ Jmp Pd 3 acres/Sh Jmps 6/CC Fences 8/Office/Tack Rm/Lec Rm/Vis Aids/ Video/WC/Showers/Wash Rm/Chng Rm/ Car Park
Accom: 12 – Dormitory (Children) Catering: Full
Specialities: Instruction private/shared/ and in small classes of not more than six/Instructional courses during school holidays
Location: Off A143 10 miles from Bury St Edmunds & Diss

ROSE-ACRE RIDING STABLES
Back Mundesley Road, Gimingham, Nr Mundesley, Norfolk, NR11 8HN
Tel: Mundesley (0263) 720671/Mobile: 0831 584917
Proprietor & Chief Inst: Mrs J Self (BHS(PTT))
Instruction in Riding and Jumping
Av No: Horses 10 Ponies 17 Specialist Horses: 4 JC – 1JA – 2 B & 2 C Sh Jmpers
Std of Schlg: General Purpose Std of Specialist Schlg: Sh Jmpg – A

Livery: Full/Part/School/Break/Hack – Bridleways/Beach/Country Lanes
Ev Classes
Courses: Hol/Wkg Pupils/YT – 1/BHS Stages I & II
Facilities: Out Man: 20 x 40m Fl Lit/A Full Set BSJA Sh Jmps/CC Fences/Jmp Pd/Refresh/WC/Wash Rm/Car Park
Specialities: Show Jumping
Location: Off B1159 6 miles east of Cromer

ROSEBROOK FARM EQUESTRIAN CENTRE
South Lopham, Diss, Norfolk, IP22 2JP
Tel: Bressingham (037 988) 278
Proprietors: Mr & Mrs J S Attenborough
Other Staff: 2 (BHSAI) 1 (BHSII(T)) Miss A Haylor (BHSI) – visiting
Instruction in Riding and Jumping & Students to BHSAI Exam
Av No: Horses 8 Ponies 6
Std of Schlg: General Purpose
Livery: Full/Part/Break/School/Hack – Arable Farming
Ev Classes
Courses: Resid Inst Hol/Wkg Students – 1/YT – 1
Facilities: Cov Sch: 62 x 22m* Gly Fl Lit/Out Man: 46 x 31m Seats Fl Lit/Jmp Pd*/Sh Jmps*/18 CC Fences/CC Course/Lec Rm/Vis Aids/WC/Wash Rm/Showers/Chng Rm/Shop/Video*/Car Park
Accom: 10 – Dormitory 4 – Cottage 2 – Caravan Plus new holiday accommodation Catering: Full
Specialities: Instructional Holidays
Exclusions: No unaccompanied hacking
Location: 6 miles from Diss 4 miles off A143 & 2 from A1066

RUNCTON HALL STUD
Church Farm, North Runton, King's Lynn, Norfolk
Tel: Kings Lynn (0553) 840676
Proprietors: Mr & Mrs P Kemp
Other Staff: 1 (BHSII) P/T
Instruction in Riding and Jumping
Av No: Horses 11 Ponies 11
Std of Schlg: General Purpose
Livery: Full/Part/Grass/Hunter/School/Break/Hunt/Hacking – Farmland
Ev Classes
Facilities: Cov Sch: 31 x 14m*/Out Man: 80m x 30m* Fl Lit Jmp Pd: 80m x 40m* Fl Lit/Lec Rm/Vis Aids/Refresh/Wash Rm/WC/Chng Rm/Wait Rm/Car Park
Specialities: Show Jumping
Exclusions: No YT
Location: 2 miles from Junc of A47/A10 & 4 miles from centre of King's Lynn

SALHOUSE EQUESTRIAN CENTRE
Farrer Farms Ltd, Vicarage Farm, Salhouse, Norwich, Norfolk, NR13 6RW
Tel: 0603 782749/720921
Proprietor: Farrer Farms Ltd
Managing Director & Chief Inst: R C Fielder Esq **Other Staff:** 2 (BHSAI) 1 (BHSII) P/T 1 RDA Inst
Instruction in Riding and Jumping & Students to BHSAI Exam
Av No: Horses 18 Ponies 3
Std of Schlg: General Purpose
Livery: Full/Grass/Break/School/Hunt/Hack – Broad land
Ev Classes
Courses: Resid Inst/Teaching by coloured video/YT – 2/Students – 20 – Norwich College 1 day a week
Facilities: Cov Sch: 55 x 25m* Gly 50/Out Man: 25 x 46m* Fl Lit/Jmp Pd Seats Fl Lit/Sh Jmps/26 CC F ences/CC Course/Lec Rm/Vis Aids/Club Rm/Refresh/Rest Rm/WC/Showers/Wash Rm/Chng Rm/Car Park
Accom: 12 – House/Caravan Catering: Part
Specialities: Equestrian holiday courses/RDA
Location: Off A1151 6 miles from Norwich

STANBROOK RIDING CENTRE
Paddock Farm, Lower Road, Holme Hale, Thetford, Norfolk, IP25 7EB
Tel: Holme Hale (0760) 22125
Proprietors: Mrs B A & Miss B T Bates
Principal Inst: Miss B T Bates (BHSAI)
Instruction in Riding and Jumping
Av No: Horses 6 Ponies 6
Std of Schlg: General Purpose
Livery: Full/School/Break/Hack – Woods/Country Lanes/Tracks/Bridleways/Fields
Ev Classes
Facilities: Out Man: 25 x 22m* Fl Lit/Jmp Pd/Sh Jmps/CC Jmps/Lec Rm/Vis Aids/Refreshments/Wash Rm/WC/Change Rm/Wait Rm
Specialities: Young people/Small Groups & personal attention/Breaking & Schooling Ponies
Exclusions: No unsupervised riding
Location: 1 mile off A47 5 miles from Swaffham

STIFFKEY VALLEY STABLES
Old Wells Road, Little Walsingham, Norfolk, NR22 6BZ
Tel: 0328 72 377/796
Proprietor & Chief Inst: Mr R Le-Bon Olive
Other Staff: 1 (BHSAI) P/T
Instruction in Riding and Jumping
Av No: Horses 5 Ponies 1
Std of Schlg: General Purpose School/Break/Hack – Farmland/Grass Lanes/Beaches
Courses: Resid Riding Hols
Facilities: Out Man: 37 x 20m/Jmp Pd/Lec Rm/Vis Aids/Wash Rm/WC/Chng Rm/Wait Rm/Car Park
Accom: 8 – In house (B & B)
Specialities: Horse Driving
Exclusions: No YT
Location: Off B1105 5 miles from Fakenham

STRUMPSHAW RIDING CENTRE
Buckenham Road, Strumpshaw, Norwich, Norfolk, NR13 4NP
Tel: 0603 712815
Proprietor: Mrs F Beard
Other Staff: Mr Beard (BHSAI) 2 (BHSAI) P/T
Instruction in Riding and Jumping
Av No: Horses 10 Ponies 11
Std of Schlg: General Purpose
Livery: Full/Part/Hack – Bridle paths/Fields
Ev Classes
Courses: YT – 2
Facilities: Cov Sch: 37 x 14m* Gly*/Out Man: 46 x 22m/22 CC Fences*/Jmp Pd*/Lec Rm/Vis Aids/Video/W ash Rm/Wait Rm/Car Park
Specialities: Young Children
Location: Off A47 between Norwich & Great Yarmouth

TOP FARM EQUESTRIAN CENTRE
Western Longville, Norwich, Norfolk, NR9 5JN
Tel: 0603 872247/872662
Proprietors: Mr & Mrs P Skitmore
Other Staff: Miss T Chambers (BHSAI) P/T Mr S Tibbler
Instruction in Riding and Jumping
Av No: Horses 15 Ponies 15
Std of Schlg: General Purpose Std of Specialist Schlg: CT – Basic/Sh Jmpg – Nov
Livery: Full/Part/School/Hack – Bridle paths/Country Lanes
Ev Classes
Courses: Res Childrens Hols/YT taken
Facilities: Cov Sch: 60 x 20m* Gly/Out Man: 60 x 20m*/20 Basic Small CC Fences/Jmp Pd/Refreshments/Wash Rm/WC/Showers/Changing Rm/Car Park
Accom: Caravan – 12 Catering: Full
Specialities: Childrens Riding Holidays
Exclusions: Only Children 8 – 16 yrs on Rid Hols
Location: Off A47 8 miles west of Norwich

WEST RUNTON RIDING STABLES
West Runton, Cromer, Norfolk, NR27 9QH
Tel: West Runton (026 375) 339
Proprietor: Mrs J Bakewell
Chief Inst: Miss S Dowling (BHSAI)
Basic Instruction in Riding and Jumping
Av No: Horses 10 Ponies 15
Std of Schlg: General Purpose Break/School/Hack/Trek – Forestry/Beach/National Trust
Courses: YT – 1/ET – 2
Facilities: Cov Sch: 31 x 20m* Fl Lit/Out Man: 46 x 20m*/Jmp Pd/Sh Jmps/Lec Rm/Vis Aids/Refresh/WC/Wash Rm/Showers/Chng Rm/Wait Rm/Shop/Car Park
Specialities: North Norfolk Shire Horse Centre & Collection of Native Breeds/RDA
Location: Off A149 2 miles from Cromer

WILLOW FARM RIDING SCHOOL
Ormesby St Margaret, Gt Yarmouth, Norfolk
Tel: Gt Yarmouth (0493) 730297
Proprietor & Chief Inst: Mrs J Russell (BHSAI)
Other Staff: Mrs M Martin (BHSII) P/T
Instruction in Riding and Jumping
Av No: Horses 6 Ponies 9
Std of Schlg: General Purpose
Livery: DIY/Break/School/Hunt/Hack – Beach/Farmland
Ev Classes
Courses: Inst/YT – 1/ET – 1
Facilities: Cov Sch: 12 x 25m Fl Lit/Out Man: 23 x 37m/Jmp Pd 3 acres/Sh Jmps/CC Course/CC Fences/WC/Car Park
Location: On A149 5 miles from Great Yarmouth & 20 miles from Norwich

WILLOW END EQUESTRIAN CENTRE
Kemps Corner, Pulham St Mary, Diss, Norfolk, IP21 4YH
Tel: 037 976 8296
Proprietor & Chief Inst: Mrs S I Vincent (BHSAI)

Other Staff: 1 (BHSAI) P/T
Instruction in Riding and Jumping
Av No: Horses 6 Ponies 6
Std of Schlg: General Purpose Std of Specialist Schlg: Sh Jmpg – C Break/School Hack – Tracks/Farmland
Ev Classes
Courses: Wkg Pupils
Facilities: Out Man: 20 x 40m Fl Lit/Jmp Pd/Snacks/WC/Car Park
Location: Off B1134 between Harleston & Long Stratton

SUFFOLK

BARNBY TRAINING CENTRE
Church Farm, Beccles Road, Barnby, Beccles, Suffolk, NR34 7QN
Tel: 0502 76790
Proprietor & Chief Inst: Mrs R Lambert (BHS(SM))
Other Staff: Miss K Sexton (BHSAI) Miss J Stone (BHSII) P/T Mrs H Jermy (BHSAI) P/T
Instruction in Riding and Jumping & Students to BHSAI Exam
Av No: Horses 18 Ponies 6 Specialist Horses: 1 Drg N – 1 Drg E/ 2 Sh Jmpers Grade B
Std of Schlg: General Purpose Std of Specialist Schlg: Sh Jmpg – Grade B
Livery: Full/School/Break
Ev Classes
Courses: up to BHSAI/Wkg Students – 4/YT – 1
Facilities: Cov Sch: 20 x 40m*Gly – 20/ Out Man: – 60 x 30m/Jmp Pd/Lec Rm – Film Projector/Library/Video/Seats – 12/ Refreshments/Wash Rm/WC/Waiting Rm/ Car Park
Accom: Shared Rms – 20 Catering: Full
Exclusions: No Children under 8 years/No riders over 15 stone
Location: On A146 3 miles east of Beccles

NEWTON HALL EQUITATION CENTRE
Swilland, Nr Ipswich, Suffolk, IP6 9LT
Tel: 0473 85 616 – 24 hr answering service
Proprietor & Chief Inst: Mrs R Theobald BHSI
Other Staff: 1 (BHSII) P/T 1 (BHSII) 3 (BHSAI)
Instruction in Riding and Jumping & Students to BHSII Exam
Av No: Horses 23 Ponies 15 Spec Horses: 3 Drg E/1 HT E
Std of Schlg: General Purpose
Livery: Full/Part/Break/School/Hunt/ Hack – Lanes/Bridleways
Ev Classes
Courses: Resid Inst Hol/Wkg Students – 1/YT – 8/NVQ Exams
Facilities: Cov Sch: 28 x 12m* Fl Lit/Out Man: 60 x 30m* Fl Lit/Jmp Pd* Seats Fl Lit/Sh Jmps*/CC Fences*/CC Course*/ Lec Rm*/Vis Aids*/Refresh/Chng Rm/ WC/Car Park
Accom: 12 Hostel Catering: Part/Self
Specialities: Basic Equitation/Exams/Career Cours es/RDA/ Competition Training
Location: 1 mile off B1078 6 miles from Ipswich & 6 from Woodbridge

PAKEFIELD RIDING SCHOOL
Carlton Road, Lowestoft, Suffolk,
Corres: 189 Yarmouth Road, Lowestoft Suffolk NR32 4AA
Tel: Lowestoft (0502) 572257/562410
Proprietor: Mrs T Hardy
Chief Inst: Miss D Waldock (BHSII(T))
Other Staff: Miss Hardy (BHSAI) 1 (BHSAI) P/T
Instruction in Riding and Jumping
Av No: Horses 15 Ponies 10
Std of Schlg: General Purpose School/Hack/Trek – Sands/Countryside
Ev Classes
Courses: Inst Headquarters for Lowestoft RDA/YT – 2/Wkg Pupils – 2
Facilities: Cov Sch: 23 x 15m* Gly 25/ Out Man: 46 x 15m Fl Lit/Jmp Pd/Tack Shop/WC/Car Park
Specialities: RDA/Pony Students Courses/Trekking/Gymkhanas once a month/Driving
Exclusions: No hiring for hunting
Location: On Carlton Road 1 mile from centre of Lowestoft

POPLAR PARK EQUESTRIAN CENTRE
Hollesley, Woodbridge, Suffolk
Tel: Shottisham (0394) 411425
Proprietors: Mr & Mrs R Leggett
Manager: Mrs M S Green **Chief Inst:** Mrs M Griggs (BHSII(T)) **Other Staff:** 3 (BHSAI)
Instruction in Riding and Jumping
Av No: Horses 15 Ponies 10
Std of Schlg: General Purpose
Livery: Full/Part/DIY/Hunter/School/ Break/Hunt/Hack/Common Land/Forest/ Heathland
Ev Classes
Courses: Inst Resid/YT 9/Wkg Pupils 3
Facilities: Cov Sch: 18 x 37m*/Out Man: 40m x 50m* Fl Lit/CC Course/

Jmp Pd/Sh Jmps*/Lec Rm/Vis Aids/Refresh/Showers/WC/Wash Rm
Accom: 10 – Student House – Staff & Students only Catering: Self

Specialities: Individual Attention/Excellent Hacking/Cross Country
Location: Off B1083 15 miles east of Ipswich

Riding in Greater London

GREATER LONDON

ALDERSBROOK RIDING SCHOOL LTD

Empress Avenue, Manor Park, London, E12
Tel: 081 530 4648
Proprietor: Mrs I P Thorne (BHSAI)
Chief Inst/Manager: Mr Noel Dollimore (BHSAI) **Other Staff:** 3 (BHSAI) P/T
Instruction in Riding and Jumping
Av No: Horses 4 Ponies 8
Std of Schlg: General Purpose
Livery: Full/Hack/Break/Schooling
Courses: Hol(2–4 day holiday courses)
Facilities: 2 Out Man: 61m x 44m Fl Lit/Sh Jmps/Lec Rm/WC/Refresh/Car Park
Specialities: General Instruction/Hacking/Holiday Courses/RDA/Own Shows/NVQ Students
Exclusions: No casual hire
Location: Off A117 btwn Manor Park & Wanstead

BELMONT RIDING CENTRE

The Ridgeway, Mill Hill, London, NW7
Tel: 081 959 1588/906 1255
Proprietor: Mr G Parsons
Chief Inst: (BHSI) P/T **Other Staff:** 5 (BHSAI) 2 (BHSI(T))
Instruction in Riding and Jumping & Students to BHSII Exam
Av No: Horses 15 Ponies 8
Std of Schlg: General Purpose
Livery: Full/Hack – Parkland Grass/Farmland
Evening Lessons: Tuesday–Friday inclusive
Courses: Wkg Students/YTS
Facilities: Cov Sch:40m x 20m* Gly Fl Lit/Out Man: 66m x 20m* & 70m x 25m Seats Fl Lit/Sh Jmps 20/CC Fences/Lec Rm/Vis Aids/Refresh/Wash Rm/Club Rm/WC/Showers/Car Park
Specialities: General Instruction/Student training/Livery/RDA
Exclusions: No riders over 13 stones/All rides escorted/No casual hiring
Location: Off the Ridgeway Mill Hill

CIVIL SERVICE RIDING CLUB

c/o The Royal Mews, Buckingham Palace Road, London, SW1W 0QH
Tel: 071 930 7232
Chairman: N Mitchell Esq
Chief Inst: Miss Sonia Richards (BHSI)
Other Staff: 3 (BHSAI) 1 (BHSII) 1 BHSI
Instruction in Riding and Jumping
Av No: Horses 14
Std of Schlg: General Purpose
Hack – Hyde Park/Richmond
Ev Classes Events
Facilities: Cov Sch:/Jmp Pd/Sh Jmps/CC Fences
Specialities: Riding Club Grades/Lessons/Events/Hacking/RDA
Exclusions: Membership is restricted to Civil Servants their Spouses and Children over the age of 16/Associate Members are accepted at the discretion of the Committee (generally subject to a Waiting List)/Visitors by Appointment Only

DULWICH RIDING SCHOOL

Dulwich Common, London, SE21 7EX
Tel: 081 693 2944
Proprietor: J T Bellman
Chief Insts: Miss C Tims (BHSAI) **Other Staff:** 1 (BHSAI) 1 (BHSII)
Instruction in Riding and Jumping & Students to BHSAI Exam
Av No: Horses 8 Ponies 11
Std of Schlg: General Purpose
Break/School
Ev Classes
Courses: Wkg Students
Facilities: Cov Sch:28 x 22m Fl Lit/Out Man: 31 x 22m Fl Lit*/Jmp Pd/Sh Jmps/CC Fences/CC Course/Lec Rm/Vis Aids/Wash Rm/WC/Car Park
Specialities: Career students/Pony Club Tests/Breaking for harness/Showing/Horsemaster
Exclusions: No children under 10 years/No hiring out
Location: On A205 btwn Catford & Dulwich

GOULDS GREEN RIDING SCHOOL
Goulds Green, Hillingdon, Middlesex
Tel: 0895 446256
Proprietors: Mr M W Jupp
Manageress: Miss A Mayne (BHSAI)
Chief Inst: Miss N Fleming (BHSAI)
Other Staff: 4 (BHSAI) P/T
Instruction in Riding and Jumping
Av No: Horses 4 Ponies 4
Std of Schlg: General Purpose Sh Jmpg – Novice
Livery: Full/Part/Grass/DIY/School
Ev Classes
Facilities: Out Mans: 36m x 13m* Fl Lit & 72 x 25m Fl Lit/Jmp Pd/Lec Rm/Wash Rm/WC/Tack Shop/Car Park
Specialities: Children/General Instruction/All types of Livery/RDA/ Tack Shop
Exclusions: No Casual hiring

KENTISH TOWN CITY FARM
1 Cressfield Close, Off Grafton Road, London, NW5
Tel: 071 482 2861
Proprietor: N Tuckett Esq
Farm Manager: John Langan **Asst:** Mick Magennis **Other Staff:** 1 (BHSAI)
Basic Instruction in Riding
Av No: Horses 3 Ponies 4
Std of Schlg: General Purpose
Livery: Part
Ev Classes
Courses: YT 5
Facilities: Out Man:40m x 20m Seats Fl Lit/Sh Jmps/Club Rm/Lec Rm/Refresh/ WC./Chng Rm/Wash Rm
Specialities: Facilities for deprived children of the London area/Basic riding for youngsters/RDA/Pony Club

KINGS OAK EQUESTRIAN CENTRE LTD
Theobalds Park Road, Crews Hill, Enfield, Middlesex
Tel: 081 363 7868
Directors: Mrs J P Gill & The Misses S J & G E Gill
Chief Inst: Royce Bird (BHSAI) **Other Staff:** 3 (BHSAI)
Instruction in Riding and Jumping
Av No: Horses 10 Ponies 15
Std of Schlg: General Purpose
Livery: Full/Part/DIY/Break/School/Hack
Ev Classes
Courses: Show Jumping/YTS – taken
Facilities: Cov Sch: 42m x 24m* Gly Fl Lit/Out Man :30m x 20m Fl Lit/Sh Jmps/ Lec Rm/Vis Aids/Club Rm/Refresh/WC/ Car Park
Specialities: Basic instruction/Livery facilities/Schooling/Show Jumping courses

LEA BRIDGE RIDING SCHOOL
Lea Bridge Road, Leyton, London, E10 7QL
Tel: 081 556 2629
Proprietor: Lea Valley Regional Park Authority
Manager & Chief Inst: Mrs Jeannett Garrett (BHSI) **Other Staff:** 1 (BHSAI) 4 (BHSII)
Instruction in Riding and Jumping & Students to BHSI Exam
Av No: Horses 16 Ponies 5
Std of Schlg: General Purpose Std of Spec Schlg: Drg – M
Livery: Full/DIY/Break/School – Marshland
Ev Classes
Courses: Inst Hol/Wkg Students/YT – 5
Facilities: Cov Sch: 44m x 24m Gly Fl Lit/Out Man: 56m x 20m Fl Lit/Jmp Pd 10 acres/Sh Jmps/CC Fences/Lec Rm/ Vis Aids/WC/Showers/Wash Rm/Chng Rm/Car Park
Accom: Mobile home/Flat 4 Catering: Self
Specialities: From beginners to competition riders & serious career students/Dressage/RDA/Own Pony Club
Exclusions: No hiring of horses nor unaccompanied hacking/No Children under 7 years
Location: On A104 Btwn Clapton/ Leyton

MOTTINGHAM FARM RIDING CENTRE
Mottingham Lane, London, SE9
Tel: 081 857 3003
Proprietor: W L Collins Esq
Chief Inst: Miss L Hicks (BHSAI)
Basic Instruction in Riding and Jumping
Av No: Horses 20 Ponies 20
Std of Schlg: General Purpose Hack – Own Fields
Facilities: Out Man/CC Course/WC/ Chng Rm
Specialities: Basic Equitation
Exclusions: No YT Taken
Location: Off A20 between Eltham/Sidcup

MUDCHUTE PARK & FARM RIDING SCHOOL
Pier Street, Isle of Dogs, London, E14
Tel: 071 515 5901/9271/4467
Proprietors: The Mudchute Association

Secretary: Ms L Moriton **Chief Inst:** Miss J Outram (BHSAI) **Other Staff:** 1 (BHSAI)
Basic Instruction in Riding and Jumping
Av No: Horses 4 Ponies 6
Std of Schlg: General Purpose
Hack – 30 acres parkland
Ev Classes
Courses: Inst Hol
Facilities: Out Man:25m x 50m/CC Fences 6/Sh Jmps 6/Lec Rm/Vis Aids/Refresh/WC/Wash Rm/Chng Rm/Shop/Car Park
Specialities: Basic instruction & hacking facilities in Inner London/School groups
Exclusions: No children under 7
Location: 2 miles off A13 btwn Canning Town & Poplar

NEWHAM RIDING SCHOOL & ASSOCIATION
Management Committee of Newham Riding Club, 96 Camel Road, London, E16 2DJ
Tel: 071 476 1706
Secretary: Miss L Greaves
Basic Instruction in Riding and Jumping
Av No: Horses 8 Ponies 4
Std of Schlg: General Purpose
Hack/London Park
Facilities: Cov Sch:26 x 11m/Jmp Pd/Sh Jmps/Refresh/Wash Rm/Club Rm/WC/Chng Rm
Specialities: Basic instruction in riding/RDA/Own Pony Club
Exclusions: No casual hiring

RICHARD BRIGGS RIDING STABLES
63 Bathurst Mews, London, W2 2SB
Tel: 071 723 2813/706 3806
Proprietor: Richard Briggs
Manageress: Miss J Thirkettle
Basic Instruction in Riding and Jumping
Av No: Horses 7 Ponies 4
Std of Schlg: General Purpose
Hack – Hyde Park
Ev Classes Summer Only
Specialities: Hacking/Discount rates/School Contract Work/Credit Cards taken
Exclusions: All riding escorted

ROSS NYE'S RIDING ESTABLISHMENT
8 Bathurst Mews, Hyde Park, London, W2 2SB
Tel: 071 262 3791
Proprietors: Ross Atherton Nye & Miss Kirsten Nye B A (Law) Oxon (BHSII(T))
Chief Inst: Ross Atherton Nye **Other Staff:** 1 (BHSII)
Basic Instruction in Riding and Jumping
Av No: Horses 7 Ponies 9
Std of Schlg: General Purpose
Hack – Hyde Park
Facilities: WC/Chng Rm
Specialities: Lessons in Hyde Park/RDA/Own Pony Club/NOTE: Four weeks at Easter and eight weeks in summer business transfers to: Longfrey Chilworth Guildford Surrey Tel: Guildford (0483) 35910

SNARESBROOK RIDING SCHOOL LIMITED
67/69 Hollybush Hill, Snaresbrook, London, E11 1QG
Tel: 081 989 3256
Proprietor: Miss D Parfitt
Other Staff: 2 (BHSAI) P/T 1 (BHSII)
Instruction in Riding and Jumping
Av No: Horses 10 Ponies 10
Std of Schlg: General Purpose
Hack – Epping Forest
Ev Classes
Courses: Hol Inst/YT 3
Facilities: Out Man: 31 x 17m Fl Lit/Jmp Pd/CC Fences/Chng Rm/Club Rm/WC/Car Park
Specialities: Elementary dressage/Separate junior adult classes/Own shows
Exclusions: No Riders over 14 stones
Location: On Old A11 between Snaresbrook/Woodford

SUZANNE'S RIDING SCHOOL
Brookshill Farm, Brookshill Drive, Harrow Weald, Middlesex
Tel: 081 954 3618/5592
Proprietor: Mrs S Marczak
Chief Inst: Col M Mendoza **Other Staff:** 8 (BHSAI) 5 (BHSII) P/T 1 (FBHS) 1 (FBHS) P/T
Instruction in Riding and Jumping & Students to BHSII Exam
Av No: Horses 45 Ponies 30
Std of Schlg: General Purpose/Drg – Elem/H T – Adv/Sh Jmp – I
Livery: Full/Part/Grass/Break/School/Hack – Farm Land/Woods
Ev Classes
Courses: Resid/Wkg Students/YT 12
Facilities: Cov Sch:31 x 15m Gly 100/Out Man:46 x 18m Fl Lit/Jmp Pd*/CC Course*/Lec Rm/Vis Aids/Refresh/Wash Rm/WC/Showers/Chng Rm/Wait Rm/Car park

Accom: 24 – Rooms/Catering: Residential cook & hotels locally
Specialities: Competitions/BHS Examinations/Pony Club/Riding Club activities/RDA/Junior & Senior Separate Schools
Location: Between Harrow & Bushey

TRENT PARK EQUESTRIAN CENTRE
Bramley Road, Southgate, London, N14 4XS
Tel: 081 363 8630/9005
Proprietors: Mr K Beavan (BHSI) & Mrs A Short
Other Staff: 2 (BHSI) 3 (BHSII) 3 (BHSAI) 2 (BHSAI) P/T
Instruction in Riding and Jumping & Students to BHSAI Exam
Av No: Horses 15 Ponies 14
Std of Schlg: General Purpose
Livery: Full/School/Break/Hack – Bridleways/Woodlands
Courses: Resid/Wkg Students/YT 1
Facilities: Cov Sch:68 x 25m* Gly 150/ Out Man: (2):31 x 15m Fl Lit 12 x 9m Fl Lit*/CC Fences 12/Jmp Pd/Sh Jmps/ Lec Rm/Vis Aids/WC/Refresh/Car Park
Accom: 9 – Hostel Catering: Self
Specialities: Hacking/Riding instruction/Livery/Shows/RDA
Exclusions: No Children under 5 yrs

WILLOW TREE RIDING ESTABLISHMENT
Ronver Road, London, SE12
Tel: 081 857 6438
Proprietors: E A & R I Massey
Chief Inst: Miss J Massey (BHSAI)
Other Staff: 3 (BHSAI) P/T 3 (BHSII) P/T
Instruction in Riding and Jumping
Av No: Horses 17 Ponies 14
Std of Schlg: General Purpose Std of Specialist Schlg: Drg – Nov
Livery: Full/School
Ev Classes
Courses: Hol/YTS 3
Facilities: Cov Sch:37 x 18m* Gly 20/ Out Man: 55 x 31m Fl Lit/Jmp Pd/Lec Rm/Club Rm
Specialities: Children and mentally handicapped/Nervous riders/Pony Club tests/Riding Club
Exclusions: All rides escorted
Location: Off A205 btwn Catford & Woolwich

WIMBLEDON VILLAGE STABLES
24 A/B High Street, Wimbledon, London, SW19 5DX
Tel: 081 946 8579
Manageress: Mrs C A Andrews (BHSAI)
Chief Inst: Mrs C E Stevenson (BHSI)
Other Staff: 3 (BHSAI)
Instruction in Riding and Jumping
Av No: Horses 12 Ponies 9
Std of Schlg: General Purpose
Livery: Full/Part/Hack – Wimbledon Common/Richmond Park
Ev Classes
Courses: Inst Hol Non – Resid/YT
Facilities: Lec Rm/Vis Aids/Video/ Refresh/Wash Rm/WC/Chng Rm
Specialities: Hacking/Livery/Basic Jumping Instruction/Horses available for Pony Club/Riding Club activities
Exclusions: No riders over 14 stone
Location: Centre of old Wimbledon Village

THE WORMWOOD SCRUBS PONY CENTRE (GREATER LONDON)
C/O 16 East Acton Lane, London, W3 7EG
Tel: 081 740 0573/749 5197
Proprietor & Chief Inst: Sr Mary Joy Lanzdon (BHSAI)
Other Staff: 1 (BHSAI) P/T
Instruction in Riding and Jumping
Av No: Horses 1 Ponies 10
Std of Schlg: General Purpose
Hack – Wormwood Scrubs
Ev Classes – Summer only
Courses: YT/BHS Stages I & II/Road Safety Cert/RDA Inst Cert
Facilities: Out Man: 40 x 20m*/Jmp Pd*/Lec Rm – Seating/Vis Aids/ Video/Refreshments/WC/Car Park
Specialities: General Instruction for Children/Hacking/RDA/Voltige
Exclusions: Weight limit 11 stone/No casual hire
Location: Behind Wormwood Scrubs Prison & West London Sports Centre

Riding in the South East

KENT ♦ SURREY ♦ EAST SUSSEX WEST SUSSEX

KENT

APPLETREE STABLES
Starvenden Lane, Cranbrook Common, Cranbrook, Kent, TN17 2AN
Tel: Cranbrook (0580) 713833
Proprietor: Mrs V Nuthall BHSI
Other Staff: 1 (BHSAI) P/T 1 (BHSAI) 1 BHSI
Instruction in Riding and Jumping & Students to BHSAI Exam
Av No: Horses 8 Ponies 10
Std of Schlg: General Purpose
Livery: Full/Part/Grass/School/Break/Hack – Woodl ands/Bridle paths
Courses: Inst/Wkg Students/YT 3
Facilities: Out Man(2):40m x 20m*/40m x 20m/Jmp Pd/Sh Jmps/CC Fences/Vis Aids/Wash Rm/WC/Chg Rm/Car Park
Specialities: General instruction/Children/Breaking/Schooling/Livery/Day Courses
Location: Off A229 1.5 miles north of Cranbrook

BALI – HAI STABLES
Cotmans Ash Lane, Woodlands, Kemsing, Sevenoaks, Kent, BN14 7LH
Bel: 09592 2215/5103
Proprietors: Miss A L Lyndon-Carter & Mrs M C Heilbron
Manager & Chief Inst: Mr P Milward (BHSII(T))
Livery Yard & Training Centre A
Std of Specialist Schlg: CT – Basic/Sh Jmpg – Nov
Livery: Full/Part/Grass/DIY/Hunter/School
Ev Classes
Facilities: Out Man: 60 x 20m* Fl Lit/12 Basic Schooling CC Fences*/Jmp Pd*/Refreshments/Wash Rm/WC/Showers/Chng Rm/Car Park
Specialities: Livery of all types/Instruction on own horse/Training Centre
Exclusions: No horses for hire
Location: Btwn West Kingsdown/Otford

BEDGEBURY SCHOOL RIDING CENTRE
Bedgebury School, Goudhurst, Nr Cranbrook, Kent, TN17 2SH
Tel: Goudhurst (0580) 211602
Proprietor: Church Education Corporation Ltd
Director of Riding: Mr Scott Gregory
Chief Inst: Miss M Ambler BHSI **Other Staff:** 3 (BHSII) 1 (BHSAI) 1 (BHSII) P/T 1 (BHS AI) P/T
Instruction in Riding and Jumping & Students to BHSII Exam
Av No: Horses 28 Ponies 16
Std of Schlg: General Purpose Std of Specialist Schlg: Drg – M
Livery: Full/Grass/Part/Break/Hack – Forestry
Courses: YT 1
Facilities: Cov Sch:40m x 20m* Fl Lit/2 Out Man: 44m x 22m* Fl Lit & 44x 22m/Jmp Pd/CC Fences 23*/Lec Rm/Vis Aids/WC/Car Park
Accom: 3 self contained Flats/8 – 14 Students/Cottage & Mobile Home – 16/Catering: Full
Specialities: Hacking/Hol Courses/2 years (BHSAI) Course for 6th form pupils/Career student course/General Instruction/Dressage
Exclusions: No casual hiring
Location: On B2072 Between Goudhurst/Frimwell

BLUE BARN RIDING STABLE
Blue Barn Farm, Great Chart, Ashford, Kent, TN26 1JS
Tel: Ashford (0233) 622933/621183/620199

Proprietor: Mrs S M Draper
Chief Inst: A R Draper (BHSII) **Other Staff:** 2 (BHSAI) 3 (BHSII) 2 (BHSII(T))
Instruction in Riding and Jumping & Students to BHSII Exam
Av No: Horses 15 Ponies 15
Std of Schlg: General Purpose Std of Specialist Schlg: Sh Jmp – B
Livery: Full/Part/Grass/Break/School/Hack – Bridle paths
Ev Classes
Courses: Wkg Students/YT 6
Facilities: Cov Sch:68 x 22m* Gly 100/Cov Sch:37 x 22m/Out Man: 62 x 25m* Fl Lit/Jmp Pd*/Sh Jmps*/CC Fences*/CC Course/Lec Rm*/Vis Aids*/Video/Club Rm*/Refresh/WC/Wash Rm/Wait Rm/Car Park
Accom: Cottage Catering: Self
Specialities: Show Jumping/Indoor & Outdoor Shows/Student Training
Exclusions: All rides escorted
Location: On A28 btwn Ashford/Bethersden

BRADBOURNE RIDING AND TRAINING CENTRE LIMITED
Bradbourne Vale Road, Sevenoaks, Kent, TN13 3DH
Tel: Sevenoaks (0732) 453592
Proprietor: Mr P G Felgate
Other Staff: 2 (BHSAI) 1 (BHSII)
Instruction in Riding and Jumping & Students to BHSAI Exam
Av No: Horses 19 Ponies 28
Std of Schlg: General Purpose Std of Specialist Schlg: Sh Jmpg – B
Livery: Full/Part/Break/School
Ev Classes
Courses: Wkg Students
Facilities: Cov Sch: 31 x 18m* Gly 50 Fl Lit/Out Man: 62 x 18m* Fl Lit/Jmp Pd/Sh Jmps/CC Course/Lec Rm*/Vis Aids/Club Rm*/Driving Centre/WC/Showers/Chng Rm/Wait Rm/Car Park
Specialities: Prep Pony Club Tests/One Day events/Livery/Dressage/RDA/Driving
Exclusions: No unaccompanied hacking/No Casual Hiring/No YT
Location: On A25 Junc with A21

CHAUCER RIDING AND LIVERY STABLES
Waltham, Nr Canterbury, Kent, CT4 5SB
Tel: Petham (022 770) 297/396
Proprietor: Mrs M D Mervin
Chief Inst: Miss Johnson (BHSII(T))
Other Staff: 2 (BHSAI) 1 (BHSI) P/T
Instruction in Riding and Jumping & Students to BHSAI Exam
Av No: Horses 5 Ponies 2
Std of Schlg: General Purpose
Livery: Full/Break/School/Hack/Varied
Ev Classes
Courses: Inst Hol/Wkg Students/YT 2
Facilities: Cov Sch:135 x 18m* Gly 150/2 Out Man:3 8 x 22m & 25 x 22m Seats Fl Lit/Jmp Pd/Chng Rm/H & C/Lec Rm/Vis Aids/Wash Rm/WC/Car Park
Accom: 2 - Cottage Catering: Self/Students only
Specialities: Riding Club activities/Indoor jumping shows/Own horse instruction/Private or Group
Location: In centre of Village

CHAVIC PARK FARM
Jail Lane, Biggin Hill, Kent, TN16 3AU
Tel: 0959 72090
Proprietors: Mr & Mrs N I Palmer
Chief Inst: Mrs N I Palmer (BHSII)
Other Staff: 1 (BHSAI)
Instruction in Riding and Jumping & Students to BHSAI Exam
Av No: Horses 2 Ponies 3
Std of Schlg: General Purpose
Livery: Full/Part/DIY/School/Break
Ev Classes
Courses: General – Stages etc/Wkg Pupils/YT – 2
Facilities: Cov Sch: 31 x 18m*/Gly-35/Out Man: 6 0m x 20m*/Jmp Pd/Sh Jmps*/Lec Rm*/WC/Feed Supply Shop/Car Park
Specialities: General Instruction/Livery/SchoolingRiders on own horses
Exclusions: No Casual Hiring
Location: Centre of Biggin Hill off A233

CHELSFIELD RIDING SCHOOL
Church Road, Chelsfield, Orpington, Kent, BR6 7SY
Tel: Farnborough (0689) 55603
Proprietor: Miss J M Golding
Other Staff: 2 (BHSAI) 1 (BHSI) P/T
Instruction in Riding and Jumping
Av No: Horses 11 Ponies 11
Std of Schlg: General Purpose
Livery: Full/Hack
Ev Classes
Courses: Hol/Inst
Facilities: Cov Sch:40m x20m/Out Man: 30m x 20m/Jmp Pd/Sh Jmps/CC Course/Lec Rm/Vis Aids/Refresh/Wash Rm/WC/Change Rm/Wait Rm/Car Park
Specialities: Livery/Children/General Instruction/Handicapped Riders
Exclusions: No hacking unescorted/No YT
Location: on outskirts of Village 0.5 Mile off A224

COBHAM MANOR RIDING CENTRE
Water Lane, Thurnham, Kent, ME14 3LU
Tel: 0622 38497
Proprietor: Mr & Mrs J Brumer
YT Managing Agent
Chief Inst: Mrs C Hall (BHSII) **Other Staff:** 2 (BHSAI) 1 (BHSII) 1 (BHSI) P/T 1 (BHSII) P/T 2 (BHSAI) P/T
Instruction in Riding and Jumping & Students to BHSAI Exam
Av No: Horses 19 Ponies 16
Std of Schlg: General Purpose
Livery: Full/DIY/Break/School/Hack – Bridleways/Farmland
Ev Classes
Courses: Inst Res/YT 6
Facilities: Cov Sch:40m x 20m*/2 Out Man:45m x 30m * Fl Lit & 40 x 20m/Jmp Pd/Sh Jmps/CC Course/Club Rm/ Refresh/Wash Rm/Lic Bar/WC/Wait Rm/ Saddlery Shop/Car Park
Accom: 6 – Chalet Catering – Self
Specialities: General Instruction/Livery/ Hacking
Exclusions: No casual hiring
Location: 1.5 miles Junc 7 M20 5 miles Junc 5 M2

COOMBE WOOD STABLES
Coombe Wood Lane, Hawkinge, Kent, CT18 7BZ
Tel: 0303 89 3332
Proprietors: Mr & Mrs M Fuller
Chief Inst: Miss N Parish (BHSAI)
Other Staff: 1 (BHSAI) 1 (BHSI) P/T
Instruction in Riding and Jumping
Av No: Horses 8 Ponies 5
Std of Schlg: General Purpose Std of Specialist Schlg: Sh Jmpg – Novice
Livery: Full/Part/School/Hack – Bridlepaths/Country Lanes/Woods
Ev Classes
Courses: Holiday
Facilities: Cov Sch: 24 x 42m*/Out Man: 30 x 4 5m/4 Basic Schooling CC Fences/WC/Shop/Car Park
Specialities: General Instruction/ Holiday Course/Hacking/Livery
Exclusions: No casual hire
Location: Off A260 btwn Hawkinge & Folkestone

EAGLESFIELD EQUESTRIAN CENTRE
West Yoke, Ash, Nr Sevenoaks, Kent, TN15 7HT
Tel: Ash Green (0474) 873925/872242
Proprietors: Mr G Rowland & Mrs J Clark
Chief Inst: Mrs J Clark (BHSAI) **Other Staff:** 1 (BHSAI) 1 (BHSII)
Instruction in Riding and Jumping
Av No: Horses 12 Ponies 9
Std of Schlg: General Purpose
Livery: Part/Grass/DIY/Break/School/ Hack – Varied
Ev Classes
Courses: Inst Res Hol/Stable Management
Facilities: Cov Sch: 105 x 25m* Gly Fl Lit/Jmp Pd/2 acres Fl Lit/Sh Jmps 2 full sets/CC Fences*/Lec Rm/Vis Aids/Club Rm/Members Bar/Refresh/Rest Rm/ WC/Wash Rm/Shop
Accom: 6 – House Catering: Full
Specialities: Riding instruction/Livery/Breaking/Schooling for jumping/Dressage/Full Hunter Trial course
Exclusions: No YTS taken
Location: New Ash Green 3 miles from Brands Hatch

ELLENDEN LIVERY & TRAINING CENTRE
Ellenden Farm, Foxes Cross Road, Yorkletts, Whitstable, Kent
Tel: 0227 472346
Proprietor: C Hart Esq
Manager: Mrs Pritchard (BHSHM)
Livery Service & Hacking
Std of Specialist Schlg: Drg & Sh Jmpg – Novice
Livery: Full/Part/Grass/School/Hack – Own Woodland/Bridleways
Courses: YT – 3/Wkg Pupils
Facilities: Out Man: 40 x 20m*/Jmp Pd*/Club Rm/WC/Car Park
Specialities: Livery Service/Hacking
Exclusions: No Rider over 13 stone/No casual hire
Location: 1.5 miles off the A290 between Whitstable & Canterbury

GOODNESTONE COURT EQUESTRIAN
Goodnestone Court, Goodnestone, Graveney, Nr Faversham, Kent, ME13 9BZ
Tel: 0795 532691
Proprietor & Chief Inst: Miss A L Bones(BHSAI)Regd
Instruction in Riding and Jumping
Av No: Horses 3 Ponies 1
Std of Schlg: General Purpose Std of Specialist Schlg: Grade C
Livery: Full/Grass/Hunter/School/Hack – mainly country lanes
Ev Classes
Courses: YT
Facilities: Cov Sch: 18 x 14m*/Out Man:40 x 22 m* Fl Lit/4 Basic Schooling

CC Fences/Jmp Pd*/Wash Rm/WC/Car Park
Specialities: Livery/Training
Exclusions: No casual hire
Location: Btwn Faversham & Graveney

GREENACRES RIDING SCHOOL LTD
Greenacres, Ashmore Lane, Leaves Green, Keston, Kent, BR2 6DQ
Tel: Biggin Hill (0959) 72008
Proprietors: Mrs M E Warren & Miss S M Cutts
Chief Inst: Miss S M Cutts (BHSAI)
Other Staff: 2 (BHSAI) 2 (BHSAI) P/T
Instruction in Riding and Jumping & Students to BHSAI Exam
Av No: Horses 6 Ponies 6
Std of Schlg: General Purpose
Livery: Full/Part/Break/School/50 acres own land/local
Ev Classes
Courses: Resid Inst Hol/Wkg Students
Facilities: Cov Sch: 42.6m x 21.6m Gly 100/Out Man: Fl Lit/Jmp Pd/Sh Jmps/ CC Fences/Lec Rm/Vis Aids/Club Rm/ Rest Rm/WC/Wash Rm/Chng Rm
Accom: 7 – Bungalow Catering: Full
Specialities: Four annual horse shows/ Instruction all branches equitation/Small classes/Individual lunge lessons/ Training riders' own horses
Exclusions: No YTS taken
Location: Centre of Leaves Green Off A233

HAYNE BARN RIDING SCHOOL
Hayne Barn, Saltwood, Hythe, Kent
Tel: 0303 260338
Proprietor: Mr I Record
Chief Inst: Miss S J Waters (BHSAI)
Other Staff: 2 (BHSAI) 1 (BHSII(T)) – P/T
Instruction in Riding and Jumping
Av No: Horses 10 Ponies 10
Std of Schlg: General Purpose
Livery: Full/Part/DIY/Hacking – Downland
Ev Lessons
Courses: Res Hol
Facilities: Cov Sch: 31 x 34m*/Gly/Out Man: 55 x 2 8m*/Jmp Pd/Sh Jmps/Lec Rm/Vis Aids/WC/H & C/Wait Rm/Car Park
Accom: 24 – Cottage Catering – Full/ Self
Specialities: General Instruction/Livery/ Riding Holiday
Exclusions: No YT taken
Location: Centre of Village 1 Mile from Saltwood Castle

HEIGHTS RIDING STABLES
Westerham Heights Farm, Westerham Hill, Westerham, Kent, TN16 2ED
Tel: 0959 71953/76702
Proprietor & Chief Inst: Mrs M Burton
Other Staff: 2 (BHSAI) 1 (BHSAI) P/T
Instruction in Riding and Jumping
Av No: Horses 6 Ponies 5 Specialist Horses: 1 Drg N/1 Sh Jmper Grade C/1 Eventer N
Std of Schlg: General Purpose Std of Specialist Schlg: CT – N/Sh Jmpg – C
Livery: Full/Part/Grass/DIY/Working/ School/Hack – Bridle paths
Ev Classes
Courses: Wkg Pupils
Facilities: Out Man: 46 x 30m* Fl Lit/ Novice CC Course/Jmp Pd*/Snacks/ WC/Wash Rm/Changing Rm/Car Park
Specialities: General Instruction/Show Jumping/Livery
Exclusions: No Casual Hire without assessment lesson

HORSESHOES RIDING SCHOOL
Dean Street, East Farleigh, Maidstone, Kent, ME15 0PR
Tel: 0622 46161
Proprietors: Mr & Mrs R Hargreaves
Chief Inst: Mr S Robins (BHSII) **Other Staff:** 2 UQ
Instruction in Riding and Jumping
Av No: Horses 10 Ponies 13
Std of Schlg: General Purpose
Livery: Full/Grass/Hack – Country Lanes/Woodlands/Orchards
Ev Classes
Courses: Wkg Pupil/YT – 2
Facilities: Out Man(2): 46 x 28m Fl Lit*/ 40 x 20m Fl Lit*/Jmp Pd/Vis Aids/ Snacks/Wash Rm/Car Park
Specialities: General Instruction/Hacking/ Non Residential Holiday Courses
Exclusions: Hacking for known clients only
Location: 1/4 mile off B2163 btwn Coxheath/East Farleigh

LIMES FARM EQUESTRIAN CENTRE
Limes Farm, Pay Street, Hawkinge, Kent, CT18 7DZ
Tel: Hawkinge (0303 89) 2335
Proprietor: Miss A Berry BHSI
Other Staff: 2 (BHSI) 3 (BHSAI)
Instruction in Riding and Jumping & Students to BHSII Exam
Av No: Horses 12 Ponies 6 Spec Horses: 1 Drg M/4 CT M
Std of Schlg: General Purpose
Livery: Full/Part/School/Break/Hack – Country Lane

Ev Classes
Courses: Resid Inst/Wkg Students/YT 2
Facilities: Cov Sch:49 x 25m Fl Lit/Out Man:60m x 27m*Fl Lit/Jmp Pd/Sh Jmps*/CC Course/Lec Rm/Vis Aids/ Video/Lic Bar/WC/Car Park
Accom: 23 – Student Hostel/House
Catering: Full
Specialities: Career Students/Schooling/Breaking/Training horse & rider/Residential courses/Riding Holiday Courses
Exclusions: No Casual Hiring
Location: 1/2 Mile off A260 Btween Hawkinge/Densole

LYNX PARK
Colliers Green, Goudhurst, Cranbrook, Kent, TN17 2LR
Tel: 0580 211020 (24hrs)
Proprietor & Chief Inst: Ms S K Kindersley (BHSII)
Other Staff: 2 F/T
Instruction in Riding and Jumping & Students to BHSAI Exam
Av No: Horses 4 Ponies 2
Std of Schlg: General Purpose Std of Specialist Schlg: Sh Jmpg – Grade C
Livery: Full/Part/School/Break
Ev Classes
Courses: BHS Stages – (BHSAI) Exams/Wkg Pupils – 3/YT
Facilities: Cov Sch: 40 x 20m*/Sh Jmps*/Lec Rm* – Vis Aids/Seating – 6/ Film Projector/Video/Snacks/Wash Rm/ WC/Car Park
Accom: B/B – 3 miles away – 4
Specialities: General/Private Instruction/Retraining/Holiday Courses
Exclusions: No Casual Hire
Location: 0.5 mile off A262 btwn Goudhurst/Cranbrook near Peacock Pub

MANNIX STUD
Nightingale Farm, Whiteacre Lane, Waltham, Nr Canterbury, Kent
Tel: 022770 349
Proprietor & Chief Inst: Mrs J Goddard
Other Staff: 1 (BHSI) P/T
Instruction in Riding and Jumping
Av No: Horses 6 Ponies 29
Std of Schlg: General Purpose Std of Specialist Schlg: CT – Basic/Sh Jmpg – Nov
Livery: Full/School/Hack – Bridle paths/ Woodland
Ev Classes
Courses: Resid/YT – 3
Facilities: Cov Sch: 24 x 18m/Out Man: 35 x 20 m/12 Basic Schooling CC Fences/Refreshments/Wash Rm/WC/ Showers/Tack Shop/Car Park
Accom: House – shared rms – 20
Catering: Full
Specialities: Exclusively Childrens Riding Holid ays/Hacking/General Instruction
Exclusions: Age limit 7 – 16 years
Location: Btwn Ashford & Canterbury

MOAT HOUSE
Benenden, Kent, TN17 4EU
Tel: Cranbrook (0580) 240581
Proprietor: Mr & Mrs Grindle
Chief Inst: Mr L E Walsh (BHSAI)
Livery & Facility Centre
Livery: DIY/Own land – 25 acres
Facilities: Cov Sch:61 x 24m* Gly 30/ Cov Sch: 41 x 18m/Jmp Pd Fl Lit/Sh Jmps 12/CC Fences/CC Course/Car Park
Accom: Hotel/Local Families
Specialities: Livery
Exclusions: No trekking or hacking
Location: Off B 2086 between Hartley & Benenden

NELSON PARK RIDING CENTRE
St Margaret's Road, Woodchurch, Birchington, Kent, CT7 0HJ
Tel: 0843 822251
Proprietor & Chief Inst: Mrs S J Matthews (BHSAI)
Other Staff: 1 (BHSI) P/T
Instruction in Riding and Jumping
Av No: Horses 6 Ponies 7
Std of Schlg: General Purpose Std of Specialist Schlg: Sh Jmpg – Novice
Livery: Full/Part/Grass/School/Hack – Mainly Bridle paths/Beach
Ev Classes
Courses: Childrens
Facilities: 2 Out Mans: 40 x 20m* Fl Lit & 35 x 19m* Fl Lit/Novice CC Course*/ Refreshments/Wash Rm/WC/Car Park
Specialities: General Instruction/ Childrens Courses/Summer Camps/Livery/Hacking/Riding Club
Exclusions: No casual hire
Location: 1 mile off A253 btwn Birchington & Ramsgate

OATHILL FARM RIDING CENTRE
Pound Lane, Molash, Nr Canterbury, Kent
Tel: Challock (023 374) 573
Proprietor & Chief Inst: Mr A J Doree
Other Staff: 1 (BHSI(T)) 3 (BHSAI) 2 FT
Instruction in Riding and Jumping
Av No: Horses 12 Ponies 14

Std of Schlg: General Purpose
Livery: Full/Part/Grass/Hack – Forestry Land
Ev Classes – summer only
Facilities: Out Man:40m x 20m*/Jmp Pd/Sh Jmps/CC Fences/WC/H & C/ Chng Rm/Refresh/Wait Rm/Car Park
Accom: 20 – House Catering: Full
Specialities: Riding Holidays/Hacking/ General Instruction
Exclusions: All riding escorted
Location: A252 Between Charing/Canterbury

RIDING FARM
Riding Lane, Hildenborough, Kent, TN11 9LN
Tel: Hildenborough (0732) 838717
ProprietorS: Mr R Howe
Chief Inst: Mrs M Gray (BHSAI) **Other Staff:** 8 (BHSAI) P/T
Instruction in Riding and Jumping
Av No: Horses 4 Ponies 12
Std of Schlg: General Purpose
Livery: DIY/Part/Break/School
Ev Classes
Courses: Inst
Facilities: Cov Sch: 40 x 22m*/Out Man: One-third acre/Jmp Pd/Sh Jmps/ CC Fences/Vis Aids/Lec Rm/Refresh/ Wash Rm/WC/Chng Rm/Car Park
Specialities: Livery/Shows/Riding & Pony Club Events
Exclusions: 24 hours notice of cancellation of ride to be given
Location: Off B245 on outskirks of Hildenborough

ROOTING STREET FARM RIDING CENTRE
Little Chart, Ashford, Kent, TN27 0PX
Tel: 023384 434
Proprietor & Chief Inst: Mrs J Rogers BHSI
Other Staff: Ms M Rose (BHSII(T)) P/T Miss K Waterhouse (BHSAI) P/T Miss T Ashbee (BHSAI) P/T
Instruction in Riding and Jumping & Students to BHSII Exam
Av No: Horses 5 Ponies 5 Specialist Horses: 1 E Drg/1 Int Eventer
Std of Schlg: General Purpose Std of Specialist Schlg: Drg – E/CT – Int
Livery: Full/Part/DIY/Hunter/Holiday/ School/Break
Ev Classes
Courses: Up to & including (BHSII) Exam/Wkg Pupils/Childrens Riding Holidays
Facilities: Out Man: 60 x 20m* Fl Lit/ Jmp Pd*/Wash Rm/WC/Car Park
Accom: Cottage/House Catering: Full
Specialities: Career Students/Childrens Riding Holidays/Livery
Exclusions: Weight limit 13.5 stone/ No children under 5 years
Location: On Main Road btwn Hothfield & Little Chart

ST STEPHEN'S COLLEGE RIDING SCHOOL
North Foreland, Broadstairs, Kent, CT10 3NP
Tel: Thanet (0843) 602922
Proprietor & Chief Inst: Miss L Austen (BHSAI)
Instruction in Riding and Jumping
Av No: Horses 7 Ponies 13
Std of Schlg: General Purpose
Livery: Full/Part/Hack – Sandy Beaches/ Cliff Gallop/Farmland
Ev Classes
Facilities: Out Man:31 x 18m Fl Lit/ Jmp Pd/Sh Jmps/CC Fences/Wash Rm/ WC/Car Park
Specialities: Basic Instruction/Childrens Riding Holidays/Livery/Hacking
Exclusions: No YT taken
Location: Through Town Centre out on the North Foreland Rd

TAYLOR'S RIDING ESTABLISHMENT
Casita, Waverley Avenue, Minster, Sheerness, Kent, ME12 2JL
Tel: Minster (Sheppey) (0795) 872203
Proprietor: Mr & Mrs R W Hayler
Chief Inst: Mrs Y Hayler (BHSAI) **Other Staff:** 1 (BHSAI) P/T
Instruction in Riding and Jumping
Av No: Horses 4 Ponies 10
Std of Schlg: General Purpose
Livery: Full/Grass/DIY/Break/School
Ev Classes
Courses: Resid
Facilities: Out Man:37 x 22m Fl Lit*/ Cov Sch:25 x 18m* Gly 20 Fl Lit/Jmp Pd Seats Fl Lit/Sh Jmps/CC Course/WC/ Chng Rm
Accom: 2 – Single rooms/Farmhouse Catering: Family
Specialities: Young riders/Pony Club Tests/Beginners/Adults all stages/ Competition/Own Riding Club
Exclusions: No YT taken
Location: 0.5 Mile off the main road through the town

TOLLGATE RIDING STABLES
Monks Buildings, Northumberland Bottom, Wrotham Road, Gravesend, Kent

Tel: 0474 564681/0634 718521 (Evenings)
Proprietors: Miss C Curtiss & Mr W L Prielipp
Chief Inst: Mrs B Smith (BHSII) **Other Staff:** 6 (BHSAI)
Instruction in Riding and Jumping
Av No: Horses 10 Ponies 10
Std of Schlg: General Purpose Sh Jmp: Novice
Livery: Full/Part/Hack – Lane/ Woodland/Bridleways
Ev Classes
Courses: BHS Stages 1 & 2/Wkg Pupils/YT – 2
Facilities: Cov Sch: 35 x 17m*/ Out Man: 40 x 20m Fl Lit*/Jmp Pd*/ Lec Rm/Club Rm/Vis Aids/Seating/ Snacks/Wash Rm/WC/Wait Rm/Car Park
Specialities: General Instruction/ Holiday Courses/School Contract Work/ Livery/Riding Club
Exclusions: No Casual Hiring
Location: On A277 Junc with A2

SURREY

BARNFIELD RIDING SCHOOL

Parkfields Road, Off Park Road, Kingston, Surrey, KT2 5LL
Tel: 081 546 3616/8781
Proprietor: Mrs J Grayson (BHSII)
Other Staff: 1 (BHSII) 1 (BHSAI) 4 (BHSAI) P/T
Instruction in Riding and Jumping
Av No: Horses 5 Ponies 4
Std of Schlg: General Purpose
Specialist Schlg: Sh Jmpg – Novice
School/Hack – Richmond Park
Ev Classes
Courses: up to Stage 2/YT – 1
Facilities: Out Man: 39 x 20m Fl Lt*/ Jmp Pd*/Snacks/Shop/WC/Showers/Car Park
Specialities: General Instruction/ Childrens Holiday Courses/Hacking/ RDA
Exclusions: No Riders over 14 stone/ No Casual Hire – assessment lesson

BEECHWOOD RIDING SCHOOL

Hillboxes Farm, Marden Park, Woldingham, Surrey, CR3 7JD
Tel: 0883 342266
Proprietor: Miss J Garnham (BHSAI)
Other Staff: 1UQ
Instruction in Riding and Jumping
Av No: Horses 13 Ponies 12
Std of Schlg: General Purpose
School/Hack – Parkland/Bridleways
Ev Classes
Courses: YTS
Facilities: Cov Sch: 18 x 18m/Out Mans: 60 x 20 m*/Jmp Pd/CC Fences/ Lec Rm/Video/Vis Aids/Seating/ Refreshments/Wash Rm/WC/Showers/ Changing Rm/Waiting Rm/Car Park
Specialities: General Instruction(Adults/ Children)/Long/Short term courses/ Individual instruction/Ev Classes – Horsemanship/Equitation/Theory/Practice
Exclusions: No Riders over 14 stone/No casual hire
Location: In Marden Park

BURSTOW PARK RIDING & LIVERY CENTRE

Antlands Lane, Horley, Surrey, RH6 9TF
Tel: 0293 820766
Proprietors: Mrs J Skinner & Mrs S Hart & Mrs B Avenell
Chief Inst: Mrs S Hart **Other Staff:** 1 (BHSI) P/T
Instruction in Riding and Jumping
Av No: Horses 10 Ponies 8
Std of Schlg: General Purpose
Livery: Full/Part/School
Ev Classes
Facilities: Cov Sch: 36 x 20m* Gly/ Out Man: 61 x 33m Fl Lit/Refreshments/ Wash Rm/WC/Car Park
Specialities: General Instruction/ Holiday Livery/Livery/RDA
Exclusions: No riders over 14 stone/ No casual hire
Location: Off Exit 10 M23 Follow Copthorne/East Grinstead

BUSHY PARK RIDING SCHOOL LTD

The Green, Hampton Court Road, Hampton Court, Surrey, KT8 9VW
Tel: 081 979 1748
Proprietor: Mr B Johnson
Chief Inst: Miss S Osborne (BHSAI)
Instruction in Riding
Av No: Horses 10 Ponies 1
Std of Schlg: General Purpose
Livery: Part/Hack – Parkland
Courses: YT taken
Specialities: Escorted hacks/Stable Management
Exclusions: No children under 13 years
Location: On A308 between Hampton & Hampton Court

THE CLOCK TOWER RIDING SCHOOL

Brighton Road, Kingswood, Tadworth, Surrey, KT20 6SY
Tel: Mogador (0737) 832874/833874

Proprietors: G B & J A Ayling-Rouse (BHSII)
Chief Inst: J A Ayling-Rouse (BHSII)
Other Staff: 3 (BHSAI) 1 (BHSII)
Instruction in Riding and Jumping
Av No: Horses 16
Std of Schlg: General Purpose
Livery: Full/Part/Break/School/Hack – Walton Banstead Heath/Epsom Downs
Ev Classes
Facilities: 2 Out Man:40 x 35m* & 30 x 30m* Fl Lit/Sh Jmps12/Lec Rm/ Refresh/Rest Rm/WC/Wash Rm
Specialities: Livery service/Direct access to superb riding country with no roadwork necessary
Exclusions: No YTS taken
Location: On A217 between Kingswood & Banstead Cross

THE DIAMOND CENTRE FOR HANDICAPPED RIDERS
Woodmansterne Road, Carshalton, Surrey
Tel: 081 643 7764
Chairman: Mr K Webb BEM
Exec.Chairman: Sister Chiara Hatton-Hall FBHS **Chief Inst:** Mrs P Warren (BHSAI)
Other Staff: 2 (BHSAI)
Instruction in Riding and Jumping
Av No: Horses 5 Ponies 20
Std of Schlg: General Purpose
Hack – Bridlepaths
Ev Classes
Courses: Special courses from time to time for Instructors/Helpers and Physiotherapists Hol Inst
Facilities: 2 Cov Sch: 20m x 40m* Gly Fl Lit/Sh Jmps/Lec Rm/Vis Aids/ Video/Club Rm/Rest Rm/Refresh/WC/ Showers/Wash Rm/Chng Rm/Car Park
Specialities: Riding for handicapped people/Conferences on same/Driving for the Disabled

DORKING RIDING SCHOOL
Downs Meadow, Ranmore Road, Dorking, Surrey RH4 1HW, Corres: Castre 11 Upper Rose, Hill Dorking Surrey RH4 2EB
Tel: Dorking (0306) 881718 Day/882127 Evening
Proprietor: Miss R B Fardon I of H
Other Staff: 1 (BHSAI) 1 FBHS P/T
Instruction in Riding and Jumping & Students to BHSAI Exam
Av No: Horses 8 Ponies 8
Std of Schlg: General Purpose
Hack – North Downs/Woodland/ Farmland
Courses: Inst Hol
Facilities: Cov Sch: 32 x 18m* Gly 60 Fl Lit/Sh Jmps/WC/Wash Rm/Chng Rm/ Car Park
Specialities: Mainly weekly riders – standing bookings
Exclusions: No hiring for hunting/No riders under 8 years/No YTS taken

EBBISHAM FARM LIVERY STABLES
Ebbisham Lane, Walton on the Hill, Tadworth, Surrey, KT20 7SA
Tel: 0737 812568
Proprietor: Mrs O J Rivett
Manager: Miss E Sibilim (BHSAI) **Other Staff:** 7 F/T 1 P/T
Livery Yard & Facility Centre
Livery: Full/Grass
Facilities: 2 Out Man: 40 x 45m Fl Lit & 40 x 2 0m Fl Lit/CC Courses – Novice/ Refreshments/Wash R B/WC/Car Park/ Showers
Specialities: Livery Service
Location: Between Tadworth and Walton on the Hill

FARTHING DOWN STABLES
Drive Road, Old Coulsdon, Surrey CR3 1HJ
Tel: Downland (07375) 51609
Proprietors: Mr & Mrs J Kennedy
Chief Inst: Miss A Newham (BHSAI)
Basic Instruction in Riding and Jumping
Av No: Horses 4 Ponies 4
Std of Schlg: General Purpose
Livery: Full/Part/Grass/Hack – Downland/ Parkland
Ev Classes Summer only
Courses: Inst Hol
Facilities: Out Man: 38m x 19m* Fl Lit/ Jmp Pd/Sh Jmps/CC Fences/Lec Rm/ WC
Specialities: General and private instruction/Prep for Pony Club Tests/ Children's holiday courses/Hacking/ Livery
Exclusions: No casual hire/No YTS

GREENWAYS FARM AND STABLES
Lower Eashing, Godalming, Surrey, GU7 2QF
Tel: Godalming (04868) 4741
Proprietors: Mr & Mrs M Sprake
Chief Inst: Mr M Sprake (BHSAI) **Other Staff:** 2 (BHSAI)
Basic Instruction in Riding and Jumping
Av No: Horses 8 Ponies 9
Std of Schlg: General Purpose

Livery: Full/Hunter/Hack – Common Land/Farmland
Evening Lessons
Courses: Inst/Hol
Facilities: Out Man:40m x 20m* Fl Lit/Jmp Pd/Sh Jmps/CC Fences/Lec Rm/Vis Aids/Wash Rm/WC/Chng Rm/Car Park
Specialities: Livery/Hacking/Basic instruction
Exclusions: No riders under 8 years accepted/No YTS
Location: Off A3 btwn Guildford/Hindhead

HIGHER PARK FARM EQUESTRIAN CENTRE
Halebourne Lane, West End, Chobham, Surrey, GU24 8SL
Tel: 0276 856335
Proprietor: L W Smart Esq
Manager: Miss J Rogers **Chief Inst:** Miss J Dodd (BHSAI)
Other Staff: 3 (BHSAI) P/T
Instruction in Riding and Jumping
Av No: Horses 10 Ponies 6
Std of Schlg: General Purpose Std of Specialist Schlg: Sh Jmpg – Nov
Livery: Part/School/Hack – Common Land
Ev Classes
Courses: Childrens Camps
Facilities: Cov Sch: 55 x 18m*/Out Man: 40 x 2 0m Fl Lit/Jmp Pd/Lec Rm – Vis Aids/Seating 50 – 60/Video/Refreshments/Wash Rm/WC/Showers/Waiting Rm/Car Park
Specialities: General Instruction/Children's Courses & Camps/Hacking/Side Saddle/Film Work
Exclusions: No casual hire
Location: Off A319 btwn Bagshot/Chobham 3 miles Junc 3 of M3

HUNTERSFIELD FARM RIDING CENTRE
Fairlawn Road, (off Croydon Lane), Banstead, Surrey, SM7 3AU
Tel: 081 643 1333
Proprietors: Mr & Mrs D Horley
Chief Inst: Ms M Patterson (BHSII)
Other Staff: 3 (BHSAI) 1 (BHSII)
Instruction in Riding and Jumping & Students to BHSII Exam
Av No: Horses 19 Ponies 15
Std of Schlg: General Purpose Std of Specialist Schlg: Drg Nov – E
Livery: Full/Part/School/Hack – Downs
Ev Classes
Courses: Resid Inst/Wkg Students/YTS
Facilities: Cov Sch: 37 x 65m* Fl Lit Gly 100/Out Man: 28 x 9m/Sh Jmps/Video/Vis Aids/Refresh/Rest Rm/WC/Showers/Wash Rm/Chng Rm/Shop/Car Park
Accom: 8 House Catering: Full
Specialities: Residential courses for students for (BHSAI) Exam with first class living accommodation and attention
Exclusions: Hacking regular clients only
Location: Off A2002 Between Banstead & Purley

THE KINGSTON RIDING CENTRE
38 Crescent Road, Kingston-upon-Thames, Surrey, KT2 7RG
Tel: 081 546 6361
Proprietors: Joe & Lynne Mastroianni & S Hillman
Managing Agent for YT
Chief Inst & Head Student Training: Miss A L Hyde (BHSII) **Head Girl:** Miss N Dyke (BHSAI) **Other Staff:** 7 (BHSAI) 2 (BHSII(T)) 3 (BHSI) P/T
Instruction in Riding and Jumping & Students to BHSII Exam
Av No: Horses 40 Ponies 8
Std of Schlg: General Purpose
Livery: Full/Grass/School/Hack – Richmond Park
Ev Classes
Courses: Hol/Wkg Students/YT 8/Concentrated training
Facilities: Cov Sch:32 x 18m/Out Man:60m x 20m/Jmp Pd Seats Fl Lit/Sh Jmps/Lec Rm/Club Rm/Lic Bar/Refresh/WC/Wash Rm/Car Park
Accom: 10 – shared Flats Catering: Self
Specialities: General Instruction/Riding Club/Hacking/RDA/Career Training/Private Jumping Lesson/Side Saddle
Exclusions: No beginner riders over 12.5 stone
Location: Just outside Kingston Gate – Richmond Park

LANGSHOT EQUESTRIAN CENTRE
Gracious Pond Road, Chobham, Surrey, GU24 8HJ
Tel: 0276 856949
Proprietors: Mrs L Kingsnorth & Mrs H Stevenson
Chief Inst: Miss P Heimann – Tootell
Other Staff: 1 (BHSAI) 2 (BHSII) P/T 2 (BHSAI) P/T
Instruction in Riding and Jumping
Av No: Horses 14 Ponies 10
Std of Schlg: General Purpose Std of Specialist Schlg: CT – Novice
Livery: Full/Part/School/Hack – Common Land

Ev Classes
Facilities: Cov Sch: 46 x 14m*/2 Out Mans: 40m x 20m* Fl Lit & 60 x 40m*/ CC Course* – Novice/Sh Jmps*/Lec Rm – seating 20/Refreshments/WC/Car Park
Specialities: General Instruction/School Groups/Hacking/RDA/Dressage Training
Exclusions: No casual hire/No rider over 14 stone
Location: Btwn Chertsey/Woking

LITTLE BROOK EQUESTRIAN CENTRE

East Park Lane, Newchapel, Lingfield, Surrey
Tel: 0342 832360
Proprietors: Mrs Sally-Ann Rotberg & Mr & Mrs W Marshall
Chief Inst: Mrs S Rotberg (BHSII) **Other Staff:** 2 (BHSAI) 1 (BHSII(T)) 1 FBHS
Instruction in Riding and Jumping & Students to BHSII Exam
Av No: Horses 6 Ponies 4
Std of Schlg: General Purpose
Livery: Full/Hunter/School/Break
Ev Classes
Courses: Res Inst/Wkg Students/YTS 2
Facilities: Cov Sch:37 x 18m* Gly 20/ Out Man: 43 x 22m*Fl Lit/Jmp Pd/Sh Jmps/CC Fences/Vis Aids/Offices/WC/ Wash Rm/Chng Rm/Refresh/Club Rm/ Car Park
Accom: 5 – Mobile Home Catering:Self (Students)
Specialities: Specialist Teaching/Small Classes/Student Training/Livery/YTS & ET
Exclusions: No riders over 12.5 stone
Location: 1 Mile off A22 Between Lingfield/Crawley

LOWER FARM RIDING AND LIVERY STABLES

Stoke Road, Stoke D'Abernon, Cobham, Surrey
Tel: Cobham (0932) 67545
Proprietors: Mr C Lewin and Mrs J Brown
Chief Inst: Mrs C Richens (BHSAI)
Other Staff: 2 (BHSAI) 4 (BHSAI) P/T 1 (BHSI) P/T
Instruction in Riding and Jumping
Av No: Horses 10 Ponies 9
Std of Schlg: General Purpose
Livery: Full/Part/Break/School/Hack-Woods/Common
Ev Classes
Courses: Hol/Inst
Facilities: 2 Out Man: 20m x 15m Fl Lit & 38m x 1 8m Fl Lit/Jmp Pd/Sh Jmps/ WC/Car Park
Specialities: Livery/Hacking/General/Instruction
Exclusions: No riders over 12 stone
Location: On A245 btwn Cobham & Leatherhead

THE OLD FORGE

High Road, Upper Gratton, Nr Reigate, Surrey, RH2 0TY
Tel: 07374 2341
Proprietor: Mrs B Falkner
Livery Yard
Livery: Full/Part/Grass/DIY/Hunter/ Holiday
Facilities: Out Man: 50 x 30m* Fl Lit/8 Basic Schooling CC Fences/WC/Car Park
Specialities: Livery Service of all types

OLD PARK STABLES

Old Park Lane, Farnham, Surrey, GU9 0AN
Tel: 0252 715492/726503
Proprietor: Mr J Ricketts
Manager: Miss J Wilmshurst (BHSAI)
Chief Inst: Miss V Johnston (BHSII) P/T
Other Staff: 2 (BHSAI) P/T
Basic Instruction in Riding and Jumping
Av No: Horses 10 Ponies 6
Std of Schlg: General Purpose
Livery: Full/Part/Grass/DIY/School/Hack – Bridle paths/Common Land/Country Lanes
Ev Classes
Facilities: 2 Out Man: 30m x 40m* Fl Lit/40m x 20m* Fl Lit/27 CC Fences* (Novice)/Refreshments – small canteen/ Tuck Shop at Weekends & School Holidays/WC/Car Park
Specialities: General Instruction/ Hacking/Livery
Exclusions: No Casual hire

OLDENCRAIG EQUESTRIAN CENTRE

Oldencraig Farm, Tandridge Lane, Lingfield, Surrey, RH7 6LL
Tel: 0342 833317
Proprietors: Mr & Mrs B G & Miss L Carlen
Chief Insts: Mrs B G Carlen & Miss L Carlen
Instruction in Riding and Jumping & Students to BHSAI Exam
Av No: Horses 13 Ponies 6 Specialist Horses: Med Drgs
Std of Schlg: General Purpose/Std of Specialist Schlg: Drg – Med/CT – Basic/ Sh Jmpg – Novice
Livery: Full/School
Ev Classes

Courses: Inst/1 Wkg Pupil/YT – taken
Facilities: Cov Sch: 60 x 20m* Gly/2 Out Man: 50 x45m* Fl Lit & 60 x 20m* Fl Lit/6 Schooling CC Fences/Jmp Pd/ Sh Jmps*/Lec Rm – Seating for 50/Film Projector/Library/Horse Solarium
Specialities: Dressage/Livery/ Instructional Courses/RDA
Exclusion: No casual hire
Location: On B2028 btwn Blindley Heath & Lingfield

ORCHARD COTTAGE RIDING STABLES
Babylon Lane, Lower Kingswood, Tadworth, Surrey, KT20 6XA
Tel: Reigate (0737) 241311
Proprietors: Mr & Mrs P R Howell
Principal: Mr P R Howell **Chief Inst:** Claire Hansen (BHSAI/INT TEACH CERT)
Other Staff: 1 (BHSAI)
Instruction in Riding and Jumping
Av No: Horses 9 Ponies 6
Std of Schlg: General Purpose
Hack – North Downs/Common Land
Ev Classes
Courses: Inst Hol Day
Facilities: Cov Sch: 40 x 20m/Jmp Pd 100m x 100m*/Sh Jmps 8 BSJA/11 mini for children/CC Fences/Lec Rm/ Refresh/Wash Rm/Club Rm/WC/Change Rm/Car Park
Specialities: Riding for beginners and ladies coffee mornings (A lesson or hack followed by coffee and discussion)
Exclusions: No casual hiring/No hunter hirelings/No YTS taken

PARKHURST HORSE TRAINING FACILITIES
Lodgelands, Bognor Road(A29), Beare Green, Dorking, Surrey
Tel: Dorking (0306) 711869
Proprietors: Mr & Mrs P Larrigan
Chief Inst: Marion Larrigan **Other Staff:** 1 (BHSAI)
Instruction in Riding and Jumping
Av No: Horses 8 Ponies 6
Std of Schlg: General Purpose Std of Specialist Schlg: Drg – Grand Prix
Livery: Full/Break/School
Ev Classes
Courses: Resid Inst Hol/YT 2
Facilities: Cov Sch: 49 x 25m Gly 200/Out Man:80m x 40m/Jmp Pd/Shw Jmps/Lec Rm/Club Rm/Refresh/WC/ Showers/Wash Rm/Chng Rm/Car Park
Accom: 6 Bungalow Catering: Full
Specialities: Dressage Novice to Grand Prix/Re-schooling of problem horses/Holiday Courses/Livery/Western Riding & Driving
Exclusions: No unescorted riding

PRIORY SCHOOL OF EQUITATION
Millbridge, Frensham, Farnham, Surrey, GU10 3DP
Tel: (025-125) 3697/4161
Proprietor: Mr & Mrs H Pays
Chief Inst: Miss H Dellar – Smith (BHSAI) **Manager:** Miss D Brady **Other Staff:** 3 (BHSAI) 1 (BHSII) P/T
Instruction in Riding and Jumping
Av No: Horses 8 Ponies 8
Std of Schlg: General Purpose
Livery: Full/School/Hack – Common Land
Ev Classes
Courses: Inst/Wk Students
Facilities: Cov Sch: 55 x 22m Fl Lit*/Out Man/Jmp Pd/CC Fences*/Club Rm/ Lic Bar/Wash Rm/WC/Chng Rm/ Refresh/Car park
Specialities: General instruction/ Hacking/Livery service/Indoor and outdoor shows/Courses & demonstrations
Exclusions: No YT taken
Location: On A327 Btwn Farnham/Hindhead

SOUTH WEYLANDS EQUESTRIAN CENTRE
Esher Road, Hersham, Walton-on-Thames, Surrey, KT12 4LJ
Tel: Esher (0372) 463010/463432
Proprietors: Mr & Mrs P Bushnell
Chief Inst: Mrs P Bushnell (BHSI) **Other Staff:** 4 (BHSAI) 1 BHSI
Instruction in Riding and Jumping & Students to BHSII Exam
Av No: Horses 10 Ponies 20
Std of Schlg: General Purpose Std of Spec Schlg: Drg – Elem/H T – Int/Sh Jmp – I
Livery: Break/School
Ev Classes
Courses: Wkg Students
Facilities: 2 Cov Sch: 42 x 16m Gly 50 Fl Lit & 1 8 x 16m Fl Lit Gly/2 Out Mans: 46 x 28m & 60 x 20m/Jmp Pd 1 acre/Sh Jmps/CC Fences/CC Course/Lec Rm/ Vis Aids/WC/Wash Rm/Chng Rm/Car Park
Accom: Cottage – 9 Catering: Full
Specialities: Training for Dressage & Eventing/Driving/Career Students
Exclusions: Riders weight limit 11 stone/No YT taken
Location: On A244 Between Esher & Weybridge

VALE LODGE STABLES
Downs Lane, off Dorking Road, Leatherhead, Surrey, KT22 8JG
Tel: Leatherhead (0372) 373184
Proprietor: Miss J Cooper (BHSAI)
Other Staff: 1 (BHSAI)
Instruction in Riding and Jumping
Av No: Horses 4 Ponies 6
Std of Schlg: General Purpose
Livery: Full/Part/Hack – Varied
Ev Classes
Facilities: Out Man:69 x 14m/Jmp Pd/Sh Jmps/CC Fences/WC/Chng Rm
Specialities: Teaching care of all animals/Children's/Stable Management Courses
Location: On B2045 – Dorking side of Leatherhead

WILDWOODS RIDING CENTRE
Ebbisham Lane, Walton on the Hill, Tadworth, Surrey, KT20 5BH
Tel: Tadworth (0737) 812146
Proprietor: Mrs A Chambers (BHSII)
Other Staff: 1 (BHSAI) 1 (BHSII) Freelance (BHSI) is available
Instruction in Riding and Jumping
Av No: Horses 20 Ponies 8
Std of Schlg: General Purpose
Break/School/Hack – Downland Heath/ Bridlepaths/Forestry
Ev Classes
Courses: Hol Inst
Facilities: 2 Out Mans: 40m x 20m*Fl Lit/ 20 Sh Jmps/Jmp Pd*/CC Fences/Lec Rm/ Refresh/Chng Rm/Club Rm/WC/Car Park
Specialities: General Instruction/ Hacking/Riding Club for senior and juniors
Exclusions: No casual hiring/No YTS taken
Location: Between Walton & Epsom

WOLDINGHAM EQUESTRIAN CENTRE
Southfields Road, Woldingham, Surrey
Tel: 088385 3034
Proprietor: Mrs J A Roberts
Chief Inst: Miss T Scott **Other Staff:** 1 FBHS – P/T 1 (BHSI) P/T
Basic Instruction in Riding and Jumping
Av No: Horses 12 Ponies 3
Std of Schlg: General Purpose Std of Specialist Schlg: Sh Jmpg – Novice
Livery: Full/Part/DIY/School/Hack – National Trust/North Downs/Bridle paths
Ev Classes
Facilities: Out Man: 55 x 27m* Fl Lit/10 Novice Schooling CC Fences/Jmp Pd*/Lec Rm – seating/WC/Car Park
Specialities: General Instruction/ Livery/Hacking
Exclusions: Weight limit 12.5 stone

WYVENHOE RIDING CENTRE LTD
Guildford Road, Little Bookham, Surrey, KT23 4HB
Tel: Bookham (0372) 54339
Proprietors: R A Childs J L Childs C K Childs & L L Legg
Chief Inst: Mrs L Legg (BHSII)
Other Staff: 1 (BHS T & S M)
Instruction in Riding and Jumping & Students to BHSAI Exam
Av No: Horses 9 Ponies 10
Std of Schlg: General Purpose
Livery: Full/Part/School/Break/Hack – Commonland/National Trust
Ev Classes
Courses: Resid Inst/Wkg Students
Facilities: Cov Sch: 33 x 25m* Fl Lit/ Jmp Pd/Sh Jmps/CC Course/Club Rm/ Showers/Lec Rm/Vis Aids/Video/WC/ Shop/Refresh/Wash Rm/Car Park
Accom: House – 5 Catering: Full
Specialities: RDA/General instruction/ Livery
Exclusions: No unaccompanied hacking/No YT
Location: On A246 Between Guildford & Leatherhead

EAST SUSSEX

CANTERS END RIDING SCHOOL
Hadlow Down, Nr Uckfield, East Sussex, TN22 4HP
Tel: Hadlow Down (082585) 213
Proprietor: Miss M R Thompson
Instruction in Riding and Jumping
Av No: Horses 1 Ponies 6
Std of Schlg: General Purpose
Livery: Full/Break/School/Hack
Facilities: Cov Sch: 28 x 14m* Fl Lit
Specialities: Young children/ Beginners/General Instruction
Exclusions: No casual hiring
Location: A272 Outskirts of Hadlow Down

CROCKSTEAD EQUESTRIAN CENTRE
Crockstead Farm, Halland, Nr Lewes, East Sussex, BN8 6PT
Tel: 082 584 796/7
Proprietors: East Sussex Estates Ltd – J A Lambert Esq
Other Staff: 1 (BHSII) 1 (BHSAI)
Instruction in Riding and Jumping & Students to BHSII Exam

Av No: Horses 6 Ponies 2
Std of Schlg: General Purpose Std of Specialist Schlg: Sh Jmpg – Grade B
Livery: Full/Part/Hunter/School/Break
Ev Classes
Courses: Holiday/Wkg Pupils
Facilities: Cov Sch: 60 x 25m* Gly/Out Man: 60 x 25m* Fl Lit/6 Novice Schlg CC Fences/Refreshments/Wash Rm/Lic Bar/Club Rm/WC/Tack Shop/Car Park
Specialities: Competition Centre/ Livery/Private Tuition/General Instruction
Exclusions: No Casual Hire
Location: On A22 btwn Halland & Uckfield

THE ENGLISH LANGUAGE & EQUESTRIAN CENTRE
Friars Gate Farm, Crowborough, East Sussex, TN6 1XH
Tel: 0892 661195
Proprietor: Mr D R C Forsyth
Chief Inst: Mrs H Garner (BHSII) **Other Staff:** 1 (BHS HM) 1 (BHSPTT)
Instruction in Riding and Jumping
Av No: Horses 6 Ponies 4
Std of Schlg: General Purpose
Livery: DIY/Part
Ev Classes
Courses: Resid Inst Hol/Wkg Students
Facilities: Cov Sch: 34 x 14m*/Out Man:52m x 26m*/Jmp Pd/Sh Jmps/ CC Course/Lec Rm/Vis Aids*/WC/H & C/Showers/Refresh/Car Park
Accom: 28 – House Catering: Full
Specialities: General Instruction/ Liveries/Shows/English Language Courses/Residential/Holiday Courses/ RDA
Exclusions: No unescorted rides/No YTS
Location: 1.5 miles from Crowborough off B2188

GATEWOOD STABLES
The Barn House, Robin Post Lane, Wilmington, Polegate, East Sussex, BN26 6RP
Tel: Polegate (03212) 3709
Proprietors: Mr & Mrs K Quicke
Other Staff: 3 (BHSAI) P/T
Instruction in Riding and Jumping
Av No: Horses 10 Ponies 1
Std of Schlg: General Purpose School/Hack – Forest/Downs
Ev Classes
Courses: Inst/YTS
Facilities: Cov Sch: 18 x 28m Gly 20/Out Man: 18 x 92m/Jmp Pd/Sh Jmps/CC Course/Lec Rm/Refresh/ WC/W ash Rm/Wait Rm/Car Park
Specialities: Monthly Gymkhana & Jumping/Summer Picnic Rides
Location: Off A27 2 miles from Polegate towards Lewes

HIGHAM FARM
Chapel Lane, Guestling Green, Nr Hastings, East Sussex, TN35 4HP
Tel: 0424 812636
Proprietors: Miss M Stokes FBHS Miss C Green BHSI
Training & Facility Centre & Students to BHSI
Av Horses – Ponies
Std of Schlg: General Purpose Specialist Horses: 1 Drg M/1 Sh Jmp C/1 Side Saddle Adv
Livery: Full/School/Break
Ev Classes Summer only
Courses: Up to & including BHSI/ Students only taken with own horses/ Wkg Pupil
Facilities: Out Man: 60m x 20m/Schooling Fences 6/Jmp Pd/20 x 20m Lunge Arena/ Lec Rm/Vis Aids/Video/Refreshments/ Wash Rm/WC/Showers/Car Park
Specialities: Training/Facility/Livery Centre/Side Saddle
Exclusions: No Hiring/Riders with own horses only
Location: Off A259 btwn Guestling Green & Hastings

PLUMPTON AGRICULTURAL COLLEGE
Plumpton, Lewes, East Sussex,BN7 3AE
Tel: 0273 890454
Principal: J J Wilson Esq
Head of Department: J G Campbell Esq (BHSI) **Chief Inst:** J G Campbell Esq (BHSI) **Other Staff:** 1 (BHSI SM) 1 (BHSII)
Instruction in Riding and Jumping & Students to BHSII Exam
Av No: Horses 15 ponies 2 Specialist Horses: Med & Novice Drg
Std of Schlg: General Purpose Std of Specialist Schlg: Drg & Sh Jmpg – Novice
Livery: Full/Part/Grass/School
Courses: Up to BHSAI Exam/Wkg Students
Facilities: Cov Sch: 42 x 22m*/ Out Man: 40 x 2 0m*Fl Lit/Lec Rm/ Club Rm – Seating 40/Vis Aids/ Refreshments/Wash Rm/WC/Showers/ Changing Rm/Car Park
Accom: Single Rms – 30 Catering: Full
Specialities: Career Student Training/ Livery/Stud Unit
Exclusions: No Casual Hire

SKY FARM RIDING SCHOOL
Cade Street, Old Heathfield,
East Sussex
Tel: Heathfield (043 52) 3132/2807
Proprietor: C & D Sansom
Chief Inst: Mrs J Hartwell (BHSAI)
Instruction in Riding and Jumping
Av No: Horses 13 Ponies 20
Std of Schlg: General Purpose
Livery: Full/Part/Grass/School/Break/Hack – Bridle paths/Forestry
Ev Lessons
Courses: Inst/YTS
Facilities: Cov Sch:26 x 18m*/Out Man:60m x 30m/Re freshments/WC/Car Park
Accom: House – 5 Catering: Full
Specialities: General Instruction/Children & beg inners/Livery/Hacking/Childrens courses/Competitions
Exclusions: No casual Hiring
Location: Off B2096 Between Punnets Town/Heathfield

WEST SUSSEX

ARUNDEL RIDING CENTRE
Park Place, Arundel, West Sussex
Tel: Arundel (0903) 882061
Proprietor: Mrs Joy Leggett (BHSAI)
Other Staff: 2 (BHSAI) 1 (BHSII)
Instruction in Riding and Jumping & Students to BHSAI
Av No: Horses 6 Ponies 13
Std of Schlg: General Purpose
Livery: Full/Grass/School/Hack – South Downs/Park/Woodland
Ev Classes
Courses: Resid Inst Hol/Wkg Students/YTS – 2
Facilities: Cov Sch: 20m x 40m* Gly/Out Man:32m x 26m*/Jmp Pd 100 x 75m*/Sh Jmps*/CC Fences/Lec Rm/Vis Aids/WC/Refresh/Wash Rm/Car Park
Accom: 4 Cottage Catering: Full
Specialities: Dressage/Sh Jumping and Eventing/Private & Class tuition/RDA/Driving
Exclusions: No Casual Hire
Location: Just off A27 on Outskirts of Arundel

BELMOREDEAN STUD & LIVERY STABLES
Little Champions Farm, Maplehurst Road, West Grinstead, West Sussex, RH13 6RN
Tel: 0403 864635
Proprietor: Miss L M Hartnett (BHSAI)
Facility & Livery Centre
Livery: Full/Grass/Reduced/Hunt
Facilities: Cov Sch: 44 x 20m* Gly
Specialities: Facility Centre & Livery Service
Exclusions: No horses for hire
Location: Just off A272 near Junc with the A24

COLDWALTHAM HOUSE
Nr Pulborough, West Sussex, RH20 1LY
Tel: Bury (0798) 831418
Proprietor & Chief Inst: Mrs Esme Jack (BHSI)
Training & Facility Centre & Students to BHSI Exam
Av No: horses 7
Std of Schlg: General Purpose
Livery: Full/Break/School
Courses: Wkg Students
Facilities: Cov Sch: 42 x 23m/Out Man/Jmp Pd/Sh Jmps/CC Course/Lec Rm/Vis Aids/WC/Chng Rm/Car Park
Specialities: Pupils schooled on their own horses/Training for dressage competitions/Video tape
Exclusions: No YTS
Location: Just off A29 2 miles south of Pulborough

DITCHLING COMMON STUD
Ditchling Common, Nr Burgess Hill, West Sussex, RH15 0SE
Tel: Burgess Hill (0444) 236678/871900
Proprietor & Chief Inst: Mr P J M Dudeney (BHS T & SM)
Instruction in Riding and Jumping & Students to BHSII Exam
Av No: Horses 10 Ponies 7
Std of Schlg: General Purpose
Livery: Full/Part/school/Break/Hunt
Ev Classes
Courses: Res/Inst/YTS
Facilities: Cov Sch (1): 40 x 22m Gly/Cov Sch (2): 40 x20m/Out Man: 40 x 20m*Fl Lit/CC Course/Jmp Pd/Refresh/Wash Rm/WC/Car Park
Accom: 6 – Rooms/Caravan Catering: Full
Specialities: General Instruction/Training for Competitions/Livery/Courses/Career Students
Exclusions: No casual hire
Location: Off B2112 Between Haywards Heath & Ditchling

GRANGEFIELD CHILDREN'S RIDING SCHOOL
Grangefield, Bepton, Midhurst, West Sussex, GU29 0JB
Tel: Midhurst (073 081) 3538

Proprietor: Miss W Z Sugden (BHSAI)
Other Staff: 1 (BHSAI)
Instruction in Riding and Jumping
Av No: Horses 1 Ponies 7
Std of Schlg: General Purpose
Hack – Varied
Ev Classes
Courses: In summer/Hol Inst
Facilities: Out Man: 41 x 20m/Jmp Pd/CC Fences/Refresh/WC/Chng Rm/Car Park
Specialities: Teaching Children
Exclusions: No hiring for hunting/No YTS
Location: 2 miles South of Midhurst

HANGLETON FARM LIVERY YARD
Hangleton Lane, Ferring, Worthing, West Sussex, BN12 6PP
Tel: 0903 40696/40352
Proprietor: C K Ellis Esq
Manager & Chief Inst: Miss A Todd (BHSAI)
YTS Managing Agent
Other Staff: 1 (BHSII) P/T
Livery Yard & Facility Centre
Livery: Full/School
Ev Classes
Courses: Training for NVQ/Stages I& II
Facilities: Out Man: 60 x 30m* Fl Lit/Jmpg Pd*/Lec Rm – Seating – 15/Library/Vis Aids/Video/Wash Rm/WC/Car Park
Accom: House – 16 – single Rms
Catering: Full
Specialities: Livery Service/Training for NVQ & Stages I & II
Exclusions: No Horses for Hire

NALDRETTS FARM
Bucks Green, Nr Horsham, West Sussex, RH12 3BU
Tel: Rudgwick (040 372) 2403
Proprietor & Chief Inst: Miss V D Millwood
Training Centre & Livery Yard
Av No: Horses 1 Ponies 2
Std of Schlg: General Purpose
Livery: Full/Grass/Hunter/Break/School
Facilities: Cov Sch: 12 x 18m*/Out Man:50m x 25m*/Lec Rm/WC/Wash Rm/Car Park
Accom: 4 – Guest House Catering: Full
Specialities: Schooling & preparing for the Show Ring/Side Saddle/Livery/Dressage/Instruction on own horse
Exclusions: No hiring for hacking
Location: Off A281 btwn Bucks Green/Billinghurst

WEST SUSSEX COLLEGE OF AGRICULTURE & HORTICULTURE
Brinsbury, North Heath, Pulborough, West Sussex, RH20 1DL
Tel: 079 82 3832/5222
Principal: E Hoyland Esq
Head of Department & Chief Inst: Mrs A Galloway (BHSI(T & SM))
Other Staff: 1 (BHSAI) 2 BHSI
Instruction in Riding and Jumping & Students to BHSII Exam
Av No: Horses 33 Ponies – Specialist Horses: 1 M Drg
Std of Schlg: General Purpose Std of Specialist Schlg: Sh Jmpg – Novice School
Courses: up to BHSAI Exam/YTS – 25 taken
Facilities: Out Man: 60 x 20m/Cov Sch: 42.7 x 2 4.5m/Lec Rm/Club Rm/Vis Aids/Film Projector/Library/Refreshments/Wash Rm/WC/Showers/Changing Rm/Car park
Accom: Single Rms/House – 60
Catering: Full
Specialities: Career Student Training/YTS Courses/Private Lessons
Exclusions: No Casual Hire
Location: On A29 btwn Billinghurst & Pulborough

ZARA STUD AND TRAINING CENTRE
Highleigh Road, Sidlesham, Chichester, Sussex, PO20 7NR
Tel: Sidlesham (024356) 641/662
Proprietors: Mr & Mrs P Brown
Chief Inst: Mrs P Brown (BHSAI) **Other Staff:** 1 (BHSAI)
Instruction in Riding and Jumping
Av No: Horses 6 Ponies 1
Std of Schlg: General Purpose
Livery: Full/DIY/Break/School/Hack – Beach for experienced riders
Ev Classes
Courses: Resid/YTS
Facilities: Cov Sch: 34m x 26m* Fl Lit Gly 100/Out Man: 25 x49m*/Jmp Pd/Sh Jmps/CC Fences/WC/Car Park
Accom: House 8 + Caravan Catering: Full
Specialities: Convalescent Treatment service/Western Style Riding/Riding Instruction/Physiotherapy
Exclusions: Beach Rides for Experienced Riders only
Location: 6 miles South Chichester off B 2145

Riding in the South

BERKSHIRE ♦ BUCKINGHAMSHIRE ♦ HAMPSHIRE ♦ ISLE OF WIGHT ♦ OXFORDSHIRE

BERKSHIRE

BEARWOOD RIDING CENTRE
Bear Wood, Sindlesham, Wokingham, Berkshire, RG11 5GB
Tel: 0734 760010/781865/7842208
Proprietor: The Directors of Bearwood Mariner Enterprises (Sir David Hillwood)
Secretary: Mr Manzi
Chief Inst: Miss A Rolfe (BHSAI) **Other Staff:** 3 (BHSAI) P/T
Instruction in Riding and Jumping & Students to BHSAI Exam
Av No: Horses 20 Ponies 15
Std of Schlg: General Purpose
Livery: Full/Part/Grass/Hack – Woodland/Farmland
Ev Classes
Courses: YT 1
Facilities: Cov Sch:40m x 20m*/Gly 60/ Out Man: 40 m x 20m*/Fl Lit/Sh Jmps/ Jmp Pd/Lec Rm/Vis Aids/W. C/H & C/ Wait Rm/Car Park
Specialities: General Instruction/ Individual Tuition/P C Activities/Schooling
Exclusions: All rides supervised
Location: On B3030 Btwen Arbourfield & Sindlesham

BRADFIELD RIDING CENTRE
The Maltings, Bradfield, Berkshire
Tel: Bradfield (0734) 744522
Proprietor: Mrs J White (BHSAI)
Instruction in Riding and Jumping
Av No: Horses 8 Ponies 12
Std of Schlg: General Purpose
Livery: Full/Part/Grass/DIY/School/ Break/Hunt/Hack – Parkland
Courses: YT 2/3
Facilities: Cov Sch: 26m x 20m */Out Man: 100m x 50 m*/Sh Jmps/Refresh/ Wash Rm/WC/Chng Rm/Car Park
Specialities: General Instruction/Livery/Pony Club Activities
Exclusions: No casual hiring

CANE END STABLES LTD
Cane End, Nr Reading, Berkshire, RG4 9HH
Tel: Kidmore End (0734) 724195
Proprietors: Mr & Mrs L E Hordern
Chief Inst: Miss C Bertram (BHSII)
Other Staff: 1 (BHSAI) 2 (BHSII) (BHSI SM & T)
Instruction in Riding and Jumping & Students to BHSII Exam
Av No: Horses 10 Ponies 10
Std of Schlg: General Purpose
Livery: Full/Part/Break/School
Courses: Wkg Students/YT 2
Facilities: Out Man: 37m x 23m*/Jmp Pd/Sh Jmps*/CC Course/Lec Rm/Club Room/Vis Aids/WC/Wash Rm/Chng Rm/ Car Park
Specialities: General Instruction/ Student Training/Competition livery
Exclusions: No casual hiring
Location: On A4074 Btwn Crowmarsh & Reading

CLOUD STABLES (SCHOOL OF EQUITATION)
Church Lane, Arborfield, Reading, Berkshire, RG2 9JA
Tel: Arborfield Cross (0734) 760238
Proprietors: Mr & Mrs W A Patrick
Chief Inst: Miss Kim Knightley (BHSII(T)) **Other Staff:** 2 (BHSAI) 1 (BHSII)
Instruction in Riding and Jumping & Students to BHSAI Exam
Av No: Horses 12 Ponies 4
Std of Schlg: General Purpose
Livery: Full/Part/Break/School
Ev Classes
Courses: Wkg Students
Facilities: Cov Sch: 30 x 26m Gly 60/ Cov Sch: 25 x 12m/Out Man: 37 x 18m Fl Lit/Jmp Pd/CC Fences/Vis Aids/Lec Rm/Refresh/Rest Rm/WC/Showers/Chng Rm/Car Park

Specialities: Children/Adults basic equitation/RDA
Exclusions: No casual hire/No YT
Location: Turning off A327 Btwn Shinfield & Arbourfield Cross

GREAT OAKS RIDING & LIVERY CENTRE
Great Oaks Farm, Crouch Lane, Winkfield, Berkshire
Tel: 0344 885910
Proprietor: Mrs N Waddell
Manager & Chief Inst: Miss L Standford (BHSII(T)) **Other Staff:** 1 (BHSAI) P/T
Instruction in Riding and Jumping
Av No: Horses 12 Ponies 7
Std of Schlg: General Purpose Std of Specialist Schlg: Sh Jmpg Grade C
Livery: Full/Part/School/Hack – Windsor Park Forest
Ev Classes
Courses: Wkg Pupils/Childrens
Facilities: Out Man: 44 x 20m Fl Lit/ Jmp Pd/Refreshments/WC/Car Park
Specialities: General Instruction/ Hacking/Livery/Children's Courses
Exclusion: No casual hire/Weight limit 14 stone
Location: Off B3022 btwn Ascot & Windsor

HALL PLACE RIDING STABLES
Little Heath Road, Tilehurst, Reading, Berkshire, RG3 5TX
Tel: Reading (0734) 426938
Proprietors: Mr & Mrs P Vincent
Manager: Miss S Scanlon (BHSAI)
Other Staff: 1 (BHSAI) P/T
Instruction in Riding and Jumping
Av No: Horses 15 Ponies 15
Std of Schlg: General Purpose Break/School/Hack – Woodland/Bridle paths
Ev Classes
Courses: Inst
Facilities: Cov Sch:34 x 18m Gly 50* Fl Lit/Out Man: 46 x 46m/Jmp Pd/Sh Jmps/ CC Course/Tack Shop/WC/Car Park
Specialities: RDA/General Instruction/ Hack – 1/2 Day Rides/Shows
Exclusions: No casual hiring
Location: Junc 12 M4 btwn Reading & Pangbourne

MAYS FEEDS
Ryeish Green, Three Mile Cross, Reading, Berkshire
Tel: 0734 883366/883670
Proprietors: Mr & Mrs Siviter & Mr & Mrs Clarke
Other Staff: 2 F/T & 2 P/T
D I Y Livery Yard
Livery: Grass/DIY
Facilities: Changing Rm/Car Park
Specialities: D I Y Livery
Exclusions: No riding instruction is given
Location: Btwn Three Mile Cross & Ryeish Green

PINNOCKS WOOD STABLES
Burchetts Green, Maidenhead, Berkshire
Tel: Littlewick Green (062882) 2031
Proprietor: Mrs Gilbert (BHSII)
Other Staff: 4 (BHSAI)
Training & Livery Centre
Av No: Horses – Ponies -
Std of Schlg: General Purpose Std of Specialist Horse: Drg – Med
Livery: Full/Break/School
Courses: Wkg Students/YT – 3
Facilities: Cov Sch: 40 x 18m Gly 150 Fl Lit*/Out Man: 55m x 45m*/Jmp Pd/Sh Jmps/CC Fences/Lec Rm/Vis Aids/ WC/Showers/Wash Rm/Car Park
Specialities: Student courses/Eventing/ Preparing for all aspects of showing & competitions/Livery
Location: 0.5 mile off A4 at Burchetts Green

THE SPANISH BIT RIDING SCHOOL AND LIVERY
Elm Farm, Boveney Road, Dorney Common, Nr Windsor, Berkshire, SL4 6QD
Tel: Burnham (0628) 661275
Proprietor: Mrs K Hamilton (FBHS)
Chief Inst: Miss L Collier (BHSAI) **Other Staff:** 1 (BHSII) 4 (BHSAI) 1 (BHSII) P/T
Instruction in Riding and Jumping & Students to BHSI Exam
Av No: Horses 12 Ponies 16
Std of Schlg: General Purpose Std of Specialist Schlg: Drg – Adv
Livery: Full/School/Hack – Common Land/Bridle paths/Private Escorted Hacks to Windsor Great Park
Ev Classes
Courses: Hol Inst/Wkg Pupils/ Childrens
Facilities: Cov Sch: 40m x 20m* Fl Lit Gly 150/Ou t Man: 40m x 30m* Fl Lit/ Jmp Pd/Sh Jmps*/Refresh/WC/Wash Rm/Chng Rm/Wait Rm/Car Park
Accom: Staff/Students only
Specialities: General Instruction/Livery Service/H acking/Advanced Dressage & Competition Training/T raining on own horse

Exclusions: No unescorted rides/No YT/No horses for hire
Location: 2 miles from M4 Junc 7

WOKINGHAM EQUESTRIAN CENTRE
Chapel Green House, Chapel Green, Wokingham, Berkshire, RG11 3ER
Tel: (0734) 775549
Proprietor: Mrs A C Adams
Chief Inst: Mrs Lindsay – Watts (BHSII)
Instruction in Riding and Jumping
Av No: Horses 2 Ponies 3
Std of Schlg: General Purpose
Livery: Full/Part/Grass/Hack – Forestry/Farmland
Facilities: Out Man:40m x 20m/Jmp Pd/Sh Jmps/CC Fences 90/Car Park
Specialities: Event Training
Exclusions: No YT
Location: 1 mile from Town Centre Off A321

BUCKINGHAMSHIRE

ASHLEY GREEN RIDING CENTRE
Flamstead Farm, Ashley Green, Nr Chesham, Buckinghamshire
Tel: 0494 791362/772088
Proprietor: C F Robbins – Brown Esq
Chief Inst: Miss D Spears **Other Staff:** 2 (BHSAI)
Instruction in Riding and Jumping
Av no Horses: 12 Ponies 8
Std of Schlg: General Purpose
Livery: Full/Part/Grass
Courses: Childrens Holiday Inst
Facilities: Cov Sch: 35 x 24m Gly/Sh Jmps*/Wash Rm/WC/Car Park
Specialities: Children's Inst – Holiday Courses/Livery/Horse Care
Exclusions: No casual hire/No children under 6 taken
Location: On A416 btwn Chesham/Berkhamsted

BRAWLINGS FARM RIDING CENTRE
Brawlings Lane, Horn Hill, Chalfont St Peter, Buckinghamshire, SL9 0RE
Tel: Chalfont St Giles (02407) 2132
Proprietor: Mrs J Edwards (BHSII)
Chief Inst: Mr T Elvin (BHSAI) **Other Staff:** 3 (BHSAI) 1 (BHSII) 3 (BHSII)P/T
Instruction in Riding and Jumping & Students to BHSAI Exam
Av No: Horses 20 Ponies 15
Std of Schlg: General Purpose
Livery: Full/Part/Break/School/Hack – suburban
Ev Classes
Courses: Hol Inst/Wkg Students
Facilities: Cov Sch: 42 x 20m Gly 100* Fl Lit/2 Out Mans: 37 x 18m & 60 x 20m*/Jmp Pd/Sh Jmps/CC Fences*/Wash Rm/WC/Car Park
Specialities: General Instruction/Livery/Schooling/Breaking/RDA/Holiday courses
Exclusions: No Casual Hiring
Location: Btwn Chalfont St Peter/Rickmansworth

FINMERE EQUESTRIAN CENTRE
Town Farm, Finmere, Buckingham, MK18 4AS
Tel: Finmere (02804) 7891
Proprietor: Mr D R Boyd
Chief Inst: Miss A Howes (BHSAI)
Other Staff: 1 (BHSAI)
Instruction in Riding and Jumping
Av No: Horses 4 Ponies 5
Std of Schlg: General Purpose
Livery: Full/Part/Grass/DIY/School/Break/Hack – Bridle paths
Ev Classes
Courses: Hol Inst/YT: 2
Facilities: Cov Sch:18 x 12m*/Out Man: 40m x 20m* Fl Lit/Jmp Pd/Sh Jmps/WC/Wash Rm/Refresh/Tack Shop/Car Park
Specialities: General Instruction/Livery Service/Hacking
Exclusions: All riding escorted
Location: Off A417 Centre of Village

HARTWELL RIDING STABLES
Oxford Road, Aylesbury, Buckinghamshire, HP17 8QR
Tel: Aylesbury (0296) 748641
Proprietor: Miss M L Herring (BHSAI)
Other Staff: 1 (BHSAI)
Instruction in Riding and Jumping
Av No: Horses 11 Ponies 16
Std of Schlg: General Purpose
Livery: Part/Grass/Break/School/Hack
Ev Classes
Courses: Inst Hol/YT 1
Facilities: 2 Out Mans:40m x 20m* Fl Lit & 40 x 20m/Jmp Pd/Sh Jmps/CC Fences/Rest Rm/Refresh/WC/Wash Rm/Car Park
Specialities: Teaching very young children/Riding Club/RDA
Exclusions: No unaccompanied riding
Location: On A418 Between Aylesbury & Oxford

LOUGHTON MANOR EQUESTRIAN CENTRE
Redland Drive, Childs Way, Loughton, Milton Keynes, Buckinghamshire, MK5 8AZ
Tel: Milton Keynes (0908) 666434

Proprietor: Mr D R Benson
YT Managing Agent
Chief Inst: Ms Sabrina Benson (BHSI)
Other Staff: 4 (BHSAI) 1 (BHSII) 1 (BHSI)
Instruction in Riding and Jumping & Students to BHSII Exam
Av No: Horses 17 Ponies 16 Specialist Horse: Dressage 'A'
Std of Schlg: General Purpose
Livery: Full/Part/Break/School
Ev Classes
Courses: Resid Inst Hol/Wkg Students/ Fee Paying Students
Facilities: Cov Sch:28 x 15m Gly Fl Lit/ Out Man:55 m x 20m Fl Lit/Jmp Pd Fl Lit/ Sh Jmps 25/CC Course/Lec Rm/Vis Aids/Video lessons/Wash Rm/Club Rm/WC/Change Rm/Shop/Car Park
Accom: 10 – House Catering: Part/Self
Specialities: General instruction/Event and Show Jumping instruction/ Children's riding holidays/RDA/ Dressage/YT Managing Agent
Exclusions: No casual hiring
Location: Junc 14 M1 off Childs Way

RADNAGE HOUSE RIDING SCHOOL
Radnage House, Green End Road, Radnage, Buckinghamshire, HP14 4BZ
Tel: 0494 483268
Proprietor: Mrs S M Pitt
Chief Inst: Miss S M Pilbeam (BHSII)
Other Staff: 2 (BHSII) 3 (BHSAI) 2 (BHSI) P/T
Instruction in Riding and Jumping
Av No: Horses 10 Ponies -
Std of Schlg: Advanced/General Purpose/Drg
Livery: Full/Part/Hunter/Break/ School/Hack
Ev Classes
Courses: Pre-hunting/specialist
Facilities: Cov Sch: 42 x 20m Gly/Out Man: 46 x 18m/Jmp Pd Seats/Sh Jmps/ CC Fences/CC Course/Lec Rm/Vis Aids/WC/Chng Rm/Car Park
Specialities: Pre-hunting/Specialist courses/Dressage & Horse Trials training
Exclusions: Weight limit 13 stone/No unescorted Hacking/No YT
Location: 3 miles from Junc 5 M40

SHANA RIDING SCHOOL LTD
Walters Ash, Nr High Wycombe, Buckinghamshire, HP14 4UZ
Tel: Naphill (024024) 2200
Proprietors: Mr R Huggard
Chief Inst/Manager: Miss J Sumers (BHSAI) **Other Staff:** 2 (BHSAI) P/T 1 (BHSII)
Instruction in Riding and Jumping
Av No: Horses 18 Ponies 9
Std of Schlg: General Purpose
Livery: Full/Working/Break/School/Hack – National Trust Land/Bridle Tracks
Ev Classes
Courses: Hol Inst/YT
Facilities: 2 Cov Schs: 46 x 29m* Fl Lit & 29 x 22m/Jmp Pd 25 x 25m/Sh Jmps 20/CC Fences 10/Lec Rm/Vis Aids/Club Rm/Refresh/WC/Showers/Chng Rm/Wait Rm/Car Park/Video/Saddlery Shop
Accom: House – Students – 6 Catering: Self
Specialities: General Instruction/ Shows/Livery
Exclusions: No hiring for hunting/No unaccompanied hacking
Location: Off A4010 adjacent Bradenham/ Walters Ash

SNOWBALL FARM RIDING AND LIVERY YARD LIMITED
Dorney Wood Road, Burnham, Buckinghamshire
Tel: Burnham (0628) 666222
Proprietor: Mrs S Western-Kaye
Chief Inst: Miss P Jones (BHSII) **Other Staff:** 1 (BHSII) 2 (BHSAI)
Instruction in Riding and Jumping & Students to BHSAI Exam
Av No: Horses 22 Ponies 15
Std of Schlg: General Purpose
Livery: Full/Grass/Break/School/Hack – Farmland/Bridle paths
Ev Classes
Courses: Hol Inst/Wkg Students
Facilities: Cov Sch:49 x 25m* Fl Lit/ Cov Sch:55 x 25m*/Out Man: 92 x 46m* Fl Lit/Jmp Pd/Sh Jmps/CC Course/ Rest Rm/WC/Wash Rm/Car Park
Accom: 20 – Farmhouses/Flat/Mobile Home Catering: Full
Specialities: Competition & Exam Training/Livery/Hacking
Exclusions: No Children under 7 years No riders over 13.5 stones/No YTS taken
Location: Between M4 Junc 7 & M40 Junc 2 north of Burnham

STOWE RIDINGS LTD
Black Pit Farm, Silverstone Road, Stowe, Buckingham, Bucks, MK18 5LJ
Tel: 0280 812363/823292
Proprietors: Mr & Mrs P Wheeler
Other Staff: 1 (BHSI) Visiting 1 (BHSAI)
Instruction in Riding and Jumping & Students to BHSI Exam
Av No: Horses 2 Ponies 1 Std of Specialist Horses: 2 Drg – Med/Adv
Std of Schlg: General Purpose Std of Specialist Schlg: Drg – Adv/HT INT.

Livery: Full/Part/Hunter/School/Break
Ev Classes
Courses: Up to & including (BHSI) Exam/Wkg Students – 6
Facilities: Cov Sch: 67 X 30/Gly -450/2 Out Mans: 40 x 20m* & 60 x 40M F/L/ WC/Jmp Pd/Show Jumps
Accom: Shared Room/House 6 Catering: Full
Specialities: Student & Competition Training/Livery all types/Good riding country/Off Road
Exclusions: No casual hire

HAMPSHIRE

ARNISS RIDING & LIVERY STABLES

Godshill, Fordingbridge, Hampshire
Tel: Fordingbridge (0425) 54114
Proprietor: Sandy Balls Estate
Manager & Chief Inst: Miss A Finn (BHSAI)
Instruction in Riding and Jumping
Av No: Horses 10 Ponies 10
Std of Schlg: General Purpose
Livery: Full/Grass/Break/School/Hack – New Forest
Evening Lessons
Courses: Hol Inst/YT taken
Facilities: Out Man: 20m x 40m* Seats Fl Lit/Jmp Pd/Sh Jmps/WC /Car Park
Specialities: Instruction in riding & jumping/Breaking/Schooling/Livery/RDA
Exclusions: No casual hire
Location: On B3078 Btwn Fordingbridge & Cadnam

BROADLANDS RIDING CENTRE

Broadlands, Medstead, Nr Alton, Hampshire, GU34 5PX
Tel: Alton (0420) 63382
Proprietor: Mrs S M Stratford (BHSAI)
Instruction in Riding and Jumping
Av No: Horses 4 Ponies 6
Std of Schlg: General Purpose
Livery: Full/Break/School
Courses: Inst Hol/YT – 1
Facilities: Cov Sch:32 x 18m* Fl Lit/Out Man/Sh Jmps/CC Fences/Lec Rm/Vis Aids/WC/Wash Rm/Chng Rm/Car park
Specialities: General Instruction/ Childrens holiday courses/RDA
Exclusions: No casual hire

BROCKS FARM EQUITATION LIVERY & TRAINING CENTRE

Brocks Farm, Longstock, Stockbridge, Hampshire, SO20 6EE
Tel: 0264 810090
Proprietors: Mrs J & The Misses P & L Burtenshaw
Chief Inst: Mrs A Teggin (BHSII) **Other Staff:** 1 (BHSII) 1 (BHSAI)
Instruction in Riding and Jumping & Students to BHSAI Exam
Av No: Horses 4 Ponies 8 Specialist Horses: 2 Med & 1 Adv Drg/3 Nov Sh Jmpers
Std of Schlg: General Purpose Std of Specialist Schlg: Drg – Novice/Sh Jmpg – Grade C
Livery: Full/Grass/Hunter/School
Ev Classes
Courses: Up to & including (BHSAI) Exam/YT – 2
Facilities: Out Man: 60 x 20m* Fl Lit/12 Schlg Basic CC Fences/Jmp Pd*/ Refreshments/WC/Car Park
Specialities: Instruction for Children & Novice Adults/Dressage/Livery/School for Eventing
Exclusions: No Hacking/No casual hire

BURLEY VILLA SCHOOL OF RIDING

Bashley Common Road, New Milton, Hampshire
Tel: New Milton (0425) 610278
Proprietor & Chief Inst: Miss Carter-Pennington
Manager: Mr P Cramer **Other Staff:** 2 (BHSAI)
Instruction in Riding and Jumping
Av No: Horses 10 Ponies 10 Specialist Horses: Sh Jmp Grade C
Std of Schlg: General Purpose
Livery: Full/Part/DIY/Break/School/Hack – New Forest
Ev Classes
Courses: Hol Inst/YT taken
Facilities: Cov Sch: 55 x 25m Gly* Fl Lit/Out Man: 49 x 18m* Fl Lit & 40 x 20m Fl Lit/Jmp pd/Sh Jmps/CC Fences/Vis Aids/Lec Rm/Refresh/Wash Rm/Club Rm/Lic Bar/Showers/WC/Car Park
Accom: Hotel/Dormitory 10 Catering – Full
Specialities: General instruction/Show jumping/Hacking/Regular Shows
Exclusions: No unescorted riding
Location: On B3058 north of New Milton

CATHERSTON STUD & EQUESTRIAN CENTRE

Black Knoll House, Brockenhurst, Hampshire, SO42 7QE
Tel: Lymington (0590) 22027
Fax: 0590 23805
Proprietor: A G Loriston-Clarke Esq
Chief Consultant: Mrs A Loriston-Clarke FBHS NPS Diploma

Other Staff: 1 (BHSI) 1 (BHSII) 2 (BHSAI)
Instruction in Riding and Jumping & Students to all BHS Exams including Fellowship
Av No: Horses 10 Specialist Horses: Drg Adv
Std of Schlg: General Purpose
Livery: Full/Break/School
Courses: Resid/Short intensive courses
Facilities: Cov Sch: 60m x 20m Gly 500 Fl Lit/Out Man: 60m x20m Seats 600 Fl Lit/Jmp Pd 120m x 40m/Sh Jmps 20 prs/Lec Rm/Vis Aids/Video/Rest Rm/WC/Wash Rm/Wait Rm
Accom: 10 – Shared rooms Catering: Self or Full Board
Specialities: Courses in Stud Management/All BHS Examinations/Advanced Dressage/Schooling/Side saddle/Livery
Exclusions: No horses for hire

CAUSEWAY HOUSE STABLES
Causeway House, The Causeway, Petersfield, Hampshire, GU31 4LW
Tel: Petersfield (0730) 66131
Proprietor: Mr J N Day
Chief Inst: Miss S Piper **Other Staff:** 2 (BHSAI) P/T
Instruction in Riding and Jumping
Av No Horses 4 Ponies 6
Std of Schlg: General Purpose
Livery: Part
Facilities: Cov Sch: 28 x 14m* Gly/Out Man: 40 x 20m/CC Fences/Jmp Pd/Sh Jmps/Tack Shop/Club Rm/Refreshments/Wash Rm/WC/Wait Rm/Car Park
Specialities: General Instruction/Children's Holiday Camp
Exclusions: No casual hiring
Location: Off A3 btwn Petersfield & Portsmouth

DECOY POND RIDING & LIVERY STABLES
Decoy Pond Farm, Beaulieu Road, Beaulieu, Brockenhurst, Hampshire, SO4 7YQ
Tel: Ashurst (042129) 2652
Proprietor: D N Horton (BHSAI)
Chief Inst: Mrs J M Horton (BHSII)
Instruction in Riding and Jumping
Av No: Horses 1 Ponies 1
Std of Schlg: General Purpose
Livery: Full/DIY/Holiday/Grass
Ev Classes
Facilities: Out Man: 28 x 65m Fl Lit/Jmp Pd/Sh Jmps/CC Course/CC Fences
Specialities: Livery Service including Holiday Se rvice/Facilities for hire
Exclusions: All rides escorted
Location: Off B3056 Btwn Lyndhurst & Beaulieu

FIR TREE EQUESTRIAN CENTRE
Fir Tree Farm, Ogdens, Fordingbridge, Hampshire, SP6 2PY
Tel: (0425) 654744
Proprietors: Mrs Gail Mosley (BHSII) & Mr Adrian Mosley
Other Staff: 1 (BHSII) 1 (BHSAI)
Instruction in Riding and Jumping
Av No: Horses 15 Ponies 10
Std of Schlg: General Purpose
Livery: Full/Part/School/Break/Hack – Forest
Ev Classes (Summer only)
Courses: Holiday Courses
Facilities: Out Man: 60m x 20m*/CC Fences 4/Wash Rm/WC/Car Park
Accom: 8 – House Catering: Full
Specialities: General Instruction Adult & Children/Regular Shows/Dressage Clinics/Hacking/Livery/Riding Holidays/Side Saddle
Exclusions: No Casual Hire

FLANDERS FARM RIDING CENTRE
Silver Street, Hordle, Lymington, Hampshire, SO41 6DF
Tel: Lymington (0590) 682207
Proprietor: Mrs M Rogers
Chief Inst: Miss A Carter (BHSII) **Other Staff:** 1 (BHSII) 2 (BHSAI)
Instruction in Riding and Jumping & Students to BHSAI Exam
Av No: Horses 4 Ponies 11
Std of Schlg: General Purpose
Livery: Full/Part/DIY/Break/School/Hunt/Hack – New Forest/Common Land
Ev Classes
Courses: Resid Inst Hol/Wkg Students/YT – 2
Facilities: Cov Sch:43 x 18m* Fl Lit/Jmp Pd*/Sh Jmps*/CC Course*/Lec Rm/Vis Aids/Video/WC/Refresh/Club Rm/Changing Rm/Car Park
Accom: Local Hotel Catering: Full
Specialities: Caravan & Camping Club Site/Riding Holidays/General Instruction/Shows
Location: Btwn Lymington & New Milton

FOWLERS FARM
Vernham Street, Nr Andover, Hampshire, SP11 0EL
Tel: Linkenholt (026487) 244
Proprietor: Mr & Mrs G Humphrey
Instruction in Riding and Jumping & Students to BHSAI Exam

Av No: Horses 4 Ponies 2
Std of Schlg: General Purpose
Livery: Full/Part/Grass/Hunter/School/Break
Courses: Hol with own horses only
Facilities: Cov Sch: 37 x 18m* Fl Lit/CC Fences 12/SchoolingFences/Jmp Pd/All Weather Gallop*/Lec Rm/Vis Aids/WC/Chng Rm/Car Park
Accom: 6 – House Catering – Full
Specialities: Livery service/Schooling/Showing/Accommodation for horses in transit/Students courses/Reg stallion kept/Holiday courses/Stud/Training
Exclusions: No YT owing to conditions of courses

GLENEAGLE EQUESTRIAN CENTRE
Allington Lane, West End, Southampton, Hampshire, S03 3HQ
Tel: Southampton (0703) 473164
Proprietor: Mrs E H Walsh
Chief Inst: Mrs D Day (BHSAI) **Other Staff:** 1 (BHSAI) 2 (BHSII) 1 (BHSII(SM))
Instruction in Riding and Jumping
Av No: Horses 15 Ponies 15
Std of Schlg: General Purpose
Livery: Full/Part/DIY/Hunter/School/Break/Hack – Forestry/Bridle paths
Ev Classes in Summer
Courses: YT 2
Facilities: 2 Out Mans:37 x 18m*/66 x 22m*/Jmp Pd/Sh Jmps/CC Fences/WC/Refresh/Car Park
Accom: 2 – House + Camping Hols Catering: Full
Specialities: General instruction in riding and jumping/Hacking/School contract work/RDA/Dealing
Location: Off old A27 btwn West End & Durley

HARROWAY HOUSE
Penton Mewsey, Andover, Hampshire, SP11 0RA
Tel: Weyhill (026 477) 2295
Proprietor: Mrs E C Skelton IOH NPS Dip
Chief Inst: Miss H Shearer **Other Staff:** 1 (BHSAI) 1 (BHSII)
Instruction in Riding and Jumping & Students to BHSAI Exam
Av No: Horses 10 Ponies 19
Std of Schlg: General Purpose Std of Specialist Schlg: Drg – Elem/H T – Int/Sh Jmp – B
Livery: Full/Grass/Hunter/Break/School/Hack – Woods/Downland
Ev Classes
Courses: Stage I/II & III
Facilities: Cov Sch: 605 sq m Gly 50/Jmp Pd/Sh Jmps/CC Fences/WC/Car Park
Accom: 6 – Shared rooms Catering: Family
Specialities: Children's instructional riding holidays/Side saddle instruction

HORSESHOE CENTRE FOR HANDICAPPED RIDERS
Picketts Hill, Headley, Nr Borden, Hampshire, GU35 8TB
Tel: Headley Down (0428) 713858
Proprietors: Mr & Mrs C W Turner (BHSAI)
Other Staff: 2 (BHSAI) 1 FBHS – Visiting
Instruction in Riding and Jumping
Av No: Horses 1 Ponies 14
Std of Schlg: General Purpose
Livery: Full/Hack – Woodlands/Common
Ev Classes
Courses: YT taken
Facilities: Cov Sch: 43 x 22m* Fl Lit/Jmp Pd/Sh Jmps*/CC Course/Refresh/WC/Car Park
Accom: 5 – House Catering: Full
Specialities: Riding Holidays/RDA/Children`s Instruction
Exclusions: No casual hire
Location: Off A325 signed Picketts Hill

MERRIE STUD RIDING SCHOOL
Merrie Stud, Corhampton, Southampton, Hampshire, SO3 1NB
Tel: Droxford (0489) 877564
Proprietor: Mrs J D N Shaw (BHSAI) NPS Dip
Chief Inst: Mrs Nelson (BHSI) P/T
Other Staff: 1 (BHSII) P/T
Instruction in Riding and Jumping & Students to BHSAI Exam
Av No: Horses 1 Ponies 9
Std of Schlg: General Purpose
Livery: Full/Break/School/Hack/Trek – Varied
Ev Classes
Courses: Wkg Students/YT – 1
Facilities: Cov Sch: 9 x 12m Fl Lit/Out Man:40m x 20m* Fl Lit/Sh Jmps 8/CC Course/CC Fences/Rest Rm/WC
Accom: 4 – House Catering: Full
Specialities: Nervous children/Beginners/Lightweight adults/Stud courses
Exclusions: No casual hire
Location: Btwn Corhampton & Bishops Waltham

THE NAVAL RIDING CENTRE
H M S Dryad, Southwick, Nr Fareham, Hampshire, PO17 6EJ
Tel: 0705 379974/210522 Ext 4455/6
Proprietor: Commander B W Holden-Crawfurd
Chief Inst: Mr A Noordijk (BHSI) **Other Staff:** 2 (BHSAI) 1 (BHSII(T))
Instruction in Riding and Jumping & Students to BHSI Exam
Av No: Horses 27 Ponies 13
Std of Schlg: General Purpose
Livery: Full/Part/School/Break/Hack – Estate
Ev Classes
Courses: Wkg Students/YT – 5
Facilities: Cov Schs: 20m x 60m */20m x 40m/Out Man: 65m x 55m*Fl Lit/CC Fences*/Jmp Pd*/Lec Rm*/Club Rm*/Vis Aids*/Refresh/Wash Rm/WC/Chng Rm/Bar/Car Park
Specialities: General Instruction/Shows/Career Students to BHSII Level/RDA/Riding Club
Exclusions: No Casual Hire
Location: Btwn Cosham & Wickham

NEW PARK MANOR HOTEL & STABLES
Lyndhurst Road, Brockenhurst, Hampshire
Tel: 0590 23467
Director: Mr C Cregg
Manageress: Miss E Bell (BHSAI)
Other Staff: 1 (FBHS) P/T
Instruction in Riding and Jumping
Av No: Horses 8 Ponies -
Std of Schlg: General Purpose
Livery: Full/Part/DIY/Grass/Hack/Trek – New Forest
Courses: Hol Res Inst
Facilities: Jmp Pd/Sh Jmps/Lic Bar/WC/Car Park
Accom: Hotel or Rooms/Camp Site
Specialities: Hacking and riding holidays/General Instruction
Exclusions: All Riding Escorted/No YT
Location: On A337 Btwn Brockenhurst & Lyndurst

RIDGEWAY LIVERY STABLES
Lower Baybridge Lane, Owslebury, Winchester, Hampshire
Tel: 0962 74601
Proprietor: W T Waygood Esq (BHSAI)
Livery Yard & Holiday Livery Service
Livery: Part/DIY
Facilities: Out Man: 40 x 30m* Fl Lit/Refreshments/WC/Wash Rm/Changing Rm/Car Park
Accom: Shared Rms – Caravan/House – 4 Catering Self
Specialities: DIY & Part Livery/Holiday Livery/Tuition on own horse
Exclusions: No Horses for hire

RUSSELL STABLES
Black Farm, Gatershill, West End, Southampton, Hampshire
Tel: 0703 473693
Proprietor: Mrs C Boulton (BHSI(SM))
Chief Inst: Ms W Gooch (BHSAI) **Other Staff:** 2 (BHSAI) 2 (BHSII) P/T
Basic Instruction in Riding and Jumping
Av No: Horses 10 Ponies 15
Std of Schlg: General Purpose
Livery: Full/Part/DIY/School/Break/Hack – Fields
Ev Classes
Courses: Hol Inst/YT 2
Facilities: Out Man:23 x 23m* + 22 x 27m seats Fl Lit/CC Fences/Jmp Pd/Sh Jmps*/Lec Rm/WC/Chng Rm/Refresh/Wait Rm/Car Park
Specialities: Beginner adults/Pony Club participation/Breaking & Schooling
Exclusions: All rides escorted
Location: On A27 btwn Swaythling/West End

RYCROFT SCHOOL OF EQUITATION
New Mill Lane, Eversley, Hampshire, RG27 0RA
Tel: Eversley (0734) 732761
Proprietors: Mr & Mrs W Hundley
Chief Inst: Miss B Hill (BHSII) **Other Staff:** 3 (BHSAI) 2 (BHSII) 1 (BHSI) P/T
Instruction in Riding and Jumping & Students to BHSII Exam
Av No: Horses 25 Ponies 12
Std of Schlg: General Purpose
Livery: Full/Wkg/School/Hunt/Hack – Forestry/Common
Ev Classes
Courses: Inst Hol/YT – 2
Facilities: Cov Sch:50 x 25m/Out Man: (2) 40 x 40m & 60 x 40m Fl Lit/Jmp Pd/CC Fences/WC/Riding Clothes Shop/Car Park
Specialities: Children/Adults/Hacking/Lunch Rides/General Instruction
Exclusions: No casual hire
Location: Off A327 btwn Eversley & Yately

SCHOOL FARM TRAINING CENTRE
School Farm, 1 Canefield Cottage, Romsey Road, Lockerley, Nr Romsey, Hampshire SO5 0JA
Tel: Lockerley (0794) 41196

Proprietors: Mr Aart Noordijk (BHSI) & Mrs Tessa Noordijk (BHSI)
Manager & Chief Inst: Mrs Tessa Noordijk BHSI **Other Staff:** 1 (BHSI) 1 (BHSII) 1 (BHSAI)
Livery and Training up to BHSI Exam
Av No: Horses – Ponies -
Std of Schlg: General Purpose Std of Specialist Schg: HT – N/Drg – Adv
Livery: Full/Grass/School/Break
Ev Classes
Courses: Hol Inst/YT 1
Facilities: Cov Sch: 20m x 60m* Gly/CC Course*/Out Man: 20m x 60m*/Jmp Pd*/ Horse Walker
Accom: Cottage 6 – shared Catering: Full
Specialities: Livery competition horses – private tuition/breaking/schooling/ Events/Competitions
Exclusions: No horses for general hiring

STOCKBRIDGE RIDING SCHOOL
Stockbridge Downs, Winton Hill, Stockbridge, Hampshire
Tel: Andover (0264) 810727
Proprietors: Mr & Mrs John Wrayton
Chief Inst: John Wrayton
Instruction in Riding and Jumping
Av No: Horses 9 Ponies 4
Std of Schlg: General Purpose
Livery: Full/Part/Break/School/Hack/ Trek – Downland
Ev Classes
Facilities: 2 Out Man:37 x 18m Fl Lit & 40 x 20m/Jmp Pd 1 acre Fl Lit/Sh Jmps/ Lec Rm/Vis Aids/Refresh/Rest Rm/WC/ Wash Rm/2 Horse Walkers
Specialities: Adult Beginners/Full livery
Exclusions: No Rider over 12.5 Stone/ No YT
Location: On A272 Btwn Stockbridge & Winchester

WELLINGTON RIDING LIMITED
Basingstoke Road, Heckfield, Basingstoke, Hampshire, RG27 0LJ
Tel Nos: 0734 326308/YT: 326391/ FAX: 326661
Proprietors: John & Nereide Goodman
Chief Inst: Mr R Pickles (BHSI) **Y T Manager:** Miss M Cave (BHSI(SM))
Other Staff: 6 (BHSII) 7 (BHSAI)
Instruction in Riding and Jumping & Students to BHSI Exam
Av No: Horses 37 Ponies 29
Std of Schlg: General Purpose Std of Specialist Schlg: Drg – A/Sh Jmp – A
Livery: Full/Grass/Break/School/Hunt/ Hack – Fields/Woodlands/Common
Ev Classes
Courses: Resid Inst Hol/Wkg Students/ YT – 6/Adult/Junior riding holidays
Facilities: Cov Sch:43 x 21m* Gly 250 Fl Lit/Out Man: 60m x 20m Seats Fl Lit/ Out Man:42 x 21m Fl Lit/Jmp Pd 74 x 46m/Sh Jmps/CC Fences/CC Course/ Lec Rm/Vis Aids/Video/Club Rm*/Lic Bar*/Rest Rm/Refresh/WC/Wash Rm/ Chng Rm/Tack Shop/Car Park
Accom: 26 – House/2 – Mobile Home/ 9 – Cottage/48 Log Cabins Catering: Full/Part
Specialities: Career Training for overseas students/Junior riding holidays/Competition training/Y T – Berks/Hants/Surrey
Exclusions: Maximum weight of rider – 14.5 stone/No casual hiring
Location: On A33 Btwn Reading/ Basingstoke

WOODCROFT RIDING CENTRE
Woodcroft Lane, Lovedean, Portsmouth, Hampshire, PO8 9QA
Tel: 0705 595069
Proprietors: Mr N Farndon & Miss A Dunn
Other Staff: 2 (BHSAI) P/T
Basic Instruction in Riding and Jumping
Av No: Horses 1 Ponies 15
Std of Schlg: General Purpose
Livery: Part/DIY/Hunter/School/Hack – Lanes
Ev Classes – Summer only
Courses: YT
Facilities: Out Man: 70 x 30m*/4 Schlg CC Fences/Lec Rm/Club Rm – Seating 20*/Refreshments/Wash Rm/WC/Tack Shop/Car Park
Specialities: General Instruction/ Regular Shows/Livery/Hacking
Exclusions: No casual hire
Location: 0.25 mile from centre of Village

ISLE OF WIGHT

BRICKFIELDS EQUESTRIAN CENTRE
Brickfields, Newnham Road, Binstead, Ryde, Isle of Wight
Tel: 0983 66801/615116
Proprietor: P Legge Esq
Chief Inst: Mrs P Legge **Other Staff:** 1 (BHSAI)
Basic Instruction in Riding and Jumping
Av No: Horses 20 Ponies 22
Std of Schlg: General Purpose

Livery: Full/School/Hack – Country Lanes
Ev Classes
Facilities: Cov Sch: 49 x 28m Gly 100*/ Out Mans: 55 x 28m Fl Lt* & 60 x 28m/ School fences 6/Jmp Pd*/Lec Rm*/Club Rm*/Vis Aids*/Video*/Restaurant/Lic Bar/Wash Rm/Waiting Rm/Tack Shop/ WC/Car Park
Accom: Self contained unit Catering: Full
Specialities: Basic Instruction/Shows/ Livery/Shire Horse Centre/Miniature Horse Centre
Location: Off A3054 signed – Shire Centre

ROSEMARY RIDING SCHOOL
Rosemary Lane, Ashey Road, Ryde, Isle of Wight
Tel: Ryde (0983) 63491
Proprietor: L G W Moul
Chief Inst: Mrs S Bradshaw (BHSAI)
Basic Instruction in Riding and Jumping
Av No: Horses 18 Ponies 12
Std of Schlg: General Purpose
Livery: Full/Break/School/Hack
Ev Classes
Courses: Inst Side-saddle Dressage
Facilities: Out Man: 51 x 43m Fl Lit/Jmp Pd/CC Course/Lec Rm/WC/Wash Rm/ Chng Rm/Wait Rm/Car Park
Specialities: Basic equitation & jumping
Exclusions: No YT taken
Location: Just out of Ryde signed – Sports Centre

OXFORDSHIRE

BARRINGTON RIDING CENTRE
Home Farm, Little Barrington, Nr Burford, Oxford, OX8 4TE
Tel: (045 14) 471/300
Proprietor: Mrs J E Mills
Manager: Miss C Roberts (BHSII) **Other Staff:** 1 (BHSAI) P/T
Instruction in Riding and Jumping & Students to BHSAI Exam
Av No: Horses 10 Ponies 14
Std of Schlg: General Purpose
Livery: Full/Part/School/Break/Hack – Bridle paths/Farm Land
Ev Classes – Summer only
Courses: Wkg Pupils/Non Resid Holiday Riding
Facilities: Out Man: 50 x 30m*/Jmp Pd/ CC Fences/CC Course/Wash Rm/WC/ Club Rm/Car Park
Specialities: General Instruction/RDA/ Livery/Hacking/Non Resid Holiday Riding Courses
Exclusions: No casual hire/No YT

BLENHEIM RIDING CENTRE
Benson, Nr Wallingford, Oxford, OX9 6PR
Tel: Wallingford (0491) 36057/35474
Proprietorrs: Mr & Mrs M W Jones
Manageress: Miss P Baily
Instruction in Riding and Jumping
Av No: Horses 32 Ponies 3
Std of Schlg: General Purpose
Livery: Full/Part/Hack – Lanes/ Bridleways/Forestry
Facilities: Cov Sch: 28 x 20m*/Lec Rm/ Refresh/Club Rm/WC/Car Park
Specialities: Family Riding/Riding Club/ Hacking/Livery
Exclusions: Casual hiring only after assessment Lesson
Location: 0.25 mile off A423 btwn Wallingford & Henley

BLEWBURY RIDING & TRAINING CENTRE LTD
Besselsway, Blewbury, Didcot, Oxfordshire, OX11 9NH
Tel: 0235 851016
Proprietors: Miss J E Dexter & B Knight Esq
Chief Inst: Miss A Bull (BHSII)
Manager: Mr K Hicks (BHSI(SM))
Other Staff: 1 (BHSII) 2 (BHSAI)
Instruction in Riding and Jumping & Students to BHSAI Exam
Av No: Horses 9 Ponies: 6
Std of Schlg: General Purpose
Std of Specialist Schlg: CT – Basic/Sh Jmpg – A
Livery: Full/Part/DIY/School/Hack – Downland
Ev Classes
Courses: Up to & including (BHSAI) Exam/Wkg Pupils
Facilities: 2 Cov Schs: 62 x 25m* Gly 30 & 31 x 25m/2 Out Mans: 31 x 25m* Fl Lit&40 x 28m* Fl Lit/10 Basic CC Schooling Fences/Jmp Pd*/Lec Rm/ Club Rm – Seating/Refreshments/Wash Rm/WC/Showers/Ch anging Rm/Car Park
Accom: Shared Rms/Flat – 6 Catering: Part
Specialities: General Instruction/Show Centre/Livery
Exclusions: No Casual Hire
Location: On B 4016 outside Village

COTSWOLD EQUITATION CENTRE
93 Shilton Road, Carterton, Oxford, OX8 3EN
Tel: Carterton (0993) 842262
Proprietor: Mrs C A Hogg (BHSII(T))
Other Staff: 1 (BHSAI)
Training & Livery Centre
Livery: Full/Part/Hunter/Holiday/Break/School
Ev lessons: In summer
Facilities: Out Man: 60 x 30m* Gly/Jmp Pd/Sh Jmps/CC Fences/Refresh/Wash Rm/WC/Car Park
Catering: Full
Specialities: Student Courses/Livery/Schooling for Competitions/Training Centre for persons on their own horses
Exclusions: No casual hiring
Location: On B4020 off A40 Burford

THE MALT HOUSE STUD TRAINING CENTRE
Hanney Road, Steventon, Oxfordshire
Tel: 0235 831488
Proprietor: Mr P Tuckwell
Other Staff: 1 (BHSAI)P/T 1 (BHSII)
Instruction in Riding and Jumping
Av No: Horses 20 Ponies 2
Std of Schlg: General Purpose
Specialist Horses: 4 Drg – 1 Grade B 3 Grade C
Livery: Full/Part/School/Break/Hunt
Ev Classes
Courses: Resid/YT 1
Facilities: Cov Sch: 70 x 20m* Gly/Out Man: 40 x 25m*/Fl Lit/Jmp Pd/Sh Jmps*/Club Rm/Refreshments/Licensed Bar/Showers/Wash Rm/WC/Car Park
Accom: Dormitory/Caravan Catering: Full
Specialities: Competitions/Liveries/Training Cour ses/Shows/General Instruction
Exclusions: No Casual Hiring
Location: 2 miles from Steventon towards Hanney

MANOR FARM
Hampton Poyle, Oxford
Tel: 0867 56812
Proprietors: Mr & Mrs H Kerwood
Livery: DIY
Facilities: CC Course/Out Man: 60x45m F/Lit
Specialities: DIY Livery

OAKFIELD RIDING SCHOOL
Oakfield, Great Coxwell, Faringdon, Oxfordshire
Tel: (0367) 20126
Proprietor: Mr D C Farrow
Chief Inst: Miss M A Goodwin **Other Staff:** 3 (BHSAI) 1 (BHSII) P/T
Instruction in Riding and Jumping
Av No: Horses 13 Ponies 11
Std of Schlg: General Purpose
Hack – National Trust property
Ev Classes Summer Only
Courses: Inst Hol/YT : 2
Facilities: Out Man: 40 x 20m*/Jmp Pd (2 acres)/Sh Jmps/CC Fences/WC/Car Park
Specialities: Children/Novice Adults/Hacking
Exclusions: No unaccompanied riding
Location: Off A420 signed Tythe Barn

TURVILLE VALLEY STUD RIDING SCHOOL
Turville, Henley-on-Thames, Oxfordshire, RG9 6QU
Tel: 049 163 338
Proprietor: Mrs Nan Thurman (ABRS Riding School Principal's Diploma) + (BHSAI)
Other Staff: 1 (BHSAI)
Instruction in Riding and Jumping & Students to BHSAI Exam
Av No: Horses 10 Ponies 20
Std of Schlg: General Purpose
Break/School/Hack – Chiltern Hills/Country Lanes
Ev Lessons – Summer Only
Courses: Inst Hol Wkg Students
Facilities: 2 Out Man: 50 x 20m Seats/20 x 40m/Jmp Pd 50 x 50m/Sh Jmps 6/CC Course/Lec Rm/Vis Aids/Video/Club Rm/WC/Wash Rm/Wait Rm/Chng Rm
Specialities: Children/Jumping/Dressage/Hacking/RDA/Adult Instruction Courses
Exclusions: No casual hiring/No YT

VALLEY FARM EQUESTRIAN CENTRE
Shotteswell, Nr Banbury, Oxfordshire, OX17 1HZ
Tel: 0295 730576
Proprietor: Mrs D Faulkner
Chief Inst: Mrs A Ellard (BHSII) **Other Staff:** 1 (BHSII(T))
Instruction in Riding and Jumping
Av No: Horses 15 Ponies 13 Std of Specialist Horses: 1 Adv Drg
Std of Schlg: General Purpose Std of Specialist Schlg: Drg – Adv
Livery: Full/Part/Hunt/School/Hack – Bridle paths/Fields
Ev Classes
Courses: NVQ for Warwick College of Agriculture/Non resid Camps

Facilities: Cov Sch: 46 x 24m* Gly/Out Man: 40 x 20m* Fl Lit/Jmp Pd*/Lec Rm/Wash Rm/WC/Car Park
Specialities: General Instruction/Private Lessons/Livery/Summer Courses & Camps/RDA Group
Exclusions: No casual hire

WATERSTOCK HOUSE TRAINING CENTRE
Waterstock, Nr Oxford, Oxfordshire, OX9 1JS
Tel: 0844339 616/460/401
Proprietor: L Sederholm Esq
Other Staff: 1 (BHSII) 1 (BHSI) 2 (BHSAI)
Instruction in Riding and Jumping & Students to BHSI Exam
Av No: Horses 8 Specialist Horses – Drg 'A'/Event 'A'
Std of Schlg: General Purpose
Livery: Full/Break/School
Courses: Resid Inst/Wkg Students
Facilities: Cov Sch: 42 x 21m Gly Fl Lit/ Out Man: 66 x 33m/Jmp Pd/Sh Jmps/ CC Course/Video/Vis Aids/Lec Rm/WC/ Wash Rm/Chng Rm/Tack Shop/Car Park
Accom: 26 – Rooms Catering: Full
Specialities: Eventing/Production of event horse and Rider/Show Jumping/ Career students
Exclusions: No casual hiring/No YT taken

WESTFIELD FARM RIDING CENTRE
Fenway, Steeple Aston, Oxfordshire, OX5 3SS
Tel: Steeple Aston (0869) 47421
Proprietor: Mrs A Hillier
Other Staff: 3 (BHSAI)
Instruction in Riding and Jumping
Av No: Horses 10 Ponies 15
Std of Schlg: General Purpose
Livery: Full/Part/Working/Break/School/ Hack – Woo dland/Bridleways
Ev Classes
Facilities: Cov Sch: 37 x 18m* Fl Lit/ Out Man: 41 x 20m/Jmp Pd*/CC Fences/ Wash Rm/WC/Wait Rm/Car Park
Specialities: Weekly courses school holidays/Eventing/Show Jumping/ Gymkhana/RDA

Riding in the South West

AVON ♦ CORNWALL ♦ DEVON ♦ DORSET ♦ GLOUCESTER ♦ SOMERSET ♦ WILTSHIRE

AVON

THE AVON RIDING CENTRE FOR THE DISABLED LTD
Kings Weston Road, Henbury, Nr Bristol, Avon, BS10 7QT
Tel: 0272 590266
Chairman: Mrs B Grant
Chief Inst: Miss A J Naylor (BHSAI)
Stable Manager: Mr G Haskey
Other Staff: 1 (BHSAI) 3 (BHSAI) P/T
Instruction in Riding and Jumping
Av No: Ponies 16
Std of Schlg: General Purpose
Livery: Part/School
Facilities: Cov Sch: 55m x 25m Gly-60*/ Out Man: 40m x 20m/Sh Jmps*/ Refreshments/WC/Car Park
Specialities: Riding for the Disabled Only/Instruction Facilities for Hire/Short Courses for Stages Exams
Exclusions: No Rider over 12 stone

CLEVEDON RIDING CENTRE
Clevedon Lane, Clevedon, Avon, BS21 7AG
Tel: 0272 858699
Proprietor: Mrs J A Sims
Chief Inst: Miss S Sims (BHSAI) **Other Staff:** 2 (BHSAI)
Instruction in Riding and Jumping
Av No: Horses 8 Ponies 6
Std of Schlg: General Purpose Spec Horses: Drg – E/Sh Jmp – C
Livery: Full/Part/Grass/Hack – Tracks/ Country Lanes/Common Land
Ev Classes
Courses: 2 YT
Facilities: Out Man: 60m x 25m* Fl Lit/CC Course & Fences/Jmp Pd/ Waiting Rm – Gly/Refreshments/WC/ Car Park
Specialities: General Instruction for all ages/Hacking/Creche
Exclusions: No Casual Hire
Location: Off B3124 Between Clevedon & Portishead

HARTLEY WOOD RIDING CENTRE
King Lane, Clutton Hill, Clutton Bristol, Avon BS18 4QQ, Corres: 24 The Glebe, Timsbury Avon BA3 1LT
Tel: 0761 52063
Proprietor & Chief Inst: Mrs R D Withey (BHSII)
Other Staff: 1 (BHSAI) 1 (BHSAI) P/T
Instruction in Riding and Jumping & Students to BHSAI Exam
Av No: Horses 9 Ponies 10
Std of Schlg: General Purpose Std of Specialist Schlg: Sh Jmpg – Novice
Livery: Full/Part/Hunter/School/Break/ Hack – Bridleways/Lanes
Ev Classes
Courses: Up to & including BHSAI/Wkg Pupils – 3
Facilities: Out Man: 54 x 24m* Fl Lit/ Jmpg Pd*/Lec Rm – Vis Aids/Video/ Seating for 10/Wash Rm/WC/Waiting Rm/Car Park
Specialities: General Instruction/ Training/Livery/Breaking/Schooling
Exclusions: No Casual hire

HUNSTRETE RIDING SCHOOL
Hunstrete, Nr Bristol, Avon, BS15 4NT
Tel: Compton Dando (07618) 645
Proprietors: Mr & Mrs T Warren
Chief Inst: Miss R Holt (BHSAI) **Other Staff:** 3 (BHSAI) 2 (BHSAI) P/T
Instruction in Riding and Jumping Students to BHSAI Exam
Av No: Horses 10 Ponies 10

Std of Schlg: General Purpose
Livery: Full/Part/Break/School/Hack – Woodland
Ev Classes
Courses: Wkg Students/YT – 2
Facilities: Cov Sch: 20m x 60m* Gly Fl Lit/Out Man: 40 x 20m Fl Lit/CC Fences/ Jmp Pd/Lec Rm/Club Rm/WC/Refresh/ Car Park
Specialities: Preparation for (BHSAI) Exam/Teaching novices/Dressage/Side Saddle
Exclusions: No casual hiring
Location: Off A368 midway between Bath & Bristol

KINGSWESTON STABLES
Lime Kiln Cottage, Kingsweston Road, Bristol, Avon, BS11 0UX
Tel: 0272 828929
Proprietor: R Slaughter Esq
Head Girl: Mrs A Whitefield **Other Staff:** 2 (BHSAI) P/T
Hacking & Basic Instruction in Riding Only
Av No: Horses 6 Ponies 8
Std of Schlg: General Purpose Std of Specialist Schlg: Sh Jmpg – Novice
Livery: Part/School/Hack – Bridleways/ Woodland
Ev Classes – Summer Only
Facilities: Out Man: 25 x 37m/4 Basic Schooling CC Fences/Wash Rm/WC/ Car Park
Specialities: Hacking in ideal country
Location: 4 miles north west of the centre of Bristol

LEYLAND COURT RIDING SCHOOL
Northwoods, Winterbourne, Bristol, Avon, BS17 1RY
Tel: Winterbourne (0454) 773163
Proprietors: Mr & Mrs H M Irish
Chief Inst: Mrs A Irish (BHSAI) **Other Staff:** 1 (BHSAI)
Instruction in Riding and Jumping
Av No: Horses 16 Ponies 8
Std of Schlg: General Purpose
Livery: Full/Grass/Hunter/Break/School/ Hunt/Hack
Ev Classes
Courses: YT – 2
Facilities: Out Man: 31 x 15m* Fl Lit/ Jmp Pd/Sh Jumps*/21 CC Fences*/ Lec Rm/Club Rm
Specialities: Introduction to hunting/ Breaking & Schooling/Private tuition/ RDA
Location: 2 miles from Junc of M5/M4

THE MENDIP EQUESTRIAN CENTRE
Lyncombe Lodge, Sandford, Avon, BS19 5PG
Tel: Churchill (0934) 852335
Proprietors: Mr John Lee (BHSI) & Mrs S Lee (BHSAI)
Other Staff: 1 (BHSAI) 1 (BHSI) – Visiting
Instruction in Riding and Jumping
Av No: Horses 11 Ponies 21
Std of Schlg: General Purpose
Livery: Full/Part/Hunter/Break/School/ Hunt/Hack – Trek/Hill/Moorland
Ev Classes (summer only)
Courses: Resid Hol/Wkg Students
Facilities: Out Man: 20m x 60m* Fl Lit/Jmp Pd 35 x 80m/Sh Jmps full BSJA/30 CC Fences/CC Course 1.5 miles + mini course/Lec Rm/Vis Aids/ Club Rm/Lic Bar/Refresh/Rest Rm/WC/ Wash Rm/Chng Rm/Badminton/Squash/ Indoor Pool/Youth Club etc locally/Car Park
Accom: 45 – Farmhouse & Hotel Catering: Full/Part
Specialities: Riding holidays/All Sports/ General Instruction/RDA
Exclusions: No YT
Location: 3 miles from Junc 21 on M5

URCHINWOOD MANOR
Congresbury, Nr Bristol, Avon, BS19 5AP
Tel: 0934 833248
Proprietor: Capt Peter Hall & Mrs S Hall (BHSAI)
Managing Agent YT
Chief Inst: Miss Eve Pool BHSI **Other Staff:** 2 (BHSII) 6 (BHSAI)
Instruction in Riding and Jumping & Students to BHSII Exam
Av No: Horses 12 Ponies 10
Std of Schlg: General Purpose Std of Specialist schlg: Drg M
Livery: Full/Part/Grass/Hunter/School/ Break/Hunt/Hack – Road/Tracks
Ev Classes
Courses: Resid Hol/Wkg Students/YT 30
Facilities: Cov Sch: 54m x 24m* Gly 30/Out Man:45m x 24m*Fl Lit/Jmp Pd/ Sh Jmps/CC Course/CC Fences/Video/ Club Rm/WC/H & C/Refresh/Car Park
Accom: Mobile homes – 35 Catering: Full
Specialities: General Instruction/ Facilities for hire/Livery/Student Training/Residential courses & holidays – full catering/Hanoverian/T B Stud
Location: Off A370 Between Congresbury/Bristol

VILLA FARM RIDING SCHOOL
Hewish, Weston Super Mare, Avon, BS24 6RQ
Tel: Yatton (0934) 838814
Proprietor: Mrs P M A Moss (BHS PTT)
Basic Instruction in Riding and Jumping
Av No: Horses 3 Ponies 13
Std of Schlg: General Purpose Hack/Varied
Facilities: Out Man:40m x 20m/Jmp Pd/Lec Rm/WC/Chng Rm/Vis Aids
Specialities: Beginners & Children
Exclusions: No YT taken
Location: On A370 in village of Hewish

WELLOW TREKKING CENTRE
Little Horse Croft Farm, Wellow, Bath, Avon, BA2 8QE
Tel: 0225 834376
Proprietors: Mr & Mrs F Shellard
Chief Inst: Mrs F Shellard **Other Staff:** 1 (BHSAI) P/T
Hacking & Trekking
Av No: Horses 22 Ponies 8
Std of Schlg: General Purpose
Livery: Part/Grass/DIY/School/Hack/Trek – Bridleways
Ev Classes
Courses: YT
Facilities: Out Man: 40 x 20m* Fl Lit/Refreshments/Club Rm/WC/Car Park
Specialities: Basic Riding Instruction/Livery Service/Hacking/Trekking
Location: 5 mile out of Village btwn Wellow/Hinton Charterhouse

WHITE CAT STABLES
Lyde View, Howsmoor Lane, Mangotsfield, Bristol, Avon, BS17 3AQ
Tel: Bristol (0272) 564370/560226
Proprietor & Chief Inst: Mrs P E Gough (BHSAI)
Other Staff: 2 (BHSAI) P/T
Instruction in Riding and Jumping & Students to BHSAI Exam
Av No: Horses 12 Ponies 8
Std of Schlg: General Purpose
Livery: Full/Part/DIY/Break/School
Ev Classes
Courses: Hol Inst/Wkg Students/YT – 3
Facilities: Cov Sch: 32 x 18m/Fl Lit Seats/Jmp Pd/Sh Jmps/CC Fences/Lec Rm/Refresh/WC/Chng Rm/Car Park
Specialities: Beginners and Intermediate all ages/Stable Management/Riding & Road Safety Instructors Examinations
Location: 5 miles east of Bristol

THE WORLEBURY RIDING SCHOOL
Acres, 114 Worlebury Hill Road, Weston Super Mare, Avon, BS22 9TG
Tel: Weston Super Mare (0934) 631446
Proprietors: Miss H S Tonkin IIH & Miss S M B Tonkin (BHS PTT) **Other Staff:** 2 (BHSAI)
Instruction in Riding and Jumping & Students to BHSAI Exam
Av No: Horses 10 Ponies 12
Std of Schlg: General Purpose
Livery: Full/Break/School/Hack – Sands
Courses: Wkg Students
Facilities: Cov Sch: 32 x 18m* Gly 20/Out Man/Jmp Pd/CC Fences/CC Course/Lec Room/WC/Chng Room
Specialities: Children/Riding Club/Pony Club/RDA
Exclusions: No hunting/No YT
Location: Off Milton Hill through Worlebury

CORNWALL

CHIVERTON RIDING CENTRE
Silverwell, Nr Blackwater, Truro, Cornwall
Tel: Truro (0872) 560471
Proprietors: Mrs S Fawdry & Miss V Jane
Managing Agents YT
Chief Inst: Mrs S A Fawdry (BHSAI)
Other Staff: 1 (BHSAI) 1 (BHSII) 1 (BHSAI) P/T
Instruction in Riding and Jumping & Students to BHSII Exam
Av No: Horses 10 Ponies 9
Std of Schlg: General Purpose
Livery: Full/Part/Break/School/Hack
Ev Classes
Courses: Hol/Inst/YT 12
Facilities: Cov Sch: 42 x 22m* Gly Fl Lit/Out Man: 62 x31m*/Jmp Pd/Sh Jmps 10*/CC Fences/Vis Aids/Lec Rm/Refresh/WC/Car Park
Accom: 4 Students only Catering: Full
Specialities: Career Students/General Instruction/Livery of all types/Tests/RDA/YT Managing Agent
Location: Off B3277 btwn Blackwater/St Agnes

DUCHY COLLEGE OF AGRICULTURE & HORTICULTURE
Stoke Climsland, Callington, Cornwall, PL17 8PB
Tel: 0579 370769
Director: A S Counsell Esq
Chief Inst: Miss J Batty – Smith (BHSI)
Other Staff: 1 (BHSII) 2 (BHSAI)

Instruction in Riding and Jumping & Students to BHSII Exam
Av No: Horses 9 Ponies 3
Std of Schlg: General Purpose Std of Specialist Schlg: Sh Jmp – Novice
Livery: Full/School
Courses: YT Students/BHS Stages/ NCMH – 2yr Dip in Equine Studies
Facilities: Out Man: 38 x 30m/Cov Sch: 60 x 20 m* – Seating -200/Lec Rm/Club Rm – Vis Aids/seating – 25/Film Projector/Library/Refreshments/Rm/WC/ Showers/Changing Rm/Tack Shop/Car Park
Specialities: YT/General Student Courses
Exclusions: No Hiring of horses
Location: Off A388 btwn Launceton/Callington

GOOSEHAM BARTON STABLES
Gooseham, Morwenstow, Nr Bude, Cornwall, EX23 9PG
Tel: Morwenstow (028883) 204
Proprietor: Mr R Hamilton
Chief Inst: Miss D Hamilton
Basic Instruction in Riding and Jumping
Av No: Horses 10 Ponies 12
Std of Schlg: General Purpose
Hack/Trek – Lanes/Bridlepaths/Woods/ Forestry
Courses: Resid Hol/YTS
Facilities: Jmp field/WC/Chng Rm/Club Rm/Wash Rm/Car Park
Accom: 2 Self Catering Cottages – sleeps 5/6
Specialities: Self Catering mobile home – families etc. Riding as required/ Hacking
Exclusions: No Children under 12 for Residential Holidays
Location: 2.5 miles off A39 between Bideford/Bude

THE MANOR RIDING SCHOOL
Veryan, Truro, Cornwall, TR2 5PH
Tel: 0872 501574
Proprietors: Mr & Mrs Trethowan
Chief Inst: Mrs J M Trethowan (BHSAI)
Other Staff: Miss F Jones (BHSAI)
Basic Instruction in Riding and Jumping
Av No: Horses 6 Ponies 5
Std of Schlg: General Purpose
Livery: Full/Part/Grass/School/Hack – Country Lanes/Beach for experienced riders only
Ev Classes
Courses: BHS Stages up to & including BHSAI/YT – 1
Facilities: 24 x 15m* Gly/10 Basic Schooling CC Fences/Lec Rm/WC/Car Park
Specialities: Beginners & Nervous riders

MOSS FARM RIDING
Bradford, Blisland, Bodmin, Cornwall, PL30 4LF
Tel: 0208 850628
Proprietors: Mr & Mrs P J Dibb
Chief Inst: Mrs S Corney
Riding Holidays
Av No: Horses 5 Ponies 0
Std of Schlg: General Purpose
Livery: Full/Part/DIY/Hunt/Hack – Moorland
Courses: YT 1
Facilities: Refreshments/Wash Rm/WC/ Showers/Car Park
Accom: Shared Rooms – House – 6 Catering: Full/Part
Specialities: Hacking/Hunting/Riding Holidays/Holiday Livery
Exclusions: Only Experienced Riders taken
Location: Off A30 at Temple Four turning

NINE TOR RIDING CENTRE
North Hill, Launceston, Cornwall, PL15 7PE
Tel: Coads Green (0566) 82232
Proprietors: David & Lyn Bloomfield
Other Staff: 1 (BHSAI) P/T
Basic Instruction in Riding and Jumping
Av No: Horses 15 Ponies 20
Std of Schlg: General Purpose
Hack – Open moorland
Courses: Resid Hol/YTS – 1
Facilities: Sh Jmps 2/CC Fences 15/ Refresh/WC/Showers/Wash Rm/Chng Rm/Car Park
Accom: 30 beds – Farmhouse Catering: Full
Specialities: Riding Holidays/ Unaccompanied children 10-16 (Also special over 16's weeks arranged)/ casual hacking by arrangement
Location: Btwn Launceston/Liskeard

OLD MILL STABLES
Lelant Downs, Hayle, Cornwall, TR27 6LN
Tel: Hayle (0736) 753045
Proprietors: Miss S V Renowden & Miss M M Scotting
Chief Inst: Miss A Abbey (BHSII) **Other Staff:** 1 (BHSAI)

Instruction in Riding and Jumping & Students to BHSAI Exam
Av No: Horses 11 Ponies 9
Std of Schlg: General Purpose
Livery: Full/Grass/School/Hack – Woodland/Moors/Country Lanes
Ev Classes
Courses: Res Hol Inst/YTS 2
Facilities: Out Man:20 x 41m/Jmp Pd/Sh Jmps/CC Fences/Lec Rm/Vis Aids/Refresh/WC/Car Park
Accom: Local Hotels/Cornish Cottage/Farmhouse
Specialities: Instructional adult riding holidays/Pony Master Courses/RDA/Dressage/Horse Trial Days
Exclusions: No riders over 12.5 stone
Location: Btwn Lelant/Halse town

POLPEVER RIDING STABLES

Duloe, Liskeard, Cornwall
Tel: Looe (05036) 3010
Proprietor: Mrs S Kinver
Instruction in Riding and Jumping
Av No: Horses 6 Ponies 8
Std of Schlg: General Purpose
Livery: Full/Grass/Hack/Trek – Bridlepaths/Woodlands
Courses: Day Release Students 8/YTS
Facilities: Out Man/Jmp Pd/Refresh/Club Rm/12 Cavaletti/WC/Chng Rm/Car Park
Accom: 12 – Cottages Catering: Self
Specialities: Hacking/Riding Holidays/Instruction to Pony Club'B' level
Exclusions: No Unescorted Rides/Weight limit 13.5 stone
Location: Off A387 btwn Sandplace/Looe

ST LEONARD'S EQUITATION CENTRE

Polson, Launceston, Cornwall, PL15 9QR
Tel: Launceston (0566) 5543
Proprietor: Mr A Reeve (BHSAI)
Chief Inst: Miss T Wooldrige (BHSII)
Other Staff: 2 (BHSAI)
Instruction in Riding and Jumping
Av No: Horses 5 Ponies 5 Spec Horses: 2 BSJA 'C'
Std of Schlg: General Purpose
Livery: Full/Part/DIY/Break/School/Hunt/Hack – Parkland/Moorland
Ev Classes
Courses: Resid Inst Hol/YT – 2
Facilities: Out Man: 37 x 18m/Out Man: 60 x 20m*/Sh Jmps/CC Fences/Video/Wash Rm/Chng Rm/Refresh/Car Park/Tack/Feed Store
Accom: 4 Cottages Acc – 4 – Catering: self Lic Rest & Guest House
Specialities: Event & Competition Training/Instruction on personal basis/Stud
Exclusions: No casual hiring
Location: Off A30 between Lifton & Launceston

T M INTERNATIONAL SCHOOL OF HORSEMANSHIP

Henwood, Nr Liskeard, Cornwall, PL14 5BP
Tel: (0579) 62895
Proprietor: Capt E W R Moore & Miss K M Tyrrell
Other Staff: 1 (BHSAI)
Instruction in Riding and Jumping
Av No: Horses 5 Ponies 15
Std of Schlg: General Purpose
Livery: Full/Part/Break/School/Hack/Trek – Moorland
Ev Lessons – Summer only
Courses: 3 YT
Facilities: Out Man:65 x 46m*/Jmp Pd/Sh Jmps/CC Fences/Lec Rm/Vis Aids/Club Rm/WC/Wash Rm/Showers/Refresh/Car park
Accom: 21 – House Catering – Full
Specialities: Riding instruction/Residential riding holidays/Livery service/Language Courses/Visits to local tourist attractions
Exclusions: No casual hiring
Location: 3/4 mile off B3254 btwn Launceston/Liskeard

TALL TREES RIDING CENTRE

Davidstow, Camelford, Cornwall, PL32 9XR
Tel: (08406) 249
Proprietor: Mrs M Harrison
Manager/Chief Inst: Mrs M Dray (BHSAI) **Other Staff:** 3 (BHSAI) 2 (BHSII) P/T
Instruction in Riding and Jumping & Students to BHSAI Exam
Av No: Horses 12 Ponies 16
Std of Schlg: General Purpose
Livery: Full/Part/Break/School/Hack/Trek – Open Moorland/Bridlepaths
Ev Classes
Courses: Inst Hol/Indoor Show Jumping Comps/Jumping Instruction/Wkg Students/YTS 4
Facilities: Cov Sch: 55 x 22m* Gly/2nd Cov Sch:44 x 21m*/Jmp Pd four acres/Sh Jmps 15/CC Fences/Lec Rm/Vis Aids/Club Rm/Saddlery Shop/Refresh/Rest Rm/WC/Car Park
Specialities: Riding for the

Disabled/Jumping com petitions/ General Instruction & Student Training
Exclusions: No hire for hunting or unescorted rides
Location: On A395 nr Junc with A39

TRENANCE RIDING STABLES
Trenance Lane, Newquay, Cornwall, TR7 2HS
Tel: Newquay (0637) 872699
Proprietor: Mrs J Burt
Other Staff: 1 (BHSAI) P/T
Basic Instruction in Riding and Jumping
Av No: Horses 16 Ponies 10
Std of Schlg: General Purpose
Livery: Grass/DIY/Hacking/Trek – Beach/Common land/Dunes
Courses: YT – 1
Facilities: Jmp Pd/Sh Jmps*/CC Fences/Saddlery Shop/WC/Chng Rm/ Refresh/Car Park
Specialities: Hacking/Pony Trekking only
Location: Off A3076 by Estuary

TREVILLETT RIDING CENTRE
Trevillett, Tintagel, Cornwall, PL34 0HL
Tel: 0840 770 662
Proprietor: R J Valter Esq
Chief Inst: Miss T Valter **Other Staff:** Mrs T Valter
Hacking & Trekking
Av No: Horses 5 Ponies 18
Std of Schlg: General Purpose Std of Specialist Schlg: Sh Jmpg – Novice
Livery: Part/Grass/Hack – Minor Roads/ Farm Land/Moorland
Courses: Resid
Facilities: Out Man: 70 x 25m*/Snacks/ Wash Rm/WC/Car Park
Accom: House – 6 Catering: Full
Specialities: Hacking/Trekking/Holiday Accommodation
Exclusions: No Riders over 14 stone
Location: Off A39 btwn Davidstowe/Tintagel

WHEAL BULLER RIDING SCHOOL
Buller Hill, Redruth, Cornwall, TR16 6ST
Tel: 0209 211852
Proprietors: Mr & Mrs W Vernon
Chief Inst: Miss J Moyse (BHSAI) **Other Staff:** 1 (BHSAI) 1 (BHSAI) P/T
Instruction in Riding and Jumping
Av No: Horses 15 Ponies 15 Specialist Horses: 2 Sh Jmpers C/2 Eventers Nov
Std of Schlg: General Purpose Std of Specialist Schlg: Drg & CT – Nov/Sh Jmpg C
Livery: Full/Grass/School/Break/Hack – Bridle paths/National Trust
Ev Classes
Courses: BHS Stages I/II & NVQ
Facilities: Cov Sch: 32 x 18m* Gly/Out Man: 45 x 20m* Fl Lit/Nov CC Courses*/ Jmp Pd*/Refreshments/WC/Car Park
Accom: Single/Shared – Cottage/House – 24 Catering: Full
Specialities: General Instruction/Riding Holidays/Holiday Courses/Hacking
Exclusions: No unaccompanied Riding/No unaccompanied Children under 7
Location: On B 3297 Redruth/Helston Road

DEVON

ABIGALE EQUESTRIAN CENTRE
Woodway Street, Chudleigh, Newton Abbot, South Devon, TQ13 0NE
Tel: 0626 852167
Proprietor: Mrs L M Saunders
Chief Inst: Miss G C Saunders (BHSAI)
Other Staff: 1 (BHSII) P/T
Instruction in Riding and Jumping
Av No: Horses 4 Ponies 5
Std of Schlg: General Purpose Std of Specialist Schlg: Drg – Prelim & PC/Sh Jmpg – Novice
Livery: Full/Part/Grass/DIY/School/ Break/Hunt/Hack – Moorland
Ev Classes
Courses: YT
Facilities: Cov Sch: 25 x 12m*/Jmp Pd*/Refresh/WC/Car Park
Specialities: General Instruction/ Hacking/Livery/RDA/Road Safety
Exclusions: No casual hire
Location: 1/4 mile east of town centre

BABLEIGH RIDING SCHOOL
Bableigh House, Landkey, Barnstaple, North Devon
Tel: 0271 830242
Proprietor & Chief Inst: Mrs V A Coles
Other Staff: 2 (BHSAI) P/T
Instruction in Riding and Jumping
Av No: Horses 2 Ponies 11 Specialist Horse – 1 Drgs E
Std of Schlg: General Purpose Std of Specialist Schlg Drg – E/Sh Jmpg – Novice
Livery: Part/School/Hack – Common Land/Bridle paths
Facilities: Out Man: 44 x 22m*/Jmpg Pd*/Lec Rm – Vis Aids/Seating
Specialities: General Instruction/Pony Club/Livery/Hunting

Exclusions: No casual hire/No children under 7 years
Location: Off A361 1.5 miles from centre of Landkey

BELLE VUE VALLEY EQUESTRIAN CENTRE

Argyll Road, Pennsylvania, Exeter, Devon
Tel: 0392 216928
Proprietors: Mr & Mrs A Daems
Chief Inst: Mrs C B Daems (BHSII(T))
Other Staff: 2 (BHSAI)
Instruction in Riding and Jumping & Students to BHSAI Exam
Av No: Horses 4 Ponies 6 Specialist Horses: 2 Sh Jmpers Grade B
Std of Schlg: General Purpose/ Specialist Schlg: Drg – Novice/C T – Novice/Sh Jmp – Grades C & B
Livery: Full/Part/School/Break/Hack – Bridleways
Ev Classes – Summer only
Courses: BHS Stages I/II & AI/Wkg Students
Facilities: Out Man: 40 x 25m*/Schlg Fences – 12/Jmp Pd*/Snacks/WC/Car Park
Specialities: General Instruction/Career Student Courses/Schooling/Breaking/ Livery/Dealing
Exclusions: No Casual Hire

BICTON COLLEGE OF AGRICULTURE

East Budleigh, Budleigh Salterton, Devon, EX9 7BY
Tel: Colaton Raleigh (0395) 68353
Principal of College: M Florey Esq FBIM A R Ags
Director: Mr P J Cook (BHSI) **Chief Instructor:** Mr P J Cook BHSI **Other Staff:** 3 (BHSI) (SM) 2 (BHSII)
Managing Agent YT
Instruction in Riding and Jumping & Students to BHSII Exam
Av No: Horses 28 Ponies -
Std of Schlg: General Purpose School/Break
Courses: Resid/YT – 80
Facilities: Cov Sch:44m x 22m/Out Man:44m x 22m/CC Fences/Jmp Pd/ Sh Jmps/Lec Rm/Club Rm/Vis Aids/ Video/Refresh/Wash Rm/WC/Showers/ Change Rm/Car Park
Accom: 80 – Rooms Catering: Full
Specialities: Career Students only Prepared for BHS Exams and National Certificates in Management of Horses/ BDS Driving Courses
Exclusions: No hiring
Location: On A376 Btwn Budleigh Salterton & Colaton Raleigh

BLACKSLADE RIDING AND TREKKING CENTRE

Widecombe-in-the-Moor, Nr Newton Abbot, South Devon, PQ13 7TF
Tel: Widecombe (036 42) 304
Proprietor: M E Hares
Riding Holidays
Av No: Horse 10 Ponies 20
Std of Schlg: General Purpose Trek/Moorland
Courses: Resid Hol for experienced riders & complete beginners/Groups & school parties/YT
Facilities: Jmp Pd/Sh Jmps 8/CC Fences/WC/Showers/Wash Rm/Chng Rm/Wait Rm/Tack Shop/Car Park
Accom: 17 – Manor house/Easter – September Camping Catering: Full
Specialities: Riding/Trekking/School Parties/Groups
Exclusions: Unaccompanied Children under 9
Location: 1.5 miles btwn Widdecombe/ Ashburton

BUDLEIGH SALTERTON RIDING SCHOOL

Heatherways Stables, Heatherways, Dalditch Lane, Budleigh Salterton, Devon, EX9 7AS
Tel: 039 54 2035
Proprietors: Mrs B J & Miss M Howick
Chief Inst: Miss M Howick (BHSAI)
Other Staff: 1 UQ
Instruction in Riding and Jumping
Av No: Horses 5 Ponies 10 Specialist Horses: 2 Novice Eventers
Std of Schlg: General Purpose Std of Specialist Schlg: CT – Basic/Sh Jmp – Novice
School/Hack – Heath/Common Land
Ev Classes – Summer only
Courses: Resid Hol/YT – 1
Facilities: Out Man: 55 x 25m/ Schooling Fences 5 (Basic)/Jmp Pd/ Snacks/WC/Showers/Chng Rm/Waiting Rm/Car Park
Accom: Shared Cottage/House – 10 Catering: Self
Specialities: General Instruction/ Children all ages/Hacking/Riding Holidays
Exclusions: No Casual Hiring
Location: On B3179 just outside the village of Knowle

CHAGFORD RIDING CENTRE
Waye Barton, Chagford, Devon, TQ13 8DT
Tel: 06473 3519
Proprietor & Chief Inst: Miss S J Davies (BHSII) **Other Staff:** 1 (BHSII)
Instruction in Riding and Jumping
Av No: Horses 3 Ponies 5
Std of Schlg: General Purpose Std of Specialist Schlg: CT – Novice/Sh Jmpg – Novice
Livery: Full/Part/Grass/School/Break/Hack – Dartmoor
Ev Classes – Summer only
Courses: YT – 1/up to BHS Stages III/Resid Hol
Facilities: Out Man: 60 x 20m*/CC Course – Novice/CC Fences*/Jmpg Pd*/Wash Rm/WC/Chng Rm/Car Park
Accom: Single/Shared Rms – Dorm/House – 8 Catering: Full/Part
Specialities: General Instruction/Holiday Livery/Holiday Courses/Livery/Hacking
Exclusions: No riders over 14 stone
Location: 1 mile out of Chagford on Keston Road

CHESTON FARM EQUESTRIAN CENTRE
Cheston Farm, Wrangaton, South Brent, Devon, TQ10 9HL
Tel: 036 47 3266
Proprietors:: Mrs R A Cornish & Mrs M C Berry
Other Staff: 2 (BHSAI) 2 (BHSII) P/T
Instruction in Riding and Jumping
Av No: Horses 10 Ponies 10
Std of Schlg: General Purpose Specialist Schlg: Drg – Novice/Sh Jmp – Novice
Livery: Full/Part/School/Break/Hack – Open Moorland
Ev Classes
Courses:for Beginners/Novices/Experienced Riders Specialising: Drg/Jmp/also problem horses/Wkg Students
Facilities: 2 Cov Schs: 30 x 22m* & 80 x 40m/Out Man: 30 x 20m Fl Lit */Jmp Pd*/Sh Jmps/Lec Rm/WC/Chng Rm/Tack Shop/Car Park
Accom: 12 – House Catering: Full
Specialities: Hacking/Voltige/Ranger Troop/RDA – for Children & Adults/Moor Riding/Riding Holiday
Exclusions: All Rides escorted
Location: Off A38 btwn South Brent/Ivy Bridge

COLLAFORD FARM
Plympton, Plymouth, Devon, PL7 5BD
Tel: 0752 880339
Proprietors: Mr & Mrs J Watts (A S Watts (Plymouth) Ltd)
Livery Yard
Livery: Grass/DIY/Holiday
Facilities: WC/Car Park
Specialities: DIY Livery/Holiday Livery/Good Hacking Country for Livery Owners
Exclusions: Livery Service by Contract only

COOMBE PARK EQUESTRIAN CENTRE
Little Hempston, Nr Totnes, Devon, TQ9 6LW
Tel: 0803 863473
Proprietors: Mr & Mrs I Norris & Mr & Mrs J Loffet
Manager & Chief Inst: Mrs R Mogford (BHSII) **Other Staff:** 1 (BHSAI)
Instruction in Riding and Jumping
Av No: Horses 7 Ponies 14 Specialist Horses: 4 Sh Jmpers Grade C
Std of Schlg: General Purpose Std of Specialist Schlg: Sh Jmpg – Grade C
Livery: Full/Part/Grass/DIY/School
Ev Classes
Courses: Resid/Wkg Pupils – 3/YT
Facilities: Cov Sch: 46 x 21m* Gly/Out Man: 40 x 60m* Fl Lit/CC Courses*/CC Fences – Novice/Jmp Pd*/Lec Rm* – Vis Aids/Video/Seating – 50
Accom: Shared House – 6 Catering: Full
Specialities: General Instruction/Residential C ourses/Livery/Shows/RDA
Exclusions: No casual hire
Location: Off A381 btwn Totnes/Newton Abbott

CROSSWAYS RIDING SCHOOL
Axtown Lane, Yelverton, Devon, PL20 7EB
Tel: Yelverton (0822) 853025
Proprietor: Mr & Mrs Howard
Chief Inst: Mrs C Graham (BHSAI)
Other Staff: 1 (BHSAI)
Basic Instruction in Riding and Jumping
Av No: Horses 4 Ponies 6
Std of Schlg: General Purpose
Livery: Full/Part/Hunt/Hack/Trek – Moorland/Lanes
Courses: YTS 2
Facilities: Out Man:20m x 40m Fl Lit/Lec Rm/Vis Aids/Wash Rm/WC/Car Park
Specialities: Novice riders/Hacking/Liveries/Basic Instruction/Hunter Hirelings/RDA Riding & Driving
Exclusions: No unescorted Rides
Location: Off A386 btwn Plymouth/Yelverton

DEVENISH PITT RIDING SCHOOL
Farway, Nr Colyton, Devon, EX13 6EG
Tel: 0404 87 355
Proprietors: Mrs M & Miss A Banks
Chief Inst: Miss A Banks (BHSAI) **Other Staff:** 1 (BHSAI) 1 (Unqual) 1 (Unqual) P/T
Instruction in Riding and Jumping
Av No: Horses 5 Ponies 15
Std of Schlg: General Purpose Std of Specialist Schlg: CT – Novice/Sh Jmpg – Novice
Livery: Full/Grass/School/Break/Hack – Common Land/Forestry/260 acre Farmland
Ev Classes
Courses: Resid Hol/YT
Facilities: Cov Sch: 31 x 25m*/Out Man: 25 x 2 5m/CC Course – Novice/Lec Rm/ Refreshments/Wash Rm/WC/Showers/ Car Park
Accom: Shared Rms – 2 Cottages/6 Houses Catering: Full/Self
Specialities: General Instruction/Riding Holidays/Self Accom Holidays/Holiday Livery/Hacking/Livery/RDA
Exclusions: No casual hiring/All rides escorted
Location: Off B3174 btwn Honiton & Seaton

DINGLES RIDING CENTRE
Muddiford, East Down, Barnstaple, North Devon, EX31 4HR
Tel: 0271 850258
Proprietor & Chief Inst: Mrs T M Taylor
Other Staff: 1 (BHSAI) P/T
Basic Instruction in Riding and Jumping
Av No: Horses 3 Ponies 5
Std of Schlg: General Purpose School/Hack – Farm Land/National Trust
Ev Classes
Courses: Resid Riding Hols
Facilities: Out Man/Wash Rm/WC/Car Park
Accom: House – Shared Rms – 4 Catering: Full
Specialities: Basic Instruction/Riding Holidays
Exclusions: No casual hiring

DOONE VALLEY RIDING STABLES
Parsonage Farm, Oare Brendon, Lynton, N Devon, EX35 6NU
Tel: Brendon (05987) 234
Proprietor: Miss W J Burge
Riding Holidays
Av No: Horses 20 Ponies 5
Std of Schlg: General Purpose Livery/Hack/Trek/Moorland – National Park
Facilities: Refreshments/WC/Wash Rm/ Wait Rm/Car Park
Accom: 12 – Holiday flats/4 – Caravan Catering: Self
Specialities: Rides in Doone Valley & Exmoor Day rides across moor
Exclusions: Open Whitsun Bank Holiday to October
Location: Off A39 btwn Oare & Brendon

DRYWELL FARM RIDING CENTRE
Widecombe-in-the-Moor, Newton Abbot, Devon, TQ13 7PN
Tel: 03643 349
Proprietors: Mr & Mrs D Parnell
Riding Holidays
Av No: Horses 12 Ponies 9
Std of Schlg: General Purpose Hacking/Dartmoor National Park
Courses: Hol
Facilities: WC/Showers/Chng Rm/ Refresh/Car Park
Accom: 12 Farmhouse Catering: Full
Specialities: Riding holidays for the more experienced rider
Exclusions: No riders over 14 stones/ No YT/Only open March to November
Location: 2 miles from Widdecombe towards Princetown

EXETER AND DISTRICT RIDING SCHOOL
The Shieling, Ebford, Nr Topsham, Exeter, Devon, EX3 0QT
Tel: Topsham (0392) 873472
Proprietors: Mrs J A Hewitt & Miss C M Hewitt
Chief Inst: Miss Hewitt **Other Staff:** 1 (BHSAI)
Instruction in Riding and Jumping & Students to BHSAI Exam
Av No: Horses 8 Ponies 7
Std of Schlg: General Purpose
Livery: Full/Part/Hunter/Break/School/Hunt/ Hack – Lanes/Common
Ev Classes
Courses: Resid Inst Hol/Wkg Students
Facilities: Cov Sch: 42 x 23m* Gly 200/ Out Man: half acre*/Jmp Pd/Sh Jmps*/ CC Fences/Vis Aids/Lec Rm/Wash Rm/ WC/Chng Rm/Car Park
Accom: 6 House/Caravan Catering: Full
Specialities: General Instruction/ Liveries/Schooling/Competition work/ Career Students
Exclusions: No unaccompanied Hacking
Location: In centre of village 2.5 miles Junc 30 M5 off A377

HILLTOP RIDING SCHOOL
Pennsylvania Road, Exeter, Devon
Tel: Exeter (0392) 51370/70218
Proprietor: Miss J Portbury (BHSAI)
Other Staff: 1 (BHSAI)
Basic Instruction in Riding and Jumping
Av No: Horses 5 Ponies 10
Std of Schlg: General Purpose
Livery: DIY/Break/School/Hack/Farmland
Ev Classes
Courses: YT/Basic
Facilities: Out Man: 37 x 6m* Fl Lit/Jmp Pd/Sh Jmps/CC Fences/WC/Car Park
Specialities: Beginners to Pony Club 'C' Test/Local Shows/Basic Courses

HONEYSUCKLE FARM EQUESTRIAN CENTRE
Haccombe With Combe, Newton Abbot, Devon, TQ12 4SA
Tel: 0626 55944
Proprietors: Mr & Mrs I G Mackay
Chief Inst: Miss A Bock (BHSAI)
Instruction in Riding and Jumping
Av No: Horses 10 Ponies 4
Std of Schlg: General Purpose Std of Specialist Schlg: Sh Jmpg – Novice
Livery: Full/Part/DIY/School/Hack – Bridle paths/Beach
Ev Classes
Courses: YT – 3
Facilities: Cov Sch: 12 x 19m*/Out Man: 50 x 4 0m* Fl Lit/CC Course/ Refreshments/WC/Car Park
Specialities: General Instruction/ Hacking/Livery/Holiday Livery/CC Course
Exclusions: No rider over 14 stone/ No casual hire
Location: Off B3195 between Newton Abbot/Sheldon

HORWOOD RIDING CENTRE
West Barton, Horwood, Bideford, North Devon
Tel: 027 185 244
Proprietor: Mrs J Congdon
Chief Inst: Mr A Congdon **Other Staff:** 1 (Unqual) F/T 2 (Pony Club B Tests) P/T 1 (BHSI) – Visiting
Instruction in Riding and Jumping
Av No: Horses 9 Ponies 2
Std of Schlg: General Purpose Specialist Schlg: Sh Jmp – Novice
Livery: Full/Grass/School/Break/Hunt/ Hack – Lanes/Bridlepaths/Woodland
Ev Classes
Courses: YT 2
Facilities: Out Man: 60 x 20m* Fl Lit/Snacks/WC/Car Park
Accom: Hotel
Specialities: Hacking/Hunt Hire/ Liveries/Riding Short Breaks/Hunting
Exclusions: Experienced Riders only

LYDFORD HOUSE RIDING STABLES
Lydford House Hotel, Lydford, Okehampton, Devon, EX20 4AU
Tel: Lydford (082 282) 321/347/
Fax – 082283 442
Proprietor: Mrs C Knight (BHSII(T))
Other Staff: 1 (BHSAI)
Instruction in Riding and Jumping
Av No: Horses 6 Ponies 6
Std of Schlg: General Purpose
Livery: Full/Part/School/Break/Hack – Open Moorland (Dartmoor)/Country Lanes
Courses: Hol/YT 3
Facilities: Out Man:40m x 20m*/Jmp Pd/Sh Jmps/Wash Rm/Refresh/Lic Bar/ WC/Chng Rm/Car Park
Accom: Hotel Catering – Full
Specialities: Riding holidays/Nervous & inexperienced riders/Small groups/RDA/ Riding Club
Exclusions: No unescorted riding
Location: Off A386 in Village

NEWTON FERRERS EQUESTRIAN CENTRE
Newton Downs Farm, Newton Ferrers, Plymouth, PL8 1JA
Proprietors: Elissa Hebborn Roger Harris
Chief Inst: Elissa Hebborn (BHSAI)
Other Staff 1 (BHSII) 1 (BHSAI)
Instruction: General
Av No: Horses 12 Ponies 8 Specialist Horses: 1 Drg M/1 Han Stallion
Livery: Full/Part/Grass/DIY/Hunting/ Hacking/Schooling/Breaking
Ev Classes
Working Pupils
Facilities: Cov.Sch 30x20m/Out Man: 45x25m F/Lit/Novice CC Courses/Jmp Pd
Accom: House Accomodation
Specialities: Vaulting/Dressage/Cross Country
Exclusions: No Children Under 5/ Hacking only after Assessment Lesson

OTTERDENE RIDING STABLES
Venn Ottery, Ottery St Mary, Devon, EX11 1SG
Tel: 0404 81 3574
Proprietor: Mr R Adamson
Chief Inst: Mrs L Martin (BHSII) **Other Staff:** 1 (BHSII) P/T

Instruction in Riding and Jumping
Av No: Horses 10 Ponies 8 Specialist Horses: 1 Sh Jmp Grade C
Std of Schlg: General Purpose Specialist Schlg: Sh Jmp – Novice
Livery: Full/Part/Grass/DIY/School/ Break/Hack – Common Land/ Bridleways/Trek – Common Land
Ev Classes – Summer only
Courses: Wkg Pupils/YTS 2/Riding Holidays
Facilities: Out Man: 50 x 30m*/Sh Jmp Pd*/Lec Rm/Vis Aids/Snacks/Wash Rm/ WC/Showers/Changing Rm/Car Park
Accom: Dormitory/Bunk House 8 Catering: Full
Specialities: General Instruction/Livery/ Riding Holidays/Hacking/Trekking/ Holiday Livery Service
Exclusions: 7 – 15 years Childrens Riding Holidays/Weekend Breaks/ Courses for Adults
Location: Off B3180 btwn Venn Otterway/Halfway house

SHILSTONE ROCKS STUD AND TREKKING CENTRE
Widecombe-in-the Moor, Newton Abbot, Devon, TQ13 7TF
Tel: Widecombe (036 42) 281
Proprietors: Mr & Mrs R Newbolt-Young
Manager: Mrs A Whittle
Hacking & Trekking
Av No: Horses 9 Ponies 32
Std of Schlg: General Purpose
Livery: Full/Hack/Trek – Open Moorland
Courses: YT taken
Facilities: Jmp Pd/CC Course/WC/ Chng Rm/Refresh/Wash Rm/Car Park
Specialities: Trekking for Adults/ Children/Hacking/Stud/Holiday Livery service
Exclusions: Open all year/No unescorted rides
Location: 1 mile out of Widdecombe/ Ashburton

STADDON HEIGHTS FARM
Staddon Heights, Plymstock, Plymouth, Devon, PL9 9SP
Tel: 0752 481631/403273
Proprietor: R J C Westlake Esq
Hacking & Livery Centre
Av No: Horses 1
Std of Schlg: General Purpose
Livery: DIY/School/Hack – Woodland/ Lanes
Facilities: Out Man: 46 x 28m/WC/ Car Park
Specialities: Livery/Hacking/Holiday Livery
Exclusions: No casual hire
Location: Between Plymstock & Staddiscombe

STEELE HILL RIDING CENTRE
Week St Mary, Holsworthy, Devon, EX22 6XB
Tel: 028 884 553
Proprietor & Chief Inst: Miss C A Guy (BHSAI)
Instruction in Riding and Jumping
Av No: Horses 6 Ponies 9
Std of Schlg: General Purpose Std of Specialist Schlg – Sh Jmpg – Novice
Livery: Full/Part/Grass/School/Hack – Bridle paths/Forestry
Ev Classes
Facilities: Cov Sch: 43 x 21m* Gly/Jmpg Pd*/Refreshments/WC/ Car Park
Specialities: General Instruction/ No Residential Holiday Courses/ Livery Service
Exclusions: No casual hire
Location: 1 mile north of village between Week St Mary & Whitstone

DORSET

CROFT HOUSE SCHOOL LIMITED
Shillingstone, Dorset, DT11 0QS
Tel: Childe Okeford (0258) 860 295/474
Proprietors: Mrs E A Rawlinson B A
The Bursar: P C O'Connor Esq **Chief Inst:** Miss J Beeby (BHSII) **Other Staff:** 1 (BHSAI) 1 (BHSII)
Instruction in Riding and Jumping & Students to BHSAI Exam
Av No: Horses 5 Ponies 10
Std of Schlg: General Purpose Hack/Hills and woods/Full/Part/ Schooling/Breaking
Courses: Wkg Students
Facilities: Cov Sch: 28 x 14m* Gly 20/ Jmp Pd/CC Fences/Lec Rm/Vis Aids
Accom: Girls' Boarding School
Specialities: General Instr/Prep. for Riding and Pony Club Comps/Career Students/Livery Competition & Shows.
Exclusions: No Casual Hire
Location: On A357 in centre of village

FOREST LODGE EQUESTRIAN CENTRE
Motcombe, Nr Shaftesbury, Dorset, SP7 9PL
Tel: Shaftesbury (0747) 51685

Proprietors: Mr & Mrs R I Roberts
Chief Inst: Miss L Davidson-Parker (BHSAI) **Other Staff:** 1 (BHSAI) 2 (BHSII)
Instruction in Riding and Jumping
Av No: Horses 12 Ponies 11
Std of Schlg: General Purpose
Livery: Full/Part/Grass/Hunter/Break/School/Hack – Lanes/Tracks/Fields/Woods
Ev Classes
Facilities: Out Man:23 x 30m*/Jmp Pd/Sh Jmps/CC Course/2 Cov Schs: 62 x 28m & 30 x 15m/WC/Chng Rm/Refresh/Lic Bar/Club Rm/Lec Rm/Vis Aids/Video/Showers/Wash Rm/Car Park
Accom: Farmhouse – 10 Catering: Full
Specialities: Riding instruction/Riding Holidays/Pony Club work/RDA/Regular Shows/Events
Exclusions: No unescorted hacking
Location: Between Gillingham/Shaftesbury off B3081

THE FORTUNE CENTRE FOR RIDING THERAPY

Avon Tyrell, Bransgore, Christchurch, Dorset, BH23 8EE
Tel: 0425 73297
Director/Chief Inst: Mrs Dixon-Clegg SRN (BHSAI)
Senior Riding Therapist: Miss P Longden (BHSI) **Other Staff:** 1 (FBHS) – Visiting/1 BHSI/3 (BHSII)/5 (BHSAI) & many visiting Dressage/Event Competition Riders
Instruction in Riding and Jumping & Students to BHSAI Exam
Av No: Horses 18 Ponies 10 Specialist Horses: 1M/Adv M & many E/N Drg/Nov HT & CT & Voltige
Std of Schlg: General Purpose Spec Schlg: Drg – Med/CT – Int/Sh Jmp – Nov
Courses: BHSAI/II/Resid/RDA
Facilities: Cov Schs: 40 x 20m Gly*/18m x 20m Gly*/Out Mans: 60 x 20m Fl Lit*/40 x 20m Fl Lit*/CC Course/Sh Jmp Pd/Lec Rm – Seat 20/Vis Aids/Film Projector/Library/Refreshments/Wash Rm/WC/Showers/Wait Rm/Car Park
Accom: Single/Shared House – 16 Catering: Full
Specialities: Residential Training Centre for Riding Therapists & lesser Handicapped Students/Short Courses for RDA Instructors/Helpers/RDA Affiliated Group
Exclusions: No Hiring or Riding for the General Public
Location: Burley/Bransgorse

LANEHOUSE EQUITATION CENTRE

Overbury Close, Weymouth, Dorset
Tel: Weymouth (0305) 770177
Proprietors: Mr R H Addison & Mrs Y Kennard
Principal & Chief Inst: Mr R H Addison
Instruction in Riding and Jumping
Av No: Horses 9 Ponies 13 Specialist Horses: Sh Jmper C
Std of Schlg: General Purpose
Livery: Full/Part/Break/School/Hack – Bridle paths
Ev Classes
Courses: Inst Hol/YT
Facilities: Out Man:46 x 55m Seats Fl Lit/Jmp Pd Seats Fl Lit/Sh Jmps/CC Fences/Lec Rm/Vis Aids/Refresh/WC/Wash Rm/Car Park
Specialities: General Instruction/Hacking/Private Tuition
Exclusions: All Hacks escorted
Location: West of Weymouth Nr Chickerell

LEIGH EQUESTRIAN CENTRE LTD

Three Gates, Leigh, Sherborne, Dorset, DT9 6JQ
Tel: Holnest (096321) 469
Proprietors: Mr & Mrs H Shuaib
Chief Inst: Miss S E Richards (BHSI)
Other Staff: 1 (BHSAI) 2 (BHSII)
Instruction in Riding and Jumping & Students to BHSII Exam
Av No: Horses 26 Ponies 10 Specialist Horses: Drg M
Std of Schlg: General Purpose
Livery: Full/Grass/Hunter/Break/School/Hacking/Bridleways/Downs
Ev Classes
Courses: Resid Inst Hol/Wkg Students
Facilities: Cov Sch: 31 x 18m Gly 40 Fl Lit/Out Man: 31 x18m Seats/Jmp Pd/Sh Jmps/CC Course/Lec Rm/Vis Aids/Refresh/WC/Wash Rm/Chng Rm/Tennis Court/Car Park
Accom: Shared Rms – 14 Catering: Full/Part
Specialities: Student training towards BHS examin ations/Residential holidays/Livery
Exclusions: No YTS/No Casual Hire
Location: 3 miles off the A352 south of Sherborne

LONGHAM HOUSE

Longham, Hampreston, Nr Wimbourne, Dorset, BH22 9AB
Tel: Bournemouth (0202) 572758
Proprietor: Miss S R Bush
Other Staff: 2 (BHSAI) P/T

RIDING IN THE SOUTH WEST

Basic Instruction in Riding and Jumping
Av No: Horses 8 Ponies 8
Std of Schlg: General Purpose Hack/Heath/Forestry
Facilities: Out Man: 44m x 22m/Jmp Pd/ Sh Jmps/WC/Wait Rm/Chng Rm/Car Park
Specialities: Instruction under close supervision for young riders/Hacking in Ferndown Forest/RDA
Exclusions: No hunting
Location: on the A348 btwn West Parley & Poole

LULWORTH EQUESTRIAN CENTRE
Kennel Farm, Coombe Keynes, Wareham, Dorset, BH20 5QR
Tel: 0929 41 352/439
Proprietors: Mr & Mrs W J Weld
Other Staff: 3 (BHSAI) 1 (BHSII) P/T
Instruction in Riding and Jumping
Av No: Horses 10 Ponies 10 Specialist Horse: 1 Drg Elem
Std of Schlg: General Purpose Std of Specialist Schlg: Drg – Elem/CT – Int
Livery: Full/Part/Grass/School/Hunt/ Hack – Private Estate/Heath/Downland
Ev Classes
Facilities: Out Man: 60 x 20m* Fl Lit/CC Course* – Int/Jmpg Pd/Sh Jmps*/ Refreshments/Wash Rm/WC/Showers/ Changing Rm/Waiting Rm/Car Park
Accom: Local/House – 4
Specialities: General Instruction/ Instruction in Dressage & Eventing/ Livery/Riding Holidays – Hacking & Livery
Exclusions: No casual hire
Location: Between Coombe Keynes & East Lulworth

PEAR TREE FARM RIDING STABLES
Pear Tree Farm, Organford, Poole, Dorset, BH16 6LA
Tel: 0202 624203
Proprietor & Chief Inst: Miss R E House (BHSAI)
Other Staff: 1 P/T
Instruction in Riding and Jumping
Av No: Horses 1 Ponies 11
Std of Schlg: General Purpose
Livery: Holiday/School/Hack – Forestry
Ev Classes – Summer only
Facilities: Out Man: 40 x 20m*/Jmp Pd*/ Wash Rm/WC/Car Park
Specialities: General Instruction/ Children/Hacking
Exclusions: No casual hire
Location: Off A351 btwn Lychett Minster & Sandford

POUND COTTAGE RIDING CENTRE
Luccombe Farm, Milton Abbas, Dorset DT11 0BD, Corres: Pound Cottage 13, Water Lane Durweston Nr Blandford Forum Dorset DT11 0QB
Tel: 0258 451240/880057
Proprietor & Chief Inst: Mrs J Hardy (BHSAI)
Other Staff: 1 (BHSAI) P/T 1 (BHSII)
Instruction in Riding and Jumping
Av No: Horses 3 Ponies 11
Std of Schlg: General Purpose
Livery: Full/Part/Working/DIY/Hack – Forestry/Farm Land/Breaking/Schooling/ Bridle paths
Courses: Residential Rid Hols/YT – 2/ Wkg pupils
Facilities: Out Man:15x30mF/L Jump paddock/Grazing – 16 acres/Car Park
Accom: Shared House 3 Catering – Full
Specialities: General Instruction, Novices, Liveries, Riding Holiday Courses/RDA
Exclusions: No Riders over 12 st/ No Casual Hire
Location: Off A354 Between Winterbourne, Whitchurch and Milton Abbass

STOCKS FARM EQUESTRIAN CENTRE
Christchurch Road, West Parley, Dorset, BH22 8SQ
Tel: 0202 570288
Proprietor: Mr & Mrs P G Oliver
Manageress: Mrs D Walters **Other Staff:** Miss A Heather (BHSII) P/T
Instruction in Riding and Jumping
Av No: Horses 9 Ponies 6
Std of Schlg: General Purpose Std of Specialist Schlg: HT – N
Livery: Full/Part/DIY/Grass/Hack – Common Land
Ev Lessons
Courses: Inst/Wkg Pupils/YT – 2/ Stages I & II/NVQ/Lectures
Facilities: Out Man:42m x 20m * Fl Lit/ Cov Sch: 40 m x 20m* Gly 150/ International Outdoor Dressage Arena 20m x 60m/Jmp Pd/Sh Jmps/CC Fences/CC Course/WC/H & C/Refresh/ Car Park
Specialities: General Instruction/ Students/Stages I &II/Competitions – Dressage/Show Jumping esp Juniors/Top Visiting Trainers/Exams Study Groups 2hrs/Weekly pre exams courses
Exclusions: No riders under 6 years
Location: On unnumbered Road between Hurn Airport & West Parley

GLOUCESTER

HARTPURY COLLEGE
Hartpury House, Hartpury, Gloucester, GL19 3BE
Tel: 0452 70 283
Principal: M Wharton Esq BEd (Hons) NDA MRAC
Manager & Chief Inst Mr J Michaels (FBHS) **Other Staff:** Miss J Anthony (BHS SM) Mr A Lovell (BHS SM) Mr A Mead (BHSII(T)) Miss A Horne (BHSI I)
Instruction in Riding and Jumping & Students to BHSAI Exam
Av No: Horses 40 Specialist Horses: 3 Int Eventers
Std of Schlg: General Purpose Std of Specialist Schlg: CT – Int/Sh Jmpg – C/Drg – Adv
School
Ev Classes
Courses: Up to & including BHSII Exam/Wkg Pupils/YT/Resid – for College Students only
Facilities: 2 Cov Schs: 60 x 24m & 60 x 21m/Out Man: 60 x 20m Fl Lit/16 Nov CC Fences*/Sh Jmps*/Lec Rm* – Seating/Film Projector*/Library*/Vis Aids*/Video*/Wash Rm/Chng Rm/WC/Showers/Car Park
Accom: Shared Rms – College Students only – 120 Catering: Full
Exclusions: No casual clients
Location: On A417 between Gloucester & Ledbury

HUNTLEY SCHOOL OF EQUITATION
Wood End Farm, Huntley, Gloucestershire, GL19 3EY
Tel: Gloucester (0452) 830440
Proprietor: Mrs M T Freeman (BHSI(SM))
Chief Inst: Miss C Broad (BHSI) **Other Staff:** 2 (BHSII) 1 (BHSII(T)) 2 (BHSAI)
Instruction in Riding and Jumping & Students to BHSI Exam
Av No: Horses 10 Ponies 2 Specialist Horses: 1 E & 1 M Drg/1 HT Int
Std of Schlg: General Purpose
Livery: Full/Part/Grass/Break/School
Ev Classes
Courses: Resid Inst Hol/Student – 1/Wkg Students 7
Facilities: Cov Sch: 20m x 40m* Gly Fl Lit/Out Man: 20m x 60m Jmp Pd 40m x 60m/Sh Jmps 12/CC Course*/CC Fences/Lec Rm/Video/WC/Car Park
Accom: 10 – Farmhouse Catering: Self
Specialities: Preparation for Horse Trials/RDA/Career Students
Exclusions: No Hunting/Hacking or Trekking/No Children under 10
Location: On A40 miday between Glos & Ross on Wye opposite Garden Centre

LITTLEDEAN TREKKING CENTRE
Wellington Farm, Sutton Road, Littledean, Gloucester, GL14 2TU
Tel: Dean (0594) 823955
Proprietors: Mr & Mrs T Chamberlain
Trekking
Av No: Horses 12 Ponies 11
Std of Schlg: General Purpose
Hack/Trek – Forestry/Bridleways
Facilities: Out Man: 20 x 35m Fl Lit/Refresh/WC/Car Park
Specialities: Trekking/School contract work
Exclusions: No Casual Hire
Location: Off A4151 Littledean Village Side Road signed Soudley

LONG DISTANCE RIDING CENTRE
Fosseway, Bourton-on-the-Water, Gloucester, GL54 2DX
Tel: Bourton-on-the-Water (0451)21101 – day/20358
Proprietor: Miss J Davies (BHS STM)
Chief Inst: Miss N Brown (BHSAI)
Instruction in Riding and Jumping
Av No: Horses 5 Ponies 7
Std of Schlg: General Purpose
Hack – Bridleways
Ev Classes Summer
Courses: Inst/Wkg Students
Facilities: Out Man:60m x 20m*/Sh Jmps/Lec Rm/Vis Aids/Rest Rm/Refresh/WC/Chng Rm/Car Park
Specialities: General Instruction/Long term student courses/Stable Management Courses
Exclusions: No casual hiring/No YT taken
Location: On A429 Between Stow & Burford

THE PLAYMATE RIDING SCHOOL
Hardwicke House, Elmstone Hardwicke, Cheltenham, Gloucestershire, GL51 9TD
Tel: Cheltenham (0242) 680319/680888
Proprietor: Mrs J Swambo (BHSAI)
Basic Instruction in Riding and Jumping
Av No: Horses – Ponies 12
Std of Schlg: General Purpose
Hack – Bridlepaths
Ev Classes Summer only
Courses: Inst Hol
Facilities: Jmp Pd/Sh Jmps/CC Fences/WC/Wash Rm/Car Park
Specialities: Small children & beginners

Exclusions: Only open Tues – Friday/ Closed in winter/Children only
Location: Off B4019 Cheltenham – 4 miles Tewksbury 6 miles on Stoke Orchard Road

SUMMERHOUSE EQUITATION CENTRE
Hardwicke, Gloucester, GL2 6RG
Tel: 0452 720288
Proprietor: Mrs S R Weston
Chief Inst: Mrs H Gallop (BHSI(SM))
Other Staff: Miss C Howe (BHSAI) Miss M Scriyin (BHSAI) P/T
Instruction in Riding and Jumping & Students to BHSII Exam
Av No: Horses 16 Ponies 18
Std of Schlg: General Purpose Std of Spec Schlg: – 3 Drg Nov – Med/2 Evt Nov – Int/2 Shw Jmp – Grade C
Livery: Part/School/Break/Hack – Cotswold Hills
Ev Classes
Courses: 2 Wkg Students/YT – 3
Facilities: Cov Sch:43m x 25m*/Out Man: 40m x 20m Fl Lit*/CC Fences 20/Jmp Pd/ Lec Rm/Video/Film Equip/Refresh/WC
Accom: Mobile homes – 2 (Wkg Pupils/ YT only) Catering: Self
Specialities: General Instruction/Road Safety Tests/Personal Tuition/Side Saddle(Nov)/Regular Shows
Exclusions: No Casual Hiring
Location: On A38 Between Glos & Exit 12 on M5

THE TALLAND SCHOOL OF EQUITATION
Church Farm, Siddington, Cirencester, Glos, GL7 6EZ
Tel: 0285 652318/Fax: 0285 659409
Proprietors: Colonel & Mrs R C T Sivewright (FIH FBHS) & Mrs Hutton (FBHS)
Other Staff: 8 (BHSAI) 3 (BHSII) 2 (BHSI)
Instruction in Riding and Jumping & Students to all BHS Exams including Fellowship
Av No: Horses 75 Ponies 18
Std of Schlg: General Purpose/Advanced Dressage/Novice – Advanced Event
Livery: Full/Part/Grass/Break/School/ Hunt (own horses only)/Hack – Cotswolds
Courses: Resid Inst Hol/Wkg Students
Facilities: Cov Sch: 60m x 20m* Gly 200/2 Out Mans: 40 x 20m & 40 x 20m Seats Fl Lit/Jmp Pd/CC Course/Lec Rms 2/Club Rm*/WC/Wash Rm/Vis Aids/ Video/Car Park
Accom: 40 – Students Catering: Full
Specialities: Short courses equitation/ Competition yard/RDA/Side Saddle/ Showing/Career Students – Competition Training
Exclusions: No trekking/No hunter hiring/No YT
Location: 1 mile SE Cirencester next to Siddington Church

SOMERSET

BURCOTT RIDING SCHOOL
Lower Burcott, Wells, Somerset, BA5 1NQ
Tel: Wells (0749) 73145
Proprietor: Mr N Payne (BHSAI)
Other Staff: Miss N Stevens (BHSII) 3 (BHSAI)
Instruction in Riding and Jumping
Av No: Horses 14 Ponies 21
Std of Schlg: General Purpose
Livery: Full/Part/Hunter/Break/School/ Hack – Lanes
Ev Classes
Courses: Res Inst Hol/YT – 1/Wkg Student – 1
Facilities: Out Man: 30 x 60m* Fl Lit/ Jmp Pd/Sh Jmps/CC Fences/CC Course/WC/Car Park
Specialities: Children & novice adults/ General Instruction
Exclusions: No Children Under 7/ No casual hiring
Location: 1.5 miles from Wells

CURLAND EQUESTRIAN ENTERPRISES
Crosses Farm Stud, Curland, Taunton, Somerset, TA3 5SD
Tel: Buckland St Mary (046034) 234
Proprietors: Mrs A L Brown BSc (BHSI(E & SM)) & Mrs M Baillie (BHSAI)
Other Staff: 3 (BHSAI) 2 (BHSII)
Instruction in Riding and Jumping & Students to BHSII Exam
Av No: Horses 4 Ponies 0 Specialist Horses: Drg – A/HT – A
Std of Schlg: General Purpose
Livery: Full/Part/Hunter/Break/School/ Hack – Varied
Ev Classes
Courses: Wkg Students/YT – 1
Facilities: Cov Sch: 40m x 20m Fl Lit/ Out Man:60m x 30m/Jmp Pd/Sh Jmps/ CC Fences/Lec Rm/Vis Aids/Showers/ Wash Rm/WC/Refresh/Chng Rm/Car Park
Specialities: Career Students/General Instruction/Livery
Location: Btwn Taunton/Ilminster

EBBORLANDS FARM & RIDING CENTRE
Ebborlands Farm, Wookey Hole, Nr Wells, Somerset, BA5 1AY
Tel: Wells (0749) 72550
Proprietor: Mrs E A Gibbs
Chief Inst: Miss J Penny (BHSII(T))
Instruction in Riding and Jumping
Av No: Horses 10 Ponies 5
Std of Schlg: General Purpose
Livery: Full/Part/DIY/Break/School/Hack – Mendip Hills/Somerset levels
Ev Classes
Courses: Resid Inst Hol/YT – 2
Facilities: Cov Sch: 32 x 18m/Out Man: 24 x 55m*/CC Fences/Sh Jmps 6*/WC/ Shop/Restaurant/Swimming Pool within quarter mile/Caves nearby
Accom: Self-catering at Ebborlands Farm/Full Catering elswhere
Specialities: Small groups/Riding holidays/Weekly lessons/Hacks with lovely views
Exclusions: No hiring for hunting
Location: 2 miles north west of Wells

GREENHAM EQUESTRIAN CENTRE
Ridge Farm, Greenham, Wellington, Somerset
Tel: 0823 672304
Proprietors: Mr & Mrs C Marshall
Chief Inst: Mrs C Marshall **Other Staff:** 3 (BHSAI) P/T
Instruction in Riding and Jumping
Av No: Horses 5 Ponies 5
Std of Schlg: General Purpose
Livery: Part/School/Hack – Farmland
Ev Classes
Courses: BHS Stages I & II/YT – 1
Facilities: Out Mans: both 40 x 20m* Fl Lit/6 Basic Schooling CC Fences/ Lec Rm – Video Camera/Vis Aids/ Refresh/WC/Car Park
Specialities: General Instruction/ Courses/Hacking
Exclusions: No casual hire
Location: Off A38 btwn Wellington & Whitehall

GREGGS RIDING SCHOOL
Placket Lane, Off West Coker Road, Yeovil, Somerset, BA22 2HH
Tel: Yeovil (0935) 23894
Proprietors: Mr & Mrs G Bennett
Instruction in Riding and Jumping
Av No: Horses 4 Ponies 8
Std of Schlg: General Purpose School/Hack – Country lanes/Bridleways
Evening Lessons – Summer only
Courses: Hol Inst
Facilities: Out Man:40m x 45m/Sh Jmps/Jmp Pd/CC Fences/WC/Chng Rm
Specialities: Day Courses/General Instruction/RDA
Exclusions: No Casual hiring for hacking
Location: Off A30 btwn Yeovil & West Coker

KNOWLE RIDING CENTRE
Timberscombe, Minehead, Somerset, TA24 6TZ
Tel: Timberscombe (0643) 841342
Proprietors: John & Kathryn Lamacraft
Other Staff: 2 (BHSAI) 1 (BHSII) 1 (BHSI) P/T Miss B Howett (FBHS) – when required
Riding Holidays & Hacking
Av No: Horses 35 Ponies 12
Std of Schlg: General Purpose
Livery: Holiday Livery
Courses: Resid Hol/Wkg Students
Facilities: Cov Sch:42 x 20m* Gly 30/ Jmp Pd/Sh Jmps/CC Course*/H T/Hunt/ Hack/Lec Rm – Vis Aids/Lic Bar/ Swimming Pool/WC/Car Park
Accom: 25 Countryhouse Catering: Full
Specialities: Riding Holidays (residential with i nstruction)/Escorted Hacks/Hunting
Exclusions: No unaccompanied children under 11 years/No YT
Location: Off A396 Between Dunster/ Timberscombe

MILLFIELD SCHOOL
Street, Somerset, BA16 0AA
Tel: Street (0458) 42291 (Only for pupils of Millfield School)
Headmaster: Mr C S Martin MA
Chief Inst/Riding Master: Major C R Burke **Other Staff:** 1 (BHSII) P/T 2 (BHSAI)
Instruction in Riding and Jumping & Students to BHSAI Exam
Av No: Horses 26 Ponies 5
Std of Schlg: General Purpose
Livery: Full/Hunt/Hack
Courses: Wkg Students – 5
Facilities: Cov Sch: 55 x 25m Fl Lit Gly/ Jmp Pd/CC Fences/Lec Rm/Vis Aids/ Wash Rm/WC/Chng Rm/Car Park
Specialities: Polo/Hunting/Combined training
Exclusions: For use of Millfield pupils only during term time/No YT

PORLOCK VALE EQUITATION CENTRE
Porlock Ford, Nr Minehead, Somerset, TA24 8NY
Tel: 0643 862338

Proprietor: Mr Coxhead
Chief Inst: Mr R J Hutton (BHSI)
Instruction in Riding and Jumping
Av No: Horses 15 Ponies 1
Std of Schlg: General Purpose
Livery: Full/Holiday/Break/School/Hack – Exmoor
Courses: Resid Int Hol/Wkg Students – 6
Facilities: Cov Schs: 40 x 20m* Fl Lit Gly & 30 x 15m* Fl Lit Gly/Out Man: 38 x 16m* Fl Lit/Large Jmpg Pds*/Sh Jmps 10*/CC Course/Lec Rm/Vis Aids/ Refresh/WC/Wash Rm/Chng Rm/Car Park
Accom: 26 Rms – TV/Tel Catering: Full
Specialities: General Instructing/Riding & Hunting Holidays
Location: Off B3225 2 miles from Porlock

THE QUANTOCK RIDING CENTRE
Pardlesham Farm, Kilve, Nr Bridgwater, Somerset, TA5 1SQ
Tel: Holford (027874) 374
Proprietors: Mr D Houghton & Ms R Moore
Chief Inst: Mrs S Payne (BHSAI)
Basic Instruction in Riding and Jumping
Av No: Horses 6 Ponies 23
Std of Schlg: General Purpose
Livery: Full/DIY/Hunt/Hack/Trek – Quantock Hills
Courses: Resid Hol/YT – 1
Facilities: Out Man: 18 x 9m/Jmp Pd/Sh Jmps/CC Course/Refresh/WC/Showers/ Chng Rm/Tack Shop/Car Park
Accom: 1 House – 20 Catering: Full
Specialities: Residential Riding Holidays/Unaccompanied Children/ Parties/Hacking/Day Treks/Hunting Weekends
Exclusions: No unescorted rides
Location: Off A39 at start of Village

THE WEST SOMERSET RIDING CENTRE
Moor Road, North Hill, Minehead, Somerset, TA24 5RT
Tel: 0643 705406
Proprietor: Mr C Fisher
Chief Inst: Mr K Boulter
Instruction in Riding and Jumping
Av No: Horses 8 Ponies 8
Std of Schlg: General Purpose
Specialist Horse 1 Drg – N/Sh Jmpers
Livery: Full/Part/Grass/DIY/School/ Break/Hunt/Hack – Moorland/Forest/ Coast
Ev Classes
Courses: Resid/YT taken
Facilities: Out Man: 32m x 17m*/ Jmp Pd*/Sh Jmps*-Novice/6 Schooling CC Fences/WC/Car Park
Accom: Shared Rooms(Cottage) Catering: Self
Specialities: General Instruction/Livery/ Hacking/Trekking/Riding & Hunting Holidays
Exclusions: No Pupils under 6 years
Location: At the back of town

WILTSHIRE

BRYMPTON RIDING SCHOOL
Whiteparish Common, Salisbury, Wiltshire
Tel: Whiteparish (0794) 884386
Proprietor: Mrs S A Near (BHSAI) NPSD
Instruction in Riding and Jumping
Av No: Horses 8 Ponies 15
Std of Schlg: General Purpose
Livery: Full/Part/Grass/Hunter/Hack/ Trek – National Trust/New Forest
Ev Classes Summer only
Courses: YT taken
Facilities: Out Man:45m x 30m/Jmp Pd/ Sh Jmps/CC Fences/WC/Car Park
Specialities: Pony Club tests/Basic Instruction
Location: Off A27 near centre of Village

HEDDINGTON WICK CHILDREN'S RIDING SCHOOL
3 Hillside, Heddington, Calne, Wiltshire, SN11 0PH
Tel: Bromham (0380) 850796/850182
Proprietor: Mrs I Gage (BHSAI)
Other Staff: 1 (BHSAI)
Instruction in Riding and Jumping
Av No: Horses 2 Ponies 11
Std of Schlg: General Purpose
Hack – Country lanes/Common/ Downland/Farmland
Facilities: Out Man: 111 x 55m/Jmp Pd/ Sh Jmps/CC Fences for children/Car Park
Specialities: Courses of instruction & hacking for children only/Road Safety courses
Exclusions: No casual hiring/No YT
Location: Off A3102 – Calne on outskirts of Heddington

HURDCOTT LIVERY STABLES
Winterbourne Earls, Salisbury, Wiltshire, SP4 7HR
Tel: Idmiston (0980) 611276
Proprietor: Miss C Bright

Livery Yard
Av No: Horses 4 Ponies 12
Livery: Full/Part/Grass/Hunter/ Farmland/Bridleways
Facilities: Out Man/WC/Car Park
Specialities: Liveries
Exclusions: No Hiring
Location: Off A338 in Village

THE INFANTRY SADDLE CLUB
Oxendene, Warminster, Wiltshire
Tel: 0985 214000 Ext 2395/2326
Proprietor: Major R B Sullivan-Tailyour (BHSAI)
Chief Inst: Mr J Malcolm (BHSAI) **Other Staff:** 1 (BHSI) P/T 3 (BHSAI) P/T
Instruction in Riding and Jumping
Av No: Horses 8 Ponies 10 Specialist Horses: 1 Grade C Sh Jmper
Std of Schlg: General Purpose Std of Specialist Schlg: CT – Novice/Sh Jmpg–C
Livery: Full/Part/Grass/DIY/School/Hack – Downland/Bridle path
Ev Classes
Courses: Stages I & II/YT
Facilities: Cov Sch: 40 x 20m* Gly -30 Bench/Out Man: 60 x 30m* Fl Lit/2 Novice CC Courses*/Jmp Pd*/Lec Rm* – Vis Aids/Library/Video/Seating – 20/ Refreshments/Wash Rm/WC/Showers/ Car Park
Specialities: General Instruction/Livery/ RDA/Facility Hire
Exclusions: No casual hire/weight limit 14 stone

LACKHAM COLLEGE
Joint Equestrian Centre, Lacock, Nr Chippenham, Wiltshire, SN15 2NY
Tel: 0249 443111 Ext 217/213
Proprietor: Mr P W Morris
Manager & Chief Inst: Col G Wesley (BHSI(SM & T)) **Other Staff:** Miss E Ross (BHSII) Miss J Robinson (BHSII) Miss J Pulford (BHSII) – all P/T
Instruction in Riding and Jumping & Students to BHSAI Exam
Av No: Horses 12 Ponies 8
Std of Schlg: General Purpose Std of Specialist Schlg: Sh Jmpg – Novice
Livery: Full/Part/School/Hack – Parkland
Ev Classes – Summer only
Courses: Up to & including (BHSAI) Exam/YT
Facilities: Out Man: 60 x 40m*/Lec Rm – Vis Aids/Film Projector/Library/Video/ Snacks/WC/Chng Rms/Car Park
Accom: Shared Rms Catering: Full
Specialities: Career Students/Long & Short Term Courses/Hacking/Livery/RDA
Exclusions: No Rider over 12 stone
Location: Off A350 btwn Chippenham/ Melksham

PEWSEY VALE RIDING CENTRE
Church Farm, Stanton St Bernard, Marlborough, Wiltshire, SN8 4LJ
Tel: 0672 851 400/326
Proprietor: M J Read Ltd – B Read Esq
Manager: Mrs L Shutter **Chief Inst:** J Duck (BHSII) **Other Staff:** 1 (BHSII) 2 (BHSAI)
Instruction in Riding and Jumping
Av No: Horses 60 Ponies 15 Specialist Horses: Int Eventer/Hunters
Std of Schlg: General Purpose Specialist Schlg: Drg – Elementary/ Sh Jmp – Novice
Livery: Full/Part/Grass/DIY/School/ Break/Hunt/Hack – Downs/Farm land
Ev Classes
Courses: YT 2
Facilities: Cov Schs: 15 x 24m Gly & 44 x 30m*/Out Man: 44 x 22m Fl Lit/CC Course – 26/Sh Jpg Pd/Refreshments/ Lec Rm/Wash Rm/WC/Shower/Chang Rm/Wait Rm/Car Park
Specialities: General Instruction/Livery/ Hacking/Hunters for Hire/Indoor Shows
Location: 4 miles off A4 Btwn Beckhampton & Marlborough

STONAR SCHOOL
Atworth, Melksham, Wiltshire, SN12 6LR
Tel: Melksham (0225) 702405
Proprietor & Chief Inst: Mrs A M C Davies BHSI(T)
Other Staff: 1 (BHSAI) 1 (BHSII)
Instruction in Riding and Jumping & Students to BHSAI Exam
Av No: Horses 14 Ponies 10
Std of Schlg: General Purpose
Livery: Part/Hack
Courses: Wkg Pupils – 6
Facilities: Cov Sch: 43 x 18m/Out Man: 0m x 40m/Jmp Pd/Sh Jmps/CC Fences/ Lec Rm/Video/WC/Showers/Chng Rm/ Wait Rm/Car Park
Specialities: Nervous riders/Pony Club/ Riding Club Tests/General Instruction
Exclusions: No casual hire
Location: 2 miles out of Village of Atworth

TOLLARD PARK EQUESTRIAN CENTRE
Tollard Royal, Salisbury, Wiltshire, SP5 5PU
Tel: 0725 516249
Proprietor: Major General D M Roberts

Chief Inst: Miss K L Roberts (BHSAI)
Other Staff: Miss E L Roberts Mrs S A Hassall (BHSI) P/T
Instruction in Riding and Jumping
Av No: Horses 16 Ponies 6
Std of Schlg: General Purpose Std of Specialist Schlg: Sh Jmpg – C
Livery: Full/Part/Grass/DIY/Holiday/School/Break/Hack – Parkland/Forestry
Ev Classes
Courses: Up to & including BHSAI/YT – 2/Wkg Pupils
Facilities: Cov Sch: 60 x 23m* Gly – 100/Bench/Out Man: 55 x 25m* Fl Lit/Wash Rm/WC/Showers/Car Park
Accom: Cottage/Dormitory – 4 Catering: Full
Specialities: General Instruction/Livery of all tpyes/Hacking
Exclusions: No riders over 14 stone/No hiring for Hunting
Location: Off B3081 btwn Blanford/Shaftsbury

WHITE HORSE TREKKING CENTRE
Cleeve House, Codford, Warminster, Wiltshire, BA12 0JZ
Tel: Warminster (0985) 50395
Proprietor: Mr W D Puddy
Chief Inst: Miss S Chester (BHSAI)
Other Staff: 2 (BHSAI)
Riding/Trekking Holidays
Av No: Horses 15 Ponies 15
Std of Schlg: General Purpose Hunt/Trek – Woodlands/Downlands
Courses: Resid Hol/YT
Facilities: Jmp Pd/Sh Jmps/CC Fences/Club Rm/Refresh/WC/Showers/Wash Rm/Chng Rm/Shop/Car Park
Accom: 6 – House/30 – Bunkhouse/20 – Camping Catering: Full/Part/Self
Specialities: Trekking holidays/'Leap Frog' Trekking – break at changeover points rides alternate hours accompanied by Landrover
Exclusions: No casual hiring
Location: On A36 btwn Codford St Mary & Warminster

WICKSTEAD FARM EQUESTRIAN CENTRE
Wickstead Farm, Highworth, Swindon, Wiltshire, SN6 7PP
Tel: 0793 762265
Proprietor: Mrs V Mace
Facility Centre & Livery Yard
Std of Specialist Schlg: Sh Jmpg – Novice
Livery: Full/DIY/Hunter/School/Hack – for Livery owners' use only
Ev Classes – for Livery owners
Courses
Facilities: Cov Sch: 60 x 20m* Gly – 10/Out Man: 60 x 20m* Fl Lit/15 Novice Schooling CC Fences*/Club Rm/Snacks/Wash Rm/WC/Changing Rm/Waiting Rm/Car Park
Specialities: Facility & Livery Centre/Regular Courses/Shows & Competitions
Exclusions: No horses for hire
Location: On B4019 btwn Highworth & Faringdon

WIDBROOK ARABIAN STUD AND RIDING CENTRE
Trowbridge Road, Bradford on Avon, Wiltshire
Tel: Bradford on Avon (022-16) 2608
Proprietor: Mrs D Griggs
Chief Inst: Mr C Blair (BHSII(T)) **Other Staff:** 1 (BHSII) P/T 1 (BHSAI)
Instruction in Riding and Jumping
Av No: Horses 10 Ponies 10
Std of Schlg: General Purpose
Livery: Full/Part/School/Break/Hack – Farm land
Ev Lessons
Courses: Wkg Pupil/YT – 3
Facilities: Cov Sch: 40m x 20m* Fl Lit Gly 300/Out Man: 40m x33m* Fl Lit/Jmp Pd/Sh Jmps/CC Course*/Refresh/WC/Car Park
Accom: 2 – Caravan
Specialities: General Instruction/Arabian Stud/RDA
Exclusions: No casual hiring
Location: On A363 btwn Bradford & Trowbridge

Riding in Scotland

BORDERS ♦ CENTRAL ♦ DUMFRIES AND GALLOWAY ♦ FIFE ♦ GRAMPIAN ♦ HIGHLAND ♦ LOTHIAN ♦ STRATHCLYDE ♦ TAYSIDE

BORDERS

HAZELDEAN RIDING CENTRE
Hassendeanburn, Hawick, Scotland
Tel: Denholm (045 087) 373
Proprietors: Mr & Mrs Leslie
Chief Inst: Mrs Turnbull (BHSAI)
Instruction in Riding and Jumping
Av No: Horses 5 Ponies 5
Std of Schlg: General Purpose
Livery: Full/Part/Break/School/Hack – Quiet roads/Hills
Ev Classes
Courses: Res Hol Inst/Wkg Students – 2
Facilities: Cov Sch: 43 x 22m* 60 Seats Fl Lit/Out Man: 37 x 21.5m/Jmp Pd/ Sh Jmps/CC Fences/Lec Rm/Club Rm/Rest Rm/WC/Wash Rm/Showers/ Chng Rm/Car Park
Accom: 72 – Cottages Catering: Self/Unaccompanied Children: Full
Specialities: Holiday courses/Children's courses with family/General instruction
Exclusions: Clients must be suitably dressed/No YT
Location: Off A7, 50 miles from Carlisle

WESTERTOUN FARM RIDING & HOLIDAY CENTRE
Westruther, By Gordon, Berwickshire, Scotland, TD3 6NE
Tel: 05784 270/202
Proprietors: Mr & Mrs A Isles
Chief Inst: Mrs A Isles (BHSAI) **Other Staff**: 1 (BHSAI) P/T
Instruction in Riding and Jumping
Av No: Horses 7 Ponies 13
Std of Schlg: General Purpose Std of Specialist Schlg: Sh Jmp – Novice
Livery: Full/Part/Grass/School/Break/ Hunt/Hack – Forest/Tracks/Moorland
Ev Classes
Courses: Resid Hol
Facilities: Cov Sch: 15 x 20m*/Out Man: 25 x 40m*/CC Fences 7/Refreshments/ Wash Rm/WC/Waiting Rm/Car Park
Accom: Shared Rms 6 – Children Catering: Full
Specialities: Childrens Riding Holidays
Location: 30 miles south of Edinburgh off A697 on B6456

WHISGILLS RIDING CENTRE
Newcastleton, Roxburgh, Roxburghshire, Borders, Scotland, TD9 0TQ
Tel: 03873 75675
Proprietors: Mr & Mrs W J Hayton
Manager: Mr W J Hayton **Chief Inst:** Miss T Hayton (BHSAI)
Instruction in Riding and Jumping
Av No: Horses 5 Ponies 5
Std of Schlg: General Purpose Std of Specialist Schlg: Sh Jmpg – Novice
Livery: Full/Part/School/Hack – Forestry Land/Br idleways/Moorland
Ev Classes Summer only
Courses: Resid Riding Hol
Facilities: Out Man: 40 x 20m/Snacks/ Wash Rm/WC/Showers/Changing Rm/ Sauna/Gym Rm/Games Rm/Sun Bed/ Snooker Room/Lic Bar/Car Park
Accom: Shared Rms – Family House 8 – 10 Catering: Full
Specialities: Riding Holidays/Childrens Riding Club
Exclusions: No children under 7 years/ No riders over 14 Stone
Location: Off A7 19 miles north of Carlisle

CENTRAL

DEVON RIVER RIDING CENTRE
Howe Town, By Fishcross, Alloa, Scotland, FK10 3AN
Tel: 0259 216992

Proprietor: Miss J Holley
Other Staff: 1 (BHSAI) P/T
Basic Instruction in Riding and Jumping
Av No: Horses 1 Ponies 4
Std of Schlg: General Purpose Std of Specialist Schlg: Sh Jmpg – Novice
Livery: DIY/School/Hack/Trek – Bridleways/Gartmore Dam
Ev Classes – Summer only
Facilities: Out Man: 40 x 20m/Jmpg Pd/ Wash Rm/WC/Car Park
Specialities: Children/Hacking
Location: Between Fishcross & Alva

DRUMBRAE RIDING CENTRE
Drumbrae Farm, Bridge of Allan, Stirlingshire, Scotland
Tel: (0786) 832247
Proprietor: D McNicol
Chief Inst: Ms L Merlicol (BHSII) Regd
Other Staff: Miss K McGregor (BHSAI) P/T 1 (BHSAI) P/T
Instruction in Riding and Jumping & Students to BHSAI Exam
Av No: Horses 10 Ponies 24
Std of Schlg: General Purpose Break/School/Hack – Grassland/ Moorland
Ev Classes
Courses: Inst Hol/YT – 2
Facilities: Cov Sch: 38m x 16m* Fl Lit/ Out Man: 49m x 31m Fl Lit/Sh Jmps/ CC Course/Lec Rm/Vis Aids/Caravan for Club Rm/Refresh/Rest Rm/WC/ Car Park
Specialities: Superb hacking country/ No roads/Small groups & family groups catered for
Exclusions: No riders over 13 stone
Location: 1 mile north from Bridge of Allan

LOMONDSIDE STUD EQUESTRIAN CENTRE
Buchanan Home Farm, Drymen, By Glasgow, Scotland, G63 0HU
Tel: 0360 60481
Proprietors: The Misses E & P Rennie BHSI/BHS SM
Chief Inst: Miss E Rennie (BHSI) Regd
Other Staff: 1 (BHSAI) Regd
Instruction in Riding and Jumping & Students to BHSAI Exam
Av No: Horses 5 Ponies 6 Specialist Horses: 4 Med Drg/1 Grade C Sh Jmper
Std of Schlg: General Purpose Std of Specialist Schlg: Drg – Med/Sh Jmpg – Novice
Livery: Full/Part/School/Break/Hack – Forestry/Estate Land
Ev Classes
Courses: Up to & including BHSAI Exam/Wkg Pupils/YT – 5
Facilities: Cov Sch: 20 x 50m/Lec Rm – Vis Aids/Seating/Library/Video/Wash Rm/Changing Rm/Car Park
Accom: Flat – 4 Staff & Working Students only Catering: Full
Specialities: YT Managing Agent/ Breeding/Producing Show Horses/ Native Ponies
Exclusions: For experienced riders only
Location: Off A811 15 miles north of Glasgow & 25 miles west of Stirling

DUMFRIES & GALLOWAY

BAREND RIDING CENTRE
Sandyhills, By Dalbeattie, Kirkcudbrightshire, Scotland
Tel: (038-778) 684 (day) 663 (evening)
Proprietor: Mrs S Gourlay
Chief Inst: Miss Sandra Morrison (BHSII) P/T **Other Staff:** 1 (BHSAI) YT – 4
Instruction in Riding and Jumping & Students to BHSAI
Av No: Horses 6 Ponies 10
Std of Schlg: General Purpose
Livery: Full/Part/Grass/DIY/Break/ School/Hack/Trek – Hills/Forestry Tracks
Ev Classes
Courses: Resid Inst Hol/Wkg Students/ YT
Facilities: Out Man: 55 x 25m/Jmp Pd/ Sh Jmps*/CC Fences/CC Course*/Wash Rm/Refresh/WC/Car Park
Accom: Log Houses Catering: Self
Specialities: Courses for adults and children/Visiting instructors taking courses/Hourly & two hourly treks
Exclusions: No child under 10 years accepted for treks

BRIGHOUSE BAY TREKKING CENTRE
Brighouse Bay Holiday Park, Kirkcudbright, Scotland, DG6 4TS
Tel: Borgue (055-77) 267
Proprietors: Mr & Mrs T C Gillespie
Stable Manager: Miss F Stewart
Basic Instruction in Riding and Trekking
Av No: Horses 3 Ponies 12

Std of Schlg: General Purpose Hack/Trek – Mixed Farmland/Coast/ Woodland
Courses: Resid Hol
Facilities: WC/Car Park
Accom: Family cottages/Caravans/ Camping site Catering: Self
Specialities: Outdoor activity centre – Windsurfing/Sailing/Canoeing/Water Skiing etc

FIFE

GLENROTHES RIDING CENTRE
Balgeddie Farm, Glenrothes, Fife, Scotland
Tel: (0592) 742428
Proprietors: Mr & Mrs P H Gilbert
Chief Inst: Mr P H Gilbert (BHSII(T))
Other Staff: 1 (BHSAI)
Instruction in Riding and Jumping & Students to BHSAI Exam
Av No: Horses 10 Ponies 10
Std of Schlg: General Purpose
Livery: Full/Grass/School/Break/Hack – Moorland/Farmland
Ev Classes
Courses: Inst/YTS – 3
Facilities: Cov Schs: 45 x 21.5m* Gly Fl Lit/12 x 18.5m* Gly/12 x 18.5m* Gly/ Jmp Pd/CC Fences/Lec Rm/WC/ Changing Rm/Car Park
Specialities: Children/Novice Adults/ RDA
Location: Off A911 & A92 25 miles from Edinburgh & 10 miles from Kinross

LOCHORE MEADOWS RIDING STABLES
Chapel Farm Road, Crosshill, By Lochgelly, Fife, Scotland, KY5 8LY
Tel: 0592 861596
Proprietor/Chief Inst: Dr Faith Anstey (BHSII(T))
Other Staff: 1 (BHSAI) 1 (unqual)
Instruction in Riding and Jumping
Av No: Horses 7 Ponies 12
Std of Schlg: General Purpose
Livery: Part/Hack/Trek – Country Park
Ev Classes
Courses: YT – 4
Facilities: Cov Sch: 40 x 20m*/6 small CC Fences/Jmp Pd/Lec Rm – Vis Aids/ Seating/WC/Car Park
Specialities: Managing Agent for YT/ Hacking/Trekking
Location: 5 miles south of Kinross

SHIELDBANK STUD RIDING CENTRE
North Road, Saline, Fife, Scotland, KY12 9LN
Tel: 0383 852 874
Proprietors: Mr & Mrs V F Beasley
Instruction in Riding and Jumping
Av No: Horses 6 Ponies 6
Std of Schlg: General Purpose
Livery: Full/Part/DIY/School/Working
Ev Classes
Courses: Res Inst Hol/YT
Facilities: Out Man 20 x 60m* & 30 x 60m* & 20 x 40m/Jmp Pd/Sh Jmps*/ CC Fences/Lec Rm/Vis Aids/Refresh/ Wash Rm/WC/Car Park
Accom: Local Only Catering: – Full (Students)
Specialities: Preparation for competitions
Location: Off B914 8 miles west of Junc 4 on M90

GRAMPIAN

ABERDEEN COLLEGE OF FURTHER EDUCATION SCHOOL OF RIDING
Kinellar, Aberdeen, Grampian, Scotland, AB5 0TN
Tel: 0224 790393/FAX No: 0224 790326
Farm Director: A Devonshire Esq
Manager & Chief Inst: Miss H Purvis (BHSII) **Other Staff:** Miss F Moffat (BHSII) Mrs L Bates (BHSAI) Miss S Painter (BHSAI) P/T
Instruction in Riding and Jumping & Students to BHSAI Exam
Av No: Horses 14 Ponies 0
Std of Schlg: General Purpose Std of Specialist Schlg: Sh Jmpg – Novice
Livery: Working/School
Courses: BHS Stages I/II/III/PTT/Resid – for College Students only
Facilities: Out Man: 60 x 35m/7 Basic Schooling CC Fences/Lec Rm – Vis Aids/Seating/Film Project or/Library/ Video/Refreshments/Wash Rm/WC/ Showers/Changing Rm/Car Park
Accom: For College Students & Staff only – 32 Catering: Full
Exclusions: For College Students only
Location: 8 miles west of Aberdeen off A96

GROVE RIDING CENTRE
Whiterashes, Aberdeen, Scotland, AB2 0RB
Tel: Whiterashes (0651) 82263
Proprietors: Mr R Taylor (BHSAI) Mrs E Taylor (BHSAI)

Other Staff: 1 FBHS – Visiting
Instruction in Riding and Jumping
Av No: Horses 7 Ponies 0 Spec Horses: 1 Drg A/Med/2 Med Drg
Std of Schlg: General Purpose
Livery: Full/Break/School/Hack
Ev Classes
Courses: Inst
Facilities: Cov Sch: 60 x 20m Fl Lit* Gly/Out Man: 37 x 22m Fl Lit/Jmp P 43 x 31m/CC Fences/Sh Jmps(10)/ Vis Aids/Video/Club Rm/Refresh/WC/ Wash Rm/Chng Rm/Wait Rm/Car Park
Accom: Caravan – 2
Specialities: Small classes/Lungeing/ All aspects horsemastership/Adults prepared for all R C Grade Tests/ Dressage
Location: 11 miles from Aberdeen off A947

HAYFIELD EQUESTRIAN CENTRE
Hazelhead Park, Aberdeen, Grampian, Scotland, AB1 8BB
Tel: Aberdeen (0224) 315703/ Fax No: 0224 313834
Proprietors: Mr & Mrs J A Crawford
Chief Inst: Mr J A Crawford (BHSII)
Other Staff: Miss S Hassall (BHSAI) Miss B Milne (BHSAI) Miss J Taig (BHSAI) 2 (BHSAI) P/T
Instruction in Riding and Jumping & Students to BHSAI Exam
Av No: Horses 20 Ponies 20
Std of Schlg: General Purpose
Livery: Full/Part/Grass/Break/School/ Hack – Park Ride/Forests
Ev Classes
Courses: Inst Hol/Wkg Students/YT 7/ 7 Students from Aberdeen Coll 2 days a week
Facilities: Cov Sch: 38 x 31m* Fl Lit/ 32 x 21m* Gly 80/Out Man: 40 x 20m* Fl Lit/Jmp Pd 80 x 80m/Sh Jmps 20/ CC Fences/CC Course/Lec Rm/Vis Aids/Refresh/Rest Rm/WC/Wash Rm/ Tack Shop/Car Park
Accom: Local
Specialities: Hacking/Competition teams/Basic dressage/RDA/Riding Holidays/Polo Instruction/Side Saddle/ Western Riding
Location: In Hazelhead Park/3 miles from centre of Aberdeen

LAW RIDING SCHOOL
Kennethmont, Insch, Aberdeen, Grampian, Scotland, AB5 6YT
Tel: 04643 550
Proprietor: Mrs K M Yates
Chief Inst: Miss Y Williamson (BHSAI)
Other Staff: 1 (BHSAI)
Instruction in Riding and Jumping
Av No: Horses 6 Ponies 10
Std of Schlg: General Purpose Std of Specialist Schlg: Sh Jmpg – Novice
Livery: Full/Part/Grass/Break/School/ Hack/Trek – Forestry Commission Land/ Farm Land
Ev Classes
Courses: Resid/YT – 1
Facilities: Cov Sch: 17 x 25m*/Out Man: 30 x 6 0m*/Lec Rm/Games Rm/Video Camera/Snacks/Wash Rm/WC/Car Park
Accom: Shared Chalet/Farm House – 12 Catering: Full
Specialities: Residential Riding Holidays/Trekking/RDA/Driving
Location: Off B9002 12 miles from Huntly/12 miles from Inverurie

SEAFIELD RIDING CENTRE
Forres, Moray, Grampian, Scotland
Tel: 0309 72253
Proprietors: Mr & Mrs G Sharp
Manager & Chief Inst: Mrs M Sharp BHS(E & SM) **Other Staff:** Miss C Mc Gough (BHSAI) Regd P/T
Instruction in Riding and Jumping
Av No: Horses 5 Ponies 10
Std of Schlg: General Purpose Std of Specialist Schlg: Sh Jmpg – Novice
Livery: Full/Part/DIY/School/Hack – Country Tracks
Ev Classes – Summer only
Facilities: Out Man: 25 x 25m*/Jmpg Pd/Wash Rm/WC/Car Park
Specialities: RDA/Dressage/Show Jumping
Location: Off A96 2 miles north of Forres

TOMINTOUL PONY TREKKING & TRAINING CENTRE
Richmond Arms Hotel, Tomintoul, Ballindalloch, Banffshire, Scotland, AB3 9ET
Tel: Tomintoul (080 74) 209
Proprietor: Mr C R McNiven
Manageress & Trek Leaders: hold ST & RA Cert Grade II
Trekking & Trail Riding Holidays
Av No: Horses 3 Ponies 18
Std of Schlg: General Purpose
Trek – Mountain/Moorland/Forest
Courses: Hol/Res
Facilities: Car Park
Accom: Hotel
Specialities: Excellent trekking/Good ponies/Well escorted
Exclusions: No YT
Location: 25 miles from Aviemore on A939

HIGHLAND

HIGHLAND RIDING CENTRE
Borlum Farm, Drumnadrochit, Inverness, Scotland, IV3 6XN
Tel: Drumnadrochit (04562) 220/358
Proprietors: Capt A D & Mrs H N MacDonald-Haig
Chief Inst: Mrs P Corker (BHSII)
Instruction in Riding and Jumping
Av No: Horses 12 Ponies 19
Std of Schlg: General Purpose
Livery: Grass/Break/School/Hack/Trek – Hill/Woodl and/Tracks/Forestry
Ev Lessons
Courses: Resid Inst Hol/YT – 2
Facilities: Cov Sch: 40 x 22m Gly Fl Lit/Jmp Pd 1 00 x 100m/Sh Jmps 12/ CC Fences 10/Lec Rm/Vis Aids/ Refresh/WC/Showers/Wash Rm/Car Park
Accom: Cottages – Local Catering: Self Camp Site
Specialities: Holiday riding overlooking Loch Ness/Beautiful scenery/Working farm/Families welcome/RDA
Location: On A82 15 miles south of Inverness

LOCH NESS EQUI CENTRE
Drummond Farm, Dores,Invernessshire, Scotland
Tel & Fax No: (046 375) 251
Proprietor: Mrs C Cameron (BHSAI)
Other Staff: 1 (BHSAI) 1 (BHSII) P/T
Instruction in Riding and Jumping & Students to BHSII Exam
Av No: Horses 10 Ponies 3 Specialist Horses: 2 Drg E/3 Sh Jmp C
Std of Schlg: General Purpose School/Break/Hack/Trek – Forest/Hill/ Moorland
Courses: YT – 2/ET – 3
Facilities: Cov Sch: 42 x 25m* Fl Lit Gly/Out Man 60 x 25m*/Sh Jmps/ Jmp Pd/CC Fences/Video/WC/Car Park
Accom: Log Cabins Catering: Self
Specialities: Endurance Riding/Riding Holidays/Inverness College Student Courses
Exclusions: No unaccompanied Hacking/No rider under 8 years of age
Location: On B862 10 miles south of Inverness

LOGIE FARM RIDING CENTRE
Glenferness, Nairn, Inverness, Scotland, IV12 5XA
Tel: Glenferness (03095) 226
Proprietors: Mrs S Hilleary & Mrs B Sanders
Chief Instructors: Mrs R Hilleary/Miss V Hain (BHSII(T)) **Other Staff:** Mrs C Butcher (BHSII) Regd P/T Mrs J Simpson (BHSAI) P/T
Instruction in Riding and Jumping & Students to BHSII Exam
Av No: Horses 10 Ponies 13 Specialist Horses: 1 Drg E/1 Sh Jmp C
Std of Schlg: General Purpose
Livery: Full/Part/Grass/Break/School/ Hack/Trek – Farmland/Forest
Ev Classes – Summer only
Courses: Resid Inst Hol/Wkg Students/ YT – 2/ET – 2
Facilities: Out Man: 65 x 37m/Jmp Pd/ Sh Jmps/CC Fences/CC Course/Lec Rm/Vis Aids/Rest Rm/Refresh/WC/Wash Rm/Chng Rm/Car Park
Accom: 8 – Farmhouse Catering: Full
Specialities: Childrens riding holidays(unaccompanied)/Side-saddle/ Events/Shows/Gymkhanas/Picnic rides
Exclusions: No unaccompanied Hacking
Location: 10 miles from Nairn on A939

NETHYBRIDGE RIDING CENTRE
Nethybridge, Inverness-shire, Scotland, PH25 3EB
Tel: 047 982 693
Proprietor: Mrs P M Taylor
Chief Inst: Mrs Pat Taylor (BHSII)SM
Other Staff: Mrs S Smith (BHSII(T)) Regd P/T
Instruction in Riding and Jumping & Students to BHSII Exam
Av No: Horses 3 Ponies 1 Spec Horse 2 Drsg – M
Std of Schlg: General Purpose
Livery: Full/Part/Grass/Break/School/ Hack – (By arrangement only) – Forestry/Moorland/Agricultural Land
Ev Classes (daylight only)
Courses: Inst Hol/Wkg Students
Facilities: Out Man: 21 x 45m/Jmp Pd 80 x 50m/Sh Jmps(BSJA)/CC Fences 10*/Video Camera/WC/Car Park
Accom: 2 – Family House – Catering Full Local: Guest Houses/Hotels/Self Catering
Specialities: Dressage to Medium level/Riding Holidays with individual tuition/Clients taken on weekly courses with own horse/Private & Semi Private lessons only
Exclusions: No riders over 13 stone
Location: 10 miles from A9 sign posted Nethybridge

LOTHIAN

APPIN EQUESTRIAN CENTRE
Drem, Nr North Berwick, East Lothian, Scotland, EH39 5BL
Tel: 062 088 366
Proprietors: Mr & Mrs Montgomery
Chief Inst: Mrs A Montgomery (BHSII(T)) **Other Staff:** 2 (BHSII(T))
Instruction in Riding and Jumping
Av No: Horses 11 Ponies 11 Advanced Medium 1 Spec Horses: Drg 1 N/2 E/Sh Jmpg: 1 Grade C
Std of Schlg: General Purpose
Livery: Full/Part/School/Break
Evening Lessons
Courses: Inst
Facilities: Cov Sch: 39 x 22m Gly 60*/ Jmp Pd/Sh Jmps/Lec Rm/Vis Aids/ Refresh/WC/Wait Rm/Car Park
Specialities: Dressage/Show Jumping for Clients on own horses
Exclusions: No YT & Hacking
Location: 6 miles east of North Berwick

GRANGE RIDING CENTRE
West Calder, West Lothian, Scotland
Tel 0506 871219
Proprietor: Mrs E Knight (BHSII(T))
Other Staff: Miss S Mooney (BHSAI) P/T Miss E Telfor (BHSAI) P/T
Instruction in Riding and Jumping
Av No: Horses 5 Ponies 7
Std of Schlg: General Purpose
Livery: Full/School/Break/Hack – Farm Tracks/Fields
Ev Classes
Courses: Wkg Students – 2
Facilities: Cov Sch: 46 x 22m*/Out Man: 40 x 20m* Fl Lit/Jmp Pd/Sh Jmps*/WC/ Car Park
Specialities: Beginners to Novice level/ Dressage
Location: 4 miles from Junc 4 on M8

OATRIDGE AGRICULTURAL COLLEGE
Ecclesmachan, Broxburn, West Lothian, Scotland, EH52 6NH
Tel: 0506 854387 Fax No: 0506 853373
Principal: C W Nixon Esq
Manager: Mrs F Flynn (BHSII) **Senior Lecturer**: Miss P Phillpot BHSI
Other Staff: Miss J Comrie (BHSII) P/T Miss E MacDonald (BHSII) P/T Miss T Stewart (BHSI) P/T
Instruction in Riding and Jumping & Students to BHSAI Exam
Av No: Horses 12 Ponies 3 Specialist Horses: 4 Novice Drg/1 Grade C Sh Jmper
Std of Schlg: General Purpose Std of Specialist Schlg: Drg/CT/Sh Jmpg – all Novice
School
Ev Classes
Courses: Up to & including BHSAI/ Resid/YT
Facilities: Cov Sch: 30 x 25m/Out Man: 40 x 40 m/34 CC Fences*/CC Course*/ Lec Rm – Seating/Vis Aids/Film Projector/Library/Video/Refreshments/Wash Rm/WC/Showers/Changing Rm/Car Park
Accom: Single – 130 (For Students & YT Only) Catering: Full
Specialities: Managing Agent for YT
Exclusions: No casual hire/Students only
Location: On Bathgate Hills between Edinburgh & Glasgow

TOWER FARM RIDING STABLES
85 Liberton Drive, Edinburgh, Scotland, EH16 6NS
Tel: 031 664 3375/3845
Proprietor: Mrs Judy Forrest (BHSII(T))
Other staff: 2 (BHSAI) F/T 5 (BHSAI) P/T
Instruction in Riding and Jumping & Students to BHSAI Exam
Av No: Horses 15 Ponies 20
Std of Schlg: General Purpose
Livery: Full/Part/Grass/Hunter/DIY/ Break/School/Hunt/Hack/Trek – Hill Tracks
Ev Classes
Courses: Inst/1 Wkg Students/YT 2
Facilities: Out Man: 36 x 18m* Fl Lit/ Cov Sch: 25 x 45m Fl Lit*/Jmp Pd* Fl Lit/ Sh Jmps*/CC Fences/CC Course/ Refresh/WC/Wash Rm/Chng Rm/Shop/ Car Park
Accom: 4 – Rooms Catering: Self
Specialities: Side Saddle
Location: 4 miles South of City centre

VETERINARY FIELD STATION
Easter Bush, Roslin, Midlothian, Scotland, EH25 9RG
Tel: 031 445 2001
Associate Head of Department: Mr J Kelly
Chief Inst: Miss Lyn Hickman (BHSII)
Other Staff: 1 (BHSAI)
Instruction in Riding and Jumping & Students to BHSAI Exam
Av No: Horses 9
Std of Schlg: General Purpose
Hack
Ev Classes
Courses: Inst Hol/Wkg Students – 2

Facilities: Cov Sch: 40 x 20m Fl Lit/Out Man: 40 x 20m/Jmp Pd/Sh Jmps/CC Fences/CC Course/Lec Rm – Video/ Vis Aids/Weighing Machine/Horse Walker/WC/Wash Rm/Car Park
Specialities: Riding Instruction & Stable Management – College students only/ Facilities for outside/organisations/ Courses on request
Exclusions: No YT
Location: Off A701 1 Mile from Roslin

WEFTMUIR RIDING CENTRE
Totley Wells Grange, "Weftmuir", Nr Winchburgh, South Queensferry, West Lothian, EH52 6QJ
Tel: 031 331 2990
Proprietor: Mr W J Stein
Chief Inst: Miss L Bell (BHSAI) Regd
Other Staff: Miss D Murray (BHSAI) Regd Mr P Print (BHSI) – Visiting
Instruction in Riding and Jumping & Students to BHSAI Exam
Av No: Horses 17 Ponies 18
Std of Schlg: General Purpose
Livery: Full/School/Break/Hunt/Hack – Canal towpaths/Farm Roads etc
Evening Lessons
Courses: Resid Hol Inst/YT – 7/ Employment Trainee – 2
Facilities: Cov Sch: 37 x 25m* Gly/ Out Man: 37 x 22m Fl Lit*/Jmp Pd/ CC Fences/Lec Rm/WC/Chg Rm/Wait Rm/Car Park
Accom: Cottages – 3 Bedrooms/Mobile Homes – 4 – Staff & Students
Specialities: Managing Agent for YT
Location: Btwn Winchburgh & South Queensferry

STRATHCLYDE

ARDFERN RIDING CENTRE
Via Craobh Haven, Ardfern, Argyll, Scotland, PA31 8QR
Tel: 085 25 270/632
Proprietors: Nigel & Lucia Boase
Chief Inst: Lucia Boase (BHSAI) **Other Staff:** 1 (STRA Grade II)
Basic Instruction in Riding and Jumping
Av No: Horses 14
Std of Schlg: General Purpose
Livery: Full/Grass/School/Break/Hack/ Trek – Shore of Lochs/Hills/Woods/ Fields
Courses: Inst/Hols
Facilities: Out Man: 32 x 46m*/CC Fences/WC/Car Park
Accom: Local Hotel
Specialities: Western riding/Hacking/ Trekking/Prep for PC and RC Tests/ Hiring for local events
Exclusions: Children under 8 years not taken out on general rides/Special arrangements can be made for young children
Location: Off A816 between Oban & Lochgilphead

AYRSHIRE EQUITATION CENTRE
Castle Hill Stables, Hillfoot Road, Ayr, Scotland, KA7 3LF
Tel: (0292) 266267
Proprietor: Mr J A Galbraith & Son
Chief Inst: Mr K Galbraith (BHSAI)
Other Staff: 2 (BHSAI) 2 (BHSAI) P/T
Instruction in Riding and Jumping & Students to BHSAI Exam
Av No: Horses 8 Ponies 8
Std of Schlg: General Purpose
Livery: Full/Part/Grass/Break/School/ Hunt/Hack – Beach
Ev Classes
Courses: Inst Hol/Wkg Students/YT – 6
Facilities: Out Man: 37 x 19m Seats Fl Lit/Jmp Pd/Sh Jmps/CC Course/Lec Rm/Vis Aids/Rest Rm/WC/Sh owers/ Wash Rm/Chng Rm/Car Park/Open all year
Accom: Guesthouse/Camping site Catering: Full Part/Self
Location: 1 mile from centre of Ayr

BARGOWER RIDING SCHOOL
Bargower Farm, Five Ways, Nr Kilmarnock, Ayrshire, Strathclyde, Scotland, KA1 5JX
Tel: 0563 84223
Proprietor & Chief Inst: Mrs C Cano
Manager: Mr Cano **Other Staff:** Miss P Beatie (BHSAI) P/T Miss L Munro (BHSAI) P/T
Basic Instruction in Riding and Jumping
Av No: Horses 15 Ponies 10
Std of Schlg: General Purpose Std of Specialist Schlg: Sh Jmpg – Novice
Livery: Full/School/Hack – Rolling Hills/ Bridleways/Lanes
Ev Classes
Courses: Wkg Pupils/BHS Stages I & II
Facilities: Cov Sch: 30 x 15m/Jmpg Pd/Wash Rm/WC/Car Park
Specialities: NVQ BHS Stages I & II
Exclusions: No Children under 5 years/ No riders over 13 stone
Location: On A76 5 miles south of Kilmarnock

CAIRNHOUSE TREKKING CENTRE
Cairnhouse, Blackwaterfoot, Isle of Arran, Scotland, KA27 8EU
Tel: 0770 86 256
Proprietor: Miss D MacAlister (BHSAI) Redg
Basic Instruction in Riding
Av No: Horses 6 Ponies 6
Std of Schlg: General Purpose Std of Specialist Schlg: Sh Jmp – Novice School/Hack- Beach/Moorland/Forest Land
Ev Classes
Facilities: Out Man: 40 x 20m/Wash Rm/WC/Car Park
Specialities: Hacking/Trekking in ideal Countryside – wide variety of routes
Exclusions: No YT/No unaccompanied Hacking
Location: On B880 11 miles SW of Brodick

CASTLE RIDING CENTRE & ARGYLL TRAIL RIDING
Brenfield, Ardrishaig, Argyll, Scotland, PA30 8ER
Tel: 0546 3274 Fax No: 0546 3225
Proprietors: Mrs Gray-Stephens (BHSAI) & Miss A Hay Thorburn (BHSAI)
Instruction in Riding and Jumping & Students to BHSAI Exam
Av No: Horses 18 Ponies 20
Std of Schlg: General Purpose
Livery: Full/Part/Grass/DIY/Break/ School/Hack – F ields/Woods/Hills/Open Country
Ev Classes
Courses: Resid Hol/Wkg Students – 4/ YT – 2/STR/NV Q
Facilities: Out Man: 40 x 30m*/Jmp Pd/ Sh Jmps/CC Course/Lec Rm/Vis Aids/ Video/Refresh/WC/Car Park
Accom: Local – 6 in house in 3 rms/ Hotel & Castle Catering: Full
Specialities: Residential riding holidays/Pony Club/Outdoor activities/ Water Sports/Trail Riding for experienced riders/Event Training
Exclusions: No unaccompanied children under 10 years
Location: On A83 4 miles south of Lochgilphead

DEAN CASTLE COUNTRY PARK RIDING CENTRE
Assloss Road, Dean Castle Country Park, Kilmarnock, Scotland, KA3 6BL
Tel: 0563 41123/22702
Proprietor: D Hadley Esq
Manager: Mrs S Howard (BHSAI) Regd
Other Staff: Miss S Bunyan (BHSAI) Regd
Instruction in Riding and Jumping
Av No: Horses 5 Ponies 7
Std of Schlg: General Purpose Std of Specialist Schlg: Sh Jmpg -Novice
Livery: DIY/School/Hack – Country Parks/Grassed Hills
Ev Classes – Summer only
Facilities: Out Man: 40 x 25m/Lec Rm/ Vis Aids/Seating/Film Projector/Wash Rm/WC/Showers/Changing Rm/Waiting Rm/Car Park
Specialities: RDA/Gymkhanas for Novice Riders
Location: Part of Dean Castle Country Park Complex

GLEDDOCH RIDING SCHOOL
Gleddoch Farm, Langbank, Renfrewshire, Scotland
Tel: Langbank (047 554) 350
Proprietor: Glenddoch Hotels Ltd
Director: Mr C Longdon **Chief Inst:** Mrs C Smith (BHSAI) Regd
Other Staff: Miss H McLean (BHSII(T)) Regd
Basic Instruction in Riding and Jumping
Av No: Horses 3 Ponies 8
Std of Schlg: General Purpose
Livery: Full/Part/Grass/Hack – Hilly country/No road work
Facilities: Out Man: 55.5 x 29m*/Sh Jmps/CC Fences*/WC/Wait Rm/Car Park
Specialities: Progressive instruction for regular clients and teaching beginners/ Preparation for Riding Club Grades
Location: Off A8 10 miles west of Glasgow Airport

HAZELDEN SCHOOL OF EQUITATION
Mearnskirk, Newton Mearns, Glasgow, Scotland, G77 6RR
Tel: 041 639 3011/3101
Proprietor: W Young Esq
Other Staff: 1 (BHSI) – Visiting 1 (BHSAI) P/T 2 (BHSAI)
Instruction in Riding and Jumping & Students to BHSAI Exam
Av No: Horses 8 Ponies 12
Std of Schlg: General Purpose Std of Specialist Schlg: CT – Novice/Sh Jmp – Grade C
Livery: Full/Part/Grass/School/Hack – Bridleways
Ev Classes
Courses: (BHSAI) Exam/2 Wkg Pupils/ YT – 2

Facilities: Cov Sch: 31 x 25m*/CC Course – Novice/Jmp Pd/Lec Rm/Vis Aids/Library/Video/Wash Rm/WC/ Changing Rm/Waiting Rm/Tack Shop/ Car Park
Specialities: Showing Working Hunters/ Eventing
Location: On A77 7 miles from centre of Glasgow

ISLE OF ARRAN RIDING HOLIDAYS
Shedock Farm, Shiskine, Isle of Arran, Scotland, KA27 8EW
Tel: Shiskine (0770 86) 472/230
Proprietors: Mrs G Mac Alister & Mrs J Mac Alister
Riding and Trekking
Av No: Horses 6 Ponies 6
Std of Schlg: General Purpose
Livery: Grass/Hack/Trek- Moorland/ Forestry land/Beach
Facilities: WC/Chng Rm/Car Park
Accom: Cottage 2/3 Catering: Self
Specialities: Small numbers of novices & experienced catered for/Relaxed & friendly atmosphere
Exclusions: No YT/Closed in winter
Location: On B880 1.5 miles N. E. of Blackwater Forest

LANARKSHIRE RIDING CENTRE
Race Course Stables, Lanark, Strathclyde, Scotland, ML11 9TA
Tel: 0555 61853/65652
Proprietor: Mrs E Taylor
Chief Inst: Mrs S Boyle (BHSAI) **Other Staff:** 1 (BHSAI) 1 (BHSI) – Visiting
Instruction in Riding and Jumping
Av No: Horses 20 Ponies 25
Std of Schlg: General Purpose Std of Specialist Schlg: CT & Sh Jmpg: Novice
Livery: Full/Part/School/Hunt/Hack – Woodlands/Riverside Rides
Ev Classes
Courses: Riding Holidays/Wkg Pupils/ YT – 6
Facilities: Out Man: 30 x 80m* Fl Lit/ CC Course * – Novice (Used for Riding & Pony Club events)/Jmpg Pd/Club Rm/ Lec Rm – Vis Aids/Seating/Film Projector/ Library/Video/Refreshments/Wash Rm/ Lic Bar/WC/Showers/Changing Rm/ Waiting Rm/Car Park
Accom: Shared Rms – 80 – Child or 40 Adults Catering: Full
Specialities: Childrens Riding Holidays/ Autogenic riding
Exclusions: No riders over 14 stone
Location: On Lanark Race Course

LETTERSHUNA RIDING CENTRE
Lettershuna House, Appin, Argyll, Scotland, PA38 4BN
Tel: Appin (063 173) 227
Proprietors: Mr & Mrs D R Craig
Chief Inst: Mrs Craig
Basic Instruction in Riding and Jumping
Av No: Horses 5 Ponies 7 Donkeys 1
Std of Schlg: General Purpose
Livery: Full/Hack/Trek – Shore/Hill
Courses: Hol – Non Resid
Facilities: Out Man: 6 x 12m/Jmp Pd/Sh Jmps/CC Fences/Refresh/Wash Rm/ WC/Chng Rm/Car Park
Accom: Local Caravan sites/Bed & Breakfast in Hotels nearby
Specialities: Water Sports/Fishing/ Hacking/Trekking
Location: On A828 25 miles from Oban & 25 miles from Fort William

MID DRUMLOCH FARM
By Chapelton, Hamilton, Strathclyde, Scotland, ML3 8RL
Tel: 03573 273
Proprietor: Mrs M Forbes
Chief Inst: Mrs T Crichtan (BHSII)
Other Staff: Miss J Mc Ghee (BHSAI)
Instruction in Riding and Jumping
Av No: Horses 5 Ponies 5
Std of Schlg: General Purpose Std of Specialist Schlg: Sh Jmpg – B/C/Nov
Livery: Full/School
Ev Classes
Facilities: Cov Sch: 24 x 48m* Gly/ Out Man: 31 x 46m* Fl Lit/Video/ Refreshments/Wash Rm/WC/Changing Rm/Car Park
Specialities: Full Livery/General Instruction/Unaffiliated Show Jumping Competitions
Exclusions: No riders under 4 years of age
Location: Off A726 2 miles north of Chapelton

ROCKSIDE FARM TREKKING CENTRE
Rockside Farm, Bruichladdich, Isle of Islay, Strathclyde, Scotland, PA49 7UT
Tel: 049 685 231
Proprietor & Chief Inst: Mrs R French (BHSAI)
Other Staff: 2 F/T & 2 P/T – seasonal
Trekking Centre
Av No: Horses 5 Ponies: 7
Std of Schlg: Trekking
Trekking – Beach/Hills/own Farmland
Courses: Non Resid Holiday
Facilities: Out Man: 40 x 20m/Snacks/ Wash Rm/WC/Car Park

Specialities: Trekking in ideal Countryside
Exclusions: Children under 7 years in enclosed area only
Location: On West Coast of Islay 6 miles from Bruichladdich adj to Loch Gorm

SHANDON SCHOOL OF EQUITATION
Stuckenduff Farm, Shandon, Dunbartonshire, Scotland, G84 8NW
Tel: Rhu (0436) 820 838
Proprietor: Mr B Black (BHSAI)
Chief Inst: Mrs J Black (BHSII) **Other Staff:** Miss Y Shaw (BHSAI)
Instruction in Riding and Jumping & Students to BHSAI Exam
Av No: Horses 5 Ponies 8
Std of Schlg: General Purpose
Livery: Full/Grass/Break/School/Hack/Trek – Hill/Arable fields
Ev Classes
Courses: Inst/Wkg Students – 2
Facilities: Cov Sch: 31 x 20m Fl Lit 20 Seats/Out Man: 44 x 22m/CC Course/CC Fences 12/Sh Jmps 12/Lec Rm/Rest Rm/WC/Showers/Wash Rm/Chng Rm/Refresh/Shop/Car Park
Accom: Students Flat Catering: Part
Specialities: Hacking/Dressage & Jumping Competitions/Cross Country Competitions/RDA
Exclusions: No YT
Location: Off A814 4 miles north of Helensburgh

TAYSIDE

BALNAKILLY RIDING CENTRE
Balnakilly Estate, Kirkmichael, Perthshire, Scotland, PH10 7NB
Tel & Fax No: Strathardle (025-081) 305/281
Proprietors: Mrs H Reid & Mrs D Main
Chief Inst: Mr D Main (BHSAI)
Basic Instruction in Riding and Jumping
Av No: Horses 5 Ponies 10
Std of Schlg: General Purpose
Livery: Full/Part/Grass/Hack/Pony Trek – Hills/Fo restry/Moorland/Fields
Ev Classes
Courses: Resid Inst Hol
Facilities: Jmp Pd/Sh Jmps/WC/Car Park
Accom: 50-60 in 11 Cottages Catering: Self
Specialities: Riding holiday centre/Good accommodation/Good riding country/Instruction/No traffic/Ht Swim Pool/Tennis Court/Fish/Shoot on Estate/Western Riding
Exclusions: No YT
Location: on Balnakilly Estate

BORELAND RIDING CENTRE
Fearnan, Lochtayside, By Aberfeldy, Perthshire, Scotland, PH15 2PG
Tel: Kenmore (08873) 212 Fax no – 08873 606
Proprietor: Mrs E M Menzies
Chief Inst: Miss F Menzies (BHSAI) Regd
Basic Instruction in Riding and Jumping
Av No: Horses 6 Ponies 12
Std of Schlg: General Purpose
Livery: Part/Grass/DIY/Break/School/Hack/Trek – Forestry Tracks/Farm Estate
Facilities: Jmp Pd/Sh Jmps/CC Fences/Showers/WC/Wash Rm/Chng Rm/Car Park
Specialities: Trekking
Exclusions: No YT/Only operates May to October
Location: Off A827 10 miles from Aberfeldy & 20 miles from A9

CULLODEN RIDING SCHOOL
Station Road, Stanley, Perthshire, Tayside, Scotland, PH1 4NS
Tel: 0738 827094
Proprietor: Mrs M McDonald
Chief Inst: Miss G White **Other Staff:** Miss C Gilmour (BHS(PPT)) P/T
Basic Instruction in Riding and Jumping
Av No: Horses 3 Ponies 6
Std of Schlg: General Purpose Std of Specialist Schlg: Sh Jmpg – Nov
Livery: Full/Part/School/Hack – Bridlepaths/Riverside
Ev Classes
Courses: YT
Facilities: 2 Out Mans: 30 x 25m* Fl Lit & 40 x 20m* Fl Lit/Jmpg Pd*/Wash Rm/Changing Rm/Car Park
Specialities: Sound Basic Instruction in Riding & Stable Management/Hacking
Location: 6 miles north of Perth

THE GLENEAGLES MARK PHILLIPS EQUESTRIAN CENTRE
Auchterarder, Perthshire, Tayside, Scotland, PH3 1NE
Tel: 0764 63507

Proprietor: Capt Mark Phillips MVO **General Manager:** Paul Lindsay Esq (BHSII) **Trainer:** William Micklem Esq (FBHS) **Asst Manager:** Diana Marsden (BHSI) **Senior Coach:** Miss J Stamper (BH SII(SM))/Miss N Carstairs (BHSII)/**Driving Inst:** L Bain (BHSAI) P/T/**Head Girl:** Miss A Murray **Other Staff:** 2 (BHSI) P/T 1 (BHSII) P/T 2 (BHSAI) P/T 1 (BHSI(SM)) P/T 2 (BHSAI) **Instruction in Riding and Jumping** & Students to BHS II Exam
Av No: Horses 18 Ponies 12
Std of Schlg: General Purpose Std of Specialist Schlg: 7 Sh Jmpg – Grade C/1 Drg – Med
Livery: Full/Part/School/Break/Hack – 1,500 acres of Moorland Estate
Ev Classes Courses: Resid Students
Facilities: 2 Cov Schs: 75 x 35m* Gly – 150 + 650 addit/40 x 20m*/Out Man: 60 x 40m*/Sh Jmps*/Club Rm/Lec Rm – Vis Aids/Seating/Film Projector/Library/ Restaurant/Bar/Wash Rm/Showers/WC/ Changing Rm/Wait Rm/Tack Shop/BHS Event Course(20 + fences) 2 Horse Box Parks/Blanket Drying Rm/Washing Area/Solarium/Car Park
Accom: Staff & Students – only 6 Catering: Full/Part Accom: Clients – Gleneagles Hotel
Specialities: Competitions/Full Club Membership Facilities/Riding Breaks for all levels of Rider s/Carriage Driving Tuition/Side Saddle Tuition/Western Riding/Indoor Polo Training & matches/ Vaulting
Location: 2 miles from Auchterarder

GLENFARG RIDING SCHOOL
Smiddyhill Farm, Glenfarg, Perth, Scotland, PH2 9NL
Tel: Glenfarg (05773) 262
Proprietor: Miss A M Stocks (BHSAI)
Other Staff: Visiting FBHS – once a month in summer
Basic Instruction in Riding and Jumping
Av No: Horses 2 Ponies 7
Std of Schlg: General Purpose
Livery: Part/School/Hack – varied
Evening Lessons
Facilities: Cov Sch: 31 x 22m* Fl Lit/ Jmp Pd/Sh Jmps/CC Course/WC/Chng Rm/Car Park
Specialities: Instruction for children/ Hacking/RDA
Exclusions: No YT/No riders over 10.5 stone
Location: Off B996 5 miles north of Kinross

GLENMARKIE FARM RIDING CENTRE
Glenmarkie Farm, Glensila, By Blairgowrie, Perthshire, Tayside, Scotland PH11 8QB
Tel: 057 582 341
Proprietors: Mr & Mrs S Evans
Chief Inst: Miss E Pirie **Other Staff:** 1 P/T
Trekking & Riding Holidays – Basic Instruction Only
Av No: Horses 6 Ponies 7
Std of Schlg: General Purpose
Livery: Full/Part/Grass/DIY/Hack & Trekking – Forestry/High Moorland/ Moorland
Facilities: Refreshments/WC/Car Park
Accom: 3 Shared Rms – 6 Catering: Full
Specialities: Trekking & Riding Holidays
Exclusions: Weight Limit 13 Stone
Location: 15 miles north of Blairgowrie

ROWANLEA RIDING SCHOOL LIMITED
Westcotside, Barry, Carnoustie, Scotland, DD7 7SA
Tel & Fax No: Dundee (0382) 532536
Proprietors: Mr & Mrs D Conchie
Basic Instruction in Riding and Jumping
Av No: Ponies 12
Std of Schlg: General Purpose
Livery: Full/Part/DIY/Hunter/Break/ School/Hack/Trek (Stabling for 60 – 70 Liveries)
Ev Classes – In summer
Facilities: Jmp Arena/Shw Jmps/WC/ Chng Rm/Feed Shop/Saddlery Shop/ Car Park
Specialities: Preparation of pupils for Show Jumping Competition/Liveries RDA
Exclusions: No YT
Location: 3 miles from Dundee on A930

SCOTTISH EQUITATION CENTRE
Sheriffmuir Road, Greenloaning, Dunblane, Perthshire, Scotland, FK15 OND
Tel: Braco (078 688) 278
Proprietors: Mr & Mrs J A D MacFarlane
Other Staff: Miss S Murdoch (BHSAI)
Instruction in Riding and Jumping & Students to BHSAI Exam
Av No: Horses 15 Ponies 15
Std of Schlg: General Purpose
Livery: Full/Part/Break/School/Hack – Open grass land
Courses: Inst/Wkg Students/YT 3
Facilities: Cov Sch: 37 x 19m* Fl Lit Gly 100/Out Man: 37 x 19m*/Jmp Pd/

Sh Jmps/CC Fences/Lec Rm/Vis Aids/ WC/Wash Facs/Coffee Rm/Showers/ Car Park
Accom: 6 – House – Students & YT only
Catering: Part
Specialities: Adults/Beginners & nervous riders/Holiday courses/Training courses/RDA
Exclusions: No hiring for hunting/ Weight limit 12 stone
Location: Off A9

STRATHEARN STABLES
Strathearn Hydro Limited, Crieff, Perthshire, Scotland, PH7 3LQ
Tel: Crieff (0764) 2401
Fax No: 0764 3087
Manager: Mr B Jamieson
Chief Inst: Miss L Allan
Basic Instruction in Riding and Jumping
Av No: Horses 10 Ponies 4
Std of Schlg: General Purpose
Livery: Full/Part/Grass/Break/School/ Hack – Woods/Tracks
Ev Classes – Summer only
Facilities: Out Man: 40 x 20m*/Jmp Pd 80 x 20m/Sh Jmps 8/Car Park
Accom: Hotel/Chalets
Specialities: Holiday visitors/Local school children/Hacking
Exclusions: No riders under 5 years of age/No YT/
No riders over 14 stone
Location: Off A85 at Crieff

WOODLANDS STABLES
Woodlands Road, Rosemount, Blairgowrie, Perthshire, Scotland
Tel: 0250 3475/5073
Proprietor & **Chief Inst:** Mrs A Johnston (BHSAI)
Other Staff: 1 (BHSAI) P/T
Instruction in Riding and Jumping
Av No: Horses 2 Ponies 5
Std of Schlg: General Purpose Std of Specialist Schlg: Sh Jmpg – Novice
Livery: Full/Part/Grass/School/Hack – Woodlands
Ev Classes
Courses: BHS Stages I/II/YT – 3
Facilities: Out Man: 20 x 40m* Fl Lit/ Jmpg Pd*/Wash Rm/WC/Car Park
Specialities: General Instruction/RDA
Location: Off A923/1 mile south of Blairgowrie

Riding in Wales

CLWYD ♦ DYFED ♦ GWENT ♦ GWYNEDD ♦ MID-GLAMORGAN ♦ POWYS ♦ SOUTH GLAMORGAN ♦ WEST GLAMORGAN

CLWYD

THE EQUESTRIAN CENTRE
Caeau Farm, Gresford Road, Hope, Wrexham, Clwyd, LL12 9SD
Tel: 0978 761349
Proprietor: Mr M W Tytherleigh
Chief Inst & Head Girl: Miss Y Kerr (BHSII) **Other Staff:** 3 (BHSAI) Mrs J Basil (BHSI) – Visiting Mrs R Cruthers (BHSI) – Visiting
Instruction in Riding and Jumping & Students to BHSAI Exam
Av No: Horses 15 Ponies 15
Std of Schlg: General Purpose Std of Specialist Schlg: CT – Novice/Sh Jmp – C School/Hunt/Hack – own 70 acre Farm/ Bridleways
Ev Classes
Courses: BHS Exams up to Stage III & PTT/Wkg Pupils – 5/YT/Residential
Facilities: Cov Sch: 63 x 25m* Gly – 350/Out Man: 40 x 20m*/CC Course* – 18 CC Fences – Novice/Jmpg Pd*/Lec Rm – Vis Aids/Video/Seating – 20/Film Projector/Library/Refreshments/Wash Rm/WC/Showers/Changing Rm/Waiting Rm/Car Park
Accom: for guests – Hotel – 20/for Staff – Mobile Home/Flat 6 Catering: Full
Specialities: Instructional Riding Holidays
Location: On A550 7 miles from Chester & 6 miles from Wrexham

GOLDEN PHEASANT RIDING CENTRE
Tal-y-Garth Farm, Glyn Ceiriog, Llangollen, Clwyd, LL20 7AB
Tel: (0691 72) 408
Proprietor: Mrs J Rushworth
Chief Inst: Mr A Sopwitch (BHSAI) P/T
Other Staff: 2 (BHSAI) P/T
Instruction in Riding and Jumping
Av No: Horses 12 Ponies 12
Std of Schlg: General Purpose
Livery: Full/Part/Grass/Hack/Trek – Moorland/Forestry Lanes/Drovers Tracks
Ev Classes
Courses: Resid Inst Hol
Facilities: Out Man: 40 x 20m Fl Lit seats*/Jmp Pd/Sh Jmps 7/CC Fences/ Lec Rm/Video/Vis Aids/Lic Bar/Refresh/ Club Rm/WC/Showers/Wash Rm/Chng Rm/Car Park
Accom: Dormitory – 25 Catering: Full
Specialities: Small parties/Excellent Hacking/Individual attention whenever possible
Exclusions: No YT
Location: Off A5 on B4500 6 miles from Chirk

HWYLFA DDAFYDD COUNTRY FARM HOLIDAYS
Llysfean, Colwyn Bay, Clwyd, LL29 8TW
Tel: 0492 516965
Proprietor: Mrs E Jones (PTRSW Trek Inst Grade 3)
Chief Inst: Miss J Burns (BHSAI) **Other Staff:** 1 (PTRSW Grade 3) P/T
Trekking & Residential Holidays
Av No: Horses 6 Ponies 6
Std of Schlg: Trekking
Trek/Hack: Country Lanes/Bridleways
Courses: Res Hol/YT
Facilities: Out Man: 40 x 20m*/ Restaurant/Wash Rm/Bar/WC/Changing Rm/Car Park
Accom: Cottages – 50 Catering: Self
Exclusions: No Children under 8 years
Location: Off A55 3 miles east of Abergele

PEACEHAVEN RIDING CENTRE
Terrace Lane, Penyffordd, Nr Chester, Clwyd, CH4 0HB
Tel: 0244 546819

Proprietor: Mr & Mrs G Williams
Chief Inst: Mrs V Williams (BHSAI)
Other Staff: 1 (BHSAI) P/T Mrs S Dale (BHSI) – visiting
Instruction in Riding and Jumping
Av No: Horses 7 Ponies 10
Std of Schlg: General Purpose Std of Specialist Schlg: Sh Jmpg (Pony) – Novice
School/Hack – Bridleways/Lanes
Ev Classes
Courses: Stages/NVQ/Children's one day/Holiday/YT – 2/Progressive Riding Tests/Road Safety
Facilities: Out Man: 40 x 20m Fl Lit/ Jmpg Pd/Lec Rm – Video/Snacks/Wash Rm/WC/Car Park
Specialities: Children's one day courses in Riding & Horsemanship/ Holiday Courses/Progressive Riding Tests/Stages Courses
Exclusions: No riders over 13.5 stone
Location: 7 miles from Chester (A5104) & 10 from Wrexham – 1 mile from A55

SOUTHFIELDS FARM
Stryt Isa, Penyffordd, Nr Chester, Clwyd, CH4 0JY
Tel: 0978 760496
Proprietor: Mrs B A Antliff (BHSAI)
Other Staff: 1 (BHSAI)
Livery Yard
Std of Specialist Schlg: CT – Basic/Sh Jmpg – Nov
Livery: Full/Part/School
Facilities: Out Man: 20 x 40m Fl Lit/ 9 Basic Schooling CC Fences/Jmpg Pd* – both only for livery owners use/ Snacks/Wash Rm/WC/Changing Rm/ Car Park
Specialities: To provide a high standard of Livery on a friendly private family run yard
Exclusions: No DIY Liveries/No casual clients
Location: 3 miles south of A55/12 miles from centre of Chester

DYFED

BLUE WELL RIDING CENTRE
Ffynnonlas, Llanllwni, Dyfed, SA39 9AY
Tel: 0267 202 274
Proprietors: Major & Mrs J B Gibbins (BHSAI)
Chief Inst: Mrs L Gibbins
Riding Holidays and Trekking
Av No: Horses 8 Ponies 8
Std of Schlg: General Purpose
Livery: Part/Grass/Hack/Trek – Forest/ Mountain Tracks/Moorland
Ev Classes – Summer only
Courses: Resid Hol/E T
Facilities: Out Man: 40 x 20m/Jmp Pd/ Sh Jmps/Club Rm/Refresh/WC/ Showers/Wash Rm/Car Park
Accom: 8 – Cottage – Children only/ Adults – local Catering: Full/Part
Specialities: Riding Holidays/Livery/ Hacking/Trekking/Long Distance Riding
Exclusions: No YT
Location: 2 miles from A485 between Carmarthen & Lampeter

BOWLING RIDING SCHOOL
Meadow Farm, Bowling House, Rudbaxton, Haverfordwest, Pembrokeshire, Dyfed
Tel: Treffgarne (043 787) 407/8
Proprietor: Mrs J Gibson
Chief Inst: Mrs S Noott (BHSII(T)) **Other Staff:** Miss L Morgan (BHSI) – Visiting once per week
Instruction in Riding and Jumping & Students to BHSAI Exam
Av No: Horses 19 Ponies 16
Std of Schlg: General Purpose
Livery: Part/Grass/Hunt/Hack – Fields/ Moors/Woodlands
Ev Classes
Courses: YT – 4
Facilities: Cov Sch: 25 x 18.5m* Fl Lit/ Out Man: 40 x 20m/Jmp Pd/Sh Jmps/ CC Fences*/Lec Rm/Club Rm/Refresh/ WC/Car Park
Accom: Residential – 5/Local Catering: Full
Specialities: Specialist attention all riders/360 acres beautiful riding country/CC Course/Indoor School/Show Jumping manege
Exclusions: No unaccompanied children under 8 years
Location: 0.5 mile off A40/3.5 miles north of Haverfordwest

CAE IAGO TREKKING CENTRE
Farmers, Llanwrda, Dyfed, SA19 8LZ
Tel: Pumpsaint (055 85) 303
Proprietors: Mr & Mrs C & Miss L Pollak
Chief Inst: Mrs C Pollak (BHSAI)
Riding Holidays and Trekking
Av No: Horses 10 Ponies 25
Std of Schlg: General Purpose
Hack/Trek – Mountains/Forest
Courses: Resid Hol
Facilities: Refresh/Wash Rm/WC/Car Park
Accom: 14 – Farmhouse/Dormitory – Local/YHA – Parties only Catering: Full

Specialities: Residential holidays/Pony trekking/Weekend rides/Trail riding – 2 & 3 days & 50 miles for riders over 14
Exclusions: No children under 8 years unless experienced/No YT
Location: 8 miles south east of Lampeter

CLYN-DU RIDING CENTRE
Clyn-du Farm, Burry Port, Llanelli, Dyfed
Tel: Burry Port (055-46) 2546
Proprietor/Chief Inst: Mrs R Vaughan-Jones (BHSAI)
Other Staff: 1 (BHSAI) 2 (BHSAI) P/T Miss A Philip (BHSII(T)) P/T
Instruction in Riding and Jumping & Students to BHSAI Exam
Av No: Horses 17 Ponies 11
Std of Schlg: General Purpose
Livery: Full/School/Break/Hack
Ev Classes
Courses: YT – 3
Facilities: Out Man: 22 x 46m* Fl Lit/CC Fences/Sh Jmps/Jmp Pd/WC/Refresh/Wash Rm/Car Park
Specialities: General Instruction
Location: Off A484 15 miles south of Carmarthen/4 miles from Llanelli/Junc 48 off M4

DERWEN STUD
Ynyshir, Pennant, Llanon, Dyfed, SY23 5JN
Tel: 0545 570250
Proprietor & Manager: Mr I J Roscoe-Lloyd AR AgS
Chief Inst: Miss K Fikldbo
Welsh Cob Stud
Av No: Horses 60 Ponies 2
Std of Specialist Schlg: Sh Jmp – Novice
School/Break
Courses: Grooms Certificate/YT – taken
Facilities: Cov Sch: 40 x 20m/Out Man: 30 x 12m/Jmp Pd/Lec Rm/Seating/Wash Rm/WC/Car Park
Accom: 2 Single/4 Shared – Staff & YT Catering: Part
Specialities: In Hand Showing/Breeding/Schooling
Exclusions: No Casual Hire
Location: 0ff A487 1 mile north of Aberaeron

THE DYFED RIDING CENTRE
Maes-y-felin, Bridell, Cardigan, Dyfed, SA43 3DG
Tel: Cardigan (0239) 612594
Proprietor/Principal: Mrs T Humfrey (BHSII)
Chief Inst: Mr Terence Humfrey (BHSII)
Instruction in Riding and Jumping & Students to BHSII Exam
Av No: Horses 6 Ponies 10 Specialist Horses: 1 Drg – E/1 HT – N
Std of Schlg: General Purpose
Livery: Full/Part/Break/School/Hack/Trek – Farmland/Woodland (accompanied riders only)
Ev Classes
Courses: Inst Hol/1 Wkg Student/RDA/1 ET/YT taken
Facilities: Cov Sch: 32 x 19m* Gly/Jmp Pd quarter acre* Fl Lit/Sh Jmps 10*/CC Fences*/Lec Rm/Refresh/WC/Shower/Wash Rm/Chng Rm/Car Park
Specialities: General Instruction/Training in Competitions for horses & riders
Location: Off A478 4 miles from Cardigan

EAST NOLTON RIDING STABLES
Nolton, Haverfordwest, Pembrokeshire, Dyfed, SA62 3NW
Tel: 0437 710360
Proprietors: Mr & Mrs J Owen
Manager: Mr J Owen (BHSAI) **Other Staff:** 1 BHS SM P/T
Instruction in Riding and Jumping
Av No: Horses 30 Ponies 30
Std of Schlg: General Purpose Std of Specialist Schlg: Sh Jmpg – Grade C School/Hack & Trek – Beaches/own Estate
Ev Classes
Facilities: Cov Sch: 50 x 23m* Gly/Jpg Pd/Snacks/Wash Rm/Shower/WC/Car Park
Location: Off A487 6 miles from Haverfordwest

HENDRE EYNON STABLES
Hendre Eynon, St David's, Pembrokeshire, Dyfed, SA62 6DB
Tel: St David's (0437) 720 474
Proprietor: Mr & Mrs I A Jamieson
Chief Inst: Mrs S Squire (BHSAI)
Instruction in Riding and Jumping
Av No: Horses 6 Ponies 13
Std of Schlg: General Purpose
Livery: Part/Grass/Break/School/Hunt/Hack/Trek – Farm/Moorland
Ev Classes
Courses: Inst
Facilities: Out Man: 20 x 38m/Jmp Pd/Sh Jmps/12 C C Fences/CC Course/Lec Rm/Rest Rm/WC/Showers/Wash Rm/Chng Rm/Car Park
Accom: Caravan Catering: Self
Specialities: Rides particularly suitable for beginners and nervous riders/All rides escorted

Exclusions: No YTS
Location: 2 miles north of St David's

LLANGYBI EQUESTRIAN & ADVENTURE CENTRE
Ty Hir, Llangybi, Nr Lampeter, Dyfed, SA48 8NB
Tel: 0570 45 386
Proprietor: Mrs D P Bernard (BHS HM)
Manager & Chief Inst: Miss N Goad (BHSAI) **Other Staff:** 1 (BHSAI)
Instruction in Riding and Jumping
Av No: Horses 7 Ponies 8
Std of Schlg: General Purpose Std of Specialist Schlg: Sh Jmpg – Novice
Livery: Full/Part/DIY/School/Break/Hack – Forestry/Field
Ev Classes
Courses: Wkg Pupils – 2
Facilities: Cov Sch: 24 x 26m*/Out Man: 20 x 40m*/nearby CC Course*/Club Rm – Vis Aids/Video/Refreshments/Wash Rm/WC/Showers/Heated outdoor Swimming Pool/Archery/Boating/Car Park
Accom: Shared Rms & Private with Tea/ Coffee Making Facilities/TV – 10 Catering: Full
Specialities: Residentail Riding Holidays
Exclusions: No unaccompanied Children under 8 years
Location: Off A485 3 miles from Lampeter

MAYESTON
Cosheston, Pembroke, Dyfed, SA72 4UQ
Tel: 0646 682008
Proprietor: Mrs M M Hancock
Chief Inst: Miss S Mitchell (BHSII) & Mrs R Phillips (BHSII)
Other Staff: 1 (BHSI) Visiting 1 (BHSII) P/T
Instruction in Riding and Jumping & Students to BHSAI Exam
Av No: Horses 6 Ponies 1
Std of Schlg: General Purpose Std of Specialist Schlg- Sh Jmp -Grade C/CT – Int Schlg
Courses: Resid/ET/YT Sponsor for 40 – 50
Facilities: Out Man: 60 x 20m/CC Course – Int/Jmp Pd/Wash Rm/WC/ Chng Rm/Showers/Refresh/Tack Shop/ Lec Rm/Vis Aids/Film Proj/Library/Video/ Car Park
Accom: Local Catering: Full
Specialities: Youth Training Centre
Exclusions: YT & St Mgt Courses Only/No Clients

PEMBROKESHIRE RIDING CENTRE
Pennybridge Farm, Hundleton, Pembroke, Dyfed
Tel: 0646 682513
Proprietors: Mr & Mrs E W Scourfield
Chief Inst: Mrs E W Scourfield BHS(SM)
Other Staff: 1 (BHSII(T)) P/T 1 (BHS SM) P/T
Instruction in Riding and Jumping
Av No Horses 8 Ponies 15
Std of Schlg: General Purpose Std of Specialist Schlg: Sh Jmp C/1 Drg – Novice
Livery: Full/Part/Grass/DIY/School/ Break/Hack – B ridleways/Beaches/ Lanes
Ev Classes – Summer only
Courses: Resid Rid Hols/YT – 6
Facilities: Out Man: 40 x 20m*/Cov Sch: 43 x 28m/Jpg Pd/Wash Rm/WC/ Chang Rm/Tack Shop/Car Park
Accom: Shared Rooms 6 Catering: Full
Specialities: Riding Holidays for unaccompanied Children 10 – 18 years
Exclusions: No Riders over 14 stone
Location: 2 miles south west of Pembroke

TALLY HO FARM
Troopers Inn, Haverfordwest, Pembrokeshire, Dyfed
Tel: 0437 891052
Proprietor: Mrs J Underwood (BHSAI)
Livery Yard
Std of Specialist Schlg: Sh Jmpg – Novice
Livery: Part/Grass/DIY
Courses: YT – 1
Facilities: Out Man: 35 x 20m* Fl Lit/ WC/Car Park
Specialities: Good Grazing/Baileys feed on yard
Location: Off A4076 6 miles from Haverfordwest

GWENT

EARLSWOOD RIDING CENTRE
Upper Tump Farm, Earlswood, Chepstow, Gwent, NP6 6AW
Tel: 02917 381
Proprietors: Mr & Mrs R J Raikes-May
Chief Inst: Mrs Raikes-May **Other Staff:** 1 (BHSAI) P/T 1 (BHSII) P/T
Instruction in Riding and Jumping
Av No: Horses 10 Ponies 2
Std of Schlg: General Purpose Std of Specialist Schlg: CT Basic/Sh Jmpg Novice
Livery: Full/Grass/Hack – Common Land

Ev Classes – Summer only
Facilities: Out Man: 40 x 20m*/CC Course/Jmp Pd*/WC/Car Park
Specialities: General Instruction/ Livery/Hacking/Stud Work/Childrens Holiday Courses
Exclusions: No Casual Hire/No YT

PONDEROSA RIDING STABLES
Newport Road, New Inn, Pontypool, Gwent, Corres: 33 Clarewain New Inn, Pontypool Gwent NP4 0QA
Tel: 0495 762660/762886
Proprietors: Mr & Mrs R Davies
Manager & Chief Inst: Mrs R Davies Bsc (BHSAI)
Instruction in Riding and Jumping
Av No: Horses 4 Ponies 9
Std of Schlg: General Purpose Std of Specialist Schlg: Sh Jmpg – Grade B
Livery: Full/Part/DIY/Hunter/School/ Hack – Bridleways
Ev Classes
Courses: Wkg Pupil – 1
Facilites: Cov Sch: 18 x 35m*/Jmpg Pd/Wash Rm/WC/Car Park
Specialities: Show Jumping
Location: Off A4042 5 miles north of Newport

TREWYSGOED STUD RIDING CENTRE
Fforest, Nr Abergavenny, Gwent, Wales, NP7 7LW
Tel: 0873 890296
Proprietor: Mrs M S Featherstonhaugh (BHSII(T))
Other Staff: Miss G Hutter (BHSAI)
Instruction in Riding and Jumping & Students to BHSAI Exam
Av No: Horses 9 Ponies 10
Std of Schlg: General Purpose/Long Distance Riding Horses
Livery: Full/Part/Grass/Break/School/ Hack – Mountain/Forestry
Ev Classes
Courses: Res/Hol/Inst/Wkg Students – 1
Facilities: Cov Sch: 23 x 23m Fl Lit/ Out Man: 21 x 46m/Jmp Pd/Sh Jmps/ CC Course/Lec Rm/Vis Aids/Video/WC/ Showers/Wash Rm/Car Park
Accom: Dormitory – 4/House – 10 Full: Catering
Specialities: Unaccompanied children's holidays and courses for getting horses fit for eventing and long distance riding
Exclusions: No Casual Hiring/No YT
Location: 3 miles from Abergavenny

GWYNEDD

ANGLESEY EQUITATION CENTRE LTD
Tanrallt Newydd, Bodedern, Anglesey, Gwynedd, LL64 3UE
Tel: 0407 741378/741106
Proprietors: Mrs E M Manson & Presaddfed Estate
Manager: Mrs E M Manson **Chief Inst:** Miss S Mc Inerney (BHSII)
Other Staff: 1 (BHSAI) P/T 1 (BHSI) – Visiting
Instruction in Riding and Jumping
Av No: Horses 10 Ponies 10
Std of Schlg: General Purpose Std of Specialist Schlg: Drg & CT & Sh Jmp – All Novice
Livery: Full/Part/Grass/School/Break/ Hack – Presaddfed Estate/Quiet Lanes
Ev Classes
Courses: Riding Holidays/YTS – 1
Facilities: Out Man: 35 x 30m*/Cov Sch: 40 x 25m Fl Lit/CC Fences – 20/CC Course/Lec Rm – Seating/Snacks/Wash Rm/Changing Rm/WC/Car Park
Accom: 9 Rms – Country House Catering: Full
Specialities: Side Saddle/Riding Club/ RDA/Vaulting
Location: On B5109 Just off A5 Approx 5 miles from Hollyhead & 14 miles from Bangor

COLEG GLYNLLIFON
Fford Clynnog, Caernarfon, Gwynedd, LL54 5DU
Tel: 0286 830261
Principal: W I J Davies Esq
Manager & Chief Inst: Miss S Z Thomas (BHSII) **Other Staff:** Mrs R Hardacre (BHSII) P/T Mrs D Lloyd (BHSAI) P/T Miss G Frankland (BHSAI) P/T Capt Hartley Edwards P/T
Instruction in Riding and Jumping
Av No: Horses 14
Std of Schlg: General Purpose Std of Specialist Schlg: Sh Jmpg – Novice
Livery: Working/School
Courses: ET/YT – 8/Full Time College Student/BHS Stages I/II/III/PTT
Facilities: Out Man: 60 x 20m/Jmpg Pd/Lec Rm – Vis Aids/Film Projector/ Library/Video
Accom: Single Rms Catering: Full
Exclusions: No casual clients taken

DWYFOR RANCH RIDING CENTRE
Llanystumdwy, Nr Criccieth, Gwynedd, LL52 0SU
Tel: 0766 523349

Proprietors: Mr T Wheldon & Miss J S Brown
ChiefInst: Miss L Heald (BHS(PTT))
Other Staff: Capt Hartley Edwards
Instruction in Riding and Jumping
Av No: Horses 6 Ponies 6
Std of Schlg: General Purpose Std of Specialist Schlg: Sh Jmpg – Novice
Livery: Full/Part/Wkg/School/Hack – Lanes/Farm Land
Ev Classes
Facilities: Cov Sch: 38 x 21m*/Jmpg Pd/Snacks/Wash Rm/WC/Car Park
Location: Off A497 btwn Portmadoc & Pwllhei 12 miles south of Caernarfon

PINEWOOD STABLES
Sychnant Pass Road, Conwy, Gwynedd, LL32 8BZ
Tel: 0492 59 2256
Proprietors: Miss P J & Mr J S Oldfield
Manager & Chief Inst: Miss P J Oldfield
Other Staff: 1 P/T – Weekends only/ 5 F/T & 5 P/T Trek Leaders in Summer/ 3 in Winter
Hacking & Trekking Centre
Av No: Horses 24 Ponies 14
Std of Schlg: General Purpose Std of Specialist Schlg: Sh Jmpg – Novice School/Hack/Trek – Mountains/Beach
Facilities: Out Man: 35 x 28m/Snacks/ Wash Rm/WC/Car Park
Location: Off A55 1 mile from Conwy & 5 from Llandudno

PLAS – Y – CELYN RIDING CENTRE
Ceunant, Nr Waunfawr, Caernarfon, Gwynedd, LL55 4SA
Tel: 028685 642
Proprietors: Mr & Mrs P Wesemael
Other Staff: 2 P/T in summer
Pony Trekking
Av No: Horses 4 Ponies 18
Std of Schlg: Trekking
School/Break/Hack – Mountain/ Moorland
Specialities: Trekking on Foothills of Snowdon Mountain Ranges
Exclusions: No Children under 8 years
Location: 3 miles from Caernarfon on Llanrug – Waunfawr Road

RHIWIAU RIDING CENTRE
Llanfairfechan, Gwynedd, North Wales, LL33 OEH
Tel: 0248 680094
Proprietors: Miss R M & Miss S Hill
Other Staff: 1 (BHSAI)
Instruction in Riding and Jumping
Av No: Horses 7 Ponies 8
Std of Schlg: General Purpose Hack/Trek – Snowdonia National Park
Facilities: Out Man: 28 x 12m Sh Jmps/Jmp Pd/CC Course/Lec Rm/ Vis Aids/Club Rm/Lic Bar/Refresh/WC/ Showers/Chng Rm/Tuck Shop/Car Park/Video
Accom: 24 – House + Guest House Catering: Full
Specialities: Riding and English language courses/Riding holidays/ Hacking/Trekking
Exclusions: No YT
Location: Off A55 midway between Conway & Menai Bridge

SNOWDONIA RIDING STABLES
Weirglodd Fawr, Waunfawr, Caernarfon, Gwynedd, LL55 4PQ
Tel: 0286 85 342
Proprietor: Mrs R Z Thomas
Manager & Chief Inst: Miss S Z Thomas (BHSII) P/T **Other Staff:** Mrs R Hardacre (BHSII) P/T
Instruction in Riding and Jumping
Av No: Horses 12 Ponies 12
Std of Schlg: General Purpose Std of Specialist Schlg: Drg – Novice
Livery: Part/Grass/School/Hack/Trek – Mountain/Moorland/Bridleways
Ev Classes
Courses: YT Taken
Facilities: Out Man: 40 x 20m* Fl Lit/ 2 Schooling CC Fences/Lec Rm – Vis Aids/Seating – Caravan/WC/Car Park
Specialities: Pony Trekking
Location: 3 miles from Caernarfon on A4085

MID-GLAMORGAN

GRAIG FAWR LIVERY STABLES
Caerphilly, Mid-Glamorgan
Tel: Caerphilly (0222) 883659
Proprietors: Mr & Mrs D W Jones & Mr A W Parry-Jones **Chief Inst:** A W Parry-Jones (BHSAI)
Livery & Training Centre
Av No: Horses 0 Ponies 3 – RDA use only
Std of Schlg: General Purpose
Livery: Full/DIY/Break/School
Ev Classes
Facilities: Cov Sch: 31 x 15m* Gly/Out Man: 18.5 x 37m* Fl Lit/Jmp Pd/CC Fences*/CC Course/WC/Chng Rm
Specialities: Competition Training for Livery Owners on own Horses
Exclusions: No Casual Hire/No YTS

MID GLAMORGAN COLLEGE OF AGRICULTURE & HORTICULTURE
Pencoed, Bridgend, Mid Glamorgan, CF35 5LG
Tel: 0656 860 202/635
Principal: J Thomas Esq
Manager/Chief Inst: Mrs S Bater (BHSI)
Other Staff: Mrs T Berterelli (BHSII) Miss A Hooper (BHSII) 5 (BHSAI) P/T
Instruction in Riding and Jumping & Students to BHSAI Exam
Av No: Horses 25 Ponies 5
Std of Schlg: General Purpose Std of Specialist Schlg: Sh Jmpg – C School
Ev Classes
Courses: Up to & including BHSAI/14 Students/20 YT/NVQ
Facilities: Cov Sch: 40 x 20m* Gly/Out Man: 60 x 30m/Jmpg Pd*/8 CC Fences/ Lec Rm – Seating/Film Projector/Vis Aids/Video/Library/WC/Showers/ Chnging Rm/Waiting Rm/Car Park
Accom: Local Catering: Full
Specialities: Full/Part Time Courses/ NVQ Training
Exclusions: No Casual hire
Location: 1 mile off Junc 35 on M4

POWYS

CAMNANT CENTRE
Camnant, Dolfor, Newtown, Powys, SY16 4BS
Tel: Llananno (059 783) 271
Proprietors: Miss E A Brooke & Miss M T Coyne
Chief Inst: Miss M T Coyne **Other Staff:** 1 (BHSI) – Once a week 1 Pony Trek Grade II
Instruction in Riding and Jumping
Av No: Horses 3 Ponies 3
Std of Schlg: General Purpose
Hacking – Moorland
Courses: Res Hol Inst
Facilities: Out Man: 40 x 20m*/Jmp Pd/ Sh Jmps*/Lec Rm/Club Rm/Vis Aids/ WC/Wash Rm/Chng Rm/Refresh/Car Park
Accom: 14 – Farmhouse Catering: Full
Specialities: Children/Holiday Courses/ Side Saddle/Riding Holidays for the Handicapped/RDA
Exclusions: No riders over 12 stones
Location: On A483 9 miles south of Newtown

CILWYCH FARM
Bwlch, Powys, LD3 7JJ
Tel: 0874 730460
Proprietor: Mrs V Cresswell
Livery Yard
Livery: Full/Grass/DIY/Hunter
Facilities: Out Man: 50 x 50m/18 Basic CC Fences*/Jmpg Pd*/WC/Showers/Car Park
Exclusions: Facilities for use of Livery Owners only
Location: Off A40 1 mile from Bwlch btwn Brecon & Abergavenny

CWMFFOREST RIDING CENTRE
Pengenfford, Talgarth, Brecon, Powys, Wales, LD3 0EU
Tel: Talgarth (0874) 711398
Proprietor: Michael W Turner
Instruction in Riding and Jumping
Av No: Horses 10 Ponies 5
Std of Schlg: General Purpose
Livery: Full/Part/Grass/DIY/Break/ School/Hack/Trek – Mountainous
Ev Classes
Courses: Resid Inst Hol
Facilities: Cov Sch: 43 x 21m* Gly (2) Seats 100 Fl Lit/Sh Jmps/Lec Rm/Vis Aids/ Club Rm/Lic Bar/Refresh/Rest Rm/WC/ Showers/Wash Rm/Chng Rm/Shop
Accom: 6 – in family house Catering: Full
Specialities: Residential riding holidays with instruction/Long distance riding training
Exclusions: No YT
Location: Off A479 5 miles south of Talgarth

THE LION ROYAL HOTEL & PONY TREKKING CENTRE
The Lion Royal Hotel, Rhayader, Powys, LD6 5AB
Tel: Rhayader (0597) 810202
Proprietors: E J & M E Collard
Trekking & Riding Holidays
Av No: Horses 12 Ponies 11
Std of Schlg: General Purpose
Hack/Trek – Open hills/Valleys/No main roads
Courses: Resid Hol
Facilities: Lic Bar/WC/Showers/Chng Rm/Packed lunches/Tea after trekking/ Baths/Car Park
Accom: 40 – Hotel Catering: Full
Specialities: Breeding Trekking Ponies/ Mounts allocated to riders/All horses & ponies kept for their whole lives
Exclusions: No unaccompanied riding/ Season May – September
Location: In Rhayader

LLANGORSE RIDING CENTRE
Gilfach Farm, Llangorse, Brecon, POWYS, Wales, LD3 7UG
Tel: 087484 272

Proprietor: J V M Thomas Esq
Chief Inst: Miss I Thomas **Other Staff:** 20 P/T as required – 2 (BHSAI)
Trekking & Hacking
Av no: Horses 40 Ponies 30
Std of Schlg: General Purpose
Hack – Hills
Facilities: Waiting Rm/Wash Rm/WC/Car Park
Specialities: Trekking & Hacking
Exclusions: All Rides escorted
Location: Off B4560 6 miles south of Talgarth

TREGOYD AND CADARN RIDING AND TREKKING CENTRE
Tregoyd, Three Cocks, Brecon, Powys, Wales, LD3 0SP
Tel: 04974 351
Proprietors: E L & D G Jones
Riding Holidays and Trekking
Av No: Horses 25 Ponies 75
Std of Schlg: General Purpose
Trekking – Black Mountains
Facilities: Wash Rm/WC/Change Rm/Wait Rm/Tack Shop/Car Park
Accom: 50 – Dormitory/House Catering: Full
Specialities: Trail Riding/Escorted day & half-day rides
Exclusions: Open March – October/No YT
Location: 4 miles north of Talgarth

WERN RIDING CENTRE (CRICKHOWELL) LTD
Llangattock Hillside, Crickhowell, Powys, Wales, NP8 1LG
Tel: Crickhowell (0873) 810899
Proprietors: Mr & Mrs G Holland
Riding Holidays & Trekking
Av No: Horses 18 Ponies 20
Std of Schlg: General Purpose
Hack/Trek – Grassland/Mountain/Moorland
Specialities: Riding Holidays/Hacking/Trekking
Exclusions: Open March – October
Location: 2 miles from Crickhowell

SOUTH GLAMORGAN

ARGAE HOUSE STABLES
St Andrews Major, Dinas Powys, South Glamorgan, CF6 4HD
Tel: 0222 513146
Proprietor & Chief Inst: Miss A V Roberts (BHSAI)
Other Staff: Miss S Goddard (BHSI) – 4/5 visits per week
Instruction in Riding and Jumping & Students to BHSAI Exam
Av No: Horses 10 Ponies: 5 Std of Specialist Horses: 2 Nov Drg/1 Nov Event
Std of Schlg: General Purpose Std of Specialist Schlg: CT & Drg: Nov/Sh Jmpg: Grade C
Livery: Full/Hunter/School/Hack – Country Lanes/Woodlands
Ev Classes
Courses: Up to & including BHSAI/Wkg Pupils
Facilities: Cov Sch: 40 x 20m* Gly – Bench seating/Out Man: 20 x 20m* Fl Lit/Novice CC Course* – 30 Fences/Jmpg Pd*/Snacks/Wash Rm/WC/Car Park
Specialities: Competition Training/Exam Preparation
Location: 8 miles south of Junc 33 on M4

CITY OF CARDIFF RIDING SCHOOL
Pontcanna, Cardiff, South Glamorgan, Wales
Tel: Cardiff (0222) 383908
Proprietor: Director of Leisure and Amenities Department Cardiff City Council **Manager:** Mrs P A Lockwood (BHSII(T))
Other Staff: 1 (BHSII(T)) 2 (BHSAI) 3 (BHSAI) P/T
Instruction in Riding and Jumping
Av No: Horses 16 Ponies 11
Std of Schlg: General Purpose
Livery: Full/Part/Break/School/Hack – Parkland
Ev Classes
Courses: Inst Hol/YT – 4/ET – 2
Facilities: Cov Sch: 46 x 22m* Gly Fl Lit/Out Man :Seats Fl Lit/Jmp Pd seats/Sh Jmps Full set/CC Course/Lec Rm/Vis Aids/Wash Rm/WC/Chng Rm/Car Park
Specialities: Side Saddle/Progressive Group Lessons/RDA
Exclusions: No Casual Hire
Location: On A48 one mile from centre of Cardiff

ST QUENTIN'S STABLES
Llanblethian, Nr Cowbridge, South Glamorgan, Wales
Tel: Cowbridge (04463) 2682
Proprietor: Miss M E Northway
Chief Inst: Mrs P Lewis (BHSAI)

Basic Instruction in Riding and Jumping
Av No: Horses 4 Ponies 11
Std of Schlg: General Purpose
Livery: Full/Grass/Hunter/Break/School/Hack/Trek – Lanes/Bridleways
Courses: Non-residential with accommodation arranged if required/YT – 1
Facilities: Out Man: 19 x 37m*/Jmp Pd/Sh Jmps*/CC Fences/Refresh/WC/Wash Rm/Car Park
Specialities: Children/adults of nervous disposition/RDA
Location: 1.5 miles from Cowbridge

WEST GLAMORGAN

COPLEY STABLES
Newpark Cottages, Copley, Bishopston, Swansea, West Glamorgan
Tel: Bishopston (044 128) 4428
Proprietor: Mrs W P Hemns-Tucker (BHSII)
Instruction in Riding and Jumping
Av No: Horses 4 Ponies 6
Std of Schlg: General Purpose
Livery: Full/Part/Hunter/Break/School/Hunt/Hack – Moorlands/Bridleways
Courses: Resid Hol
Facilities: Out Man: 53 x 27m*/Jmp Pd/CC Fences/Lec Rm/Refresh/Wait Rm/WC/Saddlery Shop/Car Park
Accom: Local Guesthouse or Hotel Catering: Full
Specialities: Short courses/Hacking – mainly children/Bed & Breakfast for Horses
Exclusions: Escorted hacking and hunting only
Location: On B4436 4 miles from centre of Swansea

L & A HOLIDAY & RIDING CENTRE
Goytre, Port Talbot, West Glamorgan
Tel: Port Talbot (0639) 885509
Proprietor: Mr & Mrs A G Holden
Chief Inst: Miss R Holden
Riding Holidays & Trekking
Av No: Horses 30 Ponies 34
Std of Schlg: General Purpose
Hunt/Hack/Trek – Forestry
Courses: Resid Hol
Facilities: Cov Sch: 40 x 23m Gly Fl Lit/Jmp Pd/CC Fences/Club Rm/Lic Bar/Refresh/WC/Lec Rm
Accom: 90 (16 Log Cabins) Catering: Part/Self
Specialities: Good Riding/Trekking country/Heated pool/School contract work

PANT-Y-SAIS RIDING AND TREKKING STABLES
Jersey Marine, Nr Swansea, West Glamorgan, SA10 6JF
Tel: Skewen (0792) 813213/816439
Proprietors: D S Gorvett & R E Gorvett
Chief Inst: Miss J Gorvett (BHSAI)
Basic Instruction in Riding and Jumping
Av No: Horses 4 Ponies 26
Std of Schlg: General Purpose
Livery: DIY/Break/School/Hack/Trek – Fenland/Beach/Open Country
Ev Classes
Courses: Hol
Facilities: Cov Sch: 37 x 19m* Gly/Out Man: 37 x 19m*/Jmp Pd/Sh Jmps/Lec Rm/Vis Aids/WC/Car Park
Accom: 32 – Dormitory (Purely for Children)
Specialities: RDA/General Instruction/Hacking/Trekking Holidays – August only

PARC-LE-BREOS TREKKING CENTRE
Parkmill, Gower, Nr Swansea, West Glamorgan, SA3 2EA
Tel: 0792 371636
Proprietor: Mr J Edwards
Riding Holidays & Trekking
Av No: Horses 8 Ponies 27
Std of Schlg: General Purpose
Trek – Hill/Moors/Beach/Forestry
Courses: Resid Hol
Facilities: Club Rm/Refresh/WC/Showers/Wait Rm
Accom: 26 – Dormitory/Double Rooms/Ensuite Rooms/Farmhouse Catering: Full
Specialities: Trekking holidays/Family seaside holidays/All rides escorted
Location: Off A4118 10 miles from centre of Swansea

WOODLANDS RIDING SCHOOL
Vennaway Lane, Parkmill, Gower, Nr Swansea, West Glamorgan, SA3 2EA
Tel: Bishopston (044 128) 2704
Proprietor: Miss T D Watts BHSI
Other Staff: 2 (BHSAI) P T 1 (BHSII) P T
Instruction in Riding and Jumping & Students to BHSII Exam
Av No: Horses 10 Ponies 5
Std of Schlg: General Purpose Std of Spec Schlg: Drsg – Elem/H T – Int/1 Sh Jmper Grade B
Livery: Full/Grass/Hunter/Break/School/Hack

Ev Classes
Courses: Resid/Inst/1 Wkg Students
Facilities: Cov Sch: 31 x 15m Gly 100/Out Man: 34 x 31m/Jmp Pd/CC Course/Lec Rm/Vis Aids*/Club Rm/Refresh/WC/Chng Rm
Accom: Hostel Catering: Full
Specialities: RDA/Riding Club events/Indoor & outdoor shows/Lecture demonstration evenings/Stable Management courses
Location: Off A4118 6 miles from centre of Swansea

Riding in Ireland

COUNTY ANTRIM ♦ COUNTY DONEGAL ♦ COUNTY DOWN ♦ COUNTY DUBLIN ♦ COUNTY KILKENNY ♦ COUNTY MONAGHAN ♦ COUNTY SLIGO ♦ COUNTY TIPPERARY ♦ COUNTY TYRONE ♦ COUNTY WICKLOW

COUNTY ANTRIM

ASHFIELD RIDING CENTRE
Middle Road, Islandmagee, Larne,
Co Antrim, Northern Ireland, BT40 3SL
Tel: Whitehead (096 03) 72609/72744
Proprietor: Mrs S Laird (BHSAI)
Other Staff: 1 (BHSAI)
Instruction in Riding and Jumping
Av No: Horses 3 Ponies 12
Std of Schlg: General Purpose
Livery: Full/Part/Grass/Break/School/Hack – Country Lanes/Estate
Ev Classes
Courses: Resid Inst Hol/YTS – 1
Facilities: Out Man: 40 x 20m Fl Lit*/Jmp Pd*/Sh Jmps/CC Fences 10/Lec Rm/Vis Aids/Refresh/WC/Wash Rm/Chng Rm/Tack Shop/Car Park
Accom: 6 Cottage Catering: Full
Specialities: Ponies for PC activities/Small residential courses during school holidays/Riding Club activities/tests/RDA
Exclusions: No unsupervised riding
Location: Off A2 btwn Carrickfergus/Larne

DRUMAHEGLIS RIDING SCHOOL
89 Glenstall Road, Ballymoney,
County Antrim, Northern Ireland
Tel: 02656 65500
Proprietor & Chief Inst: Miss C Morton (BHSAI)
Instruction in Riding and Jumping
Av No: Horses 3 Ponies 6
Std of Schlg: General Purpose Std of Specialist Schlg: Sh Jmpg – Novice
Livery: Full/Part/School/Hack – Country Lanes/Beach
Ev Classes
Courses: YT
Facilities: Out Man: 40 x 20m* Fl Lit/Jmpg Pd*/Refreshments/Wash Rm/WC/Car Park
Specialities: General Instruction/Hacking/Livery
Exclusions: No casual hire
Location: Btwn Ballymoney Nr Macfinn

GALGORM PARKS RIDING SCHOOL
112 Sand Road, Ballymena, Co Antrim,
Northern Ireland
Tel: Culleybackey (0266) 880269
Proprietor: Ms S R Kyle (BHSAI)
Instruction in Riding and Jumping
Av No: Horses 8 Ponies 8
Std of Schlg: General Purpose School/Break
Evening Lessons
Facilities: Cov Sch: 16 x 9m/Out Man: 60 x 40m Fl Lit*/Sh Jmps/Jmp Pd/WC/Wash Rm/Shop/Car Park
Accom: 30 – House or Camping/Dormitory Catering – Full
Specialities: General Instruction/Riding Holidays/RDA
Exclusions: No Casual Hiring
Location: Btwn Ballymena/Cullybackey

KILLOAN RIDING CENTRE
40 Killyless Road, Cullybackey,
Ballymena, Co Antrim, Northern Ireland,
BT42 1HB
Proprietor & Chief Inst: Mrs Valerie Getty
General instruction given
Av No: Horses 5 Ponies 5 Specl*: 1 Adv Drs 1 Int HT 1Grade B SJ
Std of Schlg: Med Drs/SJ Adv

Livery: Full/Part/Grass/Schooling/Breaking/Hacking/Hills/Country Roads
Ev Classes
Courses: BTec Nat. Dip Equestrian/Business
Facilities: Indoor School 20 x 40m/Gallery 50/Out Man 25 x 45m Fl Lit/Sh Jumps/WC/Tuck Shop
Specialities: Run Show Jumping Comps/Dressage Leagues/Prepare Horses and or Riders For Comps up to National Level
Exclusions: No Hire For Hunting/Accompanied Hacking/Closed Sundays/Assessment lesson for new Clients

COUNTY DONEGAL

LENAMORE STABLES
Muff, County Donegal, Ireland
Tel: 010 353 77 84022
Proprietor & Chief Inst: Miss G L Graham
Other Staff: Mrs V Craig (BHSAI) 2 (BHSAI) P/T
Instruction in Riding and Jumping
Av No: Horses 5 Ponies 10
Std of Schlg: General Purpose Std of Specialist Schlg: Sh Jmpg – Nov
Livery: Part/Grass/Holiday/School/Hack – Country Land/Forestry
Ev Classes
Courses: Holiday
Facilities: Cov Sch: 35 x 25m/Out Man: 50 x 25m/Jmpg Pd/Refreshments/Wash Rm/WC/Wait Rm/Car Park
Specialities: Basic Instruction/Holiday Courses/Show Jumping/Hacking
Exclusions: No casual hire
Location: Btwn Muff & Bridgend

STRACOMER RIDING SCHOOL
Bundoran, County Donegal, Ireland
Tel: 010 353 72 41787/41685/
Fax – 010 353 72 41002
Proprietor & Chief Inst: Mrs T Fergus Browne
Other Staff: Miss Belynda Brown
Instruction in Riding and Jumping
Av No: Horses 15 Ponies 12
Std of Schlg: General Purpose
Livery: Full/Part/Grass/Break/School/Hunt/Hack – Beach/Dunes
Ev Classes
Courses: Inst/Hol
Facilities: Out Man: 20 x 20m* Fl Lit/Jmp Pd/Sh Jmps/CC Course/Lec Rm/Club Rm/Refresh/Wash Rm/WC/Change Rm/Car Park
Accom: Hotel/Home Self Catering Cottages
Specialities: General Instruction/Hacking/Trekking/Trail rides/Livery/Riding Holiday (All types of Accommodation available)/Unaccompanied children welcome/Language Courses for Overseas Students/Shows/Events
Exclusions: No casual hiring
Location: Off the Ballyshannon Road btwn Bundoran/Ballyshannon

COUNTY DOWN

BALLYKNOCK RIDING SCHOOL
38 Ballyknock Road, Hillsborough, Co Down, Northern Ireland, BT26 6EF
Tel: Dromore (0846) 692144
Proprietor: Miss J J Howes (BHSAI)
Other Staff: 1 (BHSAI)
Instruction in Riding and Jumping
Av No: Horses 5 Ponies 10 Spec Horses: HT – Nov/Sh Jmp – B
Std of Schlg: General Purpose Std of Specialist Schlg: H T – Nov/Sh Jmp – B
Livery: Full/Grass/Break/School/Hack - Countryside
Ev Classes
Courses: Hol/YT
Facilities: Cov Sch: 37 x 12m* Fl Lit/Out Man: 4 0 x 20m/Jmp Pd/Sh Jmps/CC Fences/WC/Refresh/Car Park
Accom: Caravan 6
Specialities: Children's instruction/Residential holiday courses/Pony Club work/Schooling/Breaking/RDA
Exclusions: No unaccompanied Riding
Location: Btwn Hillsborough/Moria

EAST HOPE EQUESTRIAN CENTRE
71 Killynure Road West, Carryduff, County Down, Northern Ireland, BT8 8EA
Tel: 0232 813186
Proprietor & Chief Inst: Mrs L J Jamison (BHSII)
Instruction in Riding and Jumping
Av No: Horses 1 Ponies 6
Std of Schlg: General Purpose Std of Specialist Schlg: Sh Jmpg: C/Drg: M
Livery: Full/Part/Grass/DIY/School
Ev Classes
Facilities: Out Man: 40 x 25m Fl Lit*/Jmp Pd*/Snacks/Wash Rm/WC/Car Park
Specialities: General Instruction/Livery/Childrens Holiday Courses/Camps/Pony Club Tests
Exclusions: No YT taken
Location: Off A24 Btwn Carryduff & Temple

LAGAN VALLEY EQUESTRIAN CENTRE
170 upper Malone Road, Dunmurray, Belfast, Northern Ireland, BT17 9JZ
Tel: 0232 614853
Proprietors: Mr & Mrs W Cave
Manager/Chief Inst: Miss L Faloona (BHSAI IT) **Other Staff:** 2 (BHSAI) P/T
Std of Schlg: General purpose
Av No: Horses 4 Ponies 12
Livery: Full/Part/DIY/Grass/Holiday/Schooling
Ev Classes
Facilities: Cov sch: 46 x 18m/Gallery/Out Man Fl Lit 40 x 30m/Sh Jmps/Jmp Pd/ Lecture Rm/WC/Club Rm/Vis Aids/Snacks/Car Park
Specialities: General Instruction/Liveries of all Types/RDA
Exclusions: No Children Under 8 Years
Location: Off Outer Ringroad Btwn Mary Peters Track & Park

LESSANS RIDING STABLES
126 Monlough Road, Saintfield, Co Down, Northern Ireland
Tel Saintfield (0238) 510141
Proprietor: Miss Phillippa Auret (BHSII)
Other Staff: 1 (BHSAI) 1 (BHSII) P/T
Instruction in Riding and Jumping
Av No: Horses 10 Ponies 12
Std of Schlg: General Purpose
Livery: Full/Part/School/Break
Ev Classes
Courses: Hol Inst/Wkg Pupils
Facilities: Cov Sch: 43 x 19m Fl Lit Gly 20*/Out Man: 46 x 25m*/Sh Jmps/Jmp Pd/CC Fences*/Tack Shop/WC/Wash Rm/Refresh/Car Park
Accom: Flats – 6 Catering: Self
Specialities: General Instruction/Pony Camp/Riding Club/Courses/Livery/RDA/BHS Exam Centre
Exclusions: No Casual Hire
Location: Btwn Carryduff/Saintfield

MILLBRIDGE RIDING CENTRE LIMITED
Ballystockart, Comber, Co Down, Northern Ireland, BT23 5HZ
Tel: Comber (0247) 872508
Proprietor: Mrs Denise Neill (BHSAI)
Chief Inst: Mrs R McVeigh **Other Staff:** 1 (BHSI) P/T 1 (BHSII) P/T
Instruction in Riding and Jumping
Av No: Horses 12 Ponies 12
Std of Schlg: General Purpose
Livery: Full/Part/DIY/Break/School/Hack
Ev Classes
Courses: Rid Hol/YT
Facilities: Cov Sch: 37 x 20m* Fl Lit Gly 200/Jmp Pd 20 x 35m*/Sh Jmps/CC Course/Club Rm/Refresh/Wash Rm/Lic Bar/Games Room/WC/Tack Shop/Car Park
Specialities: RDA/General Instruction/Livery/Riding Club Activities
Location: Btwn Comber & Gransha

MOUNT PLEASANT TREKKING CENTRE
15 Bannanstown, Castlewellan, County Down, Northern Ireland, BT31 9BG
Tel: 039 67 78651
Proprietor: P King Esq
Chief Inst: Miss G Braggar **Other Staff:** 3 Escorts 6 P/T Staff when required
Hacking & Trekking
Av No: Horses 18 Ponies 8
Std of Schlg: General Purpose
Livery: Full/Grass/Holiday/School/Hack/Trek – Estates/Forest
Courses: Resid Hol
Facilities: Refreshments/Wash Rm/WC/Changing Rm/Waiting Rm/Car Park
Accom: Mobile Home – 6 Catering: Self
Specialities: Hacking/Trekking/Livery/Holiday Livery/Family Accommodation/School contract work
Exclusions: Hiring after assessment only/All rides escorted
Location: 0.75 mile off A25 btwn Castlewellan/Clough

NEWCASTLE RIDING CENTRE
35 Carnacaville Road, Castlewellan, Co Down, Northern Ireland, BT31 9HD
Tel: Newcastle (039 67) 22694
Proprietors: Mrs R K & Miss E S Martin B Sc BHSAI
Chief Inst: Miss S Martin (BHSAI) **Other Staff:** 1 (BHSAI)
Instruction in Riding and Jumping
Av No: Horses 15 Ponies 8
Std of Schlg: General Purpose
Livery: Full/Part/Break/School/Hack – Mountain/Beach/Forest
Ev Classes
Courses: Resid Inst Hol/YT 2
Facilities: Cov Sch: 30 x 20m* Gly 15-20/Out Man: 64 x 33m* Fl Lit/Jmp Pd/Sh Jmps/CC Course/Lec Rm/WC/Vis Aids/Video/Club Rm
Accom: Caravan Catering: 10 Full
Specialities: Riding holidays/RDA/General Instruction
Exclusions: All Hacking Escorted

COUNTY DUBLIN

ASHTON EQUESTRIAN CENTRE
Ashton Manor, Castleknock, County Dublin, Ireland
Tel: Dublin (0001) 387611/383236

Proprietors: B M Stone & David Stone
Chief Inst: Mr Neil Brown (BHSI) **Other Staff:** 1 (BHSI) P/T
Livery & Facility Centre
Av No: Horses 0 Ponies 0
Std of Schlg: General Purpose
Livery: Full/Part/DIY/School/Break
Facilities: Cov Sch: 40 x 23m* Fl Lit Gly 70/80/Out Man: 56 x 48m*/Jmp Pd/Sh Jmps/Lec Rm/Club Rm/Vis Aids/WC/ Showers/Chng Rm/Refresh – Cafeteria/ Coffee Shop/Car Park
Specialities: Livery & Facility Centre/ All types of Livery/Shows/Freelance Instruction available
Exclusions: No Children under 6
Location: Off the Navan Road btwn Castlknock/Finglass

CALLIAGHSTOWN RIDING SCHOOL

Calliaghstown, Rathcoole, County Dublin, Ireland
Tel: 0001 589236/Fax No: 588171
Proprietor & Chief Inst: Miss G Sugars BHSI(SM)
Other Staff: 2 (BHSAI) 1 (BHSII)
Instruction in Riding and Jumping
Av No: Horses 12 Ponies 10
Std of Schlg: General Purpose Specialist Horses 5 – Sh Jmpg – Grade C
Livery: Full/Part/Grass/School/Break/ Hunt/Hack – Mountain/Farm Land/ Forestry
Ev Classes
Facilities: Cov Sch: 43 x 22m/Gly*/Out Man: 40 x 20m*/Refreshments/Wash Rm/WC/Car Park/Lec Rm/Vis Aids/ Library/Video/Club Rm
Specialities: General Instruction/Livery/ Hack/Wicklow Trial Rides – May – September
Exclusions: No Casual Hiring
Location: Btwn Rathcoole/Kilteel

CARRICKMINES EQUESTRIAN CENTRE

Glenamuck Road, Foxrock, Dublin 18, County Dublin, Ireland
Tel: 0001 955990
Proprietors: Mr & Mrs F Flannelly
Chief Inst: Mr D Flannelly (BHSII) **Other Staff:** 2 (BHSAI) 2 (BHSII)
Instruction in Riding and Jumping
Av No: Horses 30 Ponies 4 Specialist Horses : 2 Drg/1 Grade B & C Sh Jmpers/3 Nov Eventers
Std of Schlg: General Purpose Std of Specialist Schlg: CT – Novice/Sh Jmpg – C
Livery: Full/Grass/Hunter/School/Hack – Own Land
Ev Classes
Facilities: Cov Sch: 35 x 23m/Out Man: 6 Basic Schooling CC Fences/Lec Rm/ Club Rm – Seating/Vis Aids/Video/ Refreshments/Wash Rm/WC/Changing Rm/Car Park
Accom: Local Guest House
Specialities: General Instruction/ Training Horses/Livery/Stud/Riding Club
Exclusions: No casual hire
Location: Btwn Enniskerry/Foxrock

SPRUCE LODGE EQUESTRIAN CENTRE LTD

Kilternan, County Dublin, Ireland
Tel: 0001 952109
Proprietor: Mrs J Keogh
Other Staff: 2 (BHSAI) 2 (BHSII) 1 FBHS P/T
Instruction in Riding and Jumping & Students to BHSAI Exam
Av No: Horses 6 Ponies 12
Std of Schlg: General Purpose
Livery: Full/School/Break
Ev Classes
Courses: Hol/Inst
Facilities: Cov Sch: 49 x 25m* Fl Lit Gly 100/Out Man: 40 x 20m/Jmp Pd/Sh Jmps/CC Fences/Lec Rm/Video/Vis Aids*/WC/Refresh/Car Park
Specialities: Children's courses/ instruction/Student Training/RDA
Exclusions: No riders over 14 stones
Location: On Dublin/Enniskerry Road

COUNTY KILKENNY

THOMASTOWN VOCATIONAL SCHOOL EQUESTRIAN CENTRE

Newtown, Thomastown, County Kilkenny, Ireland
Tel: 010 353 56 24112
Proprietor: Mr P Cronin
Manager: Miss B McCarthy (BHSII)
Chief Inst: Mrs F Posonby (BHSII) & SM P/T
Other Staff: 1 (BHSAI) P/T
Instruction in Riding and Jumping
Av No: Horses 14 Ponies 2
Std of Schlg: General Purpose Std of Specialist Schlg: CT: Novice
Livery: Full/School/Break
Ev Classes
Courses: Holiday/BHS Stage 1 & 2
Facilities: Cov Sch: 31 x 19m Gly/ Out Man: 44 x 35m/CC Course/Lec Rm/ Club Rm/Vis Aids/Library/Film Projector/ Wash Rm/Chng Rm/Car Park
Specialities: General Instruction/

Student Training/Holiday Courses/
Livery/Breaking/Schooling/RDA
Exclusions: No casual hire
Location: Outskirts of town off Kilkenny Road

COUNTY MONAGHAN

GREYSTONES EQUESTRIAN CENTRE

Castle Leslie, Glasslough, County Monaghan, Ireland
Tel: 010 353 42 88100
Proprietors: Mr & Mrs J Bellew
Chief Inst: Miss J Powell (ICES) **Other Staff:** 1 (BHSAI) 1 (BHSII) 1 (ICES)
Instruction in Riding and Jumping
Av No: Horses 24 Ponies 8 Std of Specialist Horses: 1 Sh Jmp Novice
Std of Schlg: General Purpose Std of Specialist Schlg: CT – Novice/Sh Jmp – Novice
School/Hack – Forest/Farm Land/Estate
Ev Classes
Courses: Resid
Facilities: Cov Sch: 20 x 35m*/Out Man: 25 x 45m*/CC Course/Sh Jmpg Pd*/Refreshments/Wash Rm/Bar/WC/Showers/Car Park
Accom: Shared House/Hotel 20
Catering: Full
Specialities: General Instruction/Hacking/Riding Holidays/RDA/Riding Club
Exclusions: No unaccompanied Children under 12 years
Location: Off L5 Btwn Middletown/Monaghan

COUNTY SLIGO

MONEYGOLD RIDING & LANGUAGE CENTRE LTD

Grange, County Sligo, Ireland
Tel: 010 353 71 63337
Proprietors: Mr & Mrs K Moran
Chief Inst: Mr K Moran **Other Staff:** Miss A Kennedy (BHSAI)
Basic Instruction in Riding and Jumping
Av No: Horses 2 Ponies 4 Specialist Horses: 1 Nov Drg
Std of Schlg: General Purpose Std of Specialist Schlg: Drg – Novice
School/Hack – Beach
Ev Classes
Courses: Rid Hols/English Lang
Facilities: Out Man: 50 x 20m/TV/Video/WC/Showers/Car Park
Accom: Shrd Dormitory/House – 10
Catering: Full
Specialities: Riding Holidays/RDA/Hacking on Beaches/English Language Teaching/Breeding
Exclusions: No rider over 14 stone

COUNTY TIPPERARY

ASHROE RIDING SCHOOL

Ashroe House, Nr Newport, County Tipperary, Ireland
Tel: 010 353 61 378271
Proprietors: Mr & Mrs M Mullane BHS Prelim
Chief Inst: Mr M Herbert FHBS **Other Staff:** 1 (BHSAI)
Instruction in Riding and Jumping
Av No: Horses 12 Ponies 26 Specialist Horses: 6 Nov Eventers
Std of Schlg: General Purpose Std of Specialist Schlg: Drg & CT – Nov/Sh Jmpg – C
Livery: Full/Part/Hunter/School/Hack – Country Roads/Forestry
Ev Classes
Courses: Non Resid Holiday/University of Limerick degree
Facilities: Cov Sch: 30 x 18m Gly/Out Man: 61 x 61m/20 Basic CC Fences/Jmpg Pd/Lec Rm – Vis Aids/Video/Seating – 20/Refreshments/Wash Rm/WC/Changing Rm/Car Park
Accom: Local B & B
Specialities: General Instruction/Livery/Holiday Courses
Exclusion: No riders over 12.5 stone
Location: 4.5 miles off Dublin/Limerick Road

COUNTY TYRONE

EDERGOLE RIDING CENTRE

70 Moneynore Road, Cookstown, Co Tyrone, Northern Ireland, BT80 8PY
Tel: Cookstown (06487) 62924
Proprietor: Mr D W H Short
Manager: Mr A Short (BHSII) **Chief Inst:** Mrs J Stone (BHSII)
Instruction in Riding and Jumping
Av No: Horses 6 Ponies 8
Std of Schlg: General Purpose
Livery: Full/Part/Grass/School/Break/Hack – Mountain

Ev Classes
Courses: Res Hol/YTS taken
Facilities: Out Man: 52 x 22m* Fl Lit/Sh Jmps/Refresh – Canteen/Club Rm/ Creche/Wash Rm/WC/Tack Shop
Accom: 12 – House Catering – Full
Specialities: Instruction/Riding Holidays – Camps/Hacking
Exclusions: No rides without assessment
Location: On A29 Btwn Cookstown – Moneymore

MOY RIDING SCHOOL
Derrycaw Road, Moy, Co Tyrone, Northern Ireland, BT
Tel: 086 87 84440
Proprietor & Chief Inst: Mrs M Corr (BHSAI)
Other Staff: 2 (BHSAI)
Basic Instruction in Riding and Jumping
Av No: Horses 10 Ponies 8
Std of Schlg: General Purpose
Livery: Full/Part/Grass/Hack
Ev Classes
Courses: Inst Hol
Accom: Available locally
Specialities: General riding instruction/ Hacking/RDA

COUNTY WICKLOW

BRENNANSTOWN RIDING SCHOOL LTD
Hollybrook, Bray, County Wicklow, Ireland
Tel: 0001 2863778/Fax No 2829590
Proprietor: Ms J Kennedy
Chief Inst: – Miss Cloudagh Carey (BHSII(T)) **Other Staff:** 3 (BHSAI) 3 (BHSII) P/T 1 (BHSI) P/T
Instruction in Riding and Jumping & Students to BHSII Exam
Av No: Horses 25 Ponies 25
Std of Schlg: General Purpose
Livery: Full/Part/Grass/School/Break/ Hunt/Hack – Woodland/Mountain/ Farmland
Ev Classes
Courses: Inst
Facilities: Cov Sch: 28 x 46m* Gly 50/ 2 Out Man* Fl Lit/CC Course/Jmp Pd/ Sh Jmps/Lec Rm/Vis Aids/Refresh/Wash Rm/Club Rm/WC/Chng Rm/Wait Rm/ Car Park
Accom: 10 – House Catering: Part
Specialities: Dressage/Eventing – foreign student courses/Career students/Hacking/Livery/Trekking/RDA
Exclusions: No children under 6 years
Location: On N11 btwn Bray/ Kimmacanocve

Riding in the Channel Islands

GUERNSEY ♦ JERSEY

GUERNSEY

LA CORBIERE RIDING & LIVERY STABLES
La Corbiere Forest, Guernsey, Channel Islands
Tel: 0481 64193
Proprietor & Chief Inst: Miss G Brock (BHSAI)
Other Staff: 1 (BHSAI) P/T 1 UQ
Instruction in Riding and Jumping
Av No: Horses 1 Ponies 7
Std of Schlg: General Purpose Std of Specialist Schlg: Sh Jmpg – Novice
Livery: Full/Grass/School/Break/Hack – Beaches/Cliff Paths/Quiet Lanes
Ev Classes
Facilities: Out Man: 60 x 20m* Fl Lit/ Jmp Pd/Sh Jmps*/Wash Rm/WC/ Changing Rm/Car Park
Specialities: Big clean loose boxes/ Daily turn out/Grass Liveries/Trailer Hire/ 24hrs supervision
Exclusions: No YT/No Heavy Adults unless on own horse

JERSEY

LA HAIE FLEURIE LIVERY & RIDING CENTRE
La Haie Fleurie, St Martin, Jersey, Channel Islands, JE3 6BN
Tel: 0534 52617
Proprietor: Miss C F Binet (BHSAI)
Other Staff: 3 (BHSAI)
Instruction in Riding and Jumping & Students to BHSAI Exam
Av No: Horses 3 Ponies 7 Specialist Horses: A Sh Jmp – C
Std of Schlg: General Purpose Std of Specialist Schlg: Sh Jmp – C/CC – Novice
Livery: Full/Part/School/Break
Ev Classes
Facilities: Out Man: 40 x 20m* Fl Lit/CC Course* & Fences*/Jmp Pd*/Lec Rm*/ Club Rm*/Vis Aids*/Refresh/Saddlery Shop/WC/Car Park
Specialities: General Instruction/ Career Students/Livery/Saddlery Shop/Shows
Exclusions: No Casual Hire

MULTINA RIDING SCHOOL
Ville Au Neveu, St Ouen, Jersey, Channel Islands
Tel: Jersey (0534) 81843
Proprietors: Mr & Mrs J Phillips
Basic Instruction in Riding and Jumping
Av No: Horses 2 Ponies 6
Std of Schlg: General Purpose
Livery: Full/Grass/Hunter/Break/School/ Hunt/Hack/Trek – Varied
Courses: Inst
Facilities: Out Man: 62 x 25m*/Jmp Pd/ Sh Jmps/CC Fences*/WC/Car Park
Specialities: Children/Liveries/ Schooling
Location: Off B53 Btwn St Ouen & St Mary

BHS Leaflets and Pamphlets

The Society produces many leaflets and pamphlets designed to help horse owners and riders. The following list gives the current titles together with the cost and post and packing where applicable. A full mail order list of equestrian books is available on request from the Marketing Department, The British Horse Society, Stoneleigh, Kenilworth, Warwickshire, CV8 2LR. (Tel: 0203 696697).

DEPARTMENT	TITLE	COST	P & P
Approvals	Riding School Rules Sign	£5.00	incl.
	Basic Requirements for a Riding Centre	£1.00	20p
	Construction of Outdoor Arenas	£1.00	20p
	Safety in Stables Posters	£2.50 per set	incl.
	Fire Action Sign	£5.00	incl.
	Hats Current BSI Rule Sign	£5.00	incl.
	Riding is a Risk Sport	£5.00	incl.
British Equestrian Centre	Outline Programme (bi-monthly)	£3.50 p.a.	incl.
Land Management, Access & Bridleways	Horses on Small Grazing Areas	Free	SAE
	Pathfinder Map Information	Free	SAE
	Policy on Width of Bridleways	Free	SAE
	Policy on re-classification of RUPPs	Free	SAE
	Obstruction of RoW	Free	SAE
	Policy on Diversions	Free	SAE
	Encounters with Aggressive People	Free	SAE
	Planning Concessions – Stabling within the Curtilage	Free	SAE
	Highway Margins and Verges	Free	SAE
	Bed & Breakfast for Horses – a list of stabling/accommodation	£1.25	incl.
	Surfacing of Bridleways and Riding Tracks	£2.25	incl.
	Policy on Countryside Conservation	Free	SAE
	Stallions on Bridleways	Free	SAE
	The Next 10 Years	Free	SAE
Dressage	List of Test and Score Sheets currently in use available upon application	Free	SAE
	Dressage Tests	10p each	SAE
	Dressage folder complete with all national tests	£10.00	90p
	Set of Tests without Folder	£3.75	45p
	Rule Book and Judges Panel 1990	£1.70	30p
	Omnibus Schedule		
	Summer Parts I & II	£1.50	50p
	Winter Parts I & II	£1.50	50p
Horse Trials	Omnibus Schedule	£2.75	50p
	Rule Book	£2.50	50p
	Dressage Sheets	£0.06 each	see dressage list
	Guidelines on Official BHS Horse Trials	£6.00	50p
Pony Club	Complete list and order form available from the Pony Club Office	Free	SAE

Riding Clubs	Complete list and order form of Riding Club publications available from the Riding Club Office	Free	SAE
Road Safety	Riding Safety on the Roads (BHS Riding and Road Safety Manual) revised edition	£1.50	25p
	Riding and Road Safety Test Card (incl syllabus)	£0.10	SAE
	Ride More Safely Leaflet	Free	SAE
	Accident Report Form	Free	SAE
	Trust Your Trailer	25p	SAE
	Road Safety Starter Pack (includes Riding Safely on the Roads)	£1.75	SAE
	Video Horse Sense Road Craft for the Rider	£26.92	incl. p/p & VAT
Training & Exams	Exam Starter Pack	£1.00	incl.
	Examination Syllabi	£0.10	SAE
	Working with Horses	£0.50	20p
	Examinations Dates/Examinations Centres List	Free	SAE
	Directory of Training Courses in Horse Industry by JNHETC	£3.00	incl.
	NVQ Level One Criteria	£1.00	30p
Welfare	Winter Feeding Comprehensive Requirements	Free	SAE
	Some Alternative Feeds	Free	SAE
	Horse Thefts	Free	SAE
	Winter Shelters, Needs, Hints on Construction	Free	SAE
	Livery Yard Guidelines, Requirements and Definitions	Free	SAE
	Euthanasia Do's and Don'ts	Free	SAE
	Well Shod Horse, Reasons for Fitting, and Types of Shoeing	Free	SAE
	The Simple Rules of Saddle Fitting	Free	SAE
	Safety in the saddle	Free	SAE
	Code of Practice for Tethering Horses and Ponies	Free	SAE
	Buying, Leasing or Borrowing Horses	Free	SAE
	Castration of Horse, Advice to Owners	Free	SAE
	The Cost of a Foal's Life	Free	SAE
	Simple Guidelines on Bits and Bitting	Free	SAE
	Control Those Worms	Free	SAE
	Poisonous Plants and Trees	Free	SAE
	Code of Practice for Horse, Pony & Donkey Sales	Free	SAE
	Ragwort	Free	SAE
	The Cost of Keeping a First Horse or Pony	Free	SAE
	Safety Stirrup Irons	Free	SAE
	How to Look After and Care for Your Donkey	Free	SAE
	Stable Fires	Free	SAE
Endurance Riding	E.R. Group Omnibus Schedule and Rule Book	£2.40	incl. p/p

If you require any of the above leaflets please send your request to the department named in the left-hand column, using the above address.

Index of BHS-Approved Establishments

Membership Application Form

Why not take advantage of British Horse Society Membership? The British Horse Society works for the well-being of all horses and ponies. If you would like to help us and yourself the best way is to join the Society. If you are already a member why not persuade a friend to join. Simply fill in the form below and return it with the first year's subscription.

Help us to ensure that it is safe for you and your animals to be out and about by joining the B.H.S.

21 years of age and over

FULL ADULT MEMBERS		£22.50
*JOINING FEE (also payable if rejoining)		£5.00
	TOTAL	£27.50

Under 21 years of age

FULL JUNIOR MEMBERSHIP	TOTAL	£15.75

* The joining fee is not applicable to Full Junior Members or applicants aged 60 or over providing the date of birth is included on the application form.

(The rates quoted above include VAT) Cheques or Postal Orders should be made payable to: **The British Horse Society** and sent with this application form.

Please use BLOCK CAPITALS

Name ....

Address ....

....

....

Post Code ....

Date of birth ....
(required if applying for Full Junior Membership or if applicants are aged 60 years or over.)

Signature ....

Tel No ....

Return your application form to Membership Department, British Horse Society, British Equestrian Centre, Kenilworth, Warwickshire CV8 2LR. Telephone Coventry (0203) 696697

Please help us enrol more members!

BHS Quest for Safer Off-Road Riding

One of the aims of the British Horse Society is to preserve existing rights of way for horses and ponies, and to open up more safe, off-road riding routes in the countryside. To help achieve this aim, the Society has a nationwide network of extremely active regional and country bridleways officers, organised by the BHS Access and Rights of Way Committee.

In addition, in 1991 the Society initiated an exciting new project – ARROW (Access and Rights of Way) – to open up linked routes for riders, and where possible, for carriage drivers.

Through the work of volunteers circular rides of up to twenty miles are now being developed in most counties in the British Isles. Progress is also being made in the forming of inter-county links so that several routes can be joined up to create a network.

The safety of horses and riders is of the utmost importance to the British Horse Society and it is hoped that the development of these ARROW trails will result in a significant reduction in horse-related road accidents, which currently stand at over five thousand per annum.

To find out about these circular rides and linked routes and/or if you can spare time to help survey, clear and maintain routes – contact the British Horse Society Access and Rights of Way Department, Stoneleigh, Kenilworth, Warwickshire, CV8 2LR, (Tel: 0203 696697).

NOTES

NOTES

NOTES

NOTES